The
Last
Dalai Lama

The
Last
Dalai Lama

·A BIOGRAPHY·

Michael Harris Goodman

SHAMBHALA
Boston
1987

Shambhala Publications, Inc.
314 Dartmouth Street
Boston, Massachusetts 02116

The Library of Congress catalogues the hardcover
edition of this work as follows:

Goodman, Michael (Michael Harris)
   The Last Dalai Lama.

Includes index.
  1. Bstan-'dzin-rgya-mtsho, Dalai Lama XIV, 1935–
  2. Dalai lamas—Biography. I. Title.
BQ7935.B777G66   1986   294.3'923'0924 [B]   85-27906
ISBN 0-87773-355-4
     0-394-55246-6 (Random House)
     0-87773-400-3 (pbk)

The photographs on the front cover and on pages 32, 56,
178, 238, and 266 are reproduced by permission of
AP/Wide World Photos. The photograph on page 6 is
from the Collection of The Newark Museum and is
reproduced by permission of the museum. The
photographs on pages 20, 44, 72, 88, 104, 118, 134, 150,
164, 192, 206, 222, 252, 280, 294, 302, and 314 are by
Michael Harris Goodman.

To Molly Immaculata Ferrara Goodman,
who lit the way

Contents

Contents

Preface

M Y FIRST ENCOUNTER WITH the people of Tibet took place in the spring of 1978 on a wooded hilltop in the Kathmandu Valley of Nepal. I had come there to visit an ancient Buddhist shrine, the Swayambhu stupa. It was an awe-inspiring structure; but I left even more impressed with the Tibetan refugees who lived in its shadow: people like Dawa, the *thonka* painter; Neten, the carpet-weaver; Paljor, the shop-keeper; Chime, the laborer; Thinley, the monk.

The Tibetans seemed to me a wonderful people: cheerful, generous, and open. Over endless cups of tea and plates of *momo*, they told me of life in their native land before its invasion by the Chinese, of their flight to freedom, and of their difficulty in adjusting to a new and alien land. As they spoke I marveled at how they had managed to retain both their sense of purpose and their sense of humor. What was it that bound these people together, that gave them such strength and determination? I found that it was their complete love for—and trust in—their spiritual and temporal leader, the Dalai Lama.

Curious to learn more about the man who inspired such faith, I found upon my return to the United States that, aside from his 1962 autobiography, *My Land and My People*, precious little had been written about him; or, since the Tibetan National Uprising of March 1959, about Tibet. The little I did find out was so fascinating that I decided to write this book.

I met the Dalai Lama and told him of my determination. He promised me his complete cooperation and was as good as his word: much of the material in the following pages was gathered in interviews with him over a five-year period in the United States and Switzerland, as well as during a two-month stay in Dharamsala, India, the seat of his government-in-exile. Thanks to the efforts of his representatives around the world, I was also able to record the voices of the Tibetan people: religious leaders and government officials, monks and laymen, peasant farmers and nomadic herdsmen, aristocrats and traders, soldiers and guerrilla fighters—the last living representatives of that free mountain kingdom on the Roof of the World.

It would appear that these words and memories were preserved none too soon. During the last several years many of these people, including the Dalai Lama's mother, immediate elder brother, foreign minister, lord chamberlain, and two most venerated spiritual advisors—all of whom contributed generously to the making of this book—have passed away. At the same time the Chinese government is continuing its systematic extermination of Tibetan culture. Having failed to obliterate the Tibetan identity by levelling monasteries, torturing monks and lamas, imprisoning and murdering dissidents, and even butchering Lhasa Apsos as undesirable relics of the past society, Peking has now launched a far more insidious assault on the people of Tibet. What it failed to achieve through force of arms it has set out to do by cultural lobotomy.

In a land where every aspect of life was permeated by religion, Peking has mandated that the word for "religious faith" be replaced with one meaning "blind faith" or "the faith of ignorance." Landholding and taxation records, religious histories and biographies of the Dalai Lamas, treaties between Tibet and China, Great Britain, and India and other countries—anything, in short, that would demonstrate that Tibet was for much of its existence before the coming of Mao an independent country—all have been destroyed. Peking has dictated that the Tibetan word for "history" be used only in reference to *Chinese* history. Tibetan history must be referred to by the word for "legend" or "story." The following account of the Dalai Lama's life, of his commitment to preserve the civilization of his country in exile, and of the remarkable courage of the Tibetan people is, most assuredly, no legend. It demonstrates the fragile nature of all our civilizations: one day an independent Tibet, the next a Tibet Autonomous Region, and the next somewhere called "Xiazang." And it suggests that unless we move toward the Dalai Lama's vision of a freedom that transcends nationality, we will continue to live in a world where everything we value may suddenly be swept away by the violent winds of our own human nature.

Acknowledgments

I WOULD LIKE TO thank the many people who contributed so generously to the making of this book. In Dharamsala, India: the late Lobsang Samden for the story of his childhood in the Potala with his little brother, the Dalai Lama; and for his warmth, encouragement, and friendship; Namlha Samden, Lobsang's widow and granddaughter of Tsarong Shappé, for spending many hours in a Himalayan cave with me, discussing practice of the Dharma with a hermit monk; the late Gyayum Chenmo for her many wonderful tales of old Tibet, as a young bride in Amdo and as mother of the Dalai Lama; Ngari Rinpoche for his good humor and tales of the years leading to the Tibetan National Uprising through the eyes of a teenaged monk; Rinchen Khando, Ngari Rinpoche's wife, for her warmth and hospitality; Pema Gyalpo, for the account of her visit to Tibet in 1980; P. T. Takla, former commander of the Dalai Lama's royal bodyguard, for his story of the Dalai Lama's escape and flight to India; the late Ling Rinpoche and the late Trijang Rinpoche, the Dalai Lama's tutors for over four decades, for their observations of his spiritual development; Dorjee Tseten Tashi-Para of the Tibetan army for the story of how he helped organize and safeguard the Dalai Lama's flight; T. T. Liushar, last head of the Tibetan foreign ministry, for his personal account of Sino-Tibetan relations during the Chinese occupation; Ven. Thupten Thonyo, monk assistant to Lhalu in Kham (1946–1950), for the story of his part in arranging Ngabo's surrender to the Chinese.

I am also grateful to Lobsang Tenzin, soldier of the Kusung Regiment, for his description of the taking of the Norbulingka by the Chinese army after the Dalai Lama's escape; Ngodup Tesur, for his tireless work arranging interviews, transcribing tapes, and interpreting, and for his welcome companionship over a few bottles of *chang* on the eve of my departure from Dharamsala; Kunsang Paljor, author, shopkeeper, and former cadre, for his incisive portrait of life in post–1959 Tibet; Elliot Sperling, for his superb interpreting in Chinese and Tibetan and for his most helpful account of

Sino–Tibetan relations for the past 1,000 years; Dr. Yeshi Thonden, the Dalai Lama's physician, and Lobsang Norbu of the Tibetan Medical Center, for their enlightening discussion of Tibetan medicine; W. Dorjee and Tashi Topgye, for their humorous and tragic tales of the founding of Tibetan settlements in India; Ratuk Ngawang, Chushi Gangdrug leader, for his account of the guerrilla campaign against the Chinese (1958–1959); Jamyang Norbu, Tempa Gyaltsen, and Kunchok Dorjee for stories of the post–Uprising guerrilla campaign in Mustang; and N. N. Nowrojee, for his superb account of McLeod Ganj over the past century.

In Darjeeling, India: Tenzin Geyche Tethong, long-time private secretary to the Dalai Lama and cabinet minister since 1980, for his description of the workings of the Tibetan government-in-exile; Lobsang Wanchuk, director of the Tibetan Self-Help Centre, for demonstrating how one group of refugees is making its way in exile; Tenzing Norgay, first person to ascend Mt. Everest, who helped found the Self-Help Centre; Dhondup, a master weaver from Gyantse whose regiment guarded the northern entrance to the Norbulingka just prior to the Dalai Lama's escape, for his account of those fateful days; Tamdrin Tsepel Andrugtsang of Kham for the memories of his uncle, the guerrilla chieftain Gompo Tashi Andrugtsang; Kesang Dorjee, master metal craftsman from Kham who fought with Gompo Tashi Andrugtsang and later in Mustang, for his stories of the Tibetan resistance movement; Dorjee Lodu, a former monk from the Nechung monastery, and his wife Tsering Dolma, a farmer's daughter from the village of Dakpo in central Tibet (birthplace of the late Reting Rinpoche), proprietors of a tea-stall, for teaching me the true meaning of the word *generosity*; and their daughter Kalden Wangmo for keeping me posted on refugee life in Bengal.

In Kalimpong, India: Tespon T. W. Shakabpa, former Tibetan finance minister, for his memories as a participant in the search for the Fourteenth Dalai Lama at Lake Lhamoi Latso and discussion of Tibetan politics. In Gangtok, Sikkim: Kunga Yonten Hochotsang of the Institute of Tibetology for his enlightening explanation of Tibetan Buddhism. In Kathmandu, Nepal: Dawa Paljor, *thonka* painter, for providing background to the Tibetan resistance movement in Mustang. In Bylakuppe and Hunsur, Tibetan settlements in south India, to Mingyur Dorjee and Champa Namgyal, for their accounts of settling some 30,000 refugees in what had been impenetrable jungle. In Bangalore, India: Yusef Naik, from the Kashmiri Muslim community of old Lhasa, for transporting me via Land Rover from Bangalore to the settlements and back, providing excellent companionship and occasional services as an interpreter.

In New York, at the Office of Tibet: Tenzin Namgyal Tethong, Acting Representative of His Holiness the Dalai Lama, whose assistance and encouragement made this project possible; Tenzin Choedok, whose good humor was as welcome as his swift translations; Ngodup Paljor, with his endless supply of books, articles, and anecdotes; Tinley Nyadank Akar, who kept me up to date with developments in Tibet; and Dhondup Namgyal, whose assistance in arranging and conducting interviews was invaluable.

In the New York–New Jersey metropolitan area: Khyongla Rato Ngawang Losang of the Dagyab in Kham for the story of his life as a Tibetan incarnation and for his account of the events leading up to the Tibetan National Uprising; Dorje Yudon Yuthok of Lhasa, widow of a former Tibetan cabinet minister, for her description of life in Lhasa during the Chinese occupation; Sherpa Tulku of Lhasa for his memories of life as an incarnate monk at Sera monastery; Thupten Norbu, a Golok nomad and *thonka* painter/restorer, for his story of the Chinese occupation in Amdo; Lama Norlha of Nangchen, Kham, for his inspiring account of how practice of the Dharma enabled him to survive internment in a Chinese prison camp; and Nima Dorjee of the Dagyab in Kham for his description of life in eastern Tibet before and during the Chinese occupation and his flight to freedom.

In St. Andrews, Scotland: H. E. Richardson of the British (and later, Indian) Mission in Lhasa, for his recollections of the Dalai Lama's arrival in 1939 and of the next turbulent decade of Tibetan history. In Kitzbühel, Austria: Heinrich Harrer, for memories of his seven years in Tibet and singular relationship with the young Dalai Lama. In Pawling, New York: the late Lowell Thomas, for the account of his visit to Tibet just prior to the Chinese invasion; and in Winterthur, Switzerland, the late Thupten Woyden Phala, the Dalai Lama's Lord Chamberlain, for his account of the Dalai Lama's last days in Tibet.

Thanks also to those who read part or all of the work in progress and offered helpful criticism: Patrick McGuire, Elizabeth Upton, John Ratti, and Joseph Judd; to my agent, Patricia Van der Leun, and my editor, Emily Hilburn Sell. And special thanks to His Holiness the Dalai Lama for making so much of his time available to me and ensuring the cooperation of so many of his people while asking only that this story be told; and to my wife, Philippa Reede Goodman, not only for her superb editing of the manuscript but also for the enthusiasm, good humor, and patience that ensured its completion.

The
Last
Dalai Lama

Prologue

T HE VILLAGE OF TEZPUR is situated on the north bank of the river Brahmaputra on the Assamese plains of northeastern India, a sleepy area of tea plantations and leech-infested swamps where planters are in the habit of wandering into the Station Club, sipping gin and tonic under an engraving of Napoleon's surrender to the British, playing a quiet game of billiards, and reminiscing about memorable tiger shoots. It has been this way for as long as anyone remembers, save for a three-week period in April 1959, when the community was jolted awake by an inundation of foreign correspondents who provided transitory prosperity for its half-dozen taxi drivers by paying the unheard-of sum of fifty rupees per day for their services, kept the telegraph operators hopping day and night with a barrage of dispatches to every corner of the globe, filled the town's only hotel and every spare bed in the Christian Mission Hospital, and drove the planters from the sacrosanct confines of their club. They had come there to cover what was being hailed as "the story of the year."

At dawn on April 18 the newsmen left Tezpur and assembled at the border of the North-East Frontier Agency, an untamed tract of craggy hills and impenetrable forests under the direct military administration of the Indian government. They waited impatiently, their eyes fixed upon the narrow track that emerged from the wilderness. Soon a procession of jeeps became visible through the dim morning light, moving solemnly in single file and coming to a halt on the other side of a hastily strung barbed-wire fence. From the lead vehicle stepped a young man of medium height and build with his head shorn, wearing tortoiseshell eyeglasses and the claret-colored robes of a Buddhist monk. With a radiant smile and palms pressed together before him in greeting, he acknowledged the gathering, walked over a path of 130 Indian army ground sheets pinned together by border soldiers of the Assam Rifles to a waiting limousine, and was whisked away into Tezpur.

The young man's name was Getsul Ngawang Lobsang Tenzin Gyatso Sisunwangyal Tsungpa Mapai Dephal Sangpo: "The Holy One, the Gentle

Glory, Powerful in Speech, Pure in Mind, of Divine Wisdom, Holder of the Faith, Ocean-Wide." To six million countrymen he was revered as Gyalwa Rinpoche or Yeshi Norbu, their "Precious Protector" and "Wish-Fulfilling Gem." To the members of the press corps and to the rest of the world he was known simply as the Dalai Lama of Tibet.

The series of catastrophic events that had brought the spiritual and temporal leader of this remote mountain kingdom into the free world after an exhausting month-long journey through inhospitable terrain had begun with the armed invasion of his homeland by the Chinese People's Republic in 1950 under the banner of "peaceful liberation," had continued with the systematic extermination of his people and culture under the banner of "democratic reforms," and had reached its apogee with the brutal suppression of the Tibetan National Uprising of 1959 under the guise of stamping out the "traitorous crimes of the Tibetan reactionary clique" and ensuring the integration of Tibet with the "Great Motherland" of China.

At Tezpur the Dalai Lama issued what under the circumstances was a remarkably dispassionate statement. It was written in the third person and outlined the course of events that had forced him to flee his country "of his own free will and not under duress." Thanking the government of India for the cordial reception accorded himself and his entourage, and stressing that his foremost concerns were "the well-being of his people" and "the perpetual flourishing of his sacred religion and freedom of his country," he expressed his "sincere regret at the tragedy that has overtaken Tibet" and heartfelt wish "that these troubles will be over soon without any bloodshed." Thereupon he boarded a special air-conditioned train sent from Calcutta to take him to Mussoorie, a tiny hill station northwest of New Delhi, where a house had been made available to him by a wealthy industrialist who had been a close friend of the late Mohandas K. Gandhi.

The Dalai Lama's presence in India placed Jawaharlal Nehru in a dilemma. To refuse asylum to the Tibetan leader would arouse a storm of criticism nationally—there had already been a series of anti-Chinese demonstrations in many cities, including one in Bombay during which a portrait of Mao Tse-tung had been pelted with eggs and tomatoes—as well as internationally. On the other hand, to grant asylum would infuriate Peking and weaken the Indian prime minister's increasingly precarious dream of peaceful coexistence with the People's Republic of China. Reluctantly he chose the latter course, and responded to the ensuing barrage of Chinese invective by opining in Parliament that what had happened in Tibet was a "clash of wills" rather than a clash of arms, and emphasizing that his government had "no intention of interfering in the internal affairs of China, with whom we have friendly relations." Within a year he made available to the Dalai Lama and his ministers a remote ghost town named Macleod Ganj in the Himalayan foothills of East Punjab some 450 miles northwest of New Delhi, where he hoped the question of Tibet would fade gracefully into obscurity and cause him no further problems.

Peking's leaders also were desirous that this should happen. The Tibetan Uprising had been a profound embarrassment to a government fond of castigating Western powers for acts of imperialist aggression, for the flight of the Dalai Lama had attracted a torrent of international condemnation. Having poured out a profusion of self-righteous commentary to convince the world that their acts of genocide against the people of Tibet had been carried out by the Tibetans themselves, nothing would have pleased them more than for Tibet to recede behind its traditional veil of mountains and mystery. The remaining members of the world community, who, with the exception of the Soviet bloc, had denounced "Red China" for its ruthless suppression of human liberties in Tibet but who had manifested no inclination to intervene militarily, were likewise content to let the matter rest.

The Dalai Lama, however, was determined that it should not.

Twenty-seven years have gone by since these events. Mao and Nehru are long dead, but this gentle and resolute Buddhist monk of fifty-one has emerged as a widely recognized and highly respected international figure, because of whom the question of Tibet is still very much alive. Ironically, much of the attention focused on this spiritual hierarch of an estimated fourteen million Tibetans and Mongolians is of a political nature.

To India, Tibet is no longer the peaceful and harmonious buffer state that had attacked none of its neighbors for more than a thousand years, the last three hundred under the rule of the Dalai Lamas. Indians have never forgiven China for invading the ancient theocracy in 1950 and using it as a launching pad in the Sino-Indian border war twelve years later. Nor have the Chinese forgiven India for providing sanctuary to the Dalai Lama and 85,000 other refugees from Tibet, and they are embittered that he presides there not only over all sects of Tibetan Buddhism but also over a Tibetan nation-in-exile. Recent attempts by Peking and New Delhi to restore diplomatic relations severed by hostilities two decades ago are reportedly focusing on the long-standing "border dispute," but there is little doubt that the future status of the Dalai Lama will be a major consideration in the outcome.

To the Soviet Union, Tibet occupies an immensely important strategic position between its eastern borders and the Chinese People's Republic. Having fought on several occasions in the past to prevent what it called the "dirty fabrication" of a "nonexistent Tibetan situation" from being discussed in the United Nations, Moscow has since changed its tune, declaring its support for the restoration of Tibet's autonomy and welcoming the Dalai Lama on a 1979 visit. In a recent book, the semi-official Soviet journalist Victor Louis has gone so far as to advance the fascinating thesis that the Dalai Lama might shift his seat of operations from India to Mongolia, and, with Russian backing, lead Tibetans, Mongolians, and Muslims from East Turkestan on a holy war against the Chinese.

To the United States, Tibet is a source of embarrassment. The paltry and half-hearted CIA assistance begun in the late 1950s ended with the thaw in Sino-American relations a decade later. In 1971 the White House ordered the suppression of a thirteen-minute United States Information Service (USIS) film entitled *Man from a Missing Land*, a documentary portraying the Chinese invasion of Tibet and the flight of the Dalai Lama, on the grounds that it might irritate China and jeopardize Richard Nixon's planned visit to Peking in February of the following year. Since that time, Washington has found it expedient to forget its earlier outrage at China's brutalization of the Tibetan people. Unlike thousands of Vietnamese, Laotians, and Cambodians, not to mention lesser numbers of Poles and Hungarians, Tibetans have never been granted refugee status in this nation of immigrants; of the 100,000 able to flee their country, barely 300 live in the United States. Only recently, after a long battle with the State Department, have U.S.-naturalized Tibetans been permitted to enter on their passports a village, region, or province of Tibet as their place of birth; prior to this they had been required to fill in "China." In the words of one of them, "Asking Tibetans to list China as their place of birth is like asking a Jew to write down Auschwitz." Likewise, the Dalai Lama was officially discouraged from applying for a visitor's visa to this country until 1979.

To the People's Republic of China, its occupation of Tibet represents three decades of utter failure and an unstable, potentially volatile future. China's invasion was not only illegal but also unwise, for her boundaries since that time have abutted those two hostile and powerful neighbors, the Soviet Union and India. Its economic policies have proven disastrous, upsetting Tibet's fragile economy and transforming a land which for centuries had known no famine into one in which there has been widespread starvation for the past two decades, and which is by far the poorest of all its territories. Its social policies have wrought equally tragic consequences. Three decades of political indoctrination, the destruction of Tibet's 3,000 monasteries, the killing of an estimated 400,000 believers, and the horrors of the Cultural Revolution have resulted neither in the eradication of the Tibetan identity nor in the conversion of Tibetans to Marxism, but rather in the deepening of inbred religious convictions and a smoldering hatred of the Chinese. Although he has been portrayed by the Chinese as a reactionary until very recently, the Dalai Lama is more beloved than ever. After years of lobbying the Western press to cover up or misrepresent its three decades of genocide in Tibet, Peking now openly acknowledges its "errors" and has promised to make Tibetans "masters in their own house." For the past several years it has intensified efforts begun in 1963 to persuade the Dalai Lama to return. Only with his help, the Chinese believe, will they be able to disentangle themselves from the chaos they have created and put that house in order.

To the people of Tibet, the Dalai Lama is a human manifestation of their patron saint, a Lord of Mercy and Compassion returned to earth to guide them on the path to enlightenment. "The Tibetans love the Dalai Lama," wrote Ippolito Desideri, a Jesuit missionary who spent five years in the Tibetan capital of Lhasa at the beginning of the eighteenth century, "because he has, an infinite number of times, become a man and taken upon himself the hardships and misery which afflict fragile, decrepit, and mortal humanity." Those living inside Tibet still look to him as their supreme ruler and pray that one day he will return to them in their Land of Snows. Those living outside Tibet also look to him as head of their nation in exile, an alternate Tibet with its own government, voluntary tax system, capital, and provinces, where under his guidance Tibetan arts, science, and religion are flourishing even while almost extinct in their native land. "Probably no leader in the world is so much loved by his followers," wrote Thomas Merton in 1973. "He means everything to them."

While the Dalai Lama's exile has been a national tragedy of unparalleled magnitude for the people of Tibet, it has not been without benefit to the rest of the world, because it has propelled this remarkable individual from his serene medieval kingdom on the Roof of the World into the turbulent twentieth century, where he personifies qualities that modern society no longer expects from its leaders. From his headquarters in the Indian Himalaya the Dalai Lama embodies the Buddha's teachings, sacrificing his personal desires for the public good and acting not only for the benefit of the Tibetan people but for the benefit of all living beings.

Although he is revered by his people as an incarnation of a deity, he is uncomfortable with excessive formality and prefers being treated as an ordinary human being. Although he possesses considerable personal wealth, he uses it to keep his ancient civilization alive in exile and lives the life of a simple Buddhist monk. Although he is a brilliant theologian and an avid student of the scriptures, he spends much of his time involved with political and mundane affairs. Although he heads the Tibetan Buddhist hierarchy, he is nondogmatic and stresses that the ultimate goals of the world's major religions are the same. Although he is one of the world's most charismatic religious figures, he has no interest in acting as a guru for the West.

Just as three decades of Communist oppression have not extinguished the faith of six million Tibetans, neither has a quarter-century of exile altered the Dalai Lama's unwavering conviction that someday he and his fellow refugees will return in peace and honor to their ancestral land. He has no economic power, no political power, and no military power: only faith that human determination is powerful enough to challenge external force. It appears that he is winning the battle.

The Thirteenth Dalai Lama   *Darjeeling 1910*

· CHAPTER I ·

A Child Is Born

T HE MUSLIN-CLAD FIGURE sat with spine erect and knees crossed in the traditional lotus posture on an ornate throne, its serene gaze directed southward over the main courtyard of the palace. As if in a trance, it maintained the same posture and contemplative expression as thousands of people passed by murmuring sacred mantras and twirling prayer wheels. Occasionally someone reached out to touch the throne or to place a flowing white ceremonial scarf at its base.

Later, when the audience hall had been cleared of visitors and locked for the night, the figure was still sitting in meditative posture; but on the following morning attendants discovered that its head had sagged slightly and turned to the east. Gently and silently, so as to cause as little disturbance as possible, they turned its face to the south again, and the day passed like the one that had preceded it. But the next morning found the head facing eastward once more.

On the northeast side of a nearby temple still under construction, a large star-shaped fungus with arms resembling the horns of a deer materialized at the base of a pillar of well-seasoned wood set into a great block of stone. A dragonflower appeared from the direction of the stairway on the east side of the main courtyard used for religious discourses. Masses of billowy white clouds resembling elephants of assorted sizes and in various postures loomed in the northeastern part of the sky.

It was nearing the end of the Tibetan Year of the Water Bird. Barely four weeks had passed since His Holiness Thupten Gyatso, the Thirteenth Dalai Lama, had passed away to the Heavenly Fields at the age of fifty-eight. There was a great, numbing sadness throughout the land. Women removed all their ornaments and wept unabashedly, and it was only with great effort that men held back their tears; some of the older ones could not. Families went into mourning. Prayer flags and banners were brought down, and butter lamps burned in every home and on every roof. Smoldering incense sent up puffs of white smoke from rooftops, and special services were held in monasteries, temples, private homes, and nomad tents. The entire nation took up a collection to build a shrine to house the mortal remains of its beloved leader; gold, silver, and precious stones poured into the holy city of Lhasa to ensure its being worthy of his greatness. All the while his hastily embalmed body, swathed in cotton, the face covered by a lifelike effigy, kept mute watch over the palace in which he had spent most of his earthly life.

Almost two years passed. Throughout Tibet there were signs of despondency, for although the government had instructed all local authorities to be on the lookout for the births of remarkable male children in their areas and the occurrence of any significant signs in connection with such births, no positive reports had been received. There was, to be sure, no way of knowing just how much time would transpire before the spirit of the late Dalai Lama could find and enter its new human abode. For, as the Buddha taught, to be reborn in human form is "as rare as for a solitary one-eyed turtle, swimming beneath the surface of the eastern oceans, to come up once every hundred years with its head through the hole of a solitary ox yoke floating in that same vast ocean."

Although the Tibetans were certain that the spirit of the Thirteenth Dalai Lama would find a suitable body in which to be reborn, a number of practical considerations made them wish it would do so sooner rather than later. The political situation in Tibet had been unstable since the death of Thupten Gyatso. Externally, there had been traditional skirmishes on the eastern frontier with the Chinese, who despite their expulsion from the country two decades earlier still refused to recognize Tibetan independence. Internally, a high-ranking lay official named Lungshar had become involved in a plot to overthrow the government and was severely punished; the repercussions of the act rocked the country. Tibet desperately needed a new Dalai Lama to provide a rallying point around which her disparate elements could unite, and to promote a return to the stability engendered and inspired by the Thirteenth Incarnation.

Ringed by lofty, snowcapped peaks, Lake Lhamoi Latso lies some ninety miles and ten days' journey southeast of Lhasa. Its crystal waters were recognized as having mystical powers by the Second Dalai Lama in the early sixteenth century, and since that time it had proven an invaluable aid in prophesying future events, including clues that led to the discovery of the Thirteenth Incarnation. To its sacred shores in the summer of the Year of the Wood Hog came a small party headed by Reting Rinpoche,[1] the regent of Tibet, who was administering the country during the interregnum. The group dispersed along the lakefront and despite intermittent rain, strong winds, and blazing sunshine, remained in deep meditation.

All at once, miraculously, the regent saw in the clear waters the Tibetan letters *a*, *ka*, and *ma* appear suddenly and then vanish. As he continued his spiritual contemplation, the vision of a three-storied temple with a gilded roof and walls clad in greenish-blue tiles became visible. To the east of the temple was a white path leading to a small mountain nearby, and at the place where the path met the mountain sat a single-storied blue house with unusual gutter pipes. After writing down these details and preserving them under the official seal, the party made its way back to Lhasa.

Although elated at the regent's revelations, Tibetan leaders were in somewhat of a quandary, for no reports had been received from any local authority of a possible Fourteenth Dalai Lama. The abbots of Drepung, Sera, and Ganden monasteries on the outskirts of Lhasa deemed it expedient to send search parties to the east in the hope of finding the new incarnation. Before doing so, however, they had first to consult the state oracle at the Nechung monastery.

Tibetan oracles are monks or nuns in whom deities known as *dharmapala* (protectors of religion) are said to return to earth. The celebrated Nechung oracle incarnates the god Pehar and has been greatly relied upon for his prophecies. It is said that the Nechung monastery was founded after an early Dalai Lama captured a particularly destructive evil spirit, sealed it in a wooden box, and cast it into the Kyichu River. Upon hearing of this, one of the abbots of Drepung sent a young disciple to fetch the box, with the admonition not to open it. But the disciple could not resist the urge to look inside. When he removed the lid, a pigeon flew out and lighted in a nearby grove of trees, and when he tried to catch it, it vanished. The disciple recounted the tale to his master, who prophesied that wherever that spirit made its abode, there prosperity would always come. So Nechung, built within that oasis of greenery, became a cloister of happiness, and its famous oracle was in regular contact with that spirit, so that he was able to advise the Tibetan government on all matters of state. One such incarnation is said to have provided certain particulars that aided in the quest for the Thirteenth Dalai Lama, including the names of his mother and father and the whereabouts of his house.

Dressed in handsome yellow brocade robes and wearing a highly polished mirror on his chest, the oracle ascended his throne to the haunting sound of monastic music. Two rows of drums beat slowly to his left, trumpets and oboes moaned to his right; facing him, a body of seated monks, their eyes half closed, chanted the sacred mantra in a deep monotone. The abbots and government officials watched in awe and reverent silence. The oracle sat for a long time in silent meditation. Suddenly he began to quiver. The monk musicians drew closer, picking up the tempo and drumming and blowing directly into his ears. He sprang from the throne, breaking from the grip of his four attendants. Then his eyes closed tightly, his face contorted into a frightening grimace, and he went into a trance.

Two attendants came forward, staggering under the weight of a golden headdress encrusted with gems, which they placed upon his head. Shaking with convulsions, he continued to dance wildly to the increasingly strident tempo of the drums. Finally, with perspiration streaming down his face, he muttered a pronouncement that was immediately taken down by a monk scribe. Three search parties should leave Lhasa, he said, to find the new Dalai Lama. One must proceed toward Dakpo in the southeast, another toward Kham in the east, and a third group toward Amdo in the northeast.

On a chill September evening in the Year of the Fire Rat, a heavy snowfall began to descend on Lhasa. Early the next morning, a slender, scholarly man in his late sixties trudged through the knee-deep accumulation on his way to offer prayers at the Jokhang Temple, a cloak pulled around his shoulders, his head bent in thought. Kyitsang Rinpoche[2] was wondering whether he and his three attendants would be able to begin their journey to Amdo as planned. The abbot knew that the day chosen for their departure had been designated an auspicious one, but as the snowflakes swirled blindingly around his head, it seemed that the venture might have to be postponed.

Nevertheless, when the group gathered at nine as arranged, the skies suddenly cleared. Brilliant sunlight began to melt the snow, and the roads leading out of the capital were soon passable. Cheered by such propitious circumstances, the quartet hastened on its way.

The journey to the province of Kham took the better part of two months and led the tiny band through a terrain dominated by barren mountains and rolling, grassy meadows dotted with small lakes. Snow fell continuously and was regarded by the group as a good omen, indicating that they would be successful in their mission. Travel was difficult and at times dangerous, but although one of the party suffered a minor case of frostbite, no serious injuries were incurred. When they reached the village of Riwoche, Kyitsang Rinpoche wrote to the exiled Panchen Lama[3] in Jyekundo and asked if recent skirmishes along the Sino-Tibetan border could impede the mission. In a letter that arrived a month later, the Panchen assured them that there should be no problems.

On the second day of the first month of the Year of the Fire Bull during Losar, the Tibetan New Year festival, the group called on the Panchen Lama and presented him with gifts and sealed documents from the Lhasa government. Over tea—a soupy mixture enhanced by the addition of butter, salt, and a pinch of borax[4]—the Panchen gave Kyitsang Rinpoche the names of three boys he had been told were likely candidates, but urged him at the same time to test any boy who seemed promising. He provided the band with two helpers, extra horses and donkeys, and a reliable guide, and aimed them northward toward Amdo with his blessing.

After a month-long trek through cold, desolate steppe land, the party was met a short distance from the Kumbum monastery by a welcoming committee made up of the abbot and some sixty horsemen chosen from the eighty nomadic tribes in the area. White ceremonial scarves (khata) were exchanged, and they all retired to a large tent that had been pitched in the center of the plain in anticipation of the arrival. Large quantities of rice and butter tea were consumed around a fire stoked with yak dung, whose acrid fumes kept everyone at a respectable distance.

Several hours later, the party from Lhasa, accompanied by this colorful and exuberant retinue, made a grand entrance into Kumbum. Just inside the monastery grounds, Kyitsang Rinpoche gasped in astonishment and drew in the reins of his horse. Directly in their path stood a three-storied temple clad in greenish-blue tiles with a gilded roof. It seemed to all the very temple that had appeared in the prophetic waters of Lake Lhamoi Latso. A light rain fell, and many differently shaped white clouds appeared in the sky: these were auspicious signs. They felt that they were getting closer to their goal.

The Kumbum monastery was founded by the Third Dalai Lama when he passed through the province of Amdo on his way to Mongolia in 1582, and had since grown into one of the largest and most famous in all of Tibet. The temple with greenish-blue tiles was the holiest of its many buildings and was called the Temple of the Golden Tree. Inside it was a magnificent silver *chörten*[5] decorated with turquoise and other precious stones, which reached almost to the roof. Surrounding this *chörten* were half a dozen smaller *chörten*s fashioned of gold. These in turn were surrounded by hundreds of gold and silver butter lamps over ten feet in circumference, each of which had no fewer than fifteen wicks. Replenished each day by monk attendants, their flickering flames illuminated the temple's inner walls, which were covered with intricate paintings of famous saints and scholars who had lived in Kumbum. Within the great silver *chörten* grew a sacred sandalwood tree known as the Tree of Ten Thousand Images. The tree was said to have sprung from the earth on the very spot where the Buddhist reformer Tsong Khapa had been born in a nomad's tent in the early fifteenth century. On its leaves could be seen mystical symbols and distinct letters of the Tibetan alphabet. These leaves had been sought so eagerly by pious souvenir hunters that the tree had been enclosed in the glittering structure to ensure its survival.[6] Nearby stood a life-sized golden statue of Tsong Khapa.

Since Amdo was under Chinese control at the time, it was necessary for Kyitsang Rinpoche to apprise the local governor, Ma Pu-feng, of the purpose of his visit and to secure his cooperation. Several weeks after their arrival at Kumbum, the group went to the Chinese bureau in the provincial capital of nearby Sining laden with fine gifts donated by local Tibetan merchants, who were only too happy to accumulate merit toward a good rebirth by aiding such a holy mission. Each member of the party carried one kind of offering: gold, silver, silk, or incense. Governor Ma greeted the Tibetans warmly. Giving them tea and fruit, he promised his assistance. Elated, the group returned to Kumbum.

Of the three children mentioned by the Panchen Lama, one had died before the party reached Amdo. The second candidate was apparently favored by the Panchen because he had grasped the Panchen's rosary during the great *Kalachakra* services some months before and then refused to let it go, an act considered a great omen. Accordingly, two of the search party—Sonam Wangdu and Khenrab Tenzin—went to the boy's house and, after resting themselves and drinking tea, asked that he be shown to them. Clad in new clothes, the lad was ushered into the room by his proud mother. Although he seemed to his visitors somewhat less than special at first glance and was, moreover, exceptionally shy, Khenrab Tenzin coiled a rosary that had belonged to the Thirteenth Dalai Lama around his wrist in the hope that the boy might show some sign of recognition. There was no such response, and the youngster soon ran from the room in tears.

While the second candidate was being examined, Kyitsang Rinpoche and Tsedrun Lobsang, accompanied by a monk attendant and an interpreter from the Kumbum monastery who had learned the Lhasa dialect while living in Sera monastery, made their way to the house of the third nominee in the tiny village of Taktser nearby. The abbot disguised himself as a servant by wearing a sheepskin cloak over his monk's robes; around his neck he wore a rosary of the late Dalai Lama's. Tsedrun Lobsang was more richly dressed and pretended to be the head of the party. They planned to introduce themselves as religious pilgrims and ask for shelter. In Tibet even the poorest home would open its doors to any who might ask, be they pilgrims, merchants, or even beggars. Kyitsang Rinpoche and the other "servant" would ask to be lodged in the anteroom, while Tsedrun Lobsang and the interpreter would proceed to the family's main living quarters and there scrutinize the boy. But it so happened that the child was playing in the anteroom when the party entered the house, and immediately sat himself down on the abbot's lap. Grasping the rosary, the child looked up at him and said softly, "I want this rosary."

"You may have it if you can guess who I am," replied Kyitsang Rinpoche. "Do you know?"

The child looked off into space, and when his eyes settled once more on the abbot's, tears had come to them. "You are a lama of Sera," he declared.

"And who is with me?" asked the abbot.

The child replied, "It is Tsedrun Lobsang."

Only with great difficulty was the group able to conceal its joy. It seemed likely that the right child had been found at last, but further tests would have to be made in order to be absolutely certain. After taking leave of the family the next day—not a simple task, for the child made quite obvious his wish to accompany them and wept profusely when finally dissuaded from doing so—the group returned to Kumbum, where Kyitsang Rinpoche sent a coded telegram to the Tibetan government in Lhasa stating what had transpired and requesting further instructions. Since there was only one telegraph line in Tibet, from Lhasa to the Indian border town of Kalimpong in Bengal, the message had to be sent from Sining, through China and India. Four weeks later came the reply from Lhasa: Kyitsang Rinpoche was to test the child further by displaying to him various possessions of the late Dalai Lama and report back as soon as possible.

From that day on, the child gave his mother no peace. Every time the family mastiff barked, he ran to the front gate to see if Kyitsang Rinpoche and his party had returned. "Please make some special tea," he would urge. "Then perhaps they will come." It seemed that the subject was never off his mind. "When they *do* come, you must give them some good food and a place to rest," he repeated at least once each day, "for they have traveled from a very distant place." His favorite pastime was gathering various household objects, placing them on the kitchen table, and announcing matter-of-factly, "I'm packing to go to Lhasa." It was almost, his mother reflected years later, as though he knew.

As Kyitsang Rinpoche and his three original attendants set out for Taktser, the resonant tones of the monastery's conch shell echoed behind them and the sweet voice of a cuckoo rang out in the balmy spring air. On the way they passed a group of men carrying vessels filled with curd, milk, and water. All of these were good signs.

As they neared the top of the pass close to the village, they encountered a Chinese youth leading three donkeys laden with wood. There were two ways to the house they were seeking, he informed them, but the lower path would prove more convenient. Following his instructions, they came presently to a clearing from which the house could be seen clearly. The late Dalai Lama had rested there while visiting the area some thirty years earlier, and it was said that he had observed the house carefully and remarked on its beauty. Since the upper path would have provided a shorter route, the party wondered if the youth might have been a celestial being who had appeared to show them the proper way. When they arrived at the main gate, their suspicions were confirmed.

The house was typically Tibetan: a single-storied rectangular structure with a broad, flat roof situated around a paved courtyard with no windows in the outside walls. In the center of the yard was a round stone base supporting a tall wooden mast from which fluttered a banner of white cotton bearing hundreds of block-printed prayers. From one of its two chimneys a wisp of smoke rose into the clear sky, indicating that it was time for evening tea. There was no doubt in their minds that this was the very house that had been seen in the waters of the sacred lake, for not only did it have blue eaves but it also had bizarre gutter pipes fashioned of gnarled juniper wood. Had they not followed the suggestion of the Chinese youth and come upon it from the other direction instead, they might have failed to recognize it.

The child's mother was astonished to see the humble servant to whom her son had taken such a liking appear at her door resplendent in the saffron and gold robes of a Grand Lama. Regaining her composure, she invited the party inside for tea and Amdo bread, apologizing for the absence of her husband, who she said was away at the mill. Kyitsang Rinpoche explained that the child had given signs of being an incarnation and that he wished to test him further. Since there were perhaps a thousand incarnate lamas in Tibet and since her eldest son had been identified as one several years earlier and was now living at Kumbum, the possibility that her youngest son might also be an incarnation did not surprise the woman. Had she known which lama her son was suspected of reincarnating, her reaction might have been different.

On an earthen sleeping platform (*kang*) in the bedroom adjacent to the kitchen, under which was a small furnace, articles that had belonged to the Thirteenth Dalai Lama were laid side by side with clever imitations. Kyitsang Rinpoche and Khenrab Tenzin stood to the right of the platform, Sonam Wangdu and Tsedrum Lobsang to the left. The abbot took two black rosaries in his hand and asked the child to express his preference. Without hesitation he chose the correct one and put it around his neck. He did likewise when confronted with a pair of yellow rosaries.

Two walking sticks were then shown to the child, one with a handle of iron and the other with a handle of bronze. Slowly and deliberately he reached out and grasped the first, then paused and let it drop back in place and chose the second. The men began to breathe more easily, for the test had been an intentionally difficult one. Both walking sticks had belonged to the Thirteenth Dalai Lama, but he had given the first one to a lama who in turn gave it to Kyitsang Rinpoche; the reason the boy had touched it was clearly to indicate its previous history.

Finally the child was presented with two small ivory drums. The one belonging to the late Dalai Lama was simple in design and inlaid with turquoise, while the other was beautifully ornamented with variegated silks and an elaborate floral design. He immediately selected the correct drum and began beating it with his right hand while he gazed at the group with a beatific smile. "Now that we had witnessed these miraculous performances," wrote Sonam Wangdu some years later, "our minds were filled with deep devotion, joy, and gaiety. Indeed we were so moved that tears of happiness filled our eyes; scarcely able to breathe, we could neither sit properly on the mat nor speak a word. Then, unable to think what to do next, we just sat gazing fondly at each other, praying no obstacles would arise." They would soon discover that their prayers were in vain.

Now that the new incarnation had been found, the remaining pieces of the puzzle fell into place. With regard to the visions from the sacred lake, the house at the foot of the path had already been identified as that in which the child was living and the temple as the one at Kumbum. The letter *a* indicated the province of Amdo in which the discovery had taken place, while the letter *ka* had a dual significance. First it denoted the name of the Kumbum monastery (of which the letter *ka*, approximated by the *k* in English, is the main letter of the initial consonant cluster) and likewise the nearby hermitage of

Karma Shar-Ston, the first letter of whose name was identical with that of the name of its famous founder, Karmapa Rolpai Dorje, Tibet's first recognized incarnation. Finally, the letter *ma* was seen as the second letter of the hermitage's name.

Although the child's parents could remember nothing remarkable about the circumstances of his birth, villagers pointed out that the boy's father had been seriously ill for a long time but was completely cured on the day his son was born, at which time a rainbow had shone upon the house. The birth of an incarnate lama is frequently accompanied by many difficulties in the locality where it takes place, they added, and for the past four years their crops had failed and many of their most valuable livestock had died. All this was reported by ciphered telegram to Lhasa, and several days later came the reply. "It is now certain that the true incarnation of His Holiness the Dalai Lama is the infant Lhamo Dhondup who was born to Choekyong Tsering and Sonam Tsomo on the fifth day of the fifth month of the Tibetan Wood Hog Year. It is essential to find a way of bringing him back immediately." The order was more easily given than followed.

General Ma Pu-feng, the Muslim warlord who administered Amdo as part of the Chinese province of Chinghai, was a greedy and ruthless man who saw to it that his domain was virtually independent of the Nationalist government at Nangking. It was widely believed that he had plotted the murder of the former abbot of Kumbum, whose friendship with Chiang Kai-shek might have proven inimical to his ambitions; and there were rumors that he had succeeded to the governorship by bribing a Kuomintang military commander with three tins labeled "Elephant Brand Scented Saffron" which were in fact filled with gold.

Kyitsang Rinpoche approached the general and advised him that he had already examined two promising candidates but that there were a dozen more whose names had been brought to his attention. It would take many days and considerable time to visit each in his home, he continued, but if some provision were made to gather them together at a central point—like Kumbum, for instance—the necessary tests could be conducted quickly. Ma seized the bait. He agreed that the children should be examined together but insisted that it should be at his headquarters in Sining. While disclaiming any interest in the affair ("The manner of testing them and so on are religious matters with which we have no concern at all"), he stipulated that he and four of his officials be present ("As this is something we have never seen or heard before, you must allow some of us to watch").

On the appointed date the Tibetans arranged the real possessions of the Thirteenth Dalai Lama, paired with their imitations as before, on a long table at the Chinese Bureau and invited the children to approach one by one and make known their choices. The event was carried off with great panache. Kyitsang Rinpoche made an impressive show of solemnly examining the children's ears and the veins of their tongues, while Sonam Wangdu and

Khenrab Tenzin pretended to note their auspicious and inauspicious signs. None of the children chose correctly more than two of the four items, and some were so shy that they made no choice at all. The monks presented the parents with *khata*s and rolls of the finest woollen cloth and sent the group to their homes.

When the general asked if anything had been decided, Kyitsang Rinpoche answered solemnly that he was empowered only to notify Lhasa and await further instructions. Ma nodded, then went over to the parents of Lhamo Dhondup. "It is obvious your son is the reincarnation of some famous lama, although the Rinpoche tells me it is too soon to know which one," he told them. "In the meantime I think it advisable that he be placed in Kumbum monastery." The advice was properly regarded as an order.

Fortunately two of their sons, Lobsang Samden and Thupten Jigme Norbu,[7] were already at Kumbum. "My parents arrived on a crisp winter morning with Lhamo Dhondup," the latter remembers. "We spent a few happy days together until it was time for my parents to go back to their farm. My mother went first, consoling Lhamo Dhondup by telling him that she was going to visit her parents. But then early one morning my father went off too, and Lobsang Samden and I were left to look after our small brother, who was naturally very upset when he noticed that his parents were missing and that he was to stay on in the monastery without them. Dissolved in tears, he begged us to take him home. I was almost seventeen years old, but I was still helpless in the face of such misery. Lobsang Samden was the first to join little Lhamo Dhondup in his sobs, but it was not long before I, too, dissolved into tears. A last attempt to distract my small brother by getting him to look at the dancing snowflakes outside the window naturally failed, and then we were all three in tears."

Lhamo was placed in the care of his paternal uncle Changchub Jimpa, who had returned to the monastery to look after him and his brother Lobsang. But most of the time he remained at the monastery while negotiations dragged on between General Ma and the Tibetan government in Lhasa, Lhamo was alone. Lobsang and several other boys his age had daily sessions with an elderly monk tutor who taught them the scriptures, and Lhamo had to wait impatiently for the classes to end while constantly trying to attract his brother's attention. The tutor was not unaware of this and, although he usually maintained strict discipline among his students by means of a bamboo rod, sometimes placed Lhamo on his lap, wrapped him in the folds of his gown, and fed him dried apricots from a wooden bowl. Those occasions, and the playtimes with his brother Lobsang, were the only bright spots during Lhamo's residence at Kumbum.

Several months passed. Despite Kyitsang Rinpoche's diligent efforts to conceal the discovery, rumors were flying thick and fast. Inquisitive visitors began to descend on Kumbum with increasing frequency, among them Chinese and European photographers. The abbot knew that the time had come for him to approach Ma Pu-feng and admit that the incarnation he had been seeking was that of the Dalai Lama, that the child from Taktser was the most likely local candidate, and that the Tibetan government sought permission to have him brought to Lhasa as soon as possible. He approached the Chinese Bureau filled with apprehension, for it was entirely possible that the general would seize the boy and attempt to establish his own rule over Tibet.

General Ma was exceptionally pleased—although under the circumstances not surprised—when told that the Taktser boy might be the next incarnation of the Dalai Lama, and pressed for details about his selection. The abbot made his replies as vague as he dared. He stressed that two other candidates were already in Lhasa and that only after further examinations had been carried out by the holy lamas and spiritual beings would the final choice be made. The general listened politely and then replied: if it were necessary that the boy leave immediately, permission would be granted upon payment of 100,000 silver dollars to Kumbum monastery, the local government of Sining, and the commander in chief—Ma himself. Kyitsang Rinpoche wired Lhasa for the ransom money and, hoping to begin the long westward journey before winter's onset, began hiring camels and donkeys from Mongol chieftains in the Kokonor region and supervising the construction of wooden packs for the animals to carry. Then he and the others waited impatiently for the funds to arrive and permission to depart.

The money came shortly thereafter, but the permission did not. Ma Pu-feng maintained that he would gladly send the group on its way but was constrained from doing so by the monks of Kumbum, who insisted that the child be officially proclaimed the Fourteenth Dalai Lama then and there.

It was a clever excuse, for what he said was not without truth. By providing shelter for a Dalai Lama and being the site of his official recognition, the monastery would have its reputation enormously enhanced, and financial contributions from pilgrims and devotees would increase proportionately. It should also be pointed out that through the centuries the government of Tibet's eastern frontier areas was in a constant state of flux, administrative control passing back and forth between Tibetans, Mongols, Manchus, and Chinese. Over the years the Chinese had the foresight to cultivate amicable relations with key monks and lamas by contributing generously to the support of important monasteries in those regions, so it came as no surprise to Kyitsang Rinpoche when loyal sources informed him that behind Kumbum's intransigence lay the wily General Ma.

When the Tibetan government appealed directly to Nanking to instruct the general to release the child, it discovered that he was a law unto himself and would have to be dealt with directly. Evidently it had become apparent to Ma and his cohorts at Kumbum that their insistence on the child's being brought to Lhasa as a mere candidate had been a bluff. He demanded additional ransom: 300,000 silver dollars, full sets of the Thirteenth Dalai Lama's robes and throne ornaments, and complete editions of two sacred Tibetan Buddhist texts, the *Kangyur* and *Tengyur*, inscribed in gold letters. The Tibetans had no choice but to pay, and did so through a group of Chinese Muslim merchants who were en route to Lhasa as the first stage of their pilgrimage to Mecca and would be repaid at an extremely favorable exchange rate.

When everything had been settled at last, little Lhamo Dhondup was clad in new robes and, in the privacy of Kyitsang Rinpoche's quarters, was set upon a throne that had been used by the Thirteenth Dalai Lama. In a brief ceremony the child was offered tea and rice, and Kyitsang Rinpoche performed a ritual known as the mandala offering. After receiving blessings from the boy, the group offered 100,000 butter lamps at the Temple of the Golden Tree and spent the rest of the day making meritorious offerings to the monks and novices of the monastery, handing each of them a silver dollar. Then Lhamo Dhondup was taken to the Congregation Hall, where the Abbot of Kumbum offered him tea and rice followed by fruits. The weather was fine and the day passed auspiciously.

Finally, after a year of negotiations and two and a half years from Kyitsang Rinpoche's visit to the little house in Taktser, the party was able to leave for the holy city of Lhasa. The child destined to become the spiritual and temporal leader of the Tibetan nation had just celebrated his fourth birthday.[8]

Notes

1. The word *rinpoche* (pronounced rin'-poe-shay), translated roughly as "precious one" or "precious like a jewel" and signifying the highest titular honor in Tibet, was conferred on persons believed to be reincarnations of famous religious teachers. Frequently the first name of a Rinpoche referred to the monastery in which he took up residence after his discovery as a young child. The Regent, for instance, came from the Reting monastery some sixty miles northeast of Lhasa.
2. Clinging like an eagle's nest to a sheer cliff and thereby deriving its evocative name, the Kyitsang monastery was located just west of Sera monastery. Kyitsang Rinpoche was its abbot.
3. The Panchen Lama is, after the Dalai Lama, the highest and most revered incarnation in Tibet. The one referred to here died within a year of the above incident, but his reincarnation, the Seventh Panchen, played an important role in subsequent Tibetan history and will be discussed at length in later chapters.
4. Chinese rather than Indian tea was preferred and came into the country through the southeastern province of Kham in the form of pressed bricks weighing approximately one kilogram apiece and frequently containing whole leaves and even stalks. Salt and soda, gathered by nomads on the Chang Tang (Northern Plains), were used to flavor it and to draw out the color; and the butter was that of the *dri*, or female yak. The mixture was boiled and then churned in a long wooden cylinder affixed with a plunger before serving. Tibetans are enthusiastic tea drinkers and can consume from thirty to eighty cups a day.

5. Similar to the stupa of Indian Buddhism, the *chörten* is a cone-shaped masonry structure of various sizes and usually contains religious relics or the ashes of deceased lamas or monks who were great teachers. The word is a combination of *mchod* (offering) and *rten* (receptacle).

6. In the middle of the nineteenth century, the French Lazarist missionary Abbé Huc approached the tree with a great deal of skepticism. His report: "Our eyes were first directed with earnest curiosity to the leaves, and we were filled with an absolute consternation of astonishment at finding that, in point of fact, there were upon each of the leaves well-formed Thibetian characters, all of a green colour, some darker, some lighter than the leaf itself. Our first impression was a suspicion of fraud on the part of the Lamas; but after a minute examination of every detail, we could not discover the least deception. The characters all appeared to us portions of the leaf itself, equally with its veins and nerves; the position was not the same in all . . . the younger leaves represented the characters only in a partial state of formation. . . . More profound intellects than ours may, perhaps, be able to supply a satisfactory explanation of the mysteries of this singular tree; but as to us, we altogether give it up. Our readers may smile at our ignorance; but we care not, so that the sincerity and truth of our statement be not suspected." E. Huc, *Travels in Tartary, Thibet, and China (1844–1848)*, 2 vols. (London, 1879), II, 52–54.

7. Born in 1922 and the eldest of the Dalai Lama's four brothers, Norbu was recognized at the age of eight to be the reincarnation of a famous monk named Taktser Rinpoche.

8. There are two primary written sources for the Dalai Lama's discovery: Sonam Wangdu, *The Discovery of the XIVth Dalai Lama* (Bangkok, 1975), and Basil Gould, *Report on the Discovery, Recognition and Installation of the Fourteenth Dalai Lama* (New Delhi, 1941).

Lake Lhamoi Latso   *Ü-Tsang 1980*

· CHAPTER 2 ·

The Land of Snows

O NCE, over a thousand years ago, it was called Khawachen, the Land of Snows. Surrounded on three sides by towering snowcapped peaks of the tallest mountains on earth, it stood alone atop the roof of the world, proud and impregnable. Today it is known as Tibet.[1] It has proven a vulnerable land, as invasions by the Mongols, the Manchus, and most recently the Chinese will attest. But the majestic mountains endure, as does the pride of its people.

Ethnographic Tibet is bordered on the south by the mighty Himalaya, on the west by the Karakoram and Ladakh mountains, and on the north by the Altyn Tagh range. Only to the northeast, where the land slopes gradually into China, is there a gap in the imposing barrier that encloses an area greater than Alaska and California combined. It is located north of India, Nepal, Bangladesh, and Burma; east of Pakistan and Kashmir; south of the Soviet Union, Sinkiang (Chinese Turkestan), and Mongolia; and west of China. Tibet is the highest country in the world, and three-quarters of it lies at an elevation of 16,000 feet and upward, higher than Mont Blanc, the loftiest summit in Europe, and too cold for crops or even trees to grow.

Tibet is made up of three provinces. A large portion of the central province of Ü-Tsang lies in the Chang Tang (Northern Plain), a terrain so desolate that Tibetans call it "the land of no man and no dog." The Chang Tang is studded with saltwater lakes, the highest in the world, which glisten like gemstones. Around their shores are found rich deposits of borax, soda, and potash, and vast areas in the vicinity are so white with saline incrustation that the unwary traveler might suffer as from snow blindness. On the fringe of the plateau live nomadic shepherds, and until recent years bands of mounted brigands preyed on unprotected caravans crossing its uninhabitable interior.

Southern and western Tibet complete Ü-Tsang. Here flow the rushing waters of the Tsangpo,[2] at 12,000 feet above sea level probably the highest navigable river in the world, and its tributaries. Here, too, converge ancient trading routes from China, India, Nepal, Kashmir, Mongolia, Turkestan, and Siberia, along which once passed caravans of horses, mules, sheep, yaks, and camels accompanied by traders, monks, and religious pilgrims. Unlike the barren plateau to its north, many towns and villages are scattered here, including three of the four largest in the land. The pre-1951 population of the capital city of Lhasa was 35,000 to 40,000, Shigatse 13,000 to 20,000, and Gyantse approximately 8,000.

In eastern Tibet, or Dokham, are the two other provinces: Kham in the southeast and Amdo, where the present Dalai Lama was discovered, in the northeast. Although differing somewhat in dress and dialect the Khampas and Amdoas are similar in many ways, especially in contrast with their brethren from Ü-Tsang. Unlike the latter, who have high cheekbones, flat noses, and round heads, the people of Dokham are tall, broad-shouldered, and long-headed with more angular noses.[3] Possibly the central Tibetans derive from the same ancestral stock as the Chinese, the Burmese, and the Thais, and the eastern Tibetans from the Mongoloid race; but for a number of reasons a systematic study has been out of the question.[4] Another characteristic distinguishing the easterners from the generally easygoing central Tibetans, and one that will be seen later in this book to play a critical role in Tibetan history, is their more demonstrative and often volatile nature. The Khampas in particular have a history of clan warfare: quite possibly these resolute warriors fought each other as often as they did the Chinese along their borders. Dokham is more populous than central Tibet and its soil is more fertile. It has forests, an abundant supply of water, and good grazing lands; for centuries its peoples dwelt mainly in scattered villages and engaged in farming, cattle breeding, and herding. Tibetans say that the best religion comes from Ü-Tsang, the best warriors from Kham, and the best horses from Amdo.

Tibet's climate is dry and cold and the air extraordinarily clear and rarefied, so much so that in recent years the handful of Westerners permitted to visit Lhasa—a mere 12,000 feet above sea level—have been provided with a preliminary medical checkup and oxygen containers next to their beds as a matter of course. Much of the Indian monsoon is blocked by the Himalayan range, so Lhasa averages but eighteen inches of rainfall annually and the Chang Tang plateau to its north only one-third as much. Similarly, most of the snowfall in the Land of Snows is confined to the lofty mountains encircling it. The heaviest accumulations rarely exceed four feet on the plateau or eight feet along the southern border; on the opposite side of the Himalaya, by way of contrast, they tend to be considerably greater. The sun is extremely strong, but when it sets the temperature drops markedly; a visitor to Lhasa in 1921 noted that the difference between the temperature in the sun during the day and the temperature at night frequently exceeded eighty degrees Fahrenheit.[5] In winter the bitter cold is intensified by ferocious winds that sweep across the land with a fury, creating blinding sand and dust storms and forcing man and beast alike to seek shelter.

Despite the dryness of the climate, however, the land is not devoid of water for drinking or cultivation: from the Tibetan highlands flow some of Asia's greatest rivers. Four rise near the sacred Mount Kailash in the southwest. The Sengye Khabab (Out of the Lion's Mouth) flows westward through Kashmir to become the Indus of Pakistan; the Lanchen Khabab (Out of the Elephant's Mouth) southward through the Himalaya to become the Sutlej of India; the Mapcha Khabab (Out of the Peacock's Mouth) a similar route to become the sacred Ganges; and the Tachok Khabab (Out of the Horse's Mouth) eastward, merging with the Kyichu south of Lhasa to form the Tsangpo, which winds through Assam and Bengal. In the east rise the Salween, which flows through Burma; the Mekong, through Laos and Thailand; the Huang Ho (Yellow River), through China; and the Yangtse, running through Kham into China and frequently serving as a natural *de facto* border separating ethnographic from political Tibet.

Tibet's political boundaries have shifted recurrently through the ages. During the reign of the Chöegyal, or Religious Kings, from the seventh to the ninth century A.D., it possessed a vast Central Asian empire encompassing parts of China, Nepal, Turkestan, India, Pakistan, and Burma. Later, owing to a combination of practical considerations and the pacifist nature of Buddhist teachings, it withdrew behind its lofty mountain barriers. Until the establishment of a Manchu protectorate over Tibet in 1720, Ü-Tsang, Kham, and Amdo were subject to Lhasa's political control. When the Thirteenth Dalai Lama proclaimed Tibetan independence after the overthrow of the Manchu Ch'ing dynasty in 1911, however, only in Ü-Tsang and western Kham was the Lhasa government able to extend its authority, for it lacked the military might to expel the Chinese—particularly local Muslim warlords like Ma Pu-feng—from eastern Kham and Amdo. Despite frequent border skirmishes in Kham, the situation remained basically unchanged until the Chinese Communist invasion in October 1950.

Roughly half of Tibet's six million people were nomadic, not a remarkable figure when one considers that the vast majority of the land was situated at altitudes where traditional methods of cultivation would have been futile. The mountain nomads, or Drokpa as they called themselves, lived on remote, windswept tablelands in black tents fashioned from woven yak hair. These often voluminous structures, some of which were able to accommodate as many as two hundred people, were partitioned into separate rooms and secured to the ground by iron pins or animal horns. Low walls of mud and stone or, more frequently, of yak dung were built around their bases to keep out wind and snow; to their sloping roofs were attached scores of colorful prayer flags, which fluttered in the breeze and offered up continual invocations to the heavens. At the entrance of each tent was a fire pit straddled by a stove large enough to hold two or three large cauldrons, and lining the

nearby walls were wooden chests containing foodstuffs and personal be-
longings. Opposite the entrance, at the far end of the tent, was the family
altar, holding images of the Buddha and other sacred objects, the whole illuminated by a cluster of butter lamps kept burning day and night. Outside,
where all but the most elderly of this hardy people preferred to sleep on
sheepskins and covered with coarse yak-hair blankets, a ferocious mastiff
could always be found tethered to a stake and maintaining a vigilant watch.
Upon observing some of these unique habitations during his expedition to
Tibet in the middle of the nineteenth century, the Lazarist missionary Abbé
Huc commented that they seemed to him like enormous black spiders with
long, thin legs, their bodies resting upon the ground.

During summer months the nomads moved from one pasture to another within the ancestral territory of their respective tribes, where their isolation was relieved only when a caravan passed by; individual encampments
were at least a mile apart because grasses were never so plentiful in any given
area to permit a greater concentration of animals. Each day the women and
children remained in camp, the former spinning, weaving, churning, and
cooking and the latter looking after newborn calves and lambs, while the
men took herds of cattle, sheep, goats, horses, and yaks up into the grazing
lands.

The domesticated yak (for there were great herds of their fierce and dangerous wild cousins, called *drongs*, roaming the land) was unquestionably
the most useful animal in Tibet. This bisonlike ox with long, shaggy black
hair lived under the most difficult conditions and usually managed to find its
own forage; in a land devoid of machinery it was used extensively for both
plowing and transport. The *dri*, its female counterpart, provided abundant
supplies of milk, cream, cheese, and butter; and the butter was used not
only for altar lamps but also as an ingredient in Tibetan-style tea, for the
sculpting of religious images, and even for polishing stone floors. A *dri*
crossed with a bull produced a hybrid of legendary strength called a *dzo*, an
indefatigable animal invaluable for agricultural work; the female hybrid, or
dzomo, produced even greater quantities of milk than the *dri*. In a country
where no coal was mined and much of the land was above the tree line, yak
dung was used occasionally as manure but with far greater frequency as fuel.
Nor was the yak valuable only when alive. From its flesh came excellent
meat to be eaten fresh or dried for later use; from its hide sturdy boots and
saddlebags as well as the outer covering for the canoelike Tibetan boat called
a coracle;[6] from its hair tents, blankets, rope, and clothing; from its horns
snuffboxes; and from its bushy tail not only fly whisks but also, until the
Communist invasion, most of the Santa Claus beards delighting children in
Europe and America. "The yak is the most extraordinary animal," wrote a
British visitor to Lhasa in 1904. "He carries 160 pounds, and consumes
nothing. He subsists solely on stray blades of grass, tamarisk, and tufts of
lichen, that he picks up on the road. He moves slowly, and bears a look of

ineffable resignation. He is the most melancholy disillusioned beast I have ever seen, and dies on the slightest provocation."[7]

With the exception of a few tribes like the ferocious Goloks of Amdo, the nomads were a shy and gentle people. They were also deeply religious, probably because their livelihood depended upon killing animals and, as Buddhists, they knew that taking any form of life was wrong. Although they accepted their lot in the belief that it had been caused through bad deeds committed in their previous lives, they tried to atone for their sins by doing meritorious deeds. "Our place in life has been determined beforehand," states an old Tibetan proverb, "but our clean deeds are the products of our own hands." Those able to afford it paid a monastery for a monk to live in their camp, read aloud the scriptures, and offer prayers. They were hospitable to travelers and contributed generously to religious institutions. At least once in their lifetime they tried to make a pilgrimage to the holy city of Lhasa; many, when they grew older, came down from the mountains to take vows and become monks, spending the rest of their lives in spiritual contemplation.

When the chill of winter made itself felt, the nomads moved down from their snow-encrusted plateaus to the foothills, where they encamped until spring. Some went on pilgrimages to places like Lhasa or Kumbum, for this was a time of religious festivals throughout the land. Others set off with livestock, butter, cheese, and meat to the nearest market—often a three-week journey—where they exchanged their goods for barley, rice, tea, and dried fruit with farmers who had just brought in their harvest. Six months later, when the snows had melted and a new, bright green carpet dotted with brilliant wildflowers had sprung from the earth, they ascended to their secluded highlands and began the cycle once again.

Agriculturalists accounted for approximately one-third of Tibet's labor force. Some were farmers, others herders, and a third group, the *samadrok* (literally, "neither peasant nor grazier") were agro-pastoralists on land of marginal utility. In most of the country long winters and high altitudes combined to allow only one crop to be grown each year. Especially in central Tibet, where the soil was not so fertile as in Kham and Amdo, the land benefited from the rest it gained. That the extreme dryness of the atmosphere could make cultivation impossible had long been recognized; it is said that when the famed Buddhist teacher Atisha came to Tibet from India in the eleventh century, he caused a dam to be built "for the benefit of the people." Farmlands were watered by irrigation ditches from streams and rivers, but if the rainfall was unusually light, even this could not save the crops. In the critical fourth Tibetan month (approximately mid-May to mid-June), a dearth of rain caused teams of claret-robed monks to be dispatched from monasteries throughout the land to sacred springs in their vicinity, where they held *cham-be* (Rain-Bringing Services) to propitiate the *lu*, subterranean serpent spirits responsible for crops and rain, offering invocations and feeding the fish in nearby ponds with handfuls of grain. Faith in the efficacy of this monastic intercession was rooted more in superstition than in the Buddha's teachings. Many believed, like Aku (Uncle) Tömpa, the legendary comic writer of Tibetan folklore, that the services should be conducted only when clouds were drifting from south to north and the likelihood of rain was greatest; "When the southern clouds go northward," went a common Tibetan proverb, "Aku Tömpa prays for rain." Indeed, a particularly severe drought would summon forth Tibet's most famous rainmaker, the oracle of Gadong, to the summer palace of the Dalai Lama. There, in the presence of the ruler and high government and monastic officials, the monk medium would permit the protecting deity to enter his body so that it could respond to the entreaties of the assemblage. The oracle's performance was followed inevitably by at least a modicum of precipitation; perhaps, like Aku Tömpa, he studied the clouds before going into his trance, for he did so only during the rainy season.

The valley farmers occupied more permanent habitations than the nomads. Usually rectangular structures with walls of stone or sun-dried brick, these houses in the uplands were ordinarily built around a central courtyard like the house in Taktser where the Fourteenth Dalai Lama was born. Flat roofs of beaten earth were most common, and on them might have been found a few sticks of precious firewood, stacks of grain drying in the sun before threshing, potted flowers growing in the protection of warm chimneys, and perhaps a few onion plants from the mountains. Frequently, multicolored prayer flags flew from each of the four corners, and a large earthenware receptacle for burning aromatic herbs and shrubbery as incense offerings occupied a central position. Each dwelling contained an altar illuminated by at least one tiny butter lamp, and larger homes ordinarily had separate altar rooms.

Just as the crop yield in Tibet was limited by the unique climatic conditions, so too was crop variety. Green vegetables did not fare well and were rarely available. Fruits such as apricots, pears, peaches, and apples were grown in the southern and eastern districts but were available elsewhere generally only in dried form. The most common root vegetables were radishes, turnips, and potatoes, but the bulk of the land was given over to the cultivation of barley, peas, wheat, and mustard.

The staple food of all Tibet was *tsampa* flour. Although it could be obtained from wheat, peas, or maize, the preferred variety and the one most widespread came from the barley plant. First the barley was roasted in a red-hot iron frying pan coated with a layer of sand to prevent it from scorching. Upon touching the sand, the barley burst open, and moments later it was poured into a sieve to separate its golden-brown, aromatic grains from the sand. Finally the roasted grains were shoveled into sacks and taken to the miller, who ground them into flour, one-tenth of which he retained as his fee. *Tsampa* was mixed most commonly with tea, but also with beer or plain water, until it reached a doughy consistency. The diner would then knead it with the fingers of one hand into bite-sized balls—a performance requiring a certain degree of expertise developed only through constant practice—and eat it with dried cheese, or vegetables, or on its own. Simple but nourishing fare, it had the added advantage of being virtually imperishable: the climate was so dry that under proper conditions the *tsampa* could be kept indefinitely. In both monasteries and government storehouses great quantities of *tsampa* were hoarded as insurance against the ever-present threat of crop failure. Famine was unknown in Tibet.

Tibetan social organization prior to the flight of the Dalai Lama in 1959 can be described most simply, although perhaps not most accurately, as feudal in nature.[8] All territory within Tibet's political borders belonged to the state, and approximately half the tillable land was granted on a hereditary basis in the form of manorial estates to aristocratic families (*zhi-ga*) and important monasteries (*chö-zhi*). The government retained a few similar holdings for its own use, but the majority of the remaining arable land was leased directly to smallholding peasants living in villages known as *shung-gyu-ba*—literally, villages of "landed government serfs." These villages were relatively autonomous internally and affected by Lhasa only in terms of tax collection, which was in the form of agricultural produce, or unpaid services, or a combination of both.

As in medieval Europe, the manorial estate was divided into tenement land, alloted by the lord to his serfs for their personal sustenance, and demesne land, from which all produce belonged to him. Lords were vested by the central government with rights over their serfs which included the collection of taxes and unpaid labor, the adjudication of disputes and crimes, and the authority to fine, whip, or imprison offenders.[9] That the system incorporated opportunities for cruelty and oppression is undeniable, but in practice this occurred only infrequently; there was no tradition of peasant uprisings in Tibet. Perhaps the most important reason for this was that the bonds betwen lords and serfs transcended landlord–tenant or ruler–subject relationships. Buddhists believe that all sentient beings are reborn after death and that the character of each successive life on the path toward ultimate enlightenment is determined by one's deeds in past lives. This is known as the law of karma, and the inequality of social positions in Tibet was explained and accepted in accordance with it. Only by leading a virtuous life could one aspire to a higher rebirth, and the possession of wealth was viewed merely as an indicator of past actions. Nor, for that matter, was it necessarily desirable: the Tibetan saying "On foot without a horse, sleep is pleasant" expressed the value of not being a slave to one's possessions.

Moreover, it was an unwise lord who made a practice of abusing his serfs. Much of the land lay fallow because of a chronic manpower shortage caused by a high rate of infant mortality, the custom of adelphic polyandry in which several brothers shared one wife to keep hereditary land parcels from being broken up, and the persistent drain on the male population by the largely celibate monasteries. Consequently the demand for labor outstripped its supply, and an unhappy or mistreated serf could always mitigate his circumstances either by subtly threatening to run away or by actually doing so. In a country with no police force worthy of note, his apprehension was unlikely, and other lords, always in need of laborers, frequently concealed runaways to their own advantage. Finally, there was room for economic mobility within the serf strata. New land was available for leasing to anyone willing to work it, and day-labor jobs were easy to come by; the diligent serf could often improve his situation dramatically. "The poor are not oppressed," wrote a British visitor to Tibet at the beginning of the twentieth century. "They and the small tenant farmers work ungrudgingly for their spiritual masters, to whom they owe a blind devotion. They are not discontented. Each family contributes one of its members to the monkhood, [and] when we are inclined to abuse the monks for consuming the greater part of the country's produce, we should remember that the laymen are not the victims of class prejudice, the plebians groaning under the burden of the patricians, so much as the servants of a community chosen from among themselves, and with whom they are connected by family ties." [10]

After the nomads and agriculturalists, the most numerous group in Tibet were the monks, who made up some 15 percent of the population. Although playing a major role in Tibetan life, they were not really an occupational group, and will be discussed in a later chapter. There was also a small "middle class" of mercantilists who carried on trade with India and China. To the former country the main export was wool and the main imports were cotton goods and precious stones; to the latter, musk, furs, and medicinal herbs were sent in exchange for tea and silks. Total imports fell far short of exports, and the balance was paid in Indian rupees. Other occupational classes were often itinerant and included muleteers, tailors, goldsmiths, silversmiths, weavers, cobblers, carpenters, and, especially on the Chang Tang plateau, brigands. [11] Three other groups are worthy of mention because of the special role they played in Tibetan life: butchers, beggars, and a unique group known as the *ragyapa*.

Owing to the rigorous climate and the limited variety of available food, meat formed an essential part of the diet of most Tibetans. Buddhism, however, teaches that the taking of life is a sin; and butchers who slaughtered animals for human consumption were regarded as sinners and outcastes despite the necessity for their actions. Wherever possible non–Buddhists were recruited for the task. In Lhasa the field was dominated by members of a small colony of Kashmiri Muslims who had lived in the holy city for centuries, while in Amdo, Chinese Muslims known as Hui-Hui were frequently called into service. Conversely, it was not unusual for Tibetans to spare the lives of animals destined for the cooking pot by purchasing them from their owners and either setting them free or retaining them as household pets. A European resident of Lhasa in the late 1940s remembers that in the home of an aristocratic friend lived one such animal, a plump white goose that since its rescue had developed a rather proprietary air and waddled about quite regally. Saving the life of a living creature in this manner was considered a highly meritorious deed that would help the purchaser secure a better rebirth.[12]

Professional beggars were also a familiar sight in Tibet, especially in Lhasa, where scores of them lined the three sacred paths of the holy city.[13] Their status was usually inherited, although to their ranks sometimes came recently disabled laborers. Begging was a recognized way of life with a definite set of traditions, the first of which was that a mendicant must not ask a stranger for alms more than once a season. Another was that one must give, or else be subject to a stream of curses—and everyone feared the curses of a beggar. Moreover, Tibetans believed that the beggar fulfilled a useful function in society since almsgiving was one of the fundamental obligations of their faith. "If the crop is a good one, the beggars will have plenty of food" was a familiar proverb.

There was also a special community of beggars, the *ragyapa*,[14] scavengers to whom was assigned the disposal of the dead. To Tibetans, a body is of importance only while it houses the soul, after which no trace of it should remain. Corpses were usually taken to nearby peaks and cut apart, their flesh laid out in strips and their bones pulverized to be eaten by vultures and wild animals. Most of the poor were deposited into swiftly flowing streams to be devoured by fish; in death as in life, the body could provide service to its fellow creatures. The lack of firewood made cremation impractical, but the ashes of great teachers were often set into *chörtens* because it was believed that these relics would serve to future generations as a reminder of their teachings. For the most renowned incarnations, like the Dalai and Panchen lamas, embalmment was the customary method and was entrusted to members of the monastic community.

Sequestered behind imposing mountain barriers and fortified by a faith that produced a determined conservatism and a dislike of change of any sort, Tibetans were by all accounts contented with their rugged lives in the Land of Snows. Although it was a feudal society, never in thirteen hundred years of recorded history was there an instance of general agrarian discontent. Once Buddhism took root in the country's social fabric, militaristic and expansionist traditions withered and died. For over one thousand years Tibet invaded no one and asked only to be left alone. But as the little child from Taktser was preparing to leave for the holy city of Lhasa the winds of change had already begun to blow.

Notes

1. Tibetans call their country *Bod* and themselves *Bod-pa*. "Tibet" is adapted from the Kashmiri *Tibbat*, a corruption of the word for upper Tibet, or *Tö-bod*, the part of Tibet adjoining Kashmir and Ladakh. L. Austine Waddell, *Lhasa and Its Mysteries: With a Record of the Expedition of 1903–1904* (London, 1906), 66.
2. In the Tibetan language *Tsangpo* means the "Purifier" and is applied to any large river; the Tibetans have different names for it on different parts of its course. In India it is known as the Brahmaputra.
3. There is a distinct physical similarity between the easterners and members of Tibetan aristocratic families; it is possible that the central Tibetans comprised the original population and were later invaded and dominated by peoples from Dokham.
4. Traditional Tibetan methods of disposing of the dead, which will be discussed later in this chapter, have resulted in a dearth of skeletal material; and since the Chinese invasion of 1950, access to the country to Westerners has been until quite recently severely restricted.
5. Although situated on a lofty plain, Lhasa lies at a latitude south of Cairo.
6. A fragile vessel drawing only a few inches of water, the coracle could accommodate up to ten passengers or a heavy load of goods. It could be paddled only downstream or from one river bank to another; a common sight in Tibet was a solitary boatman carrying his coracle upstream on his back, accompanied by a solitary sheep bearing food and other necessities. The only other form of water transport was the large and cumbersome ferry barge, which was drawn from one bank to another by means of strong yak-hair ropes.
7. Edmund Candler, *The Unveiling of Lhasa* (New York, 1905), 94.
8. According to the seminal work in the field, "the Tibetan political system can be seen as one which moved from a type of late feudalism to an incipient form of centralized bureaucracy" when the Fifth Dalai Lama assumed secular control of the country in the middle of the seventeenth century. Melvyn C. Goldstein, "An Anthropological Study of the Tibetan Political System," unpublished Ph.D. dissertation, University of Washington, 1963, p. 255.
9. Theoretically, serfs had the right to take complaints against their lords to the Lhasa government for adjudication. They rarely did so, however: it was an expensive process, and the manorial estate-holding nobles themselves dominated the lay segment of the government.
10. Candler, *The Unveiling of Lhasa*, 246.
11. Brigandage was practiced only in certain seasons; during the rest of the year these same tribes would bring salt for sale to southern Tibet. They were frequent visitors to Lhasa and generous contributors to monasteries. It was noted by a British consular officer in China who traveled extensively in eastern Tibet in 1918 that there was more brigandage and unrest in parts of Tibet under Chinese control than in those areas subject to the Lhasa government. Sir Eric Teichman, *Travels of a Consular Officer in Eastern Tibet* (Cambridge, 1922), p. 193.
12. Fishing was forbidden except in one area where the Tsangpo ran through a sandy desert good for neither crops nor pasturage. Although the local people were granted a special dispensation to fish for their sustenance, they were regarded as somewhat tainted for doing so. Coracle owners and blacksmiths also fell into this category.
13. The Nangkhor (Inner Circle) ran around a cloister within the grounds of the Tsuglakhang, the most famous temple in Tibet. The Barkhor (Intermediate

Circle) enclosed all the temple's buildings and was also the main marketplace of Lhasa. The Lingkhor (Park Circle) was almost five miles long and encircled all of Lhasa as well as two hills nearly a mile from its center: on one stood the Potala, winter palace of the Dalai Lama, and on the other the school of Tibetan medicine. The largest circle would have been named the Chikor (Outside Circle) but for the fact that the word "outside" was considered inauspicious and therefore inappropriate for the most sacred path of the holy city.

14. The derivation of the word *ragyapa* is uncertain. One theory maintains that it is best translated as "corpse-vulture" (*ro* means "corpse" and *go-vo* means "vulture"). Another asserts it means "the horny ones" since in Lhasa the *ragyapas'* dwellings had walls fashioned in part from animal horns. Sarat Chandra Das, *Journey to Lhasa and Central Tibet* (London, 1902), 63n, 163.

Parents of the Fourteenth Dalai Lama   *Lhasa 1940*

· CHAPTER 3 ·

The Farmer's Wife

T HE VILLAGE OF TAKTSER was situated on a small plateau in Amdo on the
caravan route between the Chinese provincial capital of Sining and the
region's second largest monastery. Its cluster of some thirty mud-brick cottages was encircled by lush fields of wheat and barley and pasturelands dotted with flowers, herbs, and grasses. Rolling hills surrounded the fields,
wonderfully green in summer and deep with snow in winter. To the south
one snowcapped mountain stood out above the others. Its name was Kyeri.
The local people called it the Mountain That Pierces the Sky, and it was believed that high in its peaks was the abode of Kye, Taktser's protective deity.
Its northern face, which loomed benignly over the tiny community below,
ran with clear springs and sparkling waterfalls and was alive with shade and
fruit trees, fragrant wildflowers and edible berries, and an abundance of
wildlife: bears, wolves, lynxes, foxes, marmots, musk deer, leopards,
monkeys, and mountain goats.

As in all Tibetan villages, the daily life of Taktser was permeated with
religion. In each cottage was an altar where an image of the Buddha was
kept perpetually illuminated by butter lamps. Brightly colored prayer flags
emblazoned with the words *Om Mani Padme Hum*—"Hail to the Jewel in the
Lotus"—flapped on the rooftops. Each syllable of this sacred mantra, the
most popular in Tibetan Buddhism, is symbolic of rebirth in one of the six
divisions of the mandala, or Tibetan Wheel of Life: *Om*, among the gods;
Ma, in the world of Titans and spirits; *Ni*, in the human world; *Pad*, in the
world of animals; *Me*, as a Tantalus in the world of ghosts; and *Hum*, in the
depths of hell.[1]

Most villagers, once they had purchased the physical necessities of life,
spent their remaining income contributing to temples and monasteries,
building religious monuments, making offerings to the "Three Jewels"—the
Buddha, the Dharma (his teaching), and the Sangha (the monkhood)—and
giving alms to the poor.

On the outskirts of the village, half hidden by conifer trees and massive rhododendrons, stood the village temple, a simple structure in the center of which was a statue of Kye in the guise of a horseman with a pointed black beard. On a hillock behind the temple a stone altar had been erected where the villagers, after placing freshly cut flowers before the temple's effigies or affixing a new prayer flag to the flagstaff, burned incense as an offering to the gods. There was no monastery in Taktser, and thus no monk was available to look after the temple and supervise the ceremonies, so one of the village men was appointed caretaker.

Not far from the temple was Taktser's *labtse*, a large heap of stones encircled by a high wooden fence, which had been dedicated to the protective deity. Once each year, on the twelfth day of the sixth month, when all but the topmost pinnacle of Kyeri had shed its blanket of frost, all 150 villagers would march there in solemn procession. Amid the beating of gongs and sounding of bells by monks from neighboring monasteries who had been invited to conduct the ceremonies, they burned incense, hung out new prayer flags, and made offerings to Kye of coins and semiprecious stones—white quartz, turquoise, and coral—and prayed for a bountiful harvest and protection from bad weather.[2] Then laiety and monk alike would adjourn to a collection of tents that had been pitched in a nearby meadow and spend the rest of the day eating, drinking *chang* (barley beer), singing, and dancing. With the exception of Losar this was Taktser's most popular annual event.

Losar was the Tibetan New Year's festival. All who could afford it would make a pilgrimage to Kumbum monastery to admire the spectacular butter sculptures fashioned by monk artists on scaffolds up to forty feet high, intricately carved and brightly painted representations of scenes in the life of the Buddha, Buddhist saints and sages, monastic and lay dignitaries in costly robes, aristocratic women wearing jewel-encrusted headdresses, and sweeping landscapes. Similar Festivals of Light were held all over Tibet, but Kumbum's butter towers were known to be the finest in the land.

A short distance from Taktser was one of Tibet's most famous monasteries, Shartsong Ridrö. Like Kyitsang Rinpoche's hermitage a thousand miles away, it was perched precariously on the edge of a 500-foot cliff, its whitewashed buildings providing a striking contrast with the reddish-brown rock face and the crystal-clear azure sky. The monastery had been founded early in the fourteenth century by Rolpai Dorje, the Fourth Black Hat Karmapa Lama and the first recognized incarnation in Tibet. Here six hundred years earlier this lama had initiated the future reformer Tsong Khapa into the monkhood. Legend has it that he cut off the boy's locks and cast them onto a rock beside the cave in which he had been living, and on that very spot a fissure appeared from which sprang up a juniper tree whose foliage, even today, bears the unmistakable scent of human hair.

In the village of Churkha, not far from Taktser, seventeen-year-old Sonam Tsomo was roused from sleep by the peal of a distant cockerel, which cut across the chill mountain air like a silvery clarion. Daylight had begun to filter down from the mountains onto the farmstead but had yet to find its way inside the house, which was soon alight with the glow of mustard-oil lamps.

While the other members of the household scurried about getting ready for the journey to Taktser, she dressed silently. "I wonder," she thought, "how life there will be." One by one she slipped into silk blouses of red, green, and white, colors that had been carefully selected to suit her complexion. Then she donned a sleeveless jade-green *chuba* made of pure Mongolian silk and fashioned in the Amdo style. She combed her long black hair as usual into three plaits, two in the front and one in the back. From her ears she hung long earrings of coral, turquoise, and silver. Finally she put on a vase-shaped headdress stitched with jewels, which reached down to her waist. While she dressed, a neighbor sat cross-legged on a low, carpet-covered platform, singing traditional Amdoan wedding songs in a deep, husky voice. It was the eleventh day of the eleventh month of the Tibetan Fire Serpent Year, 1917: Sonam Tsomo's wedding day.

Like most Tibetan marriages, the marriage of Sonam Tsomo and Choekyong Tsering had been arranged by their families. At first her grandparents had been opposed, because it was said that in Taktser the women had to work much harder. As senior family members, they had a stronger say than her parents, but they consulted a lama before reaching a decision. After calculating that her horoscope was compatible with that of her intended husband, he told the family that although the marriage might not seem the best thing just then, the future would be very bright. The parents of Choekyong Tsering were informed that the marriage was agreeable.

The Tibetans had always been a superstitious people and consulted horoscopes for all matters of importance. An astrologer would determine, for instance, not only the day on which an important ceremony should take place, but even such details as the direction in which its participants should face and the color of the food served. The very offering of tea and food was considered to bring good luck, and no social or business meeting was begun without refreshments being first provided. The same motivation lay behind the exchanging of *khatas*, or ceremonial scarves—the longer and whiter the scarf, the better. It was also considered auspicious for ceremonies to be concluded by people with lucky names such as Namgyal (Victorious), Dhondup (Successful), or Tashi (Prosperity). A marriage required an auspicious day for two people, a day on which both their individual and mutual elements were in harmony. Such a day was often quite difficult to find, and almost two years passed while Sonam Tsomo and Choekyong Tsering awaited the day chosen by the astrologer for them to begin their life together.

The ceremonial engagement party, known as Nyenchang (*nyen* means "good relationship," and *chang* is Tibetan barley beer), was held in the altar room of Sonam Tsomo's home. Since they were inviting her to become a member of their household, Choekyong Tsering's parents brought with them a document that began with prayers to the deity of health, asking that it bless the impending union, and in the names of both sets of parents promising on behalf of the couple that they love and be faithful to each other and love and respect all members of both families. Then representatives of Choekyong Tsering's family bestowed on the parents of Sonam Tsomo a series of gifts that began with auspicious tea and rice and included butter, wheat, *tsampa*, salt, and lengths of silk. The most important offering was called *nurin* ("breast price"), which symbolized repayment to the bride's mother for having fed her. A great deal of *chang* was consumed by all, and everyone agreed that it had been so well made as to be a distinctly favorable omen.

On the eve of the day chosen for the wedding to take place, a reception party of gaily dressed horsemen from the groom's home in Taktser arrived at Sonam Tsomo's house. The leader bore the *sipaho*, an arrow-shaped banner with a painted scroll hanging from its point on which were astrological symbols depicting the stars and planets and mystical symbols for protection against evil spirits. With them was a white mare to carry the bride the next day, as well as a white stallion and a black *dzomo* for her grandparents, who would accompany her as senior family members.

Early the next morning Chusho Rinpoche, the lama who had been consulted about the marriage, conducted a short service in which he sought and received permission from the household deity to allow Sonam Tsomo to join her new family. Then the groom's representative touched the back of Sonam Tsomo's neck with an arrow decorated with five strips of different-colored silk and announced to everyone present that from then on she belonged only to her husband.

The procession to Taktser was led by the man bearing the astrological chart, behind whom rode the fifty-odd members of the reception party. Next came Sonam Tsomo, wrapped snugly in a fur-lined cloak, and taking great care to lean far forward in the saddle as she rode so as not to reveal her face—a symbolic gesture to show that a groom first saw his bride only on the day of their wedding. Often a new bride would weep or even faint when leaving home, but Sonam Tsomo was composed throughout and kept whatever apprehensions she might have had to herself. Although Taktser was not far away, the journey took some seven hours because the travelers were met, in the customary Tibetan fashion, a short distance from their point of departure by a farewell party of friends and relatives who plied them with food, tea, and *chang*. Sonam Tsomo was given a special porridge made of rice and dates, and only her sister was permitted to share it. It was part of the traditional ceremony, and helped warm her.

For Sonam Tsomo it was the first of many eventful journeys she would take during the next sixty years. It was considerably shorter than the others would be, this nuptial procession across the familar, windswept tablelands of Amdo, but it would prove to be a pivotal journey both for the young girl and for her country. Her marriage to Choekyong Tsering would produce a son who, when hardly more than an infant, would be recognized as the Fourteenth Dalai Lama of Tibet. But, hugging her cloak securely about her to ward off the numbing gusts of wintry air whipping down from the icy peaks that towered over the group of festive travelers, Sonam Tsomo never suspected how radically her life would be changed as a result of this journey. Nor is it likely that had she known what the future held this knowledge would have noticeably affected her demeanor; she rarely permitted her expression to betray her emotions.

At last the bridal party arrived at Sonam Tsomo's new home. It occupied slightly higher ground than the other houses of the village and had been given a fresh coat of whitewash in honor of the occasion. The great door leading to the interior courtyard was on the east, or lee, side as protection against the weather; its wooden pivots were wrapped in sheepskin, and it swung open noiselessly to admit them. Sonam Tsomo dismounted upon a platform of barley grain and brick tea and was led across the flagstoned yard to a stack of wood, around which she walked three times in a clockwise direction. Moving to the kitchen door, she stood with her back to it, facing east as her horoscope had indicated, and proceeded to wash her face; then she went inside to make tea. This she poured into three cups, one for the chief guest selected by her husband's family and one for the second chief guest chosen by her family; a third cup she placed on the altar as an offering. Tea was then served to the entire gathering. Some of the guests tried to steal a look at her while praising the tea she had brewed, but she kept her face hidden behind one of the sleeves of her blouse, which had been cut quite full. A few mischievous older guests tugged playfully on her arm, saying, "Let's have a look! We won't be here long, so let's see your face before we leave!" She was embarrassed but tried not to show it. The ritual was known as *nama sarpai cha*—new bride's tea.

The next part of the ceremony took place in the family chapel, a small, dimly lighted room filled with ritualistic banner paintings (*thonka*s), religious images, and butter lamps. Sonam Tsomo was seated beside her husband, whom she now saw for the first time. He was wearing a long-sleeved *chuba* of maroon brocade over a crisp white shirt, and she thought he looked very handsome. The couple were joined by members of both families, seated with them in order of seniority, and then by friends. Scarves and gifts were exchanged, and a sumptuous meal of Tibetan and Chinese delicacies was served. Afterward they went up to the roof, where incense was burned and prayers were offered for the success of the marriage.

After three days of dancing, feasting, and merrymaking, Sonam Tsomo and her family went back to Churkha. She returned a month later, on a day the lamas had designated as auspicious. Upon reaching the gate of her new home, she was greeted by her husband's elder brother, who held a white porcelain bowl of milk. Into this she placed the thumb and fourth finger of her right hand, then withdrew them and flicked little droplets into the air three times. Then she went into the kitchen and brewed tea, the first steaming cup of which she placed on the altar as an offering. From that time on she was considered a regular member of the Taktser household, and the next day began to take part in the housework and other routines.

Sonam Tsomo's new family had roots in Amdo that could be traced back to the reign of King Mangson Mangtsen, the grandson of Songtsen Gampo, who in the middle of the seventh century had stationed a central Tibetan garrison there to protect his frontiers from Chinese incursions. A century later, King Trisong Detsen sent nine of his best officers to command these troops, and the area became known as Guthup (the Capable Nine). When the commanders asked the king several years later if he wished them to return to Lhasa, they were told to await further orders; these never came, and nomadic descendants of the nine officers still live in parts of Amdo, where they are known as Kamalok ("Not to Return without Orders"). Except for the last two generations, a member of the family had always served as village headman, an unpaid elective post whose major responsibility was negotiating with the authorities about taxes and imposts.

Sonam Tsomo's father-in-law, Tashi Dhondup, was a cheerful and kind-hearted man who, in the fashion of all Tibetans who were neither monks nor aristocrats, wore his hair in a pigtail wrapped around his head and tied with a red ribbon. He was a favorite of the village children, who constantly pestered him to let them sit at his feet and hear him tell his fascinating stories or sing folk songs. She warmed to him immediately. The same cannot be said for her relations with her mother-in-law, Lhamo Dolma, a gaunt, short-tempered woman whose face was badly pitted from a childhood attack of smallpox.

Within two years Tashi Dhondup and Lhamo Dolma died. Their bodies were wrapped in white cloth and transported on the back of a corpse-carrier to a rocky, elevated area a short distance from the village, which was recognizable from afar by the swarms of vultures which hovered above it. While the corpse carrier hacked the bodies to pieces with an ax, another member of the party murmured prayers and a third chased away the birds until even the skull and bones had been crushed to pieces. Only when this had been accomplished were the remains left to be consumed by the vultures. Sonam Tsomo's sadness about the death of her in-laws was mitigated by the prospect of their rebirth. They had lived virtuous lives, and she was certain that their next incarnations would be in human forms. Butter lamps were kept burning for the forty-nine-day period of mourning, which was ended with a special prayer service.

Sonam Tsomo was not yet twenty years old when she assumed full responsibility for running the Taktser household. Each day she arose just before dawn to the rooster's call and went to the kitchen, a large bi-level room with a stamped-earth floor. In a corner were stacks of fuel: logs, dried dung, brushwood, and straw, the last of these to produce the quick, intense heat necessary for roasting barley. Then she built a fire in one of the four fireplaces in a long brick stove-oven that dominated the room, and placed on it copper kettles of water for washing and morning tea. While these were heating, she crossed the courtyard and went into the altar room. After carefully washing her hands, she twisted new wicks from cotton, filled the containers with butter freshly melted from the stove, and lit the lamps. Accompanied by the rest of the family, she prostrated herself three times and offered prayers of compassion for all sentient beings, then went out to the earthenware incense burner in the center of the courtyard and shoveled into it glowing embers and herbs, usually dried alpine roses. Only after performing these religious ceremonies would tea be served and the workday begin.

Just after breakfast the village herdsman came by, his flock growing ever larger by the inclusion of cows and sheep from each cottage yard he passed en route to the mountain pastures. Accompanied by one or two laborers, Choekyong Tsering went out at the same time to work in the fields, and as soon as they had gone, Sonam Tsomo took out her brooms and cleaned both the house and the cattle byre. Aside from the housekeeping, she fetched water from the well at the other end of the village, took her husband's lunch to where he was working, churned butter, and cooked during the day; at night she did the sewing and baking. Her pastries and Amdo-style bread were thought to be the best in the village, and she made excellent sausages of sheep and *tsampa*.

Like Sonam Tsomo's native village, Taktser was an agro-pastoral community, much of it given over to pastureland for the larger village of Balangtsa, some two hours' journey away. She and her husband owned their home and several strips of land situated in different places, an ancient custom that had arisen because much of the soil was poor and had been divided up by successive generations of peasants to provide an equal share of good land to all. Their main crops were the Tibetan staples, barley and wheat. Most of these they consumed, and the surplus was bartered for brick tea, sugar, cotton fabric, and metal utensils in the nearby towns of Sining and Kumbum. In the garden close by their home they grew peas, mustard, potatoes, tomatoes, garlic, onions, radishes, and a few green vegetables. Their livestock consisted of cows, oxen, sheep, goats, *dzomo*s, chickens, pigs, and horses. Choekyong Tsering cultivated his fields with the help of two types of laborers. Some were hired on an annual contract and provided with food, clothing, lodging, and a small wage, while others were engaged on a monthly basis during the sowing and harvesting seasons.

Sonam Tsomo soon discovered to her dismay that her husband avoided farmwork as often as he was able, preferring to rely on the hired help so that he could absent himself on trips to nearby market towns. Prior to their marriage she had heard he was an impulsive and headstrong youth, the youngest and favorite child of his parents. It seemed to her that Choekyong Tsering's only interest in life was his horses. He never tired of boasting of Amdo's reputation for producing Tibet's finest horses and took great pleasure in the fact that Taktser's temple contained their protective deity in the guise of a horseman. Sometimes she could not help thinking he was more concerned with their pea crop than with any of the others, for it was grown solely for fodder. She tried in vain to persuade him to spend less time with his horses and more doing farmwork. Finally her brother-in-law Changchub Jimpa, a monk at Kumbum, was forced to move in with them and help with the chores.

Sonam Tsomo and Choekyong Tsering had sixteen children, but only seven lived past infancy. Their first daughter, Tsering Dolma, was born in 1919 and their first son in 1922. Tibetan children were frequently left un-named at birth and addressed simply as Bu (Boy), Bu-mu (Girl), or just Tu-gu (Child) until the occurrence of some important event. Consequently the boy was already three years old when given the name Thupten Jigme Norbu by a highly respected lama who passed a night in the Taktser farmhouse. Thereafter his parents called him either Jigme (Fear Not) or the honorific Jigme-la, and his siblings called him Jo-la (Oldest), a complimentary term because in Tibetan families the eldest son enjoyed preference. A few years later Jigme was recognized as the reincarnation of Taktser Rinpoche and taken to live at Kumbum monastery, where he was initiated into the monk-hood by Chusho Rinpoche, the same white-haired lama whom his mother had consulted prior to her marriage a decade earlier, who gave him in addi-tion to his incarnation title the name Tempa Rabgye. Another son, Gyalo Dhondup, was born in 1928. He had a deep, melodious voice and his eyes were so large that the family called him Mig Chenpo (Big Eyes). In 1933 a third son, Lobsang Samden, was born. Then in 1935 came the fourth son, born like all the others in the gloomy recesses of the cattle byre. His name was Lhamo Dhondup.

The day of Lhamo Dhondup's birth was cloudy, punctuated by bursts of scattered rain and thunder. Some of Sonam Tsomo's neighbors told her ex-citedly that there was a rainbow touching her house, a highly auspicious sign. She was too tired to get up and look, for she had gotten no sleep the night before because she had been caring for her husband. Yet although Choekyong Tsering had been ill for weeks, he arose from his sickbed that morning as though nothing had been wrong with him and proceeded to make offerings at the family altar. Sonam Tsomo accused him of having stayed in bed through sheer laziness, but he insisted that although he had felt quite ill just a few hours before, he now felt completely cured. He attributed his miraculous recovery to the child's birth, and told his wife that he wished their newborn son to be a monk.

When Lhamo was an infant, Sonam Tsomo would take him with her when she went to work in the fields, carrying him on her back and leaving him to sleep in the shade of an umbrella tied to a stake in the ground. Later, when he could walk, he would accompany her when she went to milk the *dzomos*, carrying his wooden bowl so she could fill it with warm, fresh milk for him to drink. He was always asking to help with the tasks, so she gave him the job of going to the chicken coop each day to collect the eggs. One day he vanished for what must have been several hours, and the family combed the entire area looking for him. Finally they found him perched in one of the nesting boxes, clucking like a hen.

He loved his mother very much. If her *chuba* had a hole in it, he would stitck one of his little fingers in the hole and tear it open even more, saying as he did so, "Don't wear this anymore. I'll get you a new one." He was extremely possessive and forbade his siblings to call her Mother. Like his father, Lhamo was spirited, stubborn, and mischievous, and lost his temper when denied anything. He could not tolerate people, or even animals, fighting. On such occasions he would grab a stick and defend the underdog, and unless the aggressors were considerably older than he, or equally strong-willed, they invariably backed down. He was fond of pretending to shoot rifles, which he fashioned from sticks around the house. Much to his father's chagrin, he was terrified of horses and, unlike his brothers, refused to ride them.[3]

When the time arrived for Lhamo to be taken to Kumbum, Sonam Tsomo's reaction was ambivalent. It was certainly an honor to have a son in the monkhood. But their eldest son, Jigme, had been living at Kumbum for almost five years and had been joined there recently by his little brother, Lobsang. And now Lhamo, her youngest child, barely three years old, would be leaving as well. She accepted the fact with a heavy heart.

Within a year her life as a farmer's wife would be at an end, and a new life would begin in the holy city of Lhasa. She would become a member of the Tibetan aristocracy and be honored with a new name, Gyayum Chenmo— Great Mother.[4]

Notes

1. Each of the six syllables was given the distinctive color of a particular state of rebirth: *Om*, the godly white; *Ma*, the Titanic blue; *Ni*, the human yellow; *Pad*, the animal green; *Me*, the Tantalic red; and *Hum*, the hellish black. L. Austine Waddell, *The Buddhism of Tibet, or Lamaism*, 2nd ed. (Cambridge, 1934), 148–149.

2. "As the water of the Ganges, or some refreshing brook, is considered holy among the sun-scorched Hindus," wrote George Bogle, a British visitor to Tibet in 1774, "so rocks and mountains are the objects of veneration among the Lama's voteries." Clements R. Markham, ed., *Narratives of the Mission of George Bogle to Tibet and of the Journey of Thomas Manning to Lhasa* (London, 1879), 70.
3. "It is funny that the former body was so fond of horses," he remarked a few years later, "and that they mean so little to me." Heinrich Harrer, *Seven Years in Tibet* (London, 1953), 143.
4. The material in this chapter was gathered in a series of interviews with the Gyayum Chenmo in Dharamsala, India, on May 5, 8, 12, 14, 16, and 23, 1980.

Tibetan temple   *Ghoom 1980*

CHAPTER 4

The Three Jewels

S EVEN CENTURIES before the birth of Christ, in the North Indian kingdom
of Sakya, Queen Mayadevi had a dream in which the stars opened up
and from the pitch-black sky at midnight emerged a six-tusked white elephant, which entered into her womb through her right side. While she was
strolling in the garden grove at Lumbini nine months later, a great tree bent
down its limbs to support her, and in this bower she gave birth to Siddhartha. Holy men recognized the child to be a divine incarnation and
warned his father that he would remain with his family only for as long as he
did not see four things: an old man, a sick man, a corpse, and a renunciate.
The king gave orders that his son be sheltered from pain and unhappiness
and provided him with the finest of tutors and all the luxuries of life. But
one night Siddhartha heard a voice speaking to him through the notes of
music played by his queens:

> The three realms of the world are aflame with the suffering of old age
> and death.
> Leaderless living creatures remain unaware that this blazing fire of
> death arises from cyclic existence,
> And they live like bees circling about inside a vase.
> The three realms are transient like the clouds of autumn,
> The birth and death of sentient beings is like gazing upon a dance.
> Like a flash of lightning is the passing of the life of sentient beings,
> Running swiftly like a splashing stream down a steep mountain.

Hearing these words, the young prince felt compelled to explore the world
beyond his cloistered environment, and, venturing forth, he was confronted
with the inescapable truth of decay and suffering. Soon after, he fled the palace and became an ascetic searching for the truth of release.

For six years Siddhartha subjected himself to a relentless series of fasts
and mortifications before it dawned on him that he was no closer to en-

lightenment than before, that all his physical and mental energies were being drained away, and that the only thing awaiting him was death—to be followed, inevitably, by yet another rebirth in which the struggle would begin anew. No sooner had he decided to eat normally again than a young girl appeared bearing a golden tray of nourishing food, from which he partook gratefully; his body revived and he walked to Bodh Gaya. After circumambulating the Bodhi Tree three times, Siddhartha sat down beneath its branches, facing east, and vowed, "Even if my body dries up and my skin, bones, and flesh fall away, I shall not move from this place until I have reached enlightenment." So saying, he entered into deep meditation.

Thunder and lightning, fire, flood, and darkness were sent by the forces of evil to frighten him, but he paid no heed and turned them into flowers, lovely palaces, and other offerings. His body in full meditational posture rose into the sky to a height of seven palm trees; and finally, after intensive contemplation, he became a Buddha, an Enlightened One, the Fully Awakened. Then he went into the forest and pondered on that which had dawned upon his mind like a clear light. Thinking that no one else would be able to comprehend this Dharma, he decided to live out his life in solitude, but when the gods requested that he go forth and teach the truth, he set out for the holy city of Benares.

At the Deer Park in the Sarnath the Gautama Buddha delivered his first sermon, on the Four Noble Truths: the Truth of Suffering, the Origin of Suffering, the Cessation of Suffering, and the Path to the Cessation of Suffering. All sentient beings, he taught, are reborn after death and their souls remain imprisoned in the wheel of existence until they achieve release by following the Noble Eightfold Path to enlightenment, when they cease being reborn and thereby cease suffering. These eight steps are right understanding (being free from delusion and superstition), right aspirations (being worthy of human intelligence), right speech (being truthful and kindly), right conduct (being peaceful and honest), right livelihood (neither endangering nor injuring any living being), right effort (self-control), right mindfulness (having an active, watchful mind), and right concentration (in meditation on the realities of life). Just as the Apostles' Creed is the basis of various Christian denominations, so too are the Four Noble Truths and the Eightfold Path the very heart of Buddhism.

Buddhism grew and prospered largely because of its practical nature. Rather than simply accepting suffering as an inexorable fact of life, it taught that release was possible, even within a single lifetime. Unlike the great Indian schools of Yoga, moreover, it did not demand a lifelong training to the exclusion of all other worldly activities. Finally, it stressed moderation, the "Middle Way" rather than renunciation. In his eighty-first year the Buddha announced to his devotees that his body was worn out and was no longer worth trying to keep alive. Lying down at the foot of a tree on his right side with his head pointing north, he left it behind.

It is believed that a terrestrial Buddha like Gautama comes along but once every *kalpa* (approximately five thousand years). During the first half of this period the doctrine spreads and grows, but during the second half it decays and atrophies until a new Buddha, the Maitreya, even greater than Gautama, will appear on earth to lead humanity on a new and higher spiritual path. The second part of the cycle, the period of decadence in which we are now living, can be shortened by prayers; and this is the spiritual task to which Tibetans everywhere have dedicated themselves.

The Buddha's doctrine split into two schools of thought as it left India and spread toward the Far East. Hinayana (the Lesser Burden) took root in Ceylon (now Sri Lanka) and Southeast Asia. More metaphysical and consequently less easily comprehensible to the masses, its followers seek enlightenment for the individual's own sake. Mahayana (the Greater Burden), on the other hand, went directly to China and Japan. Influenced by Hinduism and more emotional than Hinayana, it is more easily understood and practiced. Mahayanists strive to attain perfection not only for the sake of the individual but also for the sake of all other sentient beings.[1]

Mahayana Buddhism was introduced to Tibet during the reign of King Songtsen Gampo in the seventh century A.D. Presiding over a vast Central Asian empire and thirty-third in the line of Chöegyal (Religious Kings), the young ruler changed the course of history when for political reasons he added two foreign wives to the three Tibetan ones he had already taken. Belsa (Nepalese Princess) and Gyasa (Chinese Princess) were devout Buddhists, and they succeeded in converting the king from the indigenous animistic religion called Bön and in having him build temples to house images of the Buddha they had brought with them; it was before one of these images that the four-year-old Dalai Lama bowed when he arrived in Lhasa. The door to Belsa's temple, the Jokhang, faced west toward Nepal; that of Gyasa, the Ramoche, east toward China.

Despite the efforts of Songtsen Gampo and his wives to propagate it, the new faith reached only a small number of people, and Bön remained the predominant spiritual force in Tibet for another one and one-half centuries, until the reign of the thirty-seventh king, Trisong Detsen. Like his royal ancestors a patron of Buddhism, the king overrode strong opposition from his pro-Bön ministers to invite to Tibet the great Indian Tantric master Padmasambhava, the Lotus-Born. Better known to Tibetans as Lopön Rinpoche or Guru Rinpoche (Precious Teacher), the latter traveled throughout the land spreading Buddha's esoteric teachings by explaining them in terms of the prevailing imagery of demons and miracles, thus making them readily comprehensible to all, whom he then placed on the path to enlightenment. Padmasambhava founded the country's first monastery at Samyé (c. 779) and there supervised the training and initiation of a trial group of seven Tibetan novice monks. Revered as the chief saint of the original sect of Tibetan Buddhism, his followers became known as Nyingmapa (One of the Old), and his image may be seen in the place of honor on Tibetan altars as often as that of the Gautama Buddha himself, for Tibetans say that the Buddha would be helpless without the monkhood to spread his doctrine.

Trisong Detsen also arranged that two Chinese Buddhist monks skilled in preaching be sent to Tibet, a well-intentioned gesture that soon produced a heated doctrinal controversy. Chinese quietism, or Ch'an (Zen in Japanese), set little store by good works and taught that enlightenment could be attained instantaneously through complete mental and physical inactivity. Indian pandits maintained to the contrary that it was possible only through a slow and gradual process requiring good deeds extending over a series of lives. To resolve the impasse the king ordered that a great debate be held at Samyé monastery (c. 792); it resulted in triumph for the Indian doctrine and banishment of the Chinese.[2] He followed this act with a proclamation establishing Buddhism as the official religion of Tibet, directing that the monastic establishment be maintained thereafter by donations from the royal family, and decreeing that the "Three Jewels"—Buddha, Dharma, and Sangha—were never to be abandoned.[3]

Barely four decades after Trisong Detsen's death pro-Bön ministers came to power through a coup and placed one of his grandsons, Lang Darma, on the throne. A period of religious persecution followed during which temples and monasteries were sacked and destroyed, the teaching of Buddha's doctrines was forbidden, and monks were forced either to adopt Bön beliefs and practices or to flee the country. Legend has it that the custom of Tibetan government officials putting up their hair in knots braided with red ribbons was begun by Lang Darma to conceal his horns, the sign of a wizard, and that the royal hairdressers were warned upon pain of death to tell no one of their existence. It is also said that the king had a black tongue; ever since, whenever Tibetans meet a high-ranking person, they scratch their heads and stick out their tongues to show they have neither horns nor black tongues.

One day some three years after Lang Darma's accession, the monk Paljor Dorje, who had taken refuge in a cave near Lhasa, had a vision instructing him to rid Tibet of Lang Darma and showing him how to do it. Smearing his white pony with charcoal and donning a black robe with white lining, the monk rode into Lhasa and sought out the apostate king, for whom he performed a fantastic dance invented for the occasion. While making the threefold prostration that protocol demanded, he drew from his broadsleeved robe a bow and arrow and shot Lang Darma through the heart. Then he quickly turned his cloak inside out and rode his horse through the nearby Kyichu River, thus washing off the charcoal so that it, too, became white; and in this way he made good his escape. The monk's dance came to be known as the Black Hat dance, and upon the resurgence of Buddhism in Tibet it was celebrated annually in commemoration of the avenger's exploit.

With Lang Darma's assassination in A.D. 842 came an end to Songtsen

Gampo's line of Religious Kings. The centralized authority effected two centuries earlier disintegrated, and for the next four hundred years the country reverted to its former pattern of internecine strife. Although Lang Darma and his ministers had managed to wipe it out in central Tibet, Buddhism still clung on in more remote parts of the country, where quietly and inobtrusively it grew and spread. Instead of the emergence of another line of dominant kings, the era witnessed an increase in the number and political importance of monasteries, the spiritual guidance of pandits like Atisha, Tilopa, and Marpa, and the establishment of two new sects: the Sakyapa and Kagyupa.

By 1959 more than three thousand Buddhist monasteries were scattered throughout Tibet, and the country's relatively small population may be explained in large part by the fact that one of every four males became a monk and that the majority of monks lived lives of celibacy. In a land where religion was the dominant force, pervading every aspect of life, at least one son from each family was expected to enter the monkhood. Moreover, it was virtually the only way for a person of humble birth to rise to a position of eminence in the prevailing social system. "If your son has the ability," went an old Tibetan proverb, "the Lion's Throne is not sealed off." These institutions have frequently been described as "lamaseries" and Tibetan Buddhism as "Lamaism," presumably because the inhabitants of the one and the practitioners of the other were all lamas. Neither term is accurate. Tibetan monasteries were occupied by monks, some of whom were lamas; but not all lamas were monks.

The English word *monk* is rendered as *bhiksu* in Sanskrit and *trapa* in Tibetan and refers to individuals who have joined a religious order. *Lama* is a Tibetan word whose English equivalent is *teacher*; in Sanskrit it is *guru*, which means "one who is heavy with knowledge" and moreover one who is benevolent with that knowledge. Within the monkhood there were different grades of lamas based on individual scholarly qualifications. Some were assigned the responsibility to look after new monks, others to give teachings, and the most highly qualified to give vows. It was not unusual, furthermore, for a qualified layman to be sought out for religious instruction and to become thereafter the personal lama of the individual or individuals taught. The form of Buddhism still practiced in Tibet, Mongolia, Kashmir, and western China, and throughout the southern foothills of the Himalaya—as well as in a host of Western nations in which Tibetans have taken refuge after fleeing into exile—may be most simply and most accurately described as Tibetan Buddhism.

The characteristic of Tibetan Buddhism that distinguishes it most obviously from the practice of Buddhism elsewhere is its system of reincarnating lamas, which was begun by the Black Hat Karmapa sect in the middle of the fourteenth century.[4] Each incarnation of an important lama—of whom there are in excess of one thousand in Tibetan Buddhism—is known as a

Tulku but may also be referred to by the honorific Rinpoche (Precious One).[5] Buddhists believe in the law of karma, that all sentient beings are reborn after death and that in each of their successive lives the proportion of pain they experience and the physical form they assume are determined by their good or evil actions in the previous life. They are certain that eventually, through practicing the virtues of tolerance, forbearance, charity, kindness, and compassion, they will attain enlightenment and cease to be reborn. Tibetan incarnations are beings who have attained that state of perfection but have nevertheless returned to earth in human form to help guide others on the path to enlightenment. Depending on the stage of enlightenment they reach, they are known either as buddhas, bodhisattvas, or arahats. Some are reincarnations of great religious scholars, others of famous abbots, and still others are identifiable manifestations of the Buddha himself.

Mahayana Buddhist doctrine stresses the threefold form of Buddha, one unmanifest and two manifest—one earthly and one spiritual. The unmanifest, conceptual form and first in order of importance in the Tibetan pantheon is the Adi (First) Buddha. This primordial Buddha has five manifestations known as dhyani buddhas (buddhas of meditation) who exist on the spiritual plane, and each of these, in turn, is further projected into the material sphere in the form of a bodhisattva. The Dalai Lama incarnates an aspect of one of these bodhisattvas, the compassionate Avalokiteswara, and is known to Tibetans as Chenresi, their patron saint.

The institution of Panchen Lama, Tibet's second most revered incarnation, is of more recent vintage and dates back to the middle of the seventeenth century, when the Fifth Dalai Lama paid homage to his spiritual adviser by appointing him abbot of Tashilhunpo monastery and pronouncing him an incarnation of the dhyani buddha Amitabha, who would thereafter continue to be reborn with the title of Panchen Lama, Great Gem of Learning. Amitabha, or Öpame, as the deity is called by Tibetans, is the dhyani buddha on the meditative or spiritual plane whose projection into the earthly world is the bodhisattva Chenresi, a metaphysical interdependence the Great Fifth wished to institutionalize out of respect and devotion to his teacher. Thus the Panchen Lamas, as reincarnations of meditative beings living only on the plane of pure thought, are prescribed to a life of spiritual contemplation and must abstain from contact with the temporal world. The Dalai Lamas, however, are not only in contact with the vortex of life but also empowered to exercise both spiritual and secular authority.

There was only one female incarnation spiritually and officially recognized in the whole of Tibet, Dorje Pamo (the Thunderbolt Sow), believed to be the earthly manifestation of Dolma, Chenresi's spiritual consort. The origin of her incarnation goes back to the year 1717, when Dzungar Mongol forces were looting central Tibet and arrived at Samding monastery, where they heard great treasures had been stored.[6] Legend has it that the abbess in charge of the monastery locked its gates and refused the Dzungars admission, and that when they broke in she miraculously transformed herself and her monk attendants into an enormous sow and some eighty hogs. Terrified and disgusted, the invaders fled, never to return, and the pigs changed back into human form. Since that time the Thunderbolt Sow has been venerated by all Tibetans and is reincarnated in each abbess of Samding; she is accorded privileges almost as great as those of the Dalai Lama and Panchen Lama.[7]

Tibetan monasteries had an organization similar to that of Western universities. Larger institutions like the Three Pillars in the vicinity of Lhasa—Drepung, Sera, and Ganden, with a combined population in excess of 20,000—were subdivided into autonomous colleges called *dratsang*, each of which had its own Khenpo, or abbot.[8] Some colleges specialized in the teaching of certain scriptures and occasionally differed from one another in disciplinary regulations. Whereas a monk was usually able to choose the *dratsang* best suited to his needs, however, his place of residence was selected according to nativity; in a *khamtsen*, or fraternal dormitory, would be others from his own country (such as Mongolia or China) or region of Tibet. Within the Three Pillars were also some twenty units called *shatsang* (*sha* indicates the residence of a monk and *tsang* a family), small and extremely wealthy monk kinship groups that maintained their identity by "adopting" cousins and nephews of the elder head and, although numerically insignificant, played a significant role in the monastic branch of the Tibetan government.

Each monastery derived the majority of its income from the possession of manorial estates vested in it by the central government. The extent of the estate was a fairly accurate indicator of a monastery's size, wealth, and prestige. Since the proceeds were never sufficient to provide for the entire monkhood, large gifts of grain, butter, dried meat, tea, and sometimes currency were contributed by the government, the nobility, religious pilgrims, and peasants. The common name for all such institutions was *gompa*, and the larger ones were known as *dansa* (seat of the head lama) or *chode* (great religious institution). Little hermitages (*ridrö*) could also be found all over Tibet, usually in extremely inaccessible locations. To these remote places, often nothing more than a tiny cluster of whitewashed cottages, monks and laymen alike went on spiritual retreat. Some even moved into pitch-black caves, becoming hermits completely shut off from the sights and sounds of the outside world and devoting all their waking hours to prayer and meditation. The opening to each cave was sealed inside and outside with small boulders, between which a tiny wooden bowl of butter tea and *tsampa* would be left each day so as not to disturb the occupant. Most of those choosing to further their quest for enlightenment in this manner did so for a period of either three months or three years, but some preferred to remain in contemplation for the rest of their lives; only when food offerings were left untouched for several successive days was a cave unsealed and the mortal remains of its tenant removed. Tibetans called those who chose to live out their lives in this manner *mts'am-s-pa*, "the packed-up ones."

A child selected to pursue a religious career was generally sent to a monastery by the time he had reached five or six years of age. There he was dressed in monastic robes and the hair was shaved from his head except for a small portion on the crown, which was offered to the abbot, who then removed it in a ceremonial manner. To become a *rapjung*, or novice, he took the first sixteen vows and was given a new name, then placed in the care of a relative of his family or a guardian who would be responsible for his preliminary spiritual training and would instruct him in reading, writing, and memorization of the scriptures. After completing two such years of elementary education, a child might request from his abbot permission to take the twenty additional vows of a *getsul* and thus to commence more advanced studies. Only after reaching twenty years of age and demonstrating a solid grasp of a wide range of religious and philosophical subjects might he be qualified to take the final 207 vows of a *gelong*, or fully ordained monk.[9]

It was possible for a *gelong* to enter a school of Tibetan medicine, pursue an ecclesiastical or government career, or simply lead a life of seclusion and meditation. Additional studies might lead to one of the monastic *geshe* degrees, the highest of which, the *geshe lharampa* (doctor of metaphysics), was a prerequisite for admission to a *ngak*, or Tantric college. Only graduates of the latter were eligible to become abbots, or possibly to be appointed to the position of Ganden Ti Rinpoche (Precious Enthroned One of Ganden Monastery), head of the dominant sect of Tibetan Buddhism and considered the most learned religious figure in all the land.

Not all monks, however, pursued careers of advanced scholarship and learning. To the contrary, the majority were workers and artisans, hardly a surprising fact considering that many monasteries had populations as great as or greater than most of Tibet's towns and villages. Institutions like Drepung with its 10,000 monks, for instance, were really sprawling monastic cities requiring the services of cooks and kitchen helpers, sweepers and personal attendants, masons and carpenters. Some monks were trained as administrators for manorial estates and as monastic disciplinarians; others manifesting artistic talent became monastic dancers, *thonka* painters, and butter sculptors. Many were successful traders and moneylenders.

Perhaps the most interesting group of these secularized monks were the *dob-dob*s, brawny individuals who constituted a rugged subculture within the larger monasteries. Some cared for theological students, doing their chores and so releasing them for study, but the majority preferred less sedentary work. *Dob-dob*s wore robes in what they felt was a more dashing manner than other monks and sported red armbands over which rosaries, sometimes fashioned of rubies, were draped. They preferred to keep their hair long, especially the sidelocks, and often smeared their faces with soot to make themselves look fierce. They fought extensively among themselves under a somewhat crude code of chivalry, and many carried a large key that could be wielded as a formidable weapon, as well as carefully concealed swords. Those from Drepung monastery served an important function at the Monlam Chenmo (Great Prayer Festival), the paramount annual event in Lhasa, which was initiated by the reformer Tsong Khapa in 1409 to commemorate the anniversary of a legendary occasion when Lord Buddha defeated six heretical teachers by performing a series of miracles. The Festival's fundamental purpose was to shorten the time remaining in the spiritual reign (*kalpa*) of Gautama Buddha, whose power has passed its zenith, and to hasten the coming of the Maitreya Buddha, known to Tibetans as Gyalwa Champa (All-Conquering Love).

During the twenty-one days of Monlam, Lhasa's two city magistrates were replaced by the two priors (*shengo*) of Drepung, thereby transferring civil and criminal jurisdiction from the lay aristocracy to the monkhood, a refinement introduced by the Fifth Dalai Lama in the seventeenth century to symbolize the dual nature of his rule. On its first day the public floggers— members of the *ragyapa*, the same class as the disposers of the dead— marched out of the main door of the courthouse and laid their whips in a heap, and some two dozen of the largest, strongest, and most belligerent *dob-dob*s armed with great staffs and clearly visible swords were appointed as *geyok*s (monk policemen) to assist in the maintenance of law and order in the holy city for the duration of the festival. The remarkable success of the *dob-dob*s in controlling riotous crowds may be attributed to the fact that they did not hesitate to use force no matter how minor the provocation, and celebrants tended to give them a wide berth. Yet any man wearing monk's robes was accorded great respect in Tibet, and the *dob-dob*s, while hardly a source of joy, were accepted rather philosophically. The Buddha taught that acrimonious individuals should not be thought to have evil natures, for there are many buddhas and bodhisattvas in the world who cannot be recognized by outward appearances. Was not the great Tilopa unpleasant to look at? Did not the learned Marpa always fight with his neighbors? The monkhood, then, was viewed by the people of Tibet as a vast ocean in which both gems and stones were to be found.

Today, Tibetans continue to take refuge in the Three Jewels: in the Buddha, who, having attained permanent cessation from suffering and having compassion for all living things equally, is a guide to spiritual enlightenment as a physician is a guide to good health; in the Dharma, the wisdom of Gautama taken like divine medicine through which one attains liberation; and in the Sangha, the monastic order which, like a nurse administering this medicine, assists humankind in the practice of religion. Whatever their station in this life, they know that by maintaining the proper mental attitude and cultivating such thoughts as will benefit all other beings, they will ultimately attain liberation; that leading a monastic life or reciting from the scriptures is a useless exercise without the proper motivation; that faith, the mother of insight and wisdom, depends not on outward signs but on inner commitment. "O you people, you have faith on your lips," said the twelfth-century Tibetan saint Milarepa, "but I have faith in my mind!"

In Tibet many years ago there was a famous lama whose name was Drom. One day Drom saw a man circumambulating a *chörten.* "It is good that you walk around a *chörten,*" he said. "But wouldn't it be better to practice religion?"

"I had better read a holy book, then," said the man to himself. And he started a laborious course of reading.

One day Drom happened to meet him again. "Reading from a holy book is of course very good," Drom said. "But wouldn't it be better still if you practice religion?"

And the man thought, "It seems even recitation is not good enough. Perhaps I should begin meditating."

Not long after, Drom saw him deep in meditation. "I admit that meditation is good," he said. "But wouldn't it really be better if you practice religion?"

The man was bewildered. "What do you mean by practicing religion?" he asked. "Tell me how it is done."

"Turn your mind away from the forms of this worldly life," Drom told him. "Turn your mind toward religion."

Notes

1. The Sanskrit word *yana* means "burden" or "responsibility." According to the *Saddharma Pundarika* (Lotus Sutra), there is ultimately only one *yana*, which is neither Hinayana nor Mahayana: "The Dharma has been preached with reference . . . to the Buddhayana, which leads to the attainment of supreme Enlightenment." Lobsang Phuntsok Lhalumpa, "Buddhism in Tibet," in Kenneth W. Morgan, ed., *The Path of the Buddha: Buddhism Interpreted by Buddhists* (New York, 1956), 274–275.

2. David Snellgrove and Hugh Richardson, *A Cultural History of Tibet* (New York, 1968), 79.

3. The Buddha is one who has attained permanent cessation from suffering, a spiritual beacon for guiding others along the path of enlightenment. The Dharma refers to Buddha's teachings and to religion, the practice of which leads individuals to liberation. In Tibetan it is rendered as *chös*, meaning "to hold" one back from disaster and also "to cut" the bonds of suffering by ending cyclic existence. The Sangha means the monastic order and, in a finer sense, those who have attained enlightenment. The corresponding Tibetan word is *gedün*, "those who have the wish for liberation." The Tibetan word for this Buddhist trinity is *kunchok-sum.*

4. Dating back to the twelfth century, the Karmapas are a subsect of the Kagyupa and arose among the devotees of the lama Karmapa Dusun Khenpa, who founded the order in 1155. Eventually they split into two groups, identified by their distinctive headgear as Red Hats and Black Hats. The Third Black Hat Karmapa Lama, Rangjung Dorje (1284–1378), is said to have predicted his fu-

ture rebirth, and the fourth of the line, Karma Rolpai Dorje, was recognized as the first reincarnation in Tibet.

5. An individual recognized as a Tulku was not thought to possess upon birth the vast knowledge of his predecessor, but only to have an innate desire to amass it within his lifetime to help others attain enlightenment. On rare occasions when a Tulku manifested no such interest, he would be permitted to offer back his vows and leave the monkhood, and the validity of his incarnation would be in question. The term *Rinpoche* may also be applied to describe highly qualified scholars such as abbots of monasteries, not all of whom were Tulkus. Kyitsang Rinpoche, the elderly lama who led the search party for the Fourteenth Dalai Lama, and Reting Rinpoche, the young lama and regent of Tibet who saw the prophetic vision in the waters of the sacred lake which led to the child's discovery, were also Tulkus.

6. Samding ("Soaring Meditation") monastery overlooked Yamdrok Lake, which occupied part of a barren plateau some 15,000 feet above sea level. The agropastoralists living near its shores were forced through dire economic necessity to fish there as a means of livelihood. Consequently the entire vicinity was considered a very sinful one, and it was believed that Dorje Pamo's incarnations came to Samding especially for its spiritual benefit.

7. Contrary to what is generally believed, Samding was not a nunnery, but a monastery. There were, to be sure, nunneries all over Tibet, but the overall population of monks outnumbered that of the nuns by a rate of approximately ten to one.

8. The word *khenpo* means "chief performer in a ritual releasing candidates from the vortex of rebirths." Usually used in reference to the abbot of a monastery, it may also be applied, in the context of an ordination, to the initiating lama.

9. *Gelong* means "he who is searching for release from the world and living on alms according to the teachings of Lord Buddha."

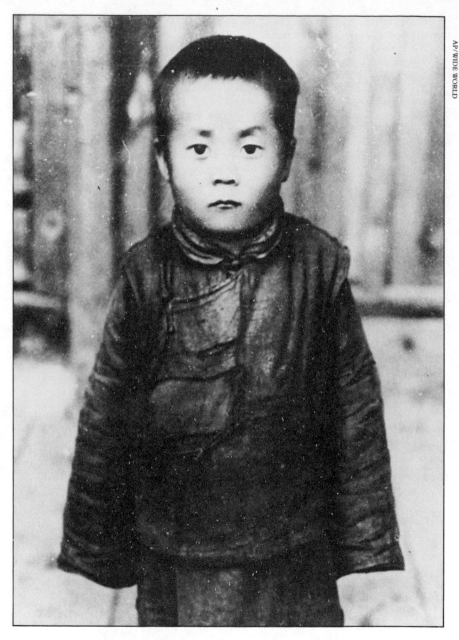

The Fourteenth Dalai Lama   *Lhasa 1940*

· CHAPTER 5 ·

Return to the Throne

O N THE FIRST DAY of the sixth month of the Year of the Earth Hare, a
party of fifty travelers with some three hundred fifty horses, mules,
yaks, and camels left Kumbum for Lhasa and an overland trek that was to
last over three months. Among them were the child incarnation and his parents, two elder brothers (Gyalo Dhondup, age eleven, and Lobsang Samden,
age six), and an uncle, the monk Taktser Garpa Loyer. Kyitsang Rinpoche
and his search party were in attendance, as was the contingent of Muslim
merchants who had extended the loan to them. They were accompanied by
a sizable bodyguard sent at the insistence of General Ma Pu-feng, who
stressed that roving bands of brigands might pose a threat to the group's security. Lest the wily warlord be suspected of harboring altruistic impulses, it
might be added that he extracted not only a further payment of five thousand dollars from the Tibetan government for these services, but also
another fifty thousand dollars from the Chinese government's Bureau of
Mongolian and Tibetan Affairs to cover the same expenses.[1] The sun shone
brightly when the journey commenced. Many different auspicious cloud
formations appeared in the sky, and a light rain fell.

The travelers followed the ancient caravan route from Amdo to the holy
city which wended through the forests of the Sandal Valley, amid scores of
tiny lakes glimmering like sapphires and surrounded by lush, verdant pastures teeming with deer, antelope, wolves, bears, and large herds of *drongs*
(wild yaks) and *kyangs* (wild asses); on to the awesome Kokonor,[2] its brilliant deep-blue waters reflecting the ring of snowcapped peaks along its
shores and so large that to follow the track around it would take three weeks;
through vast steppe lands resplendent with yellow, brown, red, and violet
vegetation; over craggy, weatherbeaten mountain passes above which eagles
and vultures loomed in their aeries; along the eastern edge of the marshy
plains of Tsaidam, where a single misstep could cause pack animals to be
swallowed up without a trace; and across the eastern reaches of the wind-

swept Chang Tang. Near a place called Little Happy Valley they saw some strange, variegated stones that bore markings like the *bodhi* seeds used for rosaries, but otherwise nothing especially remarkable was observed. As was the customary practice in Tibet, the group traveled from dawn till noon each day, then pitched yak-hair tents and encamped until the following morning on timeless camping grounds close to water and good grazing spots; some even had crudely constructed stone walls offering protection against the wind. The few habitations encountered along the way were scattered nomad tents. None was large enough to accommodate them, but from their occupants they were able to purchase butter, cheese, and meat, as well as dozens of sheep to trot along with the caravan and be slaughtered for food as needed.

The child incarnation and his brother Lobsang rode together in a litter called a *treljam*, which was attached to two poles and carried on the backs of a pair of mules walking side by side. Not infrequently the boys became bored and fretful and began to quarrel, pulling each other's hair and then crying. On such occasions Kyitsang Rinpoche rode up alongside and regaled them with jokes and stories; always smiling and playful, he even began teaching them the Tibetan alphabet to occupy some of their time. When the terrain became dangerous, the monks carried the children on their shoulders. "As we were not at all strong and had no experience in the art of carrying, we often had to be helped," reported one of them later. "However, we never felt in the least averse to the task, as carrying the little Rinpoche was a highly meritorious deed." Aside from their mother, who rode by herself in another litter, the rest of the group went on horseback. Wherever the party halted for the night, groups of Tibetan and Mongolian nomads came to pay their respects to the child. Since it was impractical to give hand-touch blessings to such a large number of devotees, Kyitsang Rinpoche devised a system whereby sacred objects and holy mantras inscribed on parchment were wrapped in ceremonial scarves (*khatas*) and the boy, seated upon a rudimentary throne fashioned from squares of turf and covered with fine silks, gave blessings to the people with them.

After more than two months the caravan finally reached the Tibetan border, where it was greeted by a small group of mounted frontier guards known as Aphors, superb horsemen and crack shots who had been recruited by the Lhasa government from the nomad tribe of Horpas and lived at the isolated checkpost in a cluster of yak-hair tents. As soon as word reached the capital that the child was safely out of Chinese hands—despite being paid for the entire journey Ma's bodyguards had been dismissed earlier, for the government had no intention of permitting an armed Chinese contingent to enter Tibet—the Tsongdu (National Assembly) convened and unanimously confirmed him to be the reincarnation of the Thirteenth Dalai Lama. Two high-ranking officials representing the lay aristocratic and monastic branches of government were dispatched hastily with ten attendants, loads of *tsampa* and fodder, a beautiful yellow tent that had belonged to the Thirteenth In-carnation, and four yak-hide coracles to greet the travelers at the Thup-topchu River and assist them in crossing it. Despite its short duration the voyage delighted the child, although he was almost as fascinated by the stout lay official accompanying him, who sported a bushy walrus mustache as well as week-old stubble on his chin.

Several days later the group crossed the Tonghor Pass and arrived at the village of Bumchen, where yellow flowers abounded; Lhasa was but a fifteen-day march away. The yellow tent was erected in this stunningly beau-tiful setting and the child seated on a throne decorated with the finest em-broidered satin. The monk official, a thirty-five-year-old Lhasan named Liushar Thupten Tharpa, made a mandala offering, and Kyitsang Rinpoche granted audiences with the child to all who had come to see him. "It was at this moment," reminisced the object of these attentions some years later, "that my father and mother first knew for certain that their son was the rein-carnation of the Dalai Lama, and they felt great joy and awe and thankful-ness, and, for the moment, incredulity—the kind of disbelief which often comes with great and happy news." It had been difficult for the monks to keep this information from the child's parents during the long journey since the father spent a great deal of time with Kyitsang Rinpoche's party. "He was a kindly man who was very fond of horses and mules," remembered one of them later. "Every day after we had put up for the night he used to sit with our retinue a great deal. This made us very uneasy and anxious as, although he was actually the father of the Dalai Lama, we had to treat him like one of ourselves." The boy's mother was more reserved than her husband and spent much of her time embroidering clothes.

Since the entire affair had been kept under a cloak of secrecy until the last possible moment, the preparations of the Tibetan government for the entry of the Dalai Lama had to be rushed through. Compounding this was the fact that it was deemed essential that the child enter the holy city before the end of the eighth month of the Tibetan calendar because the ninth month had been determined by divination and astrology to be highly inaus-picious. A large group of officials was sent by the Kashag (Council of Min-isters) to greet the new Dalai and escort him back to Lhasa with appropriate pomp and ceremony.

The welcoming party numbered about one hundred and included lay and monastic government officials, representatives of Lhasa's Three Pillars—Drepung, Sera, and Ganden monasteries—cooks, and attendants. "We hoped to greet His Holiness's party at Nagchuka, normally a ten-stage jour-ney from Lhasa," remembers T. W. Shakabpa, then a thirty-two-year-old lay secretary to the Kashag who later became head of Tibet's Finance Depart-ment, "but we were so anxious that we traveled day and night and completed the journey in half that time, arriving there at about two A.M." All changed into the proper ceremonial attire, and a small group headed by Shappé

(Council Minister) Bhondong ventured by torchlight another three miles to "The Pasture of the Four Joys," where the caravan had encamped for the night. Kyitsang Rinpoche welcomed them warmly but bade them be quiet lest they awaken the child or disturb his rest. Silently he led them to the litter and, after hesitating for a moment, drew back its curtain. To their joy they found the boy awake and not at all upset, but smiling and peering attentively at them. "The exchange of ceremonial scarves was performed by Kyitsang Rinpoche," recalled Sonam Wangdu, one of the latter's aides on the search. "Thereafter, when the little Rinpoche began bestowing the hand-touch blessing with his soft, delicate hands, dawn broke and, just as we reached the reception tents, the sun's first rays fell on them. Such were the auspicious signs that occurred spontaneously." Another member of the search party, the monk Khenrab Tenzin, lifted the boy from the litter and carried him on his shoulders into the yellow tent, where he was dressed in new robes sent by the government and seated upon a throne. T. W. Shakabpa, who had arrived at the campsite an hour after the advance party, took advantage of the confusion by surreptitiously photographing the child with his Leica. Although it was the first photograph taken of the child since he had entered Tibet and been proclaimed his country's spiritual and temporal leader by the Tsongdu, Shakabpa had to keep it a secret for years because photographing a Dalai Lama was not ordinarily permitted.[3]

A brief ceremony followed at which tea and rice were offered. Then Shappé Bhondong prostrated himself three times and handed the child a letter from the regent acknowledging him as Dalai Lama. Since in Tibet significant deeds were usually preferred to any pronouncement in words, he also offered gifts, which, although suitable for any high incarnation, could only be presented to the highest incarnation present. The child was then placed in the gilded palanquin used by the Dalai Lamas known as a *phebjam* and escorted to Nagchuka. They arrived late in the morning and went directly to the Shapten monastery, whose name signifies the "Palace of True Peace." Scores of people had been trickling in from the surrounding countryside since dawn and a huge crowd was assembled, many of whom were sprawled asleep in the courtyard. Most had dressed hurriedly in the dark, and a few of the monks and lamas elicited delighted titters of laughter for having inadvertently worn the inappropriate footwear to accompany their robes. Sitting alternately upon a throne and the familiar lap of Kyitsang Rinpoche, the new Dalai Lama held his first official reception on the top floor of the monastery. As he bestowed blessings on the exuberant crowd, they shouted gleefully, "A happy sun now shines in Tibet!"

Two days later the party, now several hundred strong, set out amid a warm and ceremonious farewell by the different monastic communities, which was punctuated by the songs and dances of villagers and nomads. It was a moving experience that the Dalai Lama would never forget: "In every village and town we passed, we encountered processions of lamas and monks carrying emblems and decorations. The people of these places also joined in the processions, while horns and flutes and drums and cymbals sounded and clouds of smoke rose from incense burners. Everyone, layman or monk, was dressed in his best clothes and welcomed me with folded hands and a happy smile on his face, as I passed through the throngs. Looking out from my palanquin, I remember people shedding tears of joy. Music and dancing followed me everywhere." At Omar-tang they were joined by the regent of Tibet, Reting Rinpoche, who had seen the vision in the sacred waters of Lake Lhamoi Latso that had led to the discovery of the new incarnation and who was ruling the land during the interregnum. A day later they arrived at the regent's monastery, some sixty miles northeast of Lhasa, where they rested for three days. Finally they reached Dögu-thang, barely three miles outside Lhasa, where new Dalai Lamas were traditionally accorded a formal welcome by the Tibetan government.

In the middle of the vast plain was erected the yellow satin Peacock Tent used solely for such occasions. Fifteen feet high and covering an area of over one hundred feet square, it had a yellow silk lining and a silk top and was used by the new Dalai Lama for religious audiences; smaller tents for him to sleep, pray, dress, and eat were pitched in a rectangular formation around it, and these in turn were surrounded by scores of other tents to accommodate monastic and lay officials as well as foreign delegations from Britain, China, Nepal, Sikkim, and Bhutan. For the better part of two days the Dalai Lama sat calmly on his throne, benignly bestowing his blessings on high dignitaries, monks, and commoners alike. The impassive yet affable manner of the child impressed all who saw him, although his family found quite amusing his apparent preoccupation with two Britons: the Londoner Reginald Fox, radio operator for the British Mission, whose sandy-colored hair was most unusual in Tibet; and Hugh Richardson, the urbane Scotsman heading the mission, who was resplendent in full diplomatic gear including plumes and spurs. The child's fascination notwithstanding, Richardson eventually gave up wearing the spurs because he could find no way to do so comfortably while sitting on cushions in the prescribed cross-legged fashion.[4]

Clusters of government workers and monks scurried about distributing ceremonial pastries and dried fruits to the thousands of celebrants, and a huge trough of dried yak meat was provided from which all were encouraged to grab what they could because doing so would bring prosperity to the land. Everywhere people were gathered in groups singing, offering prayers, and performing regional folk dances. T. W. Shakabpa even found time to compose a lengthy poem commemorating the historic occasion. "I am an old man now and have long since forgotten most of it," he says, running his fingers through his thick white hair. "But I do remember how it began:

"The day of our happiness is rising like the sun from the east,
And the camp at Dögu-thang looks as if all the stars are twinkling on
the ground."

Precisely at sunrise on the twenty-fifth day of the eighth month of the Tibetan Earth Hare Year 2066, the time and date appointed by the state astrologer, the Dalai Lama and his retinue began the last stage of their journey
to the holy city. The party, by this time swollen in size to many hundreds,
marched along a track marked with white and yellow chalked lines on which
large incense burners had been placed every thirty yards from which puffs of
aromatic smoke wafted silently into the sky. Both sides of the route were
lined with thousands of monks clad in saffron robes and holding gaily colored prayer banners aloft. Soldiers from all the regiments of the Tibetan
army were in formation to present arms, and with their bands provided a
guard of honor; and what seemed to be the entire population of the city,
bedecked in their finest clothes and ornaments, telling their rosaries, and
spinning hand-held prayer wheels, clogged the byways to welcome and
catch a glimpse of their leader. "As they watched me passing," he remembers, "I could hear them crying, 'The day of our happiness has come.' "I felt
as if I were in a dream, in the middle of a great park covered with beautiful
flowers, while soft breezes blew across it and peacocks danced elegantly before me. There was an unforgettable scent of wildflowers, and a song of freedom and happiness in the air."

The Dalai Lama's composure continued to be remarkable. Just as the
procession reached Lhasa, the Nechung oracle, deep in trance and with his
face grotesquely contorted, thrust his head into the palanquin and sprinkled
the Dalai Lama with rice, then pressed his forehead against the child's and
offered him a ceremonial scarf. So alarming was the oracle's appearance that
nearby horses took fright, but the Dalai Lama seemed entirely unperturbed
and, moreover, had the presence of mind to place a scarf around the oracle's
neck in response; it was, remarked some of those who had witnessed the
scene, as though the boy had known him all his life. The procession moved
on to the Jokhang Temple, where the child incarnation bowed humbly before
the sacred images and offered a scarf to each of the chief deities, then on to
the Norbulingka (Jewel Park), summer place of the Dalai Lamas just south
of the city, where he and his entourage were treated to a program of traditional monastic and folk dances. Here the Dalai Lama remained while arrangements for the final group of ceremonies in his honor were being completed, and his parents and siblings were installed in a small house nearby.

The culminating event in the assumption of power by a new incarnation
of the Dalai Lama is the ceremony rendered in Tibetan as *sitringasol*, roughly
translated as the "conferring of power on the golden throne" and indicating
that enthronement is the principal aspect of such an occasion and not install-
tion as is often thought. In Tibetan Buddhism the individuals who become

human embodiments of the Dalai Lama die, but the office of Dalai Lama does not. The emergence—or, more accurately, reemergence—of a Dalai Lama is believed to be the return of one who has been temporarily absent and the resumption of an authority and function already his own. Three major considerations dictated the date selected by the Tibetan government for the ceremonies to begin. Although the first, third, and fifth months of the new year had all been designated as auspicious by divination and astrology, the first was selected because it would ensure the presence of the largest possible number of Tibetans. Annual celebrations of Losar and the three-week Monlam that followed were magnificent religious observances of traditional pageantry which attracted to Lhasa tens of thousands of monks, farmers, nomads, and pilgrims and tripled or quadrupled the normal population. With the harvesting and threshing finished, the land not yet ready for cultivation, and flocks of sheep requiring little attention, it was the best time of year for Tibetans to make merry. Moreover, it was recalled that when the eastern wing of the Potala was undergoing restoration thirteen years before the death of the late Dalai Lama, the ruler had ordered an artist to paint pictures of a blue bird on the north wall and a white dragon on the east wall to either side of a stairway leading to the northern chamber. At the time the purpose of the paintings had been unclear, since they seemed to have neither legendary nor historical meaning. Now, some two decades later, it became evident that the blue bird symbolized the year of the Thirteenth Dalai Lama's death—the Water Bird—and that the white dragon indicated the enthronement of his reincarnation. For this was the Year of the Iron Dragon.[5] Finally, it had been a tradition of the Thirteenth Incarnation to move from the Norbulingka at this time each year and take up residence at the Potala, the Vatican of Tibetan Buddhism rising majestically above the vale of Lhasa, in which the enthronement was to take place.

On a bright, chilly morning a week before the ceremonies, members of the British Mission set out for their official reception at the Norbulingka by the Dalai Lama. Although the surrounding hills were covered with a powdering of fresh snow, a foretaste of spring was in the air as bar-headed geese, mallard, teal, goosander, and Brahmini ducks[6] frolicked in the icy waters of the streams flowing into the Kyichu River. Outside the gates of the summer palace had gathered a crowd of local villagers and shepherds wearing a single garment of sheepskin with the wool on the inside, the areas from which they came evident by their physical features, dialects, the styles in which the women braided their hair, and the variety of their ornaments. In the inner courtyard waited large throngs of shaven-headed monks, some on duty and others hoping to receive a blessing from the new incarnation.

The audience hall into which the group was ushered was moderate in size and lighted from a central square supported by painted pillars, its walls covered with religious frescoes barely visible in the dim light that reached them. The focal point of the chamber was the throne, vacant since the death of the Thirteenth Dalai Lama six years earlier, although attendants had maintained it precisely as it had been during his lifetime. Fresh food was brought in each day, holy water in brass bowls was replenished, and potted seasonal flowers were very much in evidence. Today, however, the throne had a new occupant. "On entering the audience room," wrote Sir Basil Gould, the political officer of Sikkim and, with Hugh Richardson temporarily out of the country, the ranking officer of His Majesty's government present for the ceremonies, "it was seen that the Dalai Lama, a solid, solemn but very wide-awake boy, red-cheeked and closely shorn, wrapped warm in the maroon-red robes of a monk and in outer coverings, was seated high on his simple throne, cross-legged in the attitude of Buddha. Below him on the graded steps of the throne, looking like giants in comparison with the child, were five Abbots." On the steps to the right and left of the throne were pots of sprouting barley and pink primula.

Gould and others who had known the Thirteenth Dalai Lama were stunned by the fact that the child seemed to recognize the close associates of his predecessor, by the "extraordinary steadiness of his gaze," and by his calm absorption in the events unfolding before him. "The next thing they noticed," he continued, "was the devotion and love, almost passing the love of women, of the Abbots who attend him. Next, perhaps, the beauty of his hands. And meanwhile all had become aware that they were in the presence of a Presence." Each then approached the throne. First came some of those few who might expect the two-handed blessing, then monks who, down to the most junior, were entitled to the blessing by one hand; and then the laity, villagers, and shepherds, each with a small offering of at least a shred of white scarf and a few coins, some to receive the blessing by two hands or by one, but most to have their foreheads touched by one of the abbots in attendance with a tassel of bright silk ribbons that had been blessed by the Dalai Lama. After a time the column of those seeking a blessing was held back and the members and staff and servants of the British Mission, not all of them Buddhists, approached the throne in turn. The leader of the party presented a scarf; a scarf that had been blessed was placed around his neck; and two small, cool, firm hands were laid steadily on his head. The other members of the party followed in turn. Tea was served twice and rice once as a form of mutual hospitality which was at the same time a sacrament. When the tea was first brought in, the Chöpon Khenpo, the abbot responsible for the Dalai Lama's food, produced a boxwood tea bowl from the folds of his gown and tasted it to make certain it had not been poisoned. Only after this precaution was the Dalai Lama served, and then the rest of the assemblage. After the second serving of tea, this time on behalf of the British Mission, gifts they had brought with them were presented to the Dalai Lama, including a gold clock with a nightingale that popped out and sang, a pedal motorcar, and a tricycle.

The audience officially ended. Lifted down from his throne and leaving the hall holding the hands of two abbots who towered on either side of him, the child was back moments later with his six-year-old brother, Lobsang Samden. "It appears that the Dalai Lama has a strong will and is already learning to exercise the privileges of his position," commented Gould. "The little monk was soon going round the smooth floor of the audience chamber in the pedal car. An outstanding virtue of Tibetans is that they hold that a place which is sacred may also be a place for fun." As they filed out of the hall and back to their residence, the Britons congratulated Kyitsang Rinpoche on his great discovery.

An auspicious sprinkling of morning snow heralded the beginning of the day selected for the Dalai Lama to leave the Norbulingka and make his official entry to the Potala for the *sitringasol* ceremonies. Lest the reader feel such interpretations of climatic conditions by Tibetans are subjective in nature or merely a matter of convenience, it should be pointed out that whereas a snowfall is regarded as highly auspicious for affairs of state, it is considered highly inauspicious for a wedding or a New Year's Day.

By dawn virtually every person in and around Lhasa had lined the mile-long route to witness the procession. From the main gates of the Norbulingka it led along an avenue of stately poplar trees, across the Lingkhor (Sacred Path) that encircled the city, over the bare hill on which stood the College of Medicine, and on to the city gate of Lhasa with its strings of tinkling bells. Here were assembled many ladies of the main aristocratic families in Lhasa, gay in headdresses set with seed pearls, coral, and turquoise, over which were looped the black coils of their long, straight hair; eight-inch earrings of turquoise cut flat and set in gold; charm boxes studded with gemstones; silk robes of every color, with silk shirtsleeves of a contrasting color turned back over the wrist; a cascade of pearls and gems over the right shoulder; and, in the case of married women, an apron in stripes of green, red, purple, and gold or whatever succession of bright colors the individual weaver had chosen.

Once inside the gate, the route swept around the base of the Potala, skirted the high walls and blue lake of the Snake Temple, proceeded along the northern face of the Potala, and finally moved up the alternating steps and stone-paved slopes of the southern approach to the magnificent thirteen-storied edifice. All along the route were men and women tending earthenware incense crocks, set on walls or carried on arm or shoulder and fed with artemisia and other fragrant herbs; troupes of strolling dancers, some wearing headdresses resembling those of American Indians; mummers; bands and drummers; clean-featured shepherds dressed in sheepskin, their broad-browed and plump wives with their hair in scores of closely plaited ringlets; monks of every age from tiny children upward in maroon robes, often tattered; beggars, farmers; countless thousands turning prayer-wheels of every device and size.

But the colorful throngs paled in comparison to the official procession of the Dalai Lama and his retinue. First came hundreds of servants, on ponies and on foot, dressed in green tunics, blue breeches, and broad red tasseled hats, carrying the Dalai Lama's food, kitchenware, garments, and bedclothes; grooms, to be ready for their masters at the Potala; attendants carrying tall banners to ward off evil spirits; some members of the Chinese delegation; high lamas followed by the Nechung oracle and the chief secretaries; the ponies of the Dalai Lama in gorgeous silk trappings; the head monks of the Potala monastery in claret robes fringed with gold and silver embroidery; junior lay officials in their long *geluche* mantles of many colors, black skirts, and white boat-shaped hats set sideways on the head and tied down under the ears; lay officials in ascending order of rank, Teijis, Dzasas, Shappés, all stiff in heavy brocade.

Then, through the clouds of incense drifting across the route and between lines of standard-bearers, came two long double lines of men in green satin uniforms and red hats with white plumes, holding draw ropes that would be needed for the long climb up the Potala; and men in red with yellow hats who moved with short, shuffling steps, bearing the yokes that supported the poles of the Dalai Lama's great golden palanquin. Directly in front of it rode the prime minister, wearing a Mongolian-style dress and a silk tasseled hat with gold bands. The child incarnation was invisible behind gold curtains and bright bunches of paper flowers. To his right was carried the tall peacock umbrella which is the privilege of the Dalai Lamas.

Next came the regent, Reting Rinpoche, under a gold umbrella, dressed in robes of golden silk and a yellow conical hat trimmed with black fox skin, his horse draped in brocade with a gold knob between its ears and led by two grooms. The family of the Dalai Lama followed: mother, father, and brothers; then abbots and incarnations from monasteries throughout Tibet, in peaked hats and wrapped in coats of gold brocade worn over maroon robes. Some incarnate lamas, boys as young as the Dalai Lama himself, were tied firmly to their saddles. Toward the end of the procession came more civil officers, the seniormost leading, in the traditional *geluche* traveling dress; more monk officials; and finally a giant monk doorkeeper of the Potala monastery, who with stentorian voice kept back the dense crowds of monks, nomads, villagers, and pilgrims. Once inside the Potala, the child was taken to his private apartments to rest, for the ceremony of his enthronement was less than twenty-four hours away, and much would be expected of him.

By three o'clock the following morning all of Lhasa was awake; indeed, there were many who had not slept at all, so great was their excitement and so joyous the occasion. Under a misty sky and an almost full moon, hundreds of monastic and lay officials, their paths illuminated by attendants carrying lanterns, trudged up the steep slope of the Potala, which loomed in all its majesty above the holy city.

The main audience hall upon which they converged was known as *si-shi-*

phuntsok, "hall of all good deeds of the spiritual and temporal worlds," and was located in the eastern part of the palace. It was a large, square room lighted from a central well supported on massive wooden pillars around which were hung the eight lucky signs of Tibetan Buddhism. Perhaps three feet in front of the north wall was a large screen covered with ritualistic banner paintings (*thonkas*) on silk or canvas, surrounded by ornate brocades, and against it was the *sengtri* (Lion Throne) of the Dalai Lamas, which had been built in accordance with the instructions of Tibetan scriptures. Fashioned of gilded wood, it was square and supported by two carved wooden lions at each of its corners. On it were five square cushions, each covered with a brocade of a different color, bringing its total height to seven feet. To its right stood a golden table inlaid with great rubies and hundreds of turquoises and pearls. The other three walls were covered with similar paintings, barely visible even by day.

The dimly lighted room began to fill up long before the child was due to make his entrance. To the right of the throne and against the north wall, the Nechung oracle and the principal monk secretaries of the Tibetan government were seated on low cushions. To the left of the throne sat the members of the Dalai Lama's family in attendance: father, brother Lobsang Samden, mother, and brother Gyalo Dhondup, also with their backs to the north wall. On the south side of the open square were raised cushions for cabinet ministers and other civil officials, in order of seniority from right to left as they faced the throne. Close to the throne on the west side of the square was the moderately raised throne of the regent and, more to the right, the seat of the prime minister. The remainder of the west side was reserved for the abbots of monasteries, incarnate lamas, and selected monks. The east side of the hall was lined with cushions for members of foreign delegations.

While the spectators filed in slowly and found their places, attendants in a long, adjacent anteroom set out the gifts that were to be offered later that day. The Maharajah of Sikkim's list included two magnificent horses, and that of the British government a brick of gold fresh from the Calcutta mint, ten bags of silver, an English saddle, a picnic case, and two pairs of parakeets. But by far the most stunning were traditional offerings from the monastery of Tashilhunpo, seat of the Panchen Lamas. Each in the care of a separate monk, there were golden figures of Lord Buddha, Chenresi,[7] and other deities, warmly wrapped in colored silks; holy books; sets of golden silk clothes; sets of the eight lucky signs in gold and in silver; a six-foot elephant tusk; a rhinoceros horn set in silver; bags of gold dust; silver ingots; countless rolls of silk and fine cloth; and provisions of every kind.

It was still an hour before dawn when a giant lictor with a voice like a foghorn and swinging a golden incense burner ordered the assemblage to be silent. All rose and watched reverently as one group of attendants entered the hall carrying warm wrappings, which they arranged carefully on the throne, and another rolled out a white carpet bearing the eight lucky symbols. After a brief pause the blare of *gyaling*s, Tibetan ceremonial horns, pierced the ear.

His tiny hands grasping those of the two abbots flanking him and clad in golden robes and a pointed yellow hat with long lappets that extended almost to his shoulders, the Dalai Lama entered the hall at a brisk pace, climbed the lower steps of his throne, and was lifted to the top of it and wrapped snugly in the warm covers. Following him were the regent, Reting Rinpoche, clad in yellow silk; the prime minister; and the abbot of Taktra monastery, who with the regent was responsible for the child's education. Next came the council ministers dressed in heavy gold brocade and fur hats, other civil officials, and the five abbots who had presided over the ceremony at the Norbulingka a week earlier. Upon entering the chamber, each prostrated himself before the Dalai Lama. The abbots assumed their stations on the steps of the Lion Throne, the regent seated himself on his throne, and the gathering took their seats.

Monks of the Potala's Namgyal monastery began the ceremony by advancing toward the throne and softly, almost inaudibly chanting special prayers praising the Dalai Lama and wishing him a long life and a prosperous reign. The regent followed, prostrated himself three times before the throne, and presented the *mendel tensum*, an offering consisting of a golden image of the Buddha of Eternal Life, a book of scriptures, and a miniature *chörten*, thereby entreating the new incarnation to enjoy a long life, to propagate the Buddhist faith, and to have thoughts like those of the buddhas. The regent, junior tutor (the abbot of Taktra), and prime minister presented scarves to the child, who blessed the first two by touching their foreheads with his own and the latter, a layman, by touching his head with both hands. The senior chamberlain led a procession of retainers bringing to the child a ceremonial sweet-tasting herb called *droma* in a small golden cup, a symbol of good luck. Finally, junior officials and the general public approached the throne in the traditional fashion: a closely packed, swaying queue of figures with knees bent, body touching body, like an enormous conga line. So great was the number seeking blessings that the ceremony lasted over five hours.

Despite their solemnity, the procedures were punctuated at regular intervals by a pair of learned abbots engaging in shrill philosophical debate and emphasizing their points in the conventional manner, which included loud hand-clapping, hitching of cloak on shoulder, and screaming in piercing tones. Nor was this the only diversion. A troupe of twelve brightly costumed dancing boys sporting jade battleaxes appeared on several occasions to perform a highly stylized mime to the accompaniment of drums, flutes, and oboes; and a procession of masked figures wended its way through the hall in robes representing deities of the oceans and heavens, chanting songs in praise of Tibet.

Befitting such an auspicious occasion, not to mention one of such great duration, refreshments were available in abundance. From time to time tea was served, first to the Dalai Lama from a golden urn with a dragon spout, and afterward to all present, each person producing a wooden bowl from the folds of his dress. Rice and *tsampa* were also handed around, and finally large portions of boiled meat. Toward the end, great piles of sweetmeats and of pastry bread molded into fantastic forms, entire dried carcasses of yaks, bulls, and sheep, often complete with horns and tails, and glistening pigs from which the bristles had been singed were set out on some fifty low tables in the middle of the hall. There was a wild rush of servants of the Potala and other poor to seize what was deemed to be food from the Dalai Lama's own table, and each secured what he could in spite of a great show of violence on the part of tall monk attendants armed with whips. The ceremonies ended with yet another dance and another debate. Then two scholarly monks approached the throne and recited to the Dalai Lama verses they had composed wishing him long life, peace and prosperity for all under his authority, and the triumph of religion throughout the world. Bestowing scarves on the pair in appreciation, the Dalai Lama was lifted from his throne, strode across the white carpet to the doorway, and withdrew as he had come.

"The main impression produced," recalled Sir Basil Gould, "was the extraordinary interest of the child in the proceedings, his presence, and his infallible skill in doing the right thing to the right person at the right time. He was perhaps the only person amongst many hundreds who never fidgeted and whose attention never wavered. It was very evident that the *sit-ringasol* was indeed the return, in response to prayer, of the Dalai Lama to a throne which by inherent authority was already his."[8]

At the age of four and a half, the little boy from Taktser was thus formally recognized as the Fourteenth Incarnation of His Holiness the Dalai Lama, the spiritual and temporal ruler of Tibet. "To all Tibetans," he remembers, "the future seemed happy and secure."

The year was 1940.

Notes

1. Despite the declaration of Tibetan independence by the Thirteenth Dalai Lama in 1913 after his return from exile in India and the overthrow of the Manchu Ch'ing dynasty, the Chinese maintained the fiction that because Tibet had been part of the Manchu Empire it automatically became upon the restoration of Chinese rule in Peking (after an absence of 267 years) an "integral" part of China. Its imposing name notwithstanding, the Bureau of Mongolian and Tibetan Affairs had no jurisdiction whatsoever in political Tibet and was simply a typical Chinese face-saving creation.

2. *Kokonor* is the Mongolian word for "Blue Lake." Situated some 10,000 feet above sea level, in the midst of its chill salt waters is a small rocky island on

which a tiny monastery stood until sometime after the Communist invasion of Tibet. The monks who lived there were riparians, but fished only in the cool months and avoided eating fish during warm weather. So completely were they cut off from the outside world that they did not even own a boat, and only when the lake froze over in midwinter were they able to tramp over the ice and beg for alms.

3. Interview with T. W. Shakabpa, Kalimpong, India, April 9, 1980.

4. Interview with Hugh Richardson, St. Andrews, Scotland, August 1979.

5. In ancient times the Tibetan calendar was based on a twelve-year cycle, each year being named after an animal: hare, dragon, serpent, horse, sheep, ape, bird, dog, pig, mouse, ox, and tiger. However, in A.D. 1027, the Buddhist religious text known in Sanskrit as *Kalachakra* was translated into Tibetan and set forth a somewhat different system, which paired the animals with five elements: fire (red), earth (yellow), iron (white), water (blue), and wood (green). Beginning that year, one element name was paired with two successive animal names to create sixty-year cycles. The element comprising the first part of the name is considered "male" the first time it is used and "female" the second. Thus the Water Dog Year (1982) is "male" and the Water Pig Year (1983) "female." We are at present living in the sixteenth such cycle, which began in 1927 and ends in 1986.

6. Brahmini ducks (ruddy sheldrakes) bred along the banks of streams and were not disturbed by the Tibetans, who considered them sacred because the color of their feathers is the same shade of yellow as the robes worn by Buddhist monks in India. L. Austine Waddell, *Lhasa and Its Mysteries: With a Record of the Expedition of 1903–1904* (London, 1906), 178–180.

7. Chenresi (Avalokiteswara) is the Buddha of Compassion and patron saint of Tibet, and is the deity that is reincarnated in the line of Dalai Lamas.

8. Basil Gould, *Report on the Discovery, Recognition and Installation of the Fourteenth Dalai Lama* (New Delhi, 1941).

Namgyal Temple   *Dharamsala 1980*

· CHAPTER 6 ·

A Celestial Dynasty

A CENTURY BEFORE COLUMBUS reached the shores of the New World, the first Dalai Lama was born in a nomad's tent on a barren plain in eastern Tibet. His arrival was greeted without fanfare; indeed it would be some time before he would come to be recognized as an incarnation of Chenresi, the Lord of Mercy and protective deity of Tibet, known in the Hindu pantheon as Avalokiteswara.

According to an ancient legend that anticipated Darwin's theory, Tibet was once a vast, beautiful land ringed by great mountains and inhabited only by invisible spirits. Into this primeval wilderness Chenresi and Dolma, his female consort, sent their incarnations. The former appeared in the form of a monkey, the latter as a cave-dwelling mountain ogress. From the union of this unusual pair emerged six offspring. These Chenresi fed on sacred grain—barley, still the staff of life to most Tibetans—with the eventual result that they shed their hair and tails and evolved into human form. According to another tradition, those who took after their father were merciful, intelligent, and sensitive, while those who emulated their mother were greedy, sinful, and stubborn. Thus the whole gamut of human behavioral traits was passed on to the Tibetans of today as an inheritance from their heavenly forebears.

The apostate King Lang Darma had been dead some five hundred years when a son was born to a couple in Amdo who had long been childless. His name was Tsong Khapa (1357–1419), and he became a monk, visiting many different monasteries and studying with the most learned scholars from the four major schools of Tibetan Buddhism: the Nyingmapa of Padmasambhava, the Kadampa of Atisha, the Kagyupa of Marpa and Milarepa, and the Sakyapa.[1] After thoroughly examining Tibetan and Sanskrit scriptures and immersing himself in deep meditation and other spiritual practices, Tsong Khapa came to the realization that Buddha's teachings had been subject to a noticeable permutation through their interaction with Bön, the primitive and shamanistic indigenous faith, and had moreover been corrupted and stripped of much of their vitality through the temporal excesses of many of the leading lamas. Spiritual discipline had grown lax and monastic reform was long overdue, so he began to restore the teachings of Atisha to their former prominence. Rather than attempt to introduce new procedures into any of the existing monasteries, he instead founded his own, twenty-eight miles from Lhasa, which he named Ganden, "Place of Joy." The members of this new Kadampa school were called Gelugpas, "those who follow the path of perfect virtue." They became known as the Yellow Hats after the distinctive color of their headgear, which set them apart from followers of the older sects, whose hats were generally red. Two other Gelugpa monasteries, Sera and Drepung, were founded near Lhasa during the next decade, and the latter became the largest monastery in Tibet and headquarters of the Gelugpas.[2] Through his monastic reforms, strict discipline, and teachings, Tsong Khapa effected major changes in the structure of Buddhist rule in Tibet that were to last until 1959.[3]

Tsong Khapa's successor as leader of the Gelugpas was one of his closest disciples, a monk named Gedün Truppa (1391–1474), who is reputed to have been a nephew of the great reformer and, like him, a native of eastern Tibet. It is said that on the night he was born in a cattle pen, Gedün Truppa was protected by a large raven during an attack by a marauding band on the family homestead. That the story might be apocryphal is less important than the infant's survival, for he later founded the famous Tashilhunpo monastery, disseminated Tsong Khapa's teachings, and greatly strengthened the new sect. Yet the Gelugpas remained a distinct minority, and Gedün Truppa was uncertain how best to keep them firmly united in the face of substantial opposition from longer-established sects. Because of their vows of celibacy the Gelugpas could not emulate the practice of hereditary succession employed by the early kings and Sakya lamas. They could, however, maintain and gradually expand their position by adopting a system of reincarnating lamas, a practice not uncommon at the time. Just before his death Gedün Truppa advised his followers not to mourn his physical passing because he would soon come back to earth in yet another human form, and two years later it was recognized that his spirit had passed into an infant born in the western province of Tsang. The new incarnation, given the name Gedün Gyatso (1475–1542), traveled widely, giving teachings throughout the land and establishing himself as a highly respected missionary and theologian despite increasing harassment by the Karmapas, a powerful offshoot of the Kagyupa sect, who had the military backing of Tibet's most powerful military force, the kings of Tsang.

The reincarnation of Gedün Gyatso was a brilliant scholar named Sonam Gyatso (1543–1588), who at the age of thirty-five visited Mongolia at the invitation of a prince of the Tumet tribe named Altan Khan. The death of Kublai Khan 300 years earlier had marked the end of the patron–lama relationship of the Mongol court and the Sakya lamas of Tibet, since which time both court and country had reverted to an ancient animistic faith similar to the Tibetan Bön.

Although Altan Khan, supreme ruler of all Mongolia, part of North China, and the Kokonor region of Tibet, was a recent convert to Buddhism, it appears that the invitation was motivated more by political than spiritual considerations. For him to remain in power, he knew it would be necessary to effect a political reunification of the disparate Mongol tribes, and a logical rallying point for such an act would be religion. He knew also that with no direct blood claim to the Mongol throne he held by virtue of military conquest, it was essential he find a way to legitimize his possession of it; and that an ideal way to do so was through "divine right."

Unfortunately, the indigenous faith was useless as an instrument of political power because, completely lacking in organization, it could not provide the careers and dignities offered by a hierarchical church. Buddhism, on the other hand, suffered from no such limitations. Moreover, it coincided with Altan Khan's aspirations that the Yellow Hats, whose influence had spread beyond Tibet into western Mongolia and northwestern China, were facing a direct military confrontation with longer-established sects and needed protection. Such was the background to his historic meeting with Sonam Gyatso in June of 1578.[4]

Wearing white robes to symbolize the light that had dawned on the "Dark Continent" of Mongolia with the arrival of the Gelugpa hierarch, Altan Khan identified himself as the reincarnation of Kublai Khan and his honored guest as the reincarnation of Kublai's spiritual guide, the Sakya lama Phagpa,[5] and proclaimed Buddhism the national religion of Mongolia. "Your visit to us has now helped the Buddhist religion to revive," he announced. "Our relationship of patron to lama can be likened to that of the sun and the moon. The ocean of blood has become an ocean of milk." To commemorate the renewal of this relationship and to honor his spiritual mentor, Altan Khan bestowed upon Sonam Gyatso the title of Dalai Lama, *Dalai* being the Mongolian translation of the Tibetan *Gyatso*, meaning "ocean" and signifying that the lama's wisdom was as deep and broad as an ocean. Because he was the third incarnation of Gedün Truppa as well as the third abbot of Drepung monastery, Sonam Gyatso came to be known as the Third Dalai Lama and his predecessors, Gedün Truppa and Gedün Gyatso, retroactively as the First and Second. Despite the deaths of Altan Khan in 1581 and Sonam Gyatso seven years later, relations betwen the Gelugpas and the house of Altan Khan became even more intimate when the great-grandson of the late Mongol leader was discovered, after an extensive examination, to be the incarnation of the Third Dalai Lama, fulfilling the latter's prophecy to his Mongolian followers that he would return as one of them in his next round of birth.

Yönten Gyatso (1589–1617) differed from his three previous and ten future incarnations in two significant ways. Born in Mongolia to Mongolian parents, he became the only non-Tibetan Dalai Lama. Whereas there is little doubt that political considerations played an important role in his discovery, it should be pointed out that Buddhist teachings maintain that bodhisattvas possess the ability to influence, by their wishes in each life, the time and place of their return. The promise made to the Mongolians by the Third Dalai Lama that he would be reborn as one of them is entirely consistent with this belief. The Fourth Dalai Lama was also the only one born to a wealthy or influential family, a fact that underscores the great strength of the Gelugpa system of spiritual and temporal succession through reincarnation. It is true that given their vows of celibacy, the Gelugpas could hardly have devised a more practical system if they were to survive as a viable force in Tibet. Furthermore, they did not assume full political and temporal authority until the middle of the sixteenth century. By making it impossible to predict precisely when, where, and in which body the next Dalai Lama would return, however, they insured against the political abuses attendant to a system of hereditary succession.

The supremacy of the Dalai Lama over both spiritual and temporal affairs in Tibet began during the reign of a remarkable individual known and revered by Tibetans as the "Great Fifth." Born to a peasant family in a village two days' journey southeast of Lhasa, Ngawang Lobsang Gyatso (1616–1682) effected an alliance with Gusri Khan of the Qośot tribe of Mongols, which paved the way for an end to hostilities and the unification of Tibet. The union came none too soon for the Gelugpas: since the death of Altan Khan the Mongols had splintered once again into dissident factions, and consequently there was no one individual to whom the Yellow Hats could turn for help. Meanwhile, attacks upon them became more and more frequent. The king of Tsang launched furious strikes against the monasteries of Sera and Drepung that claimed the lives of hundreds of monks, and seized other Gelugpa monasteries and turned them over to the Karmapas. At the same time, pro-Bön elements in the northeast were readying a massive assault whose avowed purpose was to eradicate every vestige of the reform sect from Tibet.

There are indications that even at this late date there were many on each side willing to compromise. Although his main allies were the Karmapas, it is probable that the king of Tsang would have agreed to accept all Tibetan Buddhist sects on an equal footing. Moreover, many leading Gelugpas and their lay supporters were likewise willing to arrive at a reasonable settlement. For each party, the motivation was the same: reluctance to share control of Tibet with a foreign power, even if that power were an ally. Had an agreement been worked out, Tibet might have had, like other Buddhist countries, a lay administration devoted to religion. But this was not to be.

Gusri Khan completed his military domination of Tibet in 1642 and conferred on the Fifth Dalai Lama supreme spiritual authority over the entire country, from Tachienlu in the east to the Ladakh border in the west, himself retaining responsibility for the defense of the country and the security of the Dalai Lama. With the death of the Khan thirteen years later and the reluctance of his hereditary successors as king of Tibet to exercise their political rights, the Great Fifth took all power into his own hands—the first time in Tibetan history that spiritual and temporal authority reposed in a single individual. The Dalai Lama proclaimed himself the reincarnation of Chenresi and declared that his four predecessors had likewise been earthly manifestations of Tibet's protective deity, and later honored his spiritual mentor by making him first in the line of Panchen Lamas. He shifted the headquarters of his government from Drepung to an imposing new palace overlooking Lhasa on the site where King Songtsen Gampo had built a fort a thousand years before, and named it the Potala after the spiritual abode of Chenresi. In his later years he withdrew into a life of meditation and left the actual governing of the country in the hands of his trusted regent, Sangyé Gyatso. By the time of his death in 1682, the Fifth Dalai Lama had knit his vast land into a single, cohesive, and independent unit. But trouble loomed on the horizon.

Sangyé Gyatso was quick to perceive the major weakness of the Gelugpa system of succession by reincarnation. Now that the Dalai Lama was dead, a new incarnation had to be found, and there would be an eighteen-year interregnum before the child could assume full control of Tibet's affairs. The Gelugpa system had worked well for the selection of monastic and sectarian leaders, but now for the first time the system was being applied to a head of state. Fearing that knowledge of his master's death would promote discord in the newly reunited country and bring construction of the palace to a halt, the regent Sangyé Gyatso decided to keep it a secret. Taking a few people into his confidence, he announced that the Great Fifth had retired from public life and would devote his remaining years to meditation in complete seclusion from the world. Secretly he had a stone carved with a prayer for the speedy discovery of the next incarnation built into the palace walls, where it may be seen to this day. Meanwhile, everything was done to make it appear that the Dalai Lama was alive and well. Meals were taken to his quarters as usual and a trusted monk from the Namgyal monastery was assigned to beat a hand drum and ring a bell just as the Great Fifth had done when performing his daily rituals. On public occasions the Dalai Lama's ceremonial gown was displayed on his throne in the audience hall, and attendants went through the usual routines as though he were actually present. When important visitors requested an audience, the monk, who bore a superficial resemblance to the deceased leader, dressed in the Dalai's ceremonial robes and engaged in a polite, albeit brief, ritual with his guests. Not until the Potala was finally completed in 1695 did Sangyé Gyatso announce that the Fifth Dalai Lama was dead and that his reincarnation was en route to Lhasa for enthronement ceremonies.

Although subsequently criticized for these actions and accused of selfishly and illegally seizing power, it would appear that Sangyé Gyatso was acting in Tibet's best interests. By all accounts his administration was competent, fair, and just. Had his choice of a child successor proven more suitable, the regent's gamble would most likely have worked. As it turned out, it was to change the course of Tibetan history.

The new incarnation, Tsangyang Gyatso (1683–1706), had been discovered in 1685 after a secret search and, although not formally installed in the Potala until 1697, had already taken his *getsul* vows and been provided with a rigorous scriptural education. Unlike his predecessors, however, he manifested no interest in continuing his studies and taking the vows of a *gelong*, or even in assuming his exalted station at the head of his country. Tsangyang Gyatso devoted himself to sensual rather than spiritual affairs; instead of a life of contemplation and leadership he chose one of wine, women, and song. An accomplished lyric poet, the Sixth Dalai Lama produced verses that reveal the story of his life:

> I went to my teacher, with devotion filled,
> To learn of the Lord Buddha.
> My teacher taught, but what he said escaped,
> For my mind was full of compassion,
> Full of that Compassionate One who loves me.
> She has stolen my mind.

The struggle between the sensual youth and the incarnation of Chenresi continued:

> In meditation I think of my teacher,
> I see his face before me;
> But the face is that of my lover.

Under the circumstances it is not difficult to see why a monastic existence was a difficult and trying experience for the youth. Wearing the blue silk clothes of a lay nobleman, with his hair hanging freely in long black tresses instead of the monk's tonsure, and resplendent in rings and jewelry, the young Dalai spent an inordinate amount of time dallying with eager Tibetan maidens and largely ignored his studies and the duties of his office.[6] Despite impassioned protests from the regent and leading monastic officials, who were at a loss to conduct the affairs of the country while bound by both the process of succession through reincarnation and the charming, albeit unsuitable, Dalai Lama, he at last refused to perform his final religious initiation and consecration and even renounced his original monastic vows. The significance of this action transcended its unprecedented nature: it sapped the vitality of the institution of Dalai Lama and sowed the seeds of Manchu intervention.

During the reign of the Fifth Dalai Lama relations between Tibet and the Manchu court had been excellent. The regent Sangyé Gyatso, however, abandoned the Great Fifth's restraining policy and began intriguing with the powerful Dzungar Mongols, a belligerent group posing the greatest external threat to the Manchu Empire. It was a tragic mistake; for a half century after establishing their Ch'ing dynasty in 1644, the Manchus had made only cursory efforts to extend their influence into Tibet while that country remained friendly or neutral, but the specter of a reunification of all the Mongol tribes under the banner of religion was too great a threat to ignore. Imperial control of Tibet became a necessity, and the unwitting Manchu agent for this was Lhazang Khan, the new leader of the Qośot Mongols and titular king of Tibet, who, unlike the earlier successors of Gusri Khan, was determined to restore his tribe's waning influence there.

The Manchu emperor K'ang Hsi goaded Lhazang Khan into moving on Tibet and promised military support if it should prove necessary. It did not, and after a brief war in 1705 the Khan arrived in Lhasa, assumed political control of Tibet, and had the regent put to death. These actions, however, placed him in direct opposition to the Dalai Lama, whom he decided to remove from the scene. Fearing that such a unilateral move might unite the other Mongol tribes and incite retaliation from both inside and outside Tibet, he turned again to the Manchu emperor and was accordingly promised support. In return, the wily K'ang Hsi extracted from the Khan a promise of regular payment of tribute. It was the first time tribute had been paid to the Manchus by a ruler of Tibet and likewise the first acknowledgment of Manchu supremacy.[7] It was accomplished with neither the knowledge nor the consent of the Tibetan government. In 1706 the Sixth Dalai Lama was deposed by Lhazang Khan. On the eve of his departure from Lhasa he sent a final message to his people:

> White bird in the sky,
> Lend me but one great wing
> That I too may fly eastward;
> Soon I shall return, from Lithang,
> And give you back your wing.

Tsangyang Gyatso never returned in mortal form from his eastward journey, dying—murdered, it is commonly believed—shortly afterward on his way into exile.

Once the Sixth Dalai Lama was removed from office, Lhazang Khan announced that the young poet had not been a true incarnation of Chenresi, and installed a twenty-five-year-old monk on the throne in his place. The Tibetans, however, would not recognize the puppet and were delighted to hear that shortly after the Sixth Dalai's death a new incarnation had been born in Lithang as his last poem had prophesied. In 1717 the Dzungar

Mongols, proclaiming a mission to depose the Khan and restore the rightful Dalai Lama to the throne, launched a successful invasion of Tibet and killed Lhazang Khan. They were unable to make good on the second part of their plan, however, for the canny Manchu emperor had gotten hold of the new incarnation himself.

Euphoria over the Khan's death had barely settled when disillusionment set in among the Tibetan people. They were pleased that the Dzungars had done away with the Khan and deposed his puppet Dalai Lama, but when the unruly tribe began to loot holy places and were unable to deliver the Seventh Incarnation, they awaited anxiously the help summoned from China by Lhazang Khan before his defeat. When word arrived that a large Manchu force was on its way to Lhasa with the new Dalai Lama in tow, nascent Tibetan forces rose up and chased the Dzungars from Tibet. Despite their hard-earned military victories on the march to Lhasa, the Manchus came to Tibet not as conquerors but to restore the Seventh Dalai Lama to the throne and to punish the Dzungars for killing their ally, Lhazang Khan. Yet through a combination of shrewd diplomacy and good luck, K'ang Hsi gained a foothold in Tibet; the foundation of almost two centuries of Manchu overlordship was brought about by the second non-Chinese emperor of China (the first having been the Mongol chieftain Kublai Khan five centuries earlier) to establish an affiliation with Tibet.[8]

The first thirty years of Manchu overlordship were tempestuous. The Seventh Dalai Lama, Kesang Gyatso (1708–1757), was enthroned in 1720 but exiled for seven years after his father and some influential officials were responsible for intrigues that helped spark off a civil war in 1727–28. Upon his return to Tibet he was not permitted to assume his temporal authority and the government was administered by an aristocratic lay official named Phola. To protect Manchu influence in Tibet the emperor stationed two permanent civil representatives in Lhasa known as Ambans, whose duties were to observe the affairs of the country and report them to Peking. These were backed with a sizable military garrison, which was withdrawn on two occasions after Tibetan complaints that its presence caused a shortage of supplies and subsequent rise in prices. Each withdrawal was followed by an armed uprising, the second on the heels of Phola's death and provoked by his son and successor, the hotheaded Gyurmé Namgyal. As in 1720 and 1728, the Manchu forces arrived in 1750 to discover that order had been restored—largely through the efforts of the Dalai Lama, who manifested a great degree of strength and resourcefulness now that he was in a position to do so.

It was obvious to the Manchus that they needed to create in Tibet a border state strong enough to eliminate this continual threat of internal warfare but not so strong as to pose a threat to the imperial empire. Despite Phola's successful administration, it was apparent that a lay ruler was not the answer. In 1750 they again reorganized the Tibetan government, placing the

Dalai Lama once more at its apex and restoring the temporal supremacy of the religious hierarchy as opposed to that of the lay nobility. The system lasted virtually intact for two hundred years, and was structured in the following manner.[9]

THE DALAI LAMA

In the hands of the Dalai Lama reposed both the direction of the Buddhist church and the administration of the country. He is an emanation of the bodhisattva Chenresi, the patron saint of Tibet who has returned to earth to guide mankind on the path to salvation. Normally he assumed his temporal rule at the age of eighteen, and his authority in both spheres was in theory absolute; as a divinity ruling on earth there can be no direct opposition to his orders. During his minority a regent (*gyaltsab*) was appointed to administer the government in his stead. The dual nature of the Dalai Lama's position was reflected in the governmental structure beneath him, which was divided into two branches, one civil and the other monastic. Each consisted of approximately 175 officials, but during the last two decades of Tibetan independence, from 1930 to 1950, there were approximately 200 of the former and 230 of the latter.

LAY OFFICIALS

The lay officials (*trung-khor*) were selected from an aristocracy consisting of some 150 families. In return for hereditary manorial estates granted by the state (which owned all the land), at least one male from each family was required to enter the government service. The only manner in which a commoner could aspire to such a position was through one of two infrequently trodden paths leading to ennoblement: by being a member of a new Dalai Lama's family or by performing outstanding service to the government.

Prime Minister

The post of prime minister (Silon) had its roots in remote antiquity and was revived by the Thirteenth Dalai Lama at the beginning of the twentieth century to serve as a link between him and his Council of Ministers. Held either singly by a lay official or in tandem upon the addition of a monk counterpart, the position was abolished in 1940 and briefly resurrected by the present Dalai Lama in 1950.

Council of Ministers

The highest and most important office of the Tibetan government was the Council of Ministers (Kashag), which usually consisted of three aristocratic and one monastic official. All were known as either Kalon (council minister) or Shappé ("lotus-foot"), although the monk official was also referred to as the Kalon Lama. None of the *kalons* had portfolios, and all the work and decision-making was done collectively. The council was the administrative center of the government through which all secular material had to be channeled, most of it delegated to the appropriate agencies and some brought to the attention of the Dalai Lama. Although its decisions were subject to the final authority of the latter, the council enjoyed wide authority over internal affairs.

Financial Department

The highest administrative office below the council was the Financial Department (Tsekhang), which was composed of four finance ministers (Tsepons). The duties of the Tsepons, all of whom were lay officials, consisted of maintaining revenue records, assessing taxes, and training other lay officials. Additionally they acted as presiding officers of the General Assembly.

Just below the Financial Department, but also directly subject to the council, were other specialized departments headed by one lay official and one monk official. These included the departments of foreign affairs, agriculture, the military, the judiciary, the mint, and district administration.

MONK OFFICIALS

The monk officials (Tse-drung) were selected only from the Gelugpa sect, and the majority of them came from one of the Three Pillars of Buddhism— Drepung, Sera, and Ganden monasteries. They were far more secularized than the majority of monks and because of their duties were not expected to maintain many of the normal vows. Although the higher positions tended to be dominated by monks either from aristocratic families or from wealthy monk kinship corporations known as *sha-tsang*, there were opportunities for qualified commoners to serve in various official capacities.

The Lord Chamberlain

The lord chamberlain (Chikyap Khenpo) had direct access to the Dalai Lama on matters within the jurisdiction of the monk officials. He headed the Dalai Lama's personal household and was in charge of the ruler's private treasury as well as the official Potala treasury. Although ranking slightly below the council ministers, he was often called on by them to join discussions on matters of great national interest.

Monastic Council

The function of the Monastic Council (Yiktsang) was to deal with religious matters. Its four chief secretaries (Drunyik Chenmo) took action on minor matters but were obligated to take their recommendations on more important affairs to the lord chamberlain. The Monastic Council supervised the administration of all monasteries except the Three Pillars and was in charge of the monk civil service. It was the monastic counterpart of the lay Financial Department.

THE ASSEMBLIES

There were three types of assemblies, none of which met on a regular basis. The smallest of these was a standing committee consisting of the four lay finance ministers and the four monk chief secretaries. Known as the Tru-tse-gyad (Assembly of Eight), it convened at the request of the council ministers and was frequently used by them to widen their base of support for proposals they intended to submit to the Dalai Lama. The intermediate assembly, which convened for matters of greater importance, varied in size from twenty to fifty and in addition to the eight individuals above included the abbots of the Three Pillars and selected government officials. In times of great national importance it was customary for a full assembly (the Tsongdu) to be summoned by the eight presiding officers with the inclusion of members of every occupation in Tibetan society; boatmen, soldiers, farmers, merchants, tax collectors, and so on. The Tsongdu was extremely conservative and outspoken in its assertion of Tibetan independence. Most significantly, it was a powerful vehicle through which the 20,000 monks of the Three Pillars made their views heard through their abbots.

Despite the restoration of his temporal powers, the Seventh Dalai Lama left most affairs of state in the hands of the Kashag and immersed himself in solitary religious contemplation until his death in 1757. For the next 138 years secular authority in Tibet was exercised not by his successors but by regents, high incarnate lamas appointed by the Manchu emperors until 1875, and then by the Tsongdu. The Eighth Dalai Lama was the only one of five incarnations during this period on whom full powers were conferred. Jampel Gyatso (1758–1804), however, was, like his immediate predecessor, a man of intensely spiritual nature with no interest in politics; he left his administrative responsibilities in the hands of the regent and chose to lead a life of meditation.

Of the four incarnations succeeding the Eighth Dalai Lama, only one reached the age of twenty-one. Whereas it is possible that owing to Tibet's poor sanitary facilities and medical care they succumbed to natural causes, there are indications that each may have met an unnatural death, probably by poisoning. It has been theorized that the Manchu Ambans were the likely culprits and carried out the nefarious deeds because a regent was easier to control than a Dalai Lama, but available evidence suggests otherwise. The Ambans were generally an unimpressive, vacillating lot. Moreover, the behavior of at least one regent was so ruthless that the accession of a Dalai Lama would likely have been welcomed by them with great relief. It is probable that the regents themselves, highly ambitious and lusting for power, were responsible for a series of unnaturally early deaths that could not have been entirely coincidental.

The Ninth Dalai Lama, Luntok Gyatso (1806–1815), was enthroned in the Potala in 1808. "The Lama's beautiful and interesting face and manner engrossed almost all my attention," wrote Thomas Manning, the first Englishman to reach Lhasa and likewise the first to be granted an audience with a Dalai Lama, in December 1811. "He . . . had the simple unaffected manners of a well-educated, princely child. His face was, I thought, poetically and affectingly beautiful. He was of a gay and cheerful disposition; his beautiful mouth unbending into a graceful smile, which illuminated his whole countenance. . . . I was extremely affected. . . . I could have wept."[10] Less than four years later, the child was dead. Of the Tenth, Eleventh, and Twelfth incarnations, Tsultrim Gyatso (1816–1837), Khendrup Gyatso (1838–1856), and Trinley Gyatso (1856–1875), little has been written.

Following the death of the Twelfth Dalai Lama, a traditional search was conducted for his successor and the state oracle at Nechung monastery consulted. According to Sir Charles Bell, the British political officer who later became a close friend of the Thirteenth Dalai Lama, an eminent lama went as directed to Lake Lhamoi Latso:

A wind arose—those tempestuous Tibetan winds are never far away—and dispersed the snow, leaving the ice clear before the lama, who was observing it from a nearby hill. Then he looked into it, as into a glass, and saw an image of the house and the land round it. He also saw a peach-tree in flower, several months out of season for peach blossom. That night in a dream he saw a vision of the young Dalai Lama, then somewhat less than two years old, in a woman's arms. A few days later he came to the house seen in the lake and found the child in the arms of his mother, and the face of the boy was unmistakably that seen in the dream.

The Thirteenth Incarnation not only survived his minority but also became the first Dalai Lama to exercise full political and spiritual authority since the death of the Great Fifth two centuries earlier. Thupten Gyatso (1876–1933) was responsible for a series of far-reaching reforms designed to remove abuses that were incompatible with the nation's best interests. Corrupt practices were rooted out of a number of monasteries, even if the offenders were members of his own Gelugpa sect. Monks were encouraged to refrain from too much involvement in secular affairs, and the number of lay officials was increased. The penal system was overhauled, capital punishment abolished, and corporal punishment reduced. Education, which had been reserved for monks, was extended to the children of nobility and peasants. With the introduction of electricity, telegraph, and telephone systems, and a solitary automobile in the 1920s, Tibet began to make its way slowly into the modern world. An intensely spiritual man who spent at least six hours each day in meditation and study, the Thirteenth Dalai Lama accomplished for his country as much as his illustrious predecessor, the Great Fifth. His death in 1933 was a great loss to the land and came at a critical time in Tibetan history.

Each Dalai Lama has been a unique individual, and each is revered by the Tibetan people not only for his exalted station but also for his earthly actions, all of which, they believe, were intended for their benefit. The First Incarnation, Gedün Truppa, disseminated the teachings of Tsong Khapa and nurtured the emerging Gelugpa sect. The Second, Gedün Gyatso, propagated the faith throughout the land. The Third, Sonam Gyatso, converted Altan Khan to Buddhism and lived to see the religion spread all over Mongolia. The Fourth, Yönten Gyatso, helped cement the Tibetan–Mongolian alliance. The Great Fifth, Ngawang Lobsang Gyatso, was a capable administrator and wily statesman who knit the country into a single, cohesive, independent unit before withdrawing from the secular world to the spiritual.

The Sixth Dalai Lama, Tsangyang Gyatso, contrary to what one might expect, is one of the most beloved of the line, for Tibetans believe he was sent to test the sincerity of their faith and he most certainly did so. The Seventh, Kesang Gyatso, is accorded perhaps the highest respect of all because, possibly in response to the rather tainted career of his immediate predecessor, he devoted his life to spiritual contemplation, as did the Eighth, Jampel Gyatso. The Ninth through Twelfth incarnations did not remain on this earth long enough to make their unique qualities evident, but the Thirteenth, Thupten Gyatso, was, like the Great Fifth, an activist who worked for the material benefit of his country while seeking refuge in the Buddha's teachings and providing spiritual guidance. Each Dalai Lama was born in a different time, faced different problems, and fulfilled his role in his own way. Some manifested great secular leadership, others great spiritual leadership, still others no observable leadership at all. Each, Tibetans believe, was chosen because his particular qualities were required at that particular time.

Shortly before his death, the Thirteenth Dalai Lama made a prophecy. Noting that Chinese had recently killed the highest Mongolian incarnation, demolished Buddhist monasteries, and conscripted monks into their army, he warned that similar events would soon begin in Tibet and that the Dalai Lama and other incarnations would vanish from the land. Prepare yourselves, he urged his people, for the days of brutality and horror that await you by strengthening your military forces and increasing your spiritual practices. When the People's Liberation Army invaded Tibet less than twenty years later, his ominous prophecy came true.

As little Lhamo Dhondup, now known as Tenzin Gyatso, the Fourteenth Dalai Lama of Tibet, took up residence in his winter palace, he was aware of neither his predecessor's warning nor the awesome responsibilities soon to be accorded him. Whether or not the lamas and oracles had made the right choice, whether or not the child would be able to provide the necessary earthly and spiritual leadership when he came of age, only time would tell.

Notes

1. The Sakyapa sect received its name not from the North Indian kingdom in which the Gautama Buddha had been born, but rather from the fact that its first monastery (founded in A.D. 1071) was built on a patch of gray-colored earth (*sa-kya*) and became known as the Gray Earth Monastery.
2. Ganden was founded in 1409, Drepung in 1416, and Sera in 1419.
3. Tsong Khapa has been erroneously described in a number of western books as the "Luther of Tibet." According to Snellgrove and Richardson, "This gives an entirely false impression both of Tsong Khapa himself and of the religious world in which he lived. He had no wish to interfere with the ways of others outside his monastery, and even if others were jealous of his successes, there is no sign of any open hostility between his community and others during his lifetime." David Snellgrove and Hugh Richardson, *A Cultural History of Tibet* (New York, 1968), 181.
4. For an enlightening discussion not only of this but also of the reemergence of Buddhism in Mongolia, see Larry William Moses, *The Political Role of Mongol Buddhism* (Bloomington, Ind., 1977), 83–107, and C. R. Bawden, *The Modern History of Mongolia* (New York, 1968), 26–38.
5. According to *Shing-rta*, the biography of the Third Dalai Lama, probably written by the Fourth Dalai Lama around 1615. Mongol chronicles, particularly the *Erdeni-yin Tobchi* or "Precious Summary" (1662), imply that it was Sonam Gyatso who first identified the previous incarnation. Moses, 97.
6. According to the Jesuit missionary Ippolito Desideri, "no girl or married woman or good-looking person of either sex was free from his unbridled licentiousness." In fairness to the much-maligned monk, whose rather apt name means "Ocean of Pure Melody," it should be pointed out that Desideri was a close friend of Lhazang Khan, who will enter the picture shortly.
7. K'ang Hsi was interested less in Tibet as a territory than as the home of the Tibetan Buddhism which had great influence over the tribes of Mongolia. So long as they felt the spiritual apparatus of the Buddhist church was on their side, the

Manchus made no attempt to administer Tibet directly. Alastair Lamb, *The China-India Border: The Origins of the Disputed Boundaries* (London, 1964), 28.

8. K'ang Hsi justified this action in his Edict of 1720, which maintained that the Manchus had enjoyed a privileged relationship with Tibet since 1640, when, with the outcome of the Tibetan power struggle still in doubt, representatives of the contending forces—Gusri Khan, the Fifth Dalai Lama, the king of Tsang, and the Karmapa hierarchs—were sent to solicit aid from what was then clearly the emerging power in Asia. At the time the requests were made, the Manchus had not yet established their authority in Peking and would not do so until two years after the Tibetan situation had been resolved without their aid. Moreover, the Manchus were preoccupied with conquering China and gave neither encouragement nor assistance to any faction; nor were treaties or written documents of any kind exchanged between the two nations. Nevertheless K'ang Hsi claimed that the exchange was an act of submission by Tibet, and with some 3,000 of his best troops bivouacked in and around Lhasa, there was little the Tibetans could do but acquiesce.

9. The following summary is based largely on material found in Hugh Richardson, *A Short History of Tibet* (New York, 1962).

10. Clements R. Markham, ed., *Narratives of the Mission of George Bogle to Tibet and of the Journey of Thomas Manning to Lhasa* (London, 1879), 265.

Young monk   *Bylakuppe 1980*

· CHAPTER 7 ·

The Two Brothers

RISING MAJESTICALLY some seven hundred feet above the Vale of Lhasa is the Potala, the Vatican of Tibetan Buddhism and winter palace of the Dalai Lamas. It is an enormous structure almost a quarter of a mile in length and occupies the entire top of the Marpori (Red Hill) on the edge of the holy city. Named after a craggy summit on Cape Cormorin at the southernmost tip of the Indian subcontinent, which itself was named after the spiritual abode of Chenresi, it is usually called Tse Potala (Peak Potala) or simply "the Peak" by Tibetans. So ingenious is its design that it almost seems not to have been built by human effort but instead to have materialized through some sort of celestial guidance, for as it rises from its rocky base one can barely tell where the hill ends and the Potala begins. Tibetan architecture blends with the surrounding landscape in a manner rarely found in other cultures, for to Tibetans the world is a harmonious whole. Had Tibet been less successful in keeping Western visitors from penetrating her borders, the Potala would have long since taken its place as one of the Wonders of the World. Indeed, a large, faded photograph of the Potala is said to have been the only picture of a building other than his own in Frank Lloyd Wright's studio in Oak Park, Illinois.[1]

The Potala was built on the orders of the Fifth Dalai Lama shortly after he became the first of his line to assume combined spiritual and temporal leadership of the country. In need of a place to house his new government and wishing to avoid its being regarded as an exclusively Gelugpa monopoly, he shifted his headquarters from Drepung monastery and established the court in nearby Lhasa, which he proclaimed the capital of Tibet. The new government he named after his palace at Drepung; Ganden Phodrang, "Palace of Happiness." Work on the new palace, which began on the twenty-fifth day of the third month of the year of the Wood Bird (1645), proceeded slowly, because there were no wheeled vehicles in Tibet nor would there be until the twentieth century. Each of the huge blocks of stone used in its construction had to be transported from a distant quarry by donkeys or lashed to the back of one of thousands of laborers with thongs of woven yak hair. Moreover, the sprawling structure was built without mechanical means and with only the most primitive of tools. Neither steel nor iron was used. Nor, for that matter, was mortar; the massive structure was simply a pile of blocks stacked one on top of the other, like the pyramids of Egypt.

The Potala occupies an area larger than that of many Tibetan villages. Its walls slope gently inward in typical Tibetan fashion, and the endless rows of windows, wider at the bottom than at the top, accentuate its unique symmetry. It was built in three connecting sections. The thirteen-storied central portion is painted a deep crimson to signify its special sanctity, for it houses all the tombs of the Dalai Lamas from the Fifth onward, with the conspicuous absence of the Sixth, whose death was as unusual as his life. Built on the pattern of a *chörten*, the tombs rise from the lower floor of the Red Palace and shoot up through the upper stories to the roof, where their domes, clad in sheets of solid gold, burst forth into golden canopies that glisten in the sunlight with such radiance that they can be seen for miles and provide a spiritual beacon for travelers to the holy city.

The most resplendent tombs are those of the Fifth and Thirteenth Dalai Lamas, which are both over sixty feet high. It is said that over a ton of gold was required for the tomb of the Great Thirteenth alone.[2] Both are encrusted with precious gemstones, and their interiors are filled with priceless jewels, golden religious objects, and rare Chinese porcelain. Inside the palace spiraling balconies surround the golden mausoleums, but to reach these privileged vantage points one first had to climb up a series of steep, rickety ladders, a dangerous venture, as the rungs were slippery with centuries-old grime and spillings from butter lamps.

The two nine-storied side wings are painted white. The western wing housed the Dalai Lama's personal monastery, Namgyal Dratsang (College of the Victorious Heaven) and living quarters for 175 specially selected monks whose primary function was to assist the Dalai Lama in his spiritual practices. Here also were libraries containing all the records of Tibetan culture and religion: seven thousand massive volumes weighing as much as eighty pounds apiece, some of which were written on parchment and others on palm leaves imported from India a thousand years earlier. Two thousand volumes of these scriptures were written in inks made of powdered gold, silver, iron, copper, turquoise, coral, and conch shell, each line in a different ink.[3] The eastern wing contained government offices, a school for the training of monastic officials, and the meeting chambers of the Tsongdu. Toward the summit were numerous chapels, audience halls and meeting rooms, and the spacious apartments of the Dalai Lamas and their close advisers and attendants. It was here, atop this monument to Lord Buddha, that four-year-old Lhamo Dhondup came to live in February 1940 with only his brother Lobsang for company.

It felt strange at first, living in the Potala. Not that Lobsang was used to being at home anymore: he had lived at Kumbum for half of his six years. His uncle Garpa had looked after him there and seen to it that he dressed and ate properly and studied the scriptures. His elder brother Jo-la was there too—only he couldn't call him that any longer. Ten years before, when he was eight years old, Jo-la had been recognized as the reincarnation of a great lama named Taktser Rinpoche and escorted with much ceremony to the monastery. Now he was an incarnate lama being groomed for abbothood and Lobsang an ordinary monk. Lobsang was proud that such an honor had befallen his family, but with Jo-la surrounded by tutors and attendants there was little opportunity for the brothers to be together. In the Potala it was different. Jo-la had remained in his *labrang*[4] at Kumbum and Uncle Garpa was engaged elsewhere. Like the rest of the family Lobsang called his little brother Kündün after his discovery as the reincarnation of the Thirteenth Dalai Lama. Kündün meant "the Presence," as in "the Presence of the Buddha."

The two had known each other just over a year, for Lobsang had gone off to Kumbum shortly after his brother's birth and had seen little of him until Lhamo arrived there while arrangements were being made to take him to Lhasa. Although he was quite young, Lobsang could not help being aware of the rumors that the little boy was to be the next Dalai Lama. The thought amused him, because Lhamo's mischievous behavior was anything but saintly. Now the brothers were here, ensconced on the top floor of the largest and most famous building in all of Tibet surrounded only by adult monks and no one near their own age. Lobsang missed his friends at Kumbum, and recalled how lonely his little brother had been when he went off with them to study the scriptures. He remembered, too, how Lhamo used to wait near the verandah during classes and try to attract his attention. He and his brother were alone now, but they had each other.

Lobsang was given a room of his own, near Kündün's quarters. It was a large chamber with high ceilings. He had never slept in a room by himself before and was frightened. When he asked if one of the attendants could sleep there with him, he was told he was acting like a child and would soon overcome his fear. Lying on his pallet at bedtime, the boy's attention would wander to the shadows cast on the walls through the interplay of butter lamps and religious objects. Although they frightened him, he was fascinated by the images they conjured up and stared at them for hours on end. It was months before he was able to get a good night's sleep.

Kündün never experienced any difficulty getting to sleep. During the long journey from Amdo and the ceremonies connected with his enthronement, he had almost always maintained his composure. Many who were fortunate enough to have caught a glimpse of him during that time marveled at his poise, but wiser heads saw it simply as further proof that his selection had been the correct one, that it might have been unusual behavior for an ordinary child but not for the reincarnation of Tibet's patron saint.

As befitting his exalted status, the boy occupied three other rooms in addition to his bedroom. One was a small chapel filled with banner paintings and statues of religious figures: Tsong Khapa, the great reformer from his own province of Amdo who founded the Gelugpa sect; Padmasambhava, the Indian pandit who crossed the Himalayas at the request of King Trisong Detsen in the eighth century and established the Nyingmapa sect, the oldest in Tibet; Milarepa, the renowned poet and saint and disciple of Marpa, founder of the Kagyupa sect; and, of course, the bodhisattva Chenresi, whom each Dalai Lama manifests in human form. He also enjoyed the luxury of a private bathroom. It was the only one in the entire palace and had been built for the Thirteenth Dalai Lama. In the center of the three- by six-foot area was a hole in the floor straddled by a wooden chair with a sliding lid and a seat cushioned with fur. Lobsang was intrigued by the contraption and disappointed when his little brother would not permit him to use it: "Lobsang," he was always told, "you must go outside, like the others." This was easier said than done, especially in the bitter winter weather, for there were hundreds of steps leading to the bottom, and they were quite difficult to maneuver when one was suffering from intestinal problems, a common ailment. Of his four rooms, the one the Dalai Lama used most often was also the largest. It contained his personal library of scriptures and commentaries, and its walls were covered with paintings depicting the life of the Fifth Dalai Lama, fashioned in such detail that the individual portraits were no more than an inch high. When he grew tired of reading, the boy often sat gazing at this great and elaborate mural and silently followed the life of his famous predecessor.

At the beginning of their stay in the winter palace the brothers were able to do more or less as they wished. Their favorite pastime was exploring the innermost recesses of their home, one of the largest buildings on earth. With their attendants in tow they wandered through endless mazes of winding, gloomy corridors that connected the Potala's more than one thousand rooms, assailed by an atmosphere redolent with the scent of incense, the stench of rancid butter, and the acrid fumes of yak-dung fires. It was a far cry from the pure mountain air of Amdo. With great interest Kündün and Lobsang opened every box, crate, and drawer they encountered. Once they came upon several numbered chests containing a large selection of old wooden toys: camels, elephants, yaks, snow leopards, even human figures. After they had amused themselves for several hours the monks scurried about, putting each back precisely in its proper place. Holding their claret-colored robes securely about them, the two little monks dashed from one musty room to another, frequently evading the supervision of the elder men who strove desperately to keep up with them. No matter how much they discovered one day, there were always new revelations the next, for one could never know all the palace's secrets. It abounded with ten thousand altars, twenty thousand religious images, a multitude of banner paintings, and tens of thousands of butter lamps.

Behind great padlocked doors leading to its cavernous cellars lay the greatest riches of all, for here were storerooms housing two treasuries: one, known as the Trede, was reserved for the private use of the Dalai Lamas and the other, the "Treasury of the Sons of Heaven," was a reserve to meet the expenses incident to war or other national emergencies. Entire rooms were filled with precious scrolls and the golden regalia of the kings of Tibet dating back to the time of Songtsen Gampo, and with the treasures of the Dalai Lamas who succeeded them, including priceless gifts from the emperors of China and Mongolia. Despite the opulence before them, the brothers were most interested in the collection of arms and armament from a millennium of Tibetan history, and only with great difficulty were they dissuaded from trying them on. The old monks were like shadows, following the brothers wherever they went, although they sometimes had to take the lead, as when diverting the boys' attention from a passageway leading to the deepest, dankest level of the building where the dungeons were located. The execution of criminals was forbidden in Tibet, but this did not deter magistrates from condemning offenders to a period of indefinite confinement, from which they rarely emerged alive.

Among the retinue assigned to watch over the brothers were four or five monk bodyguards known as *simga*s, enormous men often seven feet tall who wore giant shoulderpads under their robes to enhance their awesome appearance. Membership in this elite group was open to all Tibetans of the requisite physique, but in practice most were fierce Khampa warriors who would not have hesitated to lay down their lives to protect their leader.[5] On the walls just outside the Dalai Lama's apartments hung the accoutrements of their trade: grim swords, whips, and long, thick tubular pillows filled with cotton and covered with leopard skin, known as *bopchak* and probably of Mongolian origin. The presence of these pillows symbolized the guards' authority. Working twelve-hour shifts in pairs around the clock, the *simga*s provided a formidable patrol.

The grim bearing of the *simga*s frightened Kündün and Lobsang at first, but the boys eventually got used to them and not infrequently connived successfully to include these Tibetan titans as playmates. After a group of monastic officials happened upon one of these sessions and chided the bodyguards for playing like children, it was some time before Kündün was able to persuade them to participate again. There were also a large number of lay and monk sweepers called *gyapa*s and three special monk attendants assigned to minister to the specific needs of the child ruler. The Söpön Khenpo (Master of Tea) looked after his food and drink, the Simpön Khenpo

(Master of Robes) his clothing, and the Chöpön Khenpo (Master of Religious Ceremony) his religious objects.[6] The latter two positions were held by a succession of men, but the first never changed hands and was retained by a very special man named Lobsang Jimpa.

A central Tibetan from Tsang, Lobsang Jimpa had previously been the highest-ranking personal servant to the Thirteenth Dalai Lama and was thrilled when he heard that the latter's reincarnation had been discovered. Rushing out to greet his new master on the plain at Nagchuka before Kyitsang Rinpoche's retinue reached Lhasa, he was overwhelmed by the beauty and serenity of the child. He had been close by his side ever since. Both children loved the man, a kindly monk in his late forties whose graying beard made him look far older. Kündün was fascinated that Jimpa's shaven head held no hair, while on his chin he sported a bushy growth. From the very beginning the two enjoyed a warm relationship, which was terminated when the old monk died peacefully in his sleep some forty years later. The Dalai Lama remembers the day as one of the saddest in his life. A man of extraordinary composure, he remembers, too, the tears that came to his eyes.

After a year of unrestricted activity, the brothers were placed on a regular schedule and their formal education was begun. They arose early, always before sunrise. Lobsang Jimpa, his tall, gaunt frame reeling from the weight of the large wooden buckets of water he hauled all the way from the ground floor, admonished them each morning to bathe themselves thoroughly and reminded them how difficult a task it had been for him. Much to Lobsang's dismay, hot water from the kitchens below (actually, it had cooled off considerably during its long ascent and was barely tepid) was provided only for his brother, so he had to make do with icy well water. In the drafty confines of the winter palace, bathing was his least favorite chore.

Kündün and Lobsang played with their attendants until the morning meal was served in a large nearby chamber. Then each sat cross-legged on a floor cushion in front of a low rectangular table. Lobsang sat to the left of his little brother, and the three monks faced them on the opposite side. Silence was the rule, but the boys were regularly up to some sort of highly audible mischief. Breakfast usually consisted of *tsampa* and butter tea. Jimpa often produced a small lambskin bag, which he filled with the barley flour, tea, butter, and a little dried cheese. After kneading it well, he slipped his long, tapering fingers into the bag and molded tiny dough balls, which he popped into the expectant mouths of his charges one by one. Sometimes he gave them a special treat by adding some dried meat or a little brown sugar.

Playtime followed. Kündün and Lobsang took great pleasure in donning brightly painted masks and practicing monastic dances like the *shanak* or Black Hat dance first performed for King Lang Darma eleven hundred years before. Often they would prevail upon the attendants to take part in sessions of hide-and-seek, which inevitably left their elderly companions breathless.

They particularly liked a game played with a large wooden die, each facet of which was marked with one syllable of Chenresi's mantra, *Om Mani Padme Hum*. The die was rolled in conjunction with a large map on which auspicious and inauspicious places were marked. The former included Lhasa and some of the famous pilgrimage centers in Nepal and India like Lumbini, where the Gautama Buddha was born, and Bodh Gaya, where he attained enlightenment; the latter included the hot and cold hells, the lowest states in the round of existence. (It is said that the third cold hell is so cold that bodily movement is impossible and its denizens are able only to shiver and sneeze; hence its name, Ah Chu.) Lobsang was quite fond of a large collection of tin soldiers, some wearing green uniforms and others red. Despite his nascent interest in warfare, however, Kündün preferred to play with a wind-up train he had received as a gift from the British Mission. Whenever it went off the tracks, the rumpus he raised ensured that one of the attendants would hasten to set it right again.

The new Dalai Lama made his strong will felt almost from the moment he arrived in Lhasa. Having heard that the child was fond of birds, the British Mission had included in their gifts to him at the Norbulingka reception just prior to his enthronement two pairs of parakeets. After they had survived the rigors of the winter journey from India, it was thought the birds deserved rest and warmth so they were placed in the care of Reggie Fox, the mission's wireless operator, and the Dalai Lama informed they would be delivered to him after they had recuperated. Two days later there came a messenger from the Potala to request immediate delivery of the birds, then two more messengers, more senior than the latter, and then yet another two. As it was rather clear that if there was to be a battle of wills, the Dalai Lama would prove that his was the stronger, it was decided that compliance was the only possible course. Without further ado the Tibetan head clerk of the mission was dispatched with the birds, and not a moment too soon, for other messengers were already on their way. Upon his arrival at the winter palace, a fretful monk dignitary was standing in readiness. Considerably overcome, the clerk handed over the birds and began to leave but was summoned by the Dalai Lama, who, speaking the Lhasa dialect clearly and easily, questioned him about their feeding and how to keep them safe. Several days later, after being persuaded by Lobsang Jimpa that they would be better off away from the cold and drafty Potala, the child sent them back to the Mission, where they became great favorites with visitors.

At nine o'clock each morning one of Kündün's teachers arrived to coach the brothers in a two-hour study session, the first of two. After months of doing as they wished, the boys were reluctant to apply themselves but gradually became accustomed to the routine. To the delight of his elders Kündün quickly made evident a remarkable facility for learning that enabled him to progress at a considerably faster pace than his brother, a fine student in his own right. One of Kündün's earliest tutors was an old friend named Khenrab Tenzin, a highly respected monk official who had been a member of Kyitsang Rinpoche's search party and enjoyed a well-earned reputation for possessing a special gift for teaching young children, which was further enhanced by the results of his sessions with the child incarnation.

The monk's technique was the one traditionally used in Tibet. First he wrote Tibetan characters with a bamboo stick on a small wooden board that had been covered with chalk dust, and then he instructed the boy to write over them in ink. At the outset Kündün experienced great difficulty following the convolutions of the intricate characters and made little effort to conceal his impatience. Khenrab Tenzin gently took the boy's little hand in his own and guided it calmly over the tablet until he could do it without aid. Gradually Khenrab Tenzin reduced the dimensions of the characters until the child was proficient at writing in the proper size, then he had him copy whole words written at the top of the board. Finally, after about eight months of practice, he permitted Kündün to write on paper. When the child painstakingly scratched his first word onto this new medium, it is hard to say who was more satisfied, student or teacher: both were beaming. Altogether Kündün spent five years studying the written language, not a long time considering there were four distinct types of Tibetan script to be learned. At the same time he memorized a verse from the scriptures each day and spent another hour reading them, for religious training was the main purpose of his education and reading, writing, and grammar were only a means to that end.

After another play session, the brothers settled down for the main meal of the day. The fare was simple and hearty and consisted of dishes like rice and vegetables, boiled mutton stew with potatoes and white radishes, or Tibetan dumplings called *momo* served with pickle. The food was generally served either in small wooden bowls or in clay ones that kept it warm longer. Cutlery consisted of wooden spoons or chopsticks, but Kündün and Lobsang preferred to eat with their fingers. The monks rarely permitted them to eat pork, eggs, or chicken. When Kündün demanded an explanation, he was told that children needed their full powers to study and that consumption of these foods would interfere with this. A more likely justification probably lies with the religious beliefs of the monks themselves: fowls, because of the thousands of worms they eat, are guilty of the sin of taking many lives, as are pigs, to a somewhat lesser extent, from rooting in the ground. To have been reborn in those forms, these beings must have been guilty of wickedness in the previous life and would therefore be unsuitable sustenance for a young Dalai Lama. The attendants also forbade the brothers to drink milk, telling them that its high fat content might lead to liver complications. But Kündün was not to be denied. During certain rituals in the Potala when the occasion called for offerings of milk, he stole up and drank it.

A second study session occupied most of the afternoon, after which the brothers were free until bedtime. Although monks were forbidden to eat after midday, an exception was made because of their age and rank, and before retiring they were permitted a few biscuits and a little curd. In his bedroom, accessible only through an antechamber in which one of his three main attendants always slept, Kündün had the additional treat of a nightly bedtime story. Usually it was a children's tale, or perhaps a fable from the Buddhist scriptures. Many different people were required to read to the child, for once having heard a story he never forgot it, nor wished to hear it again after repeating it to Lobsang the next day.

Approximately three years after his enthronement Kündün granted an audience to Captain Ilia Tolstoy and Lieutenant Brooke Dolan, who became the fourth and fifth Americans to visit Lhasa and the first ever to meet a Dalai Lama. It was not purely a social call, for the officers were on a mission for the Office of Strategic Services in Washington. Although tranquillity prevailed within Tibet's borders, the Second World War was raging all around her. Japan had occupied the whole of Southeast Asia and invaded Burma, cutting off the famous Burma road over which the Allies were supplying China. Early attempts to airlift provisions from Calcutta to Kumming over the world's highest mountain range proved inadequate and costly. Moreover, it was an extremely dangerous endeavor; many aircraft were lost trying to traverse the Himalayan "Hump." With the Soviets occupied fighting the Germans on their western front and thus unable to supply the Chinese through Turkestan, the only alternative land route was through the southeastern corner of Tibet. The Tolstoy-Dolan expedition left India in September 1942, its destination the holy city of Lhasa.

It was a bitter winter day when Ilia Tolstoy arrived at the Potala for his audience with the child ruler bearing gifts that included a gold pocket watch, a model sailing ship fashioned of silver, and a signed photograph and letter from the American president:

His Holiness
The Dalai Lama
Supreme Pontiff of the Lama Church
Lhasa

Your Holiness:

    Two of my fellow countrymen, Ilia Tolstoy and Brooke
Dolan, hope to visit your Pontificate and the historic and widely
famed city of Lhasa. There are in the United States of America
many persons, among them myself, who, long and greatly interested in your land and your people, would highly value such an
opportunity.

    As you know, the people of the United States, in association
with those of twenty-seven other countries, are now engaged in a

war which has been thrust upon the world by nations bent on conquest, who are intent upon destroying freedom of thought, of religion, and of action everywhere. The United Nations are fighting today in defense of and for preservation of freedom, confident that we shall be victorious because our cause is just, our capacity is adequate, and our determination is unshakable.

I am asking Ilia Tolstoy and Brooke Dolan to convey to you a little gift in token of my friendly sentiment toward you.

With cordial greetings, I am

Very sincerely yours,

Franklin D. Roosevelt

Captain Tolstoy, a grandson of the Russian novelist, had the misfortune to be seated directly under a ray of brilliant sunshine that suddenly emerged from one of the small windows high above the floor of the audience hall. He was uncomfortably hot, but protocol demanded that he not move from the cushion on which he sat. Kündün watched in fascination as beads of perspiration formed on the officer's forehead, then blended into tiny rivulets that streamed down his face. "How strange it is," thought the child, "how one can be so warm on such a cold day." Owing in part to the fact that Kündün was uncharacteristically shy in the presence of the American and also because he was too young to have assumed his temporal powers, most of the conversation took place between Tolstoy and the elderly regent, Taktra Rinpoche. The captain explained that the main objective of his visit was to find a land route over which supplies could be sent from the Allies to China and to secure the permission of the Tibetan government to do so. His secondary objective was to establish official contact between the American and Tibetan governments.

Tolstoy's request was submitted through the proper channels and the response was not long in coming: Tibet wished to remain strictly neutral in the conflict. High-ranking government officials were acutely aware that Chiang Kai-shek regarded their country as an integral part of China that he planned to "restore" to Chinese rule once the Japanese invaders had been repelled from within his borders,[7] and viewed the Chinese plan to station "technicians" along the intended caravan route to "facilitate transportation" as a convenient excuse to extend their influence in eastern Tibet.[8] In response to Roosevelt's statement that America and twenty-seven other countries were engaged in a war for the preservation of freedom thrust upon them "by nations bent on conquest" who were "intent upon destroying freedom of thought, of religion, and of action everywhere," the Dalai Lama wrote in a letter composed by the regent that "Tibet also values her freedom and independence enjoyed from time immemorial and, being the great seat of the

Buddhist Religion, I am endeavoring, in spite of my tender age, to uphold and propagate our religious precepts and thereby emulate the pious work of my predecessors. I earnestly hope and pray," he added, "for a speedy termination of hostilities so that the nations of the world may enjoy a lasting and righteous peace." Seven years later the United States and its twenty-seven allies were enjoying that righteous peace when Tibet was invaded by a nation bent on conquest and intent upon destroying freedom of thought, religion, and action throughout the land. Not one nation came to her defense. Ilia Tolstoy did not see the Dalai Lama again for almost twenty years. Then, in failing health, he visited the exiled ruler in the Himalayan foothills of northern India. Although his wartime mission had proved a failure on an official level, it had resulted in an abiding affection for the Tibetan people and their leader that ended only upon his death in 1970.

Few days offered such diversion to the child ruler as the visit of Tolstoy and Dolan. There were, of course, annual celebrations of Losar and Monlam, as well as other less spectacular religious holidays. Most of all Kündün looked forward to visits from his family, who lived in a house nearby. He saw his mother once a month, although during the first few years her visits were more frequent. Their relationship, while still one of love and affection, had undergone a change almost from the moment the child was officially recognized as the reincarnation of the Thirteenth Dalai Lama. To be sure, Kündün was still his mother's son. On her visits to the Potala she brought freshly baked loaves of her Amdo-style bread which he liked so much, as well as small parcels of chicken, eggs, and, less frequently, pork. The latter items she had to carry surreptitiously, for she knew that her son's attendants would claim they were injurious to the child's health and object to her doing so. On the other hand, Gyayum Chenmo's little boy was now the supreme spiritual and temporal leader of the entire land. When she went to see Kündün, she wore her finest clothing and jewelry, and when she left she bowed before him and he laid his little hand on her head in blessing. Protocol dictated that she not receive the two-handed blessing, as that was accorded only to monks and high officials.[9]

Kündün saw his father—now known as Gyayab Chenmo, or "Great Father"—more often than he did his mother but, although he loved them both, he would have preferred it if the opposite had been the case. Before leaving home he and his mother had been almost inseparable, but his father was away much of the time tending his horses or socializing with his friends. Thus father and son never had the opportunity to get to know one another in Amdo, and once the child was enthroned as Dalai Lama there was little chance for a closer relationship to develop. Circumstances, however, conspired to throw the two of them together after they had settled in Lhasa. They often attended the *drungja*, or morning tea ceremony, a brief official function held in the Potala during the winter or in the Norbulingka in summertime, when all the government's monk officials met for their early bowls of butter tea just prior to Kündün's first tutorial session. As for his father's personal visits, the child was not unaware that their frequency was dictated largely by the season. When he moved into his summer palace each year, the number of visits increased noticeably, for on the grounds of the Norbulingka were stables where the Dalai Lama's horses were kept, some of the finest in the land.

Kündün was visited by his siblings as well, although not so often as by his parents. His sister Tsering Dolma moved to Lhasa in the autumn of 1940 with her husband, Phuntso Tashi. Brother Jo-la—Taktser Rinpoche—arrived from Kumbum a year later and took up residence at Drepung monastery, and Gyalo Dhondup was living with his parents in Lhasa. Moreover, Gyayum Chenmo had given birth to two more children since arriving in the holy city, a daughter named Jetsün Pema in 1941 and a son, Tendzin Choegyal, in 1946. Still, his favorite companion was Lobsang Samden.

The brothers fought a lot, usually at Kündün's provocation. It had always been that way, as far back as their joint residence at Kumbum. Even the stateliness of the procession from Taktser to Lhasa had been marred by frequent outbursts as the two rode side by side in Kündün's litter. Kündün had an explosive temper, and Lobsang always had his hands full trying to keep situations under control. Whereas his little brother gave full vent to his emotions, Lobsang suppressed his own. It was a difficult situation for the older child, outwardly maintaining his composure while seething inside. He might have been better off had he reacted like Lobsang Jimpa, for when the brothers fought and he was unable to separate them, the elderly monk would burst into tears and in the twinkling of an eye the boys would disentangle themselves and contemplate their beloved attendant contritely. One summer day in 1946 Kündün was chasing his brother while swinging a two-foot-long pole inlaid with ivory, when it slipped from his hand and struck Lobsang just above the eyebrow. Blood streamed down his face from the gash and the child fainted. Fortunately the wound did not prove serious and healed quickly, but the monk attendants decided the time had come for the close association of the brothers to be terminated; once he had fully recovered, Lobsang was enrolled in a public school in Lhasa. The monks had always worried that because of his access to the outside world Lobsang would bring foreign ideas to his brother, and the incident provided the excuse they needed for separating the two.

Lobsang was happy to be going to live with his parents again. For all its splendor, life at the Potala had been rigid and demanding. He loved his brother and was sad that he would be left by himself, but he looked forward to a less restrictive life. It was a cold wintry day when the two brothers bade each other goodbye. After almost eight years of constant companionship they were going their separate ways. Both were sad but neither cried. They hugged each other. Then Lobsang turned abruptly and strode from the chamber to begin the long descent to the base of the palace. Upon reaching it, he looked up and spotted his little brother peering out at him from his window high up on the top floor. They waved to each other and Lobsang struck out for Lhasa. Every so often he looked back over his shoulder, and they waved to each other once more. With each footstep the image of Kündün, wrapped in his claret-colored robes and framed like a miniature icon in his window, grew smaller and smaller. Finally Lobsang could see nothing but a tiny speck off in the distance. He waved no more. Quickening his pace, he made for his parents' home.[10]

Notes

1. Letter to Rosemary Tung from John H. Howe, a former student of Frank Lloyd Wright. "I feel certain," Howe added, "that the photograph of this remarkable building had a profound effect on Mr. Wright's work." Rosemary Tung, *A Portrait of Lost Tibet* (New York, 1980), 24.

2. "The gold, mind you, that covers it is not merely goldleaf," wrote an American visitor to Lhasa in 1938, "but slabs of gold thicker than a sturdy piece of cardboard." Theos Bernard, *Penthouse of the Gods: A Pilgrimage into the Heart of Tibet and the Sacred City of Lhasa* (New York, 1939), 173.

3. "It is not the least of the oddities of Tibet," wrote a British visitor to Tibet in 1904, "that in this unlettered country more beautiful books are produced than anywhere else in the world. . . . The covers alone present an example of beauty and loving care which Grolier could never have secured from the best of his binders." Percival Landon, *The Opening of Tibet* (New York, 1905), 200.

4. Certain incarnations inherited from their predecessors institutions known as *labrangs* ("Lama's residences"), religious corporations including not only domiciles for lamas and their staffs but also farms and pasturelands from which considerable income was often derived. The Taktser *labrang* at Kumbum was very wealthy, even after taxes had been paid to the Chinese provincial governor Ma Pu-feng. Although the majority of a *labrang*'s funds were used for religious purposes, some moneys were disbursed to enrich the family into which the incarnation had been born.

5. Contrary to what is commonly believed, the *simga*s did not come from the *dobdob* class.

6. Although the term *Khenpo* usually refers to the abbot of a monastery, in this case it is a government-bestowed honorific title for members of the Dalai Lama's personal household staff, which was headed by the Chikyap Khenpo, or lord chamberlain.

7. In his book *China's Destiny* (1943), the Generalissimo maintained the fiction that China was formed by the blending of five "clans"—Han Chinese, Mongols, Manchus, Tibetans, and Muslims—all of whom derived from a common stock and were members of the same "family." The theory is a romanticized distortion of Chinese history. To cite but one example, it would follow from it that the overthrow of the Manchu Ch'ing dynasty in 1911 was not a nationalist revolution, as Chiang claims elsewhere in the same book, but merely a civil war.

8. "Transit through Tibet is practicable by pack animal trains making one trip a year but the amount that can be transported (maximum estimates place it at

3,000 tons annually) renders the project of minor importance as a supply route to China," cabled the American ambassador Clarence E. Gauss to Secretary of State Cordell Hull from Chungking on July 13, 1942. "The round trip requires six months and about half of the year travel is impracticable." A fortnight later Gauss was informed that 700 tons was a more realistic figure. International Commission of Jurists, *Tibet and the Chinese People's Republic* (Geneva, 1960), 322–324.

9. Interview with the Gyayum Chenmo, Dharamsala, India, May 5, 1980.

10. The material in this chapter was gathered in interviews with Lobsang Samden in Dharamsala, India, on May 6, 7, 9, 10, and 16, 1980.

Ling Rinpoche   *Dharamsala 1980*

CHAPTER 8

Studies and Solitude

L OBSANG SAMDEN'S DEPARTURE ushered in a new phase of Kündün's life, for at the age of twelve Kündün was effectively isolated from his family for the first time. It is true that he was surrounded by a coterie of attendants, most notably the Söpön Khenpo, Lobsang Jimpa, who became not only a surrogate parent but, with Lobsang gone, a surrogate brother as well. It is true that any child entering a life of monastic discipline was similarly detached from his past life and routines, and that henceforth he belonged to the monastic order rather than to his family. But for the young ruler the situation was more extreme. Ensconced in his apartments at the top of the Potala or sheltered within the inner walls of the Norbulingka, he was completely cut off from all but a handful of elderly monks. Most of the outside world, beginning almost at his very doorstep, remained a mystery to him.

As the Dalai Lama, Kündün was denied the mobility enjoyed by other monks, even other incarnate lamas like his eldest brother, Jo-la. Although one of the most important lamas at Kumbum monastery and destined for abbothood, Taktser Rinpoche was nevertheless able to leave his *labrang* and move to Lhasa in the summer of 1941; while living at Drepung, furthermore, he was permitted to make a year-long pilgrimage to India and China in 1947. In contrast, Kündün's mobility from the time he arrived in Lhasa in 1939 until the Chinese invasion of Tibet some eleven years later was limited to semiannual changes of residence between his summer and winter palaces, with short stays in Lhasa's Jokhang Temple each spring and excursions to the Three Pillars nearby.

Even brother Lobsang had enjoyed a great deal of freedom when living at the Potala while Kündün was forced to remain behind. Riding the finest horses from the Dalai Lama's stables and accompanied by a few servants, he frequently went off with their father on two- and three-day journeys into the wilderness surrounding Lhasa, where they pitched tents by the banks of a lake or river and made long excursions into the hills. Upon his return, Lobsang would invariably be pestered by his little brother to describe in detail all he had seen and heard and done: where he had gone, who had gone with him, what animals he had spotted, what he had talked about. Once Lobsang was late in returning. Gyayab Chenmo was an expert horseman who constantly chided him for not riding at a swifter pace, and one day in a fit of temper he had whacked Lobsang's mount across the hindquarters with a stick. The startled animal took off like a shot and in clearing an obstacle that lay in its path pitched the boy onto the ground, where he lay unconscious from a severe concussion, which required a lengthy convalescence. Kündün considered himself fortunate for not having been present when the accident took place, for it confirmed to him his fear of horses. Thereafter he no longer envied Lobsang's excursions, or at least his brother's mode of transportation.

In his autobiography the Dalai Lama states that "some people . . . believe the Dalai Lamas were almost prisoners in the Potala Palace," and concedes that even had it been so for him, "it would have been a spacious and fascinating prison." The comment is revealing, for it indicates how, virtually from the time of his discovery, he had accepted with apparent equanimity the life to which he was predestined. Perhaps in their examination of candidates the lamas had looked beyond official tests and physical characteristics to more subtle clues of a child's emotional capacity to lead such a demanding life, especially one as intellectually rigorous and physically confining as that of a Dalai Lama. For all the fame, riches, and power that devolved on him, Kündün surrendered any chance of living a normal family life, of enjoying the camaraderie of his peers, and of having the freedom to explore the external world. For just as he had accepted his discovery and sudden adulation without question, so too did he accept the role he was being groomed to play in the life of his country.

Through his isolation he was forced to focus his energies more fully on religious studies and meditative practices. Hitherto he had learned to read and write, grasped the fundamentals of grammar and spelling, and committed to memory various portions of the scriptures. Now he was confronted with the staggering task of mastering all 108 massive volumes of the *Kangyur*, the Tibetan Buddhist bible containing the teachings of Lord Buddha, and the 225 similarly voluminous tomes of commentaries on these teachings known as the *Tengyur*. For purposes of study and learning these were subdivided into branches known as the Five Great Treatises: *Prajnaparamita*, the Perfection of Wisdom; *Madhyamika*, the Middle Path, which urges the avoidance of extremes; *Vinaya*, the Canon of Monastic Discipline; *Abhidharma*, Metaphysics; and *Pramana*, Logic and Dialectics. Strictly speaking, the last of these was not one of the scriptures but was included to emphasize the importance of logic in developing mental powers. Tantric texts were studied separately in the Gelugpa system of monastic education, and only after a pupil was thoroughly conversant with the Five Treatises.

When his elementary religious studies began in 1941, Kündün was provided with three official tutors. His senior tutor was the regent, Reting Rinpoche, and his junior tutors Taktra Rinpoche and Ling Rinpoche. Upon the resignation of Reting Rinpoche from the regency several months later, Taktra Rinpoche succeeded him as both regent and senior tutor. Since the main duty of a regent was to head the Tibetan government until the Dalai Lama reached eighteen years of age, Taktra spent most of his time in that capacity and the bulk of his teaching devolved on his assistant. Both the writing teacher, Khenrab Tenzin, and Trijang Rinpoche, a renowned scholar and one of Tibet's most popular lecturers on Buddhism, who was responsible for teaching the child grammar and spelling in those early years, were warm, easygoing men who dealt patiently with the childish antics of the two brothers while ensuring that they kept up with their studies. But Ling Rinpoche was another matter.

A brilliant scholar, the junior tutor had been born in the Year of the Water Rat (1902) in the village of Yup near Lhasa. He entered Drepung monastery at the age of ten, and through diligent study was able to pass the *geshe lharampa* (doctor of metaphysics) examinations at the early age of twenty-one. The possession of this qualification entitled him to admission at Gyudto, a famous institute for esoteric Tantric studies in Lhasa, of which he eventually became prefect and, in 1936, chief abbot. Toward the end of his third year of tenure in that position he had taken on the additional duties as tutor to the Dalai Lama.[1]

Before their initial meeting with Ling Rinpoche, Kündün and Lobsang had been warned by their attendants that during his term as prefect of Gyudto he had been a strict disciplinarian who tolerated no breach of monastic conduct and had thoroughly cowed all the monks there. The brothers were consequently on their best behavior when he strode into the tutorial room exactly on schedule and lowered his heavy form onto a cushion facing them across a low table. Two small whips hung on a nearby wall to remind the boys of the seriousness of their studies. The one reserved for Kündün was fashioned of silk, and for Lobsang of leather; although they were never used, their presence was effective. Ling Rinpoche was no less warmhearted than his colleagues but found it convenient to conceal this fact behind a forbidding exterior. Four decades after their first encounter, Ling Rinpoche recalls that although he maintained a stern expression to better maintain an air of authority, he was extremely impressed with the intelligence of the child and convinced that he was the true incarnation of Chenresi.[2] For his part, the Dalai Lama remembers keeping a poker face so as not to risk disturbing his tutor while marveling that the man had hair on his arms and knuckles but none on his head and face, and that he wrote with his left hand.

The Tibetan system of religious education employed a combination of five methods for developing the mental faculties of a student. To begin with, children learned to read and write by imitating their teacher. At the same time, more demanding courses for learning the scriptures by heart were gradually begun. The purpose of this second method was twofold, to train the memory and to provide the basis for a proper understanding of the Dharma; blind faith is not considered an admirable trait by Tibetan Buddhists. The third method of education was known as *nyam tee*, "teaching from experience." A lama such as Trijang Rinpoche, who was especially adept at this technique, would illustrate his lectures by means of concrete examples and personal stories, making frequent references to the teachings of Lord Buddha and to the commentaries of ancient sages and saints. *Nyam tee* led naturally to a fourth method, that of concentration and meditation, wherein students were exhorted to meditate at the end of each day's lectures not only on the teachings given but also on their thoughts concerning them. This was especially valuable for training the mind for the advanced study and practice of religion. Finally there was the method of highly stylized dialectical debating between students or between students and teachers. Since he had no companions, Kündün was provided with seven tutorial assistants, scholars known as *tsenchaps*—one from each of the monastic colleges within Drepung, Sera, and Ganden—who would help him prepare for examinations in Buddhist logic, metaphysics, and dialectics through a demanding series of debating sessions that dealt in ever-finer philosophical questions as he progressed with his studies. Although all of them were excellent teachers, Kündün learned the most from an outstanding Mongolian scholar named Ngodup Chognye.

Despite an initial antipathy to his new and formidable curriculum, Kündün was soon deeply immersed in it and deriving great satisfaction from all he learned. On visits to the Potala, Lobsang Samden noted that his brother's studies "occupied far more of his time and he, in turn, became more dedicated to them. He always had a very sharp, clear mind, and his powers of memorization were remarkable."[3] Ling Rinpoche discovered that although he occasionally had to prod the boy with a finger or gaze thoughtfully at the whips on the wall to encourage him to work more diligently, once Kündün was taught something, he never forgot it.

Kündün began with the *Prajnaparamita* (Perfection of Wisdom), selecting in addition to the fundamental principles of the treatise two of its more than thirty volumes of commentaries, one by the famed Indian scholar Singhbhadra and the other by the Fifth Dalai Lama. He memorized a third of a page each day but read and understood a great deal more. Additionally, he began his training in dialectical argument with the study of elementary logic. A few months after turning thirteen he was formally admitted to Drepung and Sera monasteries, an occasion requiring him to attend and participate in congregational debates at each of their five monastic colleges. It was the first time the boy had taken part in public dialectical discussions of the Great Treatises, and he remembers being "shy, excited, and a little worried." There was good reason for his concern, for his opponents were some of Tibet's most learned abbots and the debates were witnessed by hundreds of other religious scholars and by thousands of monks. Those present re-member how impressed they were by the child's poise and the acuity of his performance, but the Dalai Lama recalls merely that he conducted himself "to their satisfaction."

Upon being introduced shortly thereafter to metaphysics and logic, Kündün felt "dazed, as though I were hit on the head by a stone" but re-covered quickly; other subjects were added to his curriculum, and as he went on he experienced progressively less difficulty in grasping them. He began, moreover, to feel a growing inquisitiveness that reached far beyond his pre-scribed studies, and he derived great satisfaction from reading advanced sec-tions of the treatises and asking his tutors to explain their sophisticated con-cepts. They told him that he wished to know more than was necessary at his age, but, undaunted, he continued to bombard them with questions.

Kündün's expanding intellectual powers were paralleled closely by his spiritual development. At each stage in his training he received consecration of the mind and body in preparation for the higher doctrines. "I had the first of these initiations," he says, "when I was eight, and I still remember it viv-idly, and the feeling of peace and happiness it brought me. At each of the later ceremonies, I could feel the spiritual experience which has always been associated with them. My belief and faith in my religion became deeper, the assurance in my mind that I was following the right path became firmer." By the age of fifteen he had grown more accustomed to these experiences and was able to sense a spontaneous feeling within himself of gratitude to the Buddha. "I also felt an immense debt to those teachers, mostly Indians, who had given the Tibetans their invaluable religious doctrines, and to those Ti-betan scholars who had interpreted and preserved them in our language. I began to think less of myself and more of others and became aware of the concept of compassion. It was this sense of spiritual elevation which was attended on the mental plane by a sense of improved intellect, by better pow-ers of memory, greater proficiency in debate, and increased self-confidence."

Despite his deepening involvement with religious studies and the satis-faction derived from them, Kündün never relinquished his desire for knowl-edge of the outside world. This was not readily forthcoming, however, for as remote as Tibet was from the rest of the world, so too was he isolated from ordinary life. No doubt this very distance made it that much more at-tractive to him, but a less resolute and spirited child would have bowed to the weight of tradition and confined his interests accordingly. Ever the prag-matist, Kündün decided early on that even if he could not go out and ex-plore the world around him, he could nevertheless study it within the con-fines of his environment, and he began by doing so through the pages of a publication called *Yulchog Sosoi Sargyur Melong*, known in English as the *Tibet Mirror*.

The *Tibet Mirror* was unique on three counts. It was the only newspaper available in Tibet written in the Tibetan language; it was the only medium of information published in Tibetan that discussed the affairs of the outside world; and it was not printed in Tibet at all but rather in Kalimpong, the Indian border town and hub of the centuries-old caravan route between India and Tibet. An Indian Christian of Tibetan ancestry by the name of Gygyen Tharchin was its chief writer, editor, and publisher, and from his home in the Himalayan foothills of West Bengal it faithfully mirrored world events as he heard them over the wireless or read them in the daily press. Whenever he felt there was enough news to warrant a new issue, he went ahead and printed one. This intentionally relaxed schedule left Tharchin free with regard to both his time and his energy. Thus if the viceroy of India were to hold a noteworthy banquet, he suffered from no editorial embarrassment: the morning edition could come out any morning, and Tibetans, to whom the paper was more a novelty than an institution, would happily read it whenever it arrived. Circulation, to be sure, posed somewhat of a problem, for it could take a month or more for a caravan to ply the 300 miles from Kalimpong to Lhasa. Yet the *Tibet Mirror*, for which Tharchin charged his 150 subscribers an annual subscription of five rupees, also appeared in the provincial towns of Lithang, Kanze, Derge, Gyantse, and Shigatse. Considering the rustic nature of Tibet's postal system, it was likely conveyed to these outposts by traders or religious pilgrims.

Tharchin began publishing his newspaper in 1925. Because its editorial policy was sympathetic to Tibet and Tibetan nationalism, he received several congratulatory letters from the Thirteenth Dalai Lama, who became a regular subscriber. When Kündün moved into the Potala the subscription was still in effect, and it continued through 1959.[4]

Before he had learned to read, Kündün was attracted by the paper's last page, replete with a variety of puzzles he was able to solve by enlisting the aid of Lobsang Jimpa or his brother Lobsang. He was especially fond of those issues which featured dissecting animals and sticking them together again. Once he began to read, however, he took great interest in world affairs. One issue he remembers contained lengthy stories about Japan, Ethiopia, and Great Britain, each illustrated with a picture of its leader. Tharchin's files included photographs of Emperor Hirohito and Haile Selassie but, inexplicably, none of Neville Chamberlain; and he was thus forced to turn to a local artist whose drawing may best be termed a qualified success. It bears not the slightest resemblance to the prime minister, nor is his ubiquitous umbrella anywhere to be seen. On the other hand, Chamberlain's face from the artist's point of view gives one the unmistakable impression that it might rain at any moment.

Most of all, Kündün was fascinated with accounts of the Second World War. He was especially impressed with the pictorial array of war vehicles—tanks, armored cars, trucks, jeeps, airplanes—splashed across its pages.

This was hardly suprising, for in Tibet at the time there was a total of three automobiles: two 1927 Baby Austins, one blue and the other red and yellow, and a ponderous 1931 Dodge, painted orange. Gifts to the Thirteenth Dalai Lama that had been carried to Lhasa in pieces and then reassembled, they had been standing idle since his death in 1933 and were rusty and inoperative. Had they been in running order it would have made little difference, for there were no motorable roads in the entire country. Nor, for that matter, were there wheeled vehicles of any kind; the only wheels in Tibet were prayer wheels.

Soon Kündün was familiar with the names of Roosevelt and Eisenhower, Churchill and Montgomery, Hitler and Rommel, Stalin and Molotov. The British Mission sent him copies of the *London Illustrated News* and *Life* magazine, whose captions he had rendered into Tibetan by local noblemen who had been educated in India and were conversant with the English language. These men had traveled widely and were among the best-informed sources in Tibet on world affairs. There were many questions the boy longed to ask them about the war which could not be answered by either his attendants or tutors, but protocol dictated that he not speak directly to them or they to him, and any questions he made had to be channeled through a third person in writing. Dissatisfied with the long gaps between issues of the *Tibet Mirror*, the brief provocative accounts in Western magazines, and the cumbersome machinery of gleaning more substantive knowledge, Kündün decided to learn English.

For all its isolation, Tibet was not wholly bereft of English-language publications, thanks in large measure to a unique relationship that had developed between Kündün's predecessor and an Englishman named Sir Charles Bell. The Manchu invasion of Lhasa in 1910 had forced the Thirteenth Dalai Lama to flee to the hill station of Darjeeling, a day's journey by horseback from the trading center of Kalimpong in British India. There he met Bell, a Tibetan-speaking career diplomat serving as political liaison officer between Tibet and the Himalayan border states of Sikkim and Bhutan, who placed at the Dalai Lama's disposal a secluded cottage on the outskirts of the village, where he spent the better part of two years in exile before returning to his country. The two men shared many common interests, not the least of which were a love of Tibet and a firm belief in Tibetan independence. Two previous Dalai Lamas, the Seventh and Ninth, had each granted an audience to a visitor from the West, but never before had a personal relationship ensued. The circumstances of the Dalai Lama's exile made possible the development of a deep friendship between him and the Englishman which lasted until his death more than twenty years later. Kündün therefore had access to numerous books and maps from the estate of his predecessor, most of which had been gifts from Bell, including several volumes about Tibet written by Bell himself which are still considered classics in the field.[5] Since the Thirteenth Incarnation had no knowledge of the English language, they were in mint condition. The collection, however, was too sophisticated to be of much use to the boy at first; to learn the language he required more elementary works, and several crates of English textbooks found gathering dust in one of the Potala's storerooms suited his purposes admirably.

The presence of English schoolbooks in a musty storeroom below the Earthly Abode of Chenresi in the Forbidden City on the Roof of the World was not as remarkable as it might appear. In the early years of the Second World War, some Tibetan government officials had recognized that whatever the outcome of the conflict, Tibet, in order to retain her independence, would have to end her traditional self-imposed isolation from the rest of the world. If the Allies were victorious, it was certain that whichever force prevailed in China—the Nationalists under Chiang Kai-shek or the Communists under Mao Tse-tung—would move on Tibet, and in the less likely event of an Axis victory, there would be nothing to prevent the Japanese from launching a similar invasion. Communication with other nations leading to international recognition of Tibet's sovereign status, these officials believed, was essential to preserve the integrity of the nation. They also realized that although English-speaking Tibetans would be needed to conduct international affairs, there were only a handful of them in the country. With the aid of the British Mission a school was established in Lhasa in the spring of 1945, complete with the latest textbooks and a teacher newly arrived from England. Predictably, a strong protest was lodged by the monasteries on the grounds that the school would adversely affect the religious beliefs of the country, and it was forced to close down after only a few months of operation. The event was not without precedent, for a similar incident had occurred in 1926 when an English school established in Gyantse three years earlier was closed for the same reason.[6]

If the idea of a peaceful Buddhist monk and God of Mercy deciding to learn English in order to read about the greatest war the world has ever known seems ironic, so too is the fact that during those early years his sympathies lay with the Nazis. "Not for any other reason but because the Germans had only two allies," he explains. "Whereas the other side had so many: England, France, the Soviet Union, America. . . . So I felt good when some news item indicated that the Germans had occupied a city or won a battle. That's my nature. I am always for the underdog. When I saw the pictures of the Nuremburg trials I was quite sad. The Allied military police in their uniforms and some of the German war prisoners with whom I was familiar. It was not until later that I knew the full story. Someone sent me a complete set of volumes about the war—there were six or seven of them, I think—a pictorial set bound in Delhi. After reading them my attitude changed. Something was very wrong with Hitler."

Kündün's thirst for knowledge was not limited to books, and from an early age he manifested an aptitude for things mechanical. Lobsang Samden remembered how in the course of their daily exploration of the Potala his little brother carefully studied everything they found: how it was made, how it worked, what its purpose was. "At first he made quite a mess of things but later became expert at putting back together what he had taken apart. He opened up old clocks which had been gifts to the Thirteenth Dalai Lama and left the pieces here and there. Such behavior made our monk attendants frantic. They tried to dissuade him from doing so but he was quite stubborn. If they succeeded in stopping him one day, he was certain to resume these activities the next. I don't know how he did it, nor did anyone else, but somehow he made them all work." The child's secular reading encouraged further mechanical experimentation. "I had a very strong interest in discovering how the machines I saw in books and magazines actually worked, and a great urge to use them myself. But few such things ever reached Tibet; at that time, for instance, Lhasa had only those three inoperative cars. And one generator. A broken generator. It was at the Norbulingka and was supposed to supply electric light. I was always around it trying to make it work, often becoming so preoccupied that I forgot to eat or even to drink tea. The Söpön Khenpo, Lobsang Jimpa, used to plead with me to stop, but I would be too involved and was able to placate him only by promising to eat later. But I must say that I managed to mend it more often than not. Later I found a young Tibetan who had been trained as a driver in India, and with my eager assistance he managed to put the Dodge in running order, and also one of the Austins, by borrowing parts from the other. These were exciting moments."

There was also an old movie projector, operated by turning a handle, that once belonged to the Thirteenth Dalai Lama and provided Kündün and Lobsang with many hours of enjoyment. "There were perhaps thirty to forty reels of film," recalls the Dalai Lama. "I best remember Tarzan, the Boer War, and the coronation of one of the English kings. Also some magic films: the magician takes an egg from a hat, and all of a sudden a boy or girl appears in its place. My brother and I were fascinated." One day the projector stopped working. Kündün was unable to repair it, nor could anyone else. For months he persevered, taking it to pieces and reassembling it countless times until he was finally rewarded for his efforts. "I found the batteries which worked its electric light. That was my first introduction to electricity, and I puzzled over the connections all alone until I found the way to make it go." By then, however, the bulbs were gone. "It was my fault. When it seemed the projector would never work again, I took out the bulbs and dropped them like bombs from the upper windows of the Potala. They made a lovely explosion when they landed!" New bulbs were purchased from a Nepalese merchant in Lhasa, and, with the projector in running order, Kündün sent for a man named Heinrich Harrer.

Harrer's presence in Lhasa had come about as the result of a remarkable series of adventures. Born in Austria on July 6, 1912 (exactly twenty-three years before the birth of the Dalai Lama), he studied geography and physical education at Graz University, from which he was graduated in 1933. Although he had been selected for the Austrian Olympic ski team in 1936, he "began to feel that the only worthwhile ambition was to measure my strength against the mountains." It was the pursuit of this goal that brought him to the 27,000-foot Himalayan peak of Nanga Parbat in Kashmir with a German climbing expedition in August 1939. The Second World War broke out in Europe before the group could begin its ascent, and Harrer and the others were interned by the British. For almost four years he was incarcerated in the huge prisoner-of-war camp near Dehra Dun, in clear sight of the snowcapped Himalaya. There he studied travel books, copied and memorized maps, and learned rudimentary Hindustani, Japanese, and Tibetan before escaping in May 1943. Recaptured after eighteen days, he spent almost a year in preparation before making another escape in April 1944, disguised as an Indian laborer. Ten days out of the camp he met up with Peter Aufschnaiter, the leader of the aborted climbing expedition, and the two men crossed the Tsangchokla Pass into Tibet.

The pair spent twenty months making their way across the vast tablelands and through the treacherous mountain passes of southwestern Tibet, their goal the Forbidden City of Lhasa, which lay to the east. Several times they were ordered by district officials to leave the country, but each time they backtracked, and by a combination of tact, subterfuge, and audacity, they were able to reach Lhasa in January 1946. Ragged and hungry, they were taken in by a local nobleman who made them welcome. Soon all of Lhasa, more curious and amused than hostile, flocked to see them. It seemed at first as though they would be ordered once again to leave Tibet, but the men made themselves useful, Harrer as a gardener and Aufschnaiter as an engineer, and they were permitted to stay. Two years later Harrer was made a salaried official of the Tibetan government as a translator of foreign news and articles and as a photographer of special events. Living in a large private house complete with a stable and garden and provided with the services of a personal attendant, a messenger, and a groom, he decided to settle permanently in Tibet. It was shortly thereafter that he was summoned to the Norbulingka by the Dalai Lama. It had something to do, thought the messenger, with a movie projector.

Harrer went immediately to the summer palace, where he was greeted at the door of the inner garden by Lobsang Samden, who handed him a white ceremonial scarf and ushered him inside. There the Dalai Lama was standing with a smile. "I bowed deeply and handed him the scarf," remembers Harrer. "He took it in his left hand and with an impulsive gesture blessed me with his right. It seemed less like the ceremonial laying on of hands than an impetuous expression of a feeling." The boy burst forth with a stream of questions. "He seemed to me like a person who had for years brooded in solitude over different problems, and now that he had at last someone to talk to, wanted to know all the answers at once. I was astonished to see how much disconnected knowledge he had acquired out of books and newspapers, but as he had nobody to put questions to, he often did not know how persons and events were connected with each other."

Kündün was barely thirteen years old. "His complexion was much lighter than that of the average Tibetan," says Harrer. "His eyes, hardly narrower than those of most Europeans, were full of expression, charm, and vivacity. His cheeks glowed with excitement, and as he sat he kept sliding from side to side. His ears stood out a little from his head. This was a characteristic of the Buddha and, as I learned later, was one of the signs by which as a child he had been recognized as an incarnation. His hair was longer than is customary. He probably wore it so as a protection against the cold of the Potala. He was tall for his age and looked as though he would reach the stature of his parents, both of whom were striking figures. Unfortunately, as a result of much study in a seated posture with his body bent foward, he held himself badly. He had beautiful aristocratic hands with long fingers, which were generally folded in an attitude of peace." This initial meeting between Harrer and the young Dalai Lama set a pattern for many others over the ensuing months. They talked for hours about international politics, geography, and the sciences. Harrer assisted the boy in his studies of English and arithmetic and was in turn regaled with stories of the history of Tibet and the teachings of Lord Buddha. Gradually their early shyness disappeared and the relationship deepened into one of real friendship.[7]

Yet despite these most welcome interludes with Heinrich Harrer, the fact remained that for most of the time Kündün was without real companionship. Visits from family members continued, especially from his mother and brother. "I tried to go to the Potala at least twice each month," remembered Lobsang Samden, "and when I did, it was just like old times. Lobsang Jimpa would scurry about, providing us with tea and special sweets and biscuits and making certain we were comfortable. My brother was very interested about what I did in school and asked many questions about my schoolmates, the games we played, and what we studied. He always wanted to know if I was happy in my new life, and I told him that I was. He never complained of being either lonely or unhappy."

But lonely he was. No matter how gratifying it may have been practicing meditation, studying the scriptures, poring over publications, tinkering with mechanical apparatuses, and visiting with family members and later with Heinrich Harrer, it was no substitute for leading a normal life. Taking one of the telescopes left by his predecessor, he would often climb up to the flat roof of the Potala and spend hours peering down at the scenes unfolding before him: merchants plying their trade in the colorful stalls of the Barkhor, Lhasa's busiest commercial street; pilgrims prostrating their way along the Lingkhor, the five-mile-long Sacred Path encircling the holy city; long caravans of yaks, mules, ponies, and camels arriving with brick tea and brocades from China or cotton goods and sugar from India; women shopping, laborers working, neighbors chatting, children playing in the streets. But for all this, only rarely did he wish the circumstances of his life had been different.

Each winter Kündün spent several weeks in retreat. New chambers warmed by a southern exposure had been built for this purpose during the reign of the Thirteenth Dalai Lama, but he went instead to a cold, musty room along the northern wall of the palace that had always held a special appeal for him. It was small but its ceilings were high. One of the supporting beams sagged alarmingly and was propped up at an oblique angle by another whose end rested against the floor. Great curtains covered the walls, and when Kündün peered under them he saw that the floor was littered with dust of the ages and mouse droppings of more recent vintage. There was one large window, facing north, through which sunlight streamed in the morning, but for the rest of the day the room grew ever darker, increasingly dependent for its illumination on a few butter lamps. Yet despite its dearth of physical comfort an air of sanctity pervaded the chamber. Beginning with the Great Fifth the Dalai Lamas had all come here to pray and meditate, and the room was believed to be invested with a vast reservoir of spiritual energy.

Accompanied by one of his tutors and two monks from the Potala monastery, Kündün came here early each morning of his retreat. It was redolent with the fumes of butter and incense, and drafts made the lamps flicker and cast darting shadows on the walls. He lowered himself onto his cushion and crossed his legs, then wrapped his robes snugly about him as protection against the cold. Shutting his eyes and clasping his hands before him, he meditated on the teachings of Lord Buddha. There was complete silence, broken only when the monks chanted recitations from the scriptures in a deep, gravelly monotone. Then, silence once more.

As evening approached, one other sound became audible each day, only faintly at first and then increasingly clear. From the high, solitary window came the voices of cowherds, boys Kündün's age and even younger, bringing their animals home from pasture and singing gaily. "I wonder," he thought, "what it would be like to be happy like them."

Notes

1. Of the many Tantric colleges in Tibet, Gyudto and Gyudme (*gyud* being the Tibetan word for Tantra) in Lhasa were the most highly esteemed. Founded in the fifteenth century, they had a combined population of some 1,400 monks. For a fascinating discussion of life in Gyudto, see Rato Khyongla Nawang Losang, *My Life and Lives: The Story of a Tibetan Incarnation* (New York, 1977), 123–149.
2. Interview with Ling Rinpoche, Dharamsala, India, May 7, 1980.
3. Interview with Lobsang Samden, Dharamsala, India, May 6, 1980.

4. An American student of Buddhism who visited Tibet just before the outbreak of World War II described Tharchin, who was his "inseparable companion" on the trip to Lhasa, as "a smallish man, with a figure inclined to plumpness. He had a little fat face with a tiny moustache, and he was dressed in plus-fours and a rather loud English tweed coat. He usually held his cigarette within the palm of a closed fist, and it scarcely touched his lips. What is more important is that, a Tibetan who had been raised on the border, he had a full knowledge of the literature of his country and he had been in Lhasa many times, and had devoted many years to study. He was exceptionally competent." Theos Bernard, *Penthouse of the Gods: A Pilgrimage into the Heart of Tibet and the Sacred City of Lhasa* (New York, 1939), 36.

5. *Grammar of Colloquial Tibetan* (Calcutta, 1919), *Tibet: Past and Present* (Oxford, 1924), *The People of Tibet* (Oxford, 1928), and *The Religion of Tibet* (Oxford, 1931). A final volume, *Portrait of the Dalai Lama*, was not published until 1946 and was probably not included in the Potala collection.

6. According to a Scotsman who lived in Tibet at that time, there was constant friction between the English headmaster (on loan from the Indian Educational Service) and his assistant, who had been appointed by the Tibetan government and later became abbot of Gyantse monastery. "The lamas were against the school as they considered that if the boys' time was divided between English and Tibetan they would learn neither properly," he wrote. "Lack of study in Tibetan meant to them lack of knowledge of the tenets of the lamaist faith." David Macdonald, *Twenty Years in Tibet* (London, 1932), 221–223.

7. For a detailed account of Harrer's experiences in Tibet, see his *Seven Years in Tibet* (London, 1953).

Tsepon T. W. Shakabpa   *Kalimpong 1980*

· CHAPTER 9 ·

The Winds of Change

I N AUGUST 1949 General Chu Teh, vice-chairman of the newly formed
People's Republic of China and commander in chief of her armed forces,
announced that Tibet was part of China and that the People's Liberation
Army would march into the Roof of the World to liberate it from foreign
imperialists, sounding the death knell for Tibetan independence. Chu Teh's
assertions were entirely spurious and would have been laughable but for the
hundreds of thousands of battle-hardened troops poised to do his bidding.

Even allowing for the usual excesses of Communist rhetoric, the pronouncement that Tibet was in need of liberation from foreign imperialists
was absurd. By far the largest group of foreigners in the country were the
Chinese themselves. It is unlikely that the general was referring to them, or
to the Nepalese and Indian merchants or the staffs of their diplomatic missions in Lhasa, which constituted the next largest group. A diverse smatter-
ing of Central Asians may similarly be dismissed: Mongols and Buriats
from the Soviet Union and Mongolia, shaven-headed Bhutanese, turbaned
Muslims from Kashmir and tarbooshed Hui-Huis from Sinkiang. By the
process of elimination, then, it may be concluded that General Chu was
mustering the might of his armies to launch a massive invasion in order
to liberate Tibet from a group of hard-core European imperialists who
were holding that country in an unrelenting grip. There were exactly five
of them.

The first two of this unlikely group were the Austrian mountaineers
Heinrich Harrer and Peter Aufschnaiter, who at the time of Chu Teh's proclamation were working for the Tibetan government, the former at the Foreign Bureau translating dispatches and revising maps and the latter supervising the digging of a canal near the Norbulingka. Although the World War,
which had forced them to seek refuge in Tibet, had ended four years earlier,
both men planned to remain there for the rest of their lives. "When you look
at the aftermath of the war in Europe," Aufschnaiter told a rare visitor from

the West, "do you wonder why Heinrich and I choose to remain here with our good and faithful friends?"[1]

The third European in Tibet was the tall, dignified Scotsman Hugh Richardson. After India had achieved independence in 1947, the Britons in her civil and diplomatic service were being replaced one after the other by Indians, and Richardson, former head of the British Mission in Lhasa, had continued to fill that post for the Indian government and was the last of his countrymen in India's foreign service. "We met frequently and spoke a great deal about Tibetan politics, culture, and history," remembers Tibet's former finance minister T. W. Shakabpa. "He spoke impeccable Lhasa Tibetan with a slight Oxford accent and was extremely learned. I have never met a Westerner as knowledgeable about my country." When the Indian government asked Lord Louis Mountbatten, the last British viceroy of India, to let them keep one of his officers in their service along the northern border, Richardson, with his unparalleled knowledge of Tibet, was the logical choice. Unlike Harrer and Aufschnaiter, however, he intended to return to the West. "Much of my life has been devoted to Tibet," he explained. "It's a glorious country and the Tibetans are a superior people. I'm going to miss them and their wonderful mountains and flowers when I leave."

An affable Londoner named Reginald Fox, who had looked after the Dalai Lama's pet parakeets a decade before, had been in Tibet longer than any other Westerner. Like the two Austrians, he had settled permanently: "I like sitting on the top of the world," he said. "I like this country and its people. Tibet has been good to me, so I see no reason for leaving it." But unlike them, he had married a Tibetan woman and raised a family. Reggie Fox had always been the adventurous sort. Barely fourteen years old when the First World War broke out in 1914, he lied about his age and managed to get to France with "Kitchener's Mob," serving as a motorcycle messenger for almost five years and learning wireless transmission in his spare time. After the armistice he did communications work in Baghdad before being transferred to the Anglo-Indian railway system on the subcontinent. When a British Mission was being organized to go to Tibet in 1935, he signed on, and once he was in Lhasa, his wanderlust came to an end. Fox was hired by the Tibetan government as a radio operator when the new government of India assumed the responsibilities of the British Mission and no longer required his services. He served in a dual capacity: to monitor and condense world news of special interest to Tibet as gleaned from stations such as Radio Peking, Radio Moscow, BBC, Voice of America, Radio Delhi, and Radio Tokyo; and to train a corps of Tibetan radio operators who were then dispatched to strategic points along the border with China.[2]

The fifth European in Tibet, and the only one not living in Lhasa, was a recent arrival named Robert Ford. A former RAF radio operator from England's East Midlands, he was stationed by Fox in Chamdo, the provincial

capital of Kham and a critical outpost not far from the Sino-Tibetan frontier. Despite having only six months left on his contract at the time of Chu
Teh's proclamation, Ford opted to remain.

This quintet of European expatriates from whom the Chinese felt it
necessary to wrest Tibet by force spent their spare time not in concocting
sinister imperialist plots, but in somewhat more mundane activities. Aufschnaiter went trekking, Harrer took still photographs and motion pictures
of Tibetan festivals and religious ceremonies, Richardson played tennis and
tended his famous flower garden at the Mission, and Fox and Ford hob-
nobbed with short-wave hams all over the globe from AC4YN-Lhasa, perhaps the most remote radio station on earth.

The specter of foreign imperialism safely laid to rest, Chu Teh's second
claim—that Tibet was part of China—was equally preposterous. It is true
that at two different periods of her history Tibet had been subject to the
Mongols and later to the Manchus and furthermore had become part of their
empires, empires that also included China. But not until the People's Liberation Army invaded Tibet and the Tibetan government was coerced in May
1951 to sign an agreement for the "peaceful liberation" of their country was
Tibet ever subject to China herself. The following brief survey of Sino-
Tibetan relations will demonstrate this.

THE KINGS OF TIBET AND THE CHINESE T'ANG DYNASTY

The first verifiable contact between Tibet and China took place during the
age of the Chöegyal (Religious Kings), c. A.D. 617–842, which roughly coincided with the Chinese T'ang dynasty (618–905). For almost two centuries after Songtsen Gampo's reign, Tibet's Central Asian empire dominated parts of India, Nepal, and Burma to the south, Sinkiang to the north,
China to the east, and Swat and Hunza (parts of present-day Pakistan) to the
west. Tibetan influence was felt as far to the northwest as Ferghana and
Samarkand, both of which are now in the Soviet Union; and although relations with the Arabs were generally friendly, Tibetan power was so great
that it forced Harun al-Rashid, the caliph of Baghdad in *The Thousand and
One Nights*, to ally himself for a short time with the Chinese. In the eighth
century Tibet occupied and administered virtually all of the Chinese provinces of Kansu, Szechuan, and Yunnan, and forced the Chinese to pay an
annual tribute of 50,000 rolls of silk. When this was withheld in 763, Tibet
captured the Chinese capital of Chang'an (Sian) and installed the brother of
the Tibetan king's Chinese wife as emperor of China. The two countries
signed a pact of nonaggression in 821–822 that defined their boundaries,
stated that "all to the east is the country of Great China and all to the west is,
without question, the country of Great Tibet," and affirmed that "Tibetans
shall be happy in the land of Tibet and Chinese in the land of China."[3] The

assassination in 842 of the apostate King Lang Darma brought to an end the centralized authority of the Tibetan empire, which splintered into a number of disunited princedoms. The T'ang dynasty had also begun its decline but lasted a half century longer and was able during that time to recover most of the Chinese territory occupied by the Tibetans. For the next four hundred years, contact between the two nations was limited in large measure to frontier clashes.

TIBET AND THE YÜAN DYNASTY (1279–1368)

When Genghis Khan and his Mongol armies overran the Tangut empire in 1207, the news soon reached Tibet, where a council of leading nobles and abbots convened hastily and appointed a delegation to the Khan with an offer of submission. By this act they avoided military confrontation, but when the Tibetans ceased sending the prescribed tribute after Genghis's death, they were attacked by his grandson Godon Khan in 1239. It was the first authenticated invasion of Tibet. In 1253 Godon's successor, Kublai Khan, entered into a special relationship with a Tibetan lama named Phagpa,[4] the highest religious authority of the then-dominant Sakya sect.[5] Kublai was impressed with Phagpa's intelligence and teachings, and made him his chaplain. In return for spiritual guidance, the Sakya lama and his successors were granted authority over all of Tibet and encouraged to propagate the Buddha's doctrine throughout the Mongol empire.[6] This patron–lama relationship (Sanskrit: *danapati-bhiksu*), wherein the temporal support of the lay power was exchanged for the spiritual support of the religious power, is common to Central Asian politics and cannot be defined accurately in Western terms. After the fall of the Mongols it reasserted itself in the eighteenth century between the Manchu emperors and the Dalai Lamas.[7]

Establishment of Mongol rule over China began about 1279, when Kublai Khan created the Yüan dynasty and selected for its capital the city of Peking. Thus a new Sino-Tibetan link was established, through the conquest of China by a foreign power that had already been accepted by the Tibetans as their overlord. Tibet recovered her independence around 1350 and China two decades later, but neither took possession from the Mongols of any but their own original territories. Nor did China attempt to exercise any authority whatsoever in Tibet. The fact that the Mongols controlled Tibet from their base in Peking in no way implies, as the Chinese claimed to justify their invasion in 1950, that Tibet was in any way subject to China at any time during the Yüan dynasty. The Mongols could hardly have governed China and the rest of their sprawling empire from a nomad encampment on the Central Asian steppes, and simply adopted the highly sophisticated Chinese bureaucratic system. When the Mongolian empire collapsed there was no longer any official link between China and Tibet.

TIBET AND THE MING DYNASTY (1368–1644)

From 1350 to 1642 Tibet was ruled by a succession of lay princes and kings, none of whom made the slightest act of submission to the Chinese Ming emperors. Distant diplomatic relations existed at various times, but there was no trace of Chinese political influence over, let alone control of, Tibet. The most frequent intercourse between the two nations took the form of visits to the Imperial Court by leading Tibetan lamas, which are described in the annals of the Ming dynasty as "tribute missions." They were hardly that, being instead personal or business ventures having no connection, however tenuous, with the rulers of Tibet.[8] In fact, when the emperor Ch'eng Tsu suggested to the Fifth Karmapa Lama in 1407 that they form an alliance similar to that previously enjoyed by the Sakya Lamas and the Mongols, he was politely refused. Within Tibet, however, such patron–lama relationships were in effect during the entire period: the princes of the Pagmotra family (1350–1481) with the Kagyupa sect, and the Rimpung princes (1481–1565) and Tsang kings (1565–1642) with the Karmapas.

TIBET AND THE CH'ING DYNASTY (1644–1911)

The emperors of China had long recognized that the Great Wall was an ineffective barrier against military conquest by determined nomad tribes like the Mongols of Kublai Khan on their Central Asian frontier, and that the only satisfactory solution to the problem of perpetual harassment and invasion was the establishment of a zone of Chinese influence beyond it. Whenever possible, therefore, they put into effect a system whose purpose was not to bring these border areas under Peking's direct administration but rather to treat them as protectorates and maintain them through diplomacy and indirect rule. The system worked well when the central government was strong, but when it was in decline a weakened China risked conquest by belligerent foreigners like the Manchus, who captured Peking and established the Ch'ing dynasty in 1644. Disturbed by Sangyé Gyatso's intrigues with the always-dangerous Dzungar Mongols after the death of the Fifth Dalai Lama, the Manchus moved on Tibet and in 1720 linked it with Manchuria,[9] Mongolia, and Sinkiang to create a massive protective barrier that encircled Chinese territory from Korea in the northeast to Burma in the southwest. The ensuing relationship, it should be pointed out, was between the Manchu sovereign of a Manchu Empire and a subject Tibetan head of state; throughout the Ch'ing dynasty the status of Tibet and other non-Chinese regions of the Manchu Empire was in no way tied or subject to China. That the Chinese always viewed themselves as separate from the Manchus may be attested by one of the rallying cries of the 1911 revolution: to overthrow the foreign Manchus and restore the rule of China to the Chinese.[10]

By the end of the nineteenth century the Manchu protectorates were themselves surrounded by the great colonial empires of Britian and Russia, one consequence of the semiclandestine "Great Game" for supremacy in the Asiatic uplands.[11] The protectorates were viewed as desirable buffer regions,[12] an arrangement that did not preclude attempts to open trade with Tibet. With this in mind the British made several cautious overtures to the Manchus, applying just enough pressure to gain the necessary concessions without endangering their favorable economic position in China. It was all for naught. "We regard Chinese suzerainty over Tibet as a constitutional fiction," announced Lord Curzon, the frustrated viceroy of India, in January 1903, "a political affectation which has always been maintained because of its convenience to both parties." Curzon spoke from experience, for British–Manchu agreements in 1886, 1890, and 1893 had been either ignored or obstructed by the Tibetan government. When he addressed a pair of letters to the Dalai Lama, on the other hand, they were returned unopened with the implication that direct communication between Britain and Tibet would displease the latter's Manchu overlords. "For many years we have been the butt of the Tibetans," commented a British observer, "and China their stalking-horse."[13]

During this same period there appeared to be a growing Russian influence in Tibet through the efforts of a Buriat Mongol monk[14] named Dorjieff who had come to Lhasa on a religious pilgrimage in 1880 and taken up residence at Drepung monastery. A brilliant scholar, he had become a tutor and friend of the young Dalai Lama and acquired considerable personal influence with him. Although it is unlikely that Dorjieff originally had any official relationship with the Russian government, he eventually came to act as an emissary for Czar Nicholas II, on whose behalf he invited the Dalai Lama to Saint Petersburg. The trip, to which the young ruler had been looking forward with great anticipation, was canceled after a strong objection was voiced by the Tsongdu, which was adamant in its desire to avoid all contact with foreigners. The British followed this course of events with some concern, and when rumors of a secret alliance between Russia and Tibet began circulating in 1903, Lord Curzon ordered a military expedition under Colonel Francis Younghusband into Tibet.

After a series of skirmishes that left hundreds of poorly armed Tibetans dead, the British reached Lhasa in August 1904, only to find that the Dalai Lama had fled with Dorjieff to Mongolia, and concluded an agreement with the Tibetan regent to which the Manchu Amban was a witness but not a signatory. The Lhasa Convention called for the establishment of British trade marts in western Tibet and redefined the Tibet–Sikkim border, but of far greater importance were stipulations that without the prior consent of the British government the Tibetans were to permit no foreign power to occupy any of their territory, to interfere in any way with their affairs, or even to cross their borders. While the agreement was designed to exclude all Russian influence from Tibet, it in effect treated China as a foreign power.

Repercussions of Younghusband's actions echoed through Europe and Asia. The British, engaged in delicate negotiations they hoped would lead to reconciliation of their differences with the Russians, had originally sanctioned only a limited expedition and were embarrassed by the 300-mile penetration into Lhasa.[15] Tibet was a vital buffer between their Indian empire and the Russians and, considering the convulsions inside China during the last decade of the Ch'ing dynasty, they may be forgiven for not foreseeing that a buffer would soon be necessary between India and China instead. The new Liberal government, motivated in part by sensitivity to foreign criticism, negotiated a treaty with Peking in 1906 that almost reversed Britain's newly won concessions and stopped just short of declaring the Manchus to have sovereign rights over Tibet. A year later they entered into a similar agreement with the Russians that placed restrictions on the freedom of action of both Britain and Russia in Tibet; in it the word *suzerainty* was used to describe China's relation to Tibet for the first time. For reasons best known to themselves, the British did not see fit to inform the Tibetan government of either treaty.

In the meantime the ease with which Younghusband's forces had marched through Tibet shocked the Manchus into the realization that they could no longer maintain their influence in Central Asia by indirect rule, that to guarantee the control of the frontier they would have to bring it under their direct administration. They invaded eastern Tibet in 1905 and took Lhasa in 1910, forcing the Dalai Lama to flee to India.

TIBETAN RELATIONS WITH REPUBLICAN AND NATIONALIST CHINA (1912–1949)

The overthrow of the Manchus in the Chinese Revolution of 1911 and the forcible expulsion of their troops from Tibet a year later made possible the return of the Thirteenth Dalai Lama from two years of exile in Darjeeling and Kalimpong. Noting that the Manchu attempt to colonize his country had "faded like a rainbow in the sky," he proudly proclaimed the resumption of Tibetan independence and, to ensure its recognition, dispatched one of his ablest ministers to represent him at a tripartite conference arranged by the British at their summer capital of Simla in the Himalayan foothills of East Punjab. The Chinese, predictably, had other ideas. Conveniently ignoring the fact that they controlled no part of the Dalai Lama's domain and claiming that it had been an integral part of China since conquest by the Mongols of Genghis Khan in the thirteenth century, they countered with a claim of sovereignty over Tibet.

The British negotiators were in a quandary. They had good reason to believe that Russia was on the verge of obtaining a position of influence in Lhasa that not only would be inimical to their interests but might also prove disruptive to the future stability of the Himalayan frontier of their Asian empire. To their minds the ideal solution would be to preserve Tibet as a modified buffer state, which would "allow the development of a stable Tibetan government free from outside influence, but in closer relations than before with the British Government."[16] Unwilling to establish a protectorate over Tibet,[17] the British preferred that it remain under some sort of Chinese control rather than become independent and free to enter into relations with Russia. At the urging of the British plenipotentiary Sir Henry McMahon, therefore, the Simla convention of 1914 proposed that China be granted suzerainty over Tibet. The precise definition of this term and of its counterpart, *autonomy*, is impossible according to Richardson "because the words have to be interpreted in accordance with the circumstances of each specific case." He makes clear, however, that "authorities on international law hold that suzerainty is by no means the same as sovereignty" and that "an autonomous state under the suzerainty of another is not precluded from having an international personality." Under no circumstances was Tibet to be converted into a Chinese province, so in effect nominal suzerainty was to be conceded in exchange for practical independence.[18]

It was also proposed that the country be divided into two areas. Outer Tibet, by far the larger of the two, was to encompass all the territory west of the Yangtse River, which had been ruled almost perpetually by the Tibetan government, and to be granted autonomy under the guiding hand of the Dalai Lama and his successive reincarnations. Inner Tibet was to encompass those border areas of Kham and Amdo whose populations were predominantly Tibetan in race and religion but whose political control over the centuries had passed back and forth between the Tibetans, Chinese, Muslim warlords, and various local chieftains. Although the area was to be theoretically self-governing, there was nothing to prevent the Chinese from exerting their influence and control there.

A draft agreement was initialed by delegates of all three nations, but the Chinese government repudiated the action of their representative and demanded further concessions. The Tibetans were stunned. After approaching the conference with such high hopes, they had been pressured into conceding that thereafter their country would for the first time in its history become a part of China, even one with such a nebulous and relatively benign status as a suzerain. Having gone this far, they would concede no more. After an unsuccessful attempt to bring the Chinese to terms, the convention was signed by the British and Tibetan ministers, who declared that although it was binding as to relations between them, its benefits would be denied the Chinese until they signed. Tibet thus retained her independence, and the British, freed from the restrictions of the 1907 Anglo-Russian Convention by the downfall of the czarist regime in 1917, evinced no hesitation thereafter in carrying on diplomatic relations with the Dalai Lama's government without first consulting the Chinese. While dealing with Tibet in practice as an independent state they avoided offending China by conveniently side-stepping formal recognition of this sovereignty. British economic interests in China greatly exceeded those in Tibet, and now that Britain enjoyed a virtual monopoly of trade with Tibet, there was no reason to jeopardize those interests by insisting upon such recognition.

The major factor that permitted Tibet to maintain her independence despite recurrent border clashes on the frontier was the internal disunity of China that had followed the overthrow of the Manchus. The end of the First World War found the country in almost complete political disintegration. The attempts of Sun Yat-sen and his political party to gain control of the revolutionary government had ended in total failure, and China was mired in a period of warlordism, with large territories in the hands of local chieftains like Ma Pu-feng in Amdo. The government was in the hands of military leaders who, not under the control of a single individual with superior armies at his disposal, were divided among themselves. Each leader became autonomous within a particular area, and the government disintegrated. In the 1920s two groups came to power, the Kuomintang (which had been founded in 1912 but was ineffective until reorganized by Soviet advisers) and the Communist party (founded in Shanghai in 1921), and much of Chinese history for the next three decades revolves around their relationship to each other. Allies in the early and middle part of the decade, they squared off in a civil war from 1927 to 1937, formed a united front against Japanese invaders from 1937 until the end of the Second World War, then resumed their civil war until the Communists emerged victorious in 1949.

The contending factions during this chaotic period each visited Tibet in 1935, although under different circumstances. The Nationalist government was granted permission to send a "condolence mission" to Lhasa following the death of the Thirteenth Dalai Lama. The real purpose behind the visit, which marked the first official entry of the Chinese into the country since their expulsion in 1912, was to probe the interim government for signs of weakness. The Great Thirteenth had adamantly opposed concessions to China, and the latter hoped to find some tractable officials who could be bribed or threatened into adopting a pro-Chinese posture. A series of negotiations ensued in which the Tibetans made clear their willingness to acknowledge Chinese suzerainty only under the conditions of the 1914 Simla Convention, which guaranteed them internal autonomy and the right to conduct their own foreign affairs. This was no more satisfactory to the Chinese now than it had been twenty years earlier; the talks were suspended and their head official returned to Nanking, leaving behind two liaison officers with a wireless set, which grew in a few years into a regular diplomatic mission. A British mission followed in its wake.[19]

As for the Communists, their Long March took them through eastern

Tibet, where their actions were a shocking precursor of things to come. The retreating forces looted and destroyed monasteries and slaughtered innocent people, forcing local Tibetans to cooperate with the Nationalists in fighting against them. Another part of their otherwise heroic journey, led by such luminaries as Mao Tse-tung, Chou En-lai, and Lin Piao, was made through some of the most forbidding territories on the Chinese–Tibetan borderland peopled by the fierce Goloks and Mantzu. "A few hundred yards on either side of the road," writes Edgar Snow, "it was quite unsafe. Many a Red who ventured to forage for a sheep never returned. The mountaineers hid in the thick bush and sniped at the marching invaders. They climbed the mountains and when the Reds filed through the deep, narrow rock passes, where sometimes only one or two could pass abreast, the Mantzu rolled huge boulders down to crush them and their animals. Here were no chances to explain 'Red policies towards National minorities,' no opportunities for friendly alliances! The Mantzu queen had an implacable, traditional hatred for Chinese of any variety . . . [and] threatened to boil alive anyone who helped the travellers." Several years later Snow was told by Mao Tse-tung: "That is our only foreign debt, and some day we must pay the Mantzu and Tibetans for the provisions we were obliged to take from them." How well and in what manner Mao repaid them will be seen later.[20]

Once they had gained control of the Chinese mainland at the end of 1949, the Communists did not move immediately to invade Tibet. Instead they made evident by means of frequent broadcasts over Radio Peking that they intended to "liberate" the country while guaranteeing regional autonomy and religious freedom. They appealed for a peaceful capitulation but warned that Tibet was certain to be "liberated" in any event and that there was no one to whom they could turn for help. Harboring a centuries-old aversion to the Chinese and all too aware of the plundering and killing by the Communists during the Long March the Tibetans were not eager to welcome them into their midst.

Aside from the fact that they never had any intention of honoring their promises for freedom of religion and Tibetan regional autonomy, the Chinese appeal made sense: their invasion of Tibet was imminent, and they correctly surmised that the rest of the world would stand by while they accomplished it. Lest it be thought that by attempting to reach a peaceful settlement the Communists were motivated by altruism, it should be pointed out that their troops had been engaged in battle for over twenty years—first against the Kuomintang, then the Japanese, then the Kuomintang again—and would soon be fighting in Korea. It made good sense to try to take Tibet without the use of arms. At the same time, the Tibetan government was invited to send delegates with full negotiating powers to Peking, and pressure was brought to bear on the eldest brother of the Dalai Lama to effect a hasty settlement.

Taktser Rinpoche had returned from Lhasa to Amdo in the summer of 1948, where in the following spring he was to be installed as the abbot of Kumbum monastery. A few months later the People's Liberation Army arrived after vanquishing the troops of Ma Pu-feng in the Battle of Lanchow and forcing the Muslim warlord to flee into exile. Fugitives from the Communist forces sought asylum in Kumbum and told such frightening stories of Chinese outrages against their co-religionists in Mongolia and China that many monks thought it expedient to leave the monastery and go underground in nearby villages or join local nomad groups. Painful evidence of Chinese violence was soon in coming, when the Rinpoche heard that the 600-year-old Shartsong Ridrö, the tiny hermitage near his native village of Taktser, had been attacked by a Communist-led mob, which had forced the twenty monks who lived there to flee into the mountains. The mob had then roamed through the temples destroying religious scriptures and plundering priceless images. Two other monasteries in the vicinity suffered the same fate, and bitter complaints to the Chinese authorities notwithstanding, nothing was done to punish the guilty parties or ensure that such actions would not be repeated.

Despite assurances that the Buddhist religion would not be tampered with, Taktser Rinpoche was informed that monasteries would have to redistribute their lands among the people and that the monks would be converted into laborers. He was reproached for the fact that beggars were not forced to work, that large amounts of butter were wasted in religious ceremonies, and that money was squandered on incense and ceremonial scarves. Two Chinese escorts were assigned to stay by his side at all times whose duty it was to engage him in political discussions and ridicule his spiritual practices; he was unable even to pray without being asked derisively whether prayer had ever filled anyone's belly. The unrelenting pressure brought him to the verge of despair and made it impossible for him to carry out his duties. In the spring of 1950, one year after assuming the abbotship, he resigned in the hope that a new Khenpo, one not related to the Dalai Lama, would be permitted greater latitude than he.

If Taktser Rinpoche entertained any hopes that his resignation might lessen his personal pressure, he was disappointed, for it not only continued but grew more intense, culminating with the proposal that he should betray his people and, if necessary, his brother as well. Should the Dalai Lama not welcome the Chinese "liberators," he was warned, means would be found to get rid of him, and fratricide would be considered justifiable if there was no other way to advance their cause. He agreed to go to Lhasa and urge his brother to capitulate.

On the eve of his departure Taktser Rinpoche walked slowly through the familiar winding lanes of Kumbum, visiting the temples for the last time, running his hand over their ancient pillars, placing his feet on their time-worn steps. His last visit was to the Temple of the Golden Tree, the oldest and holiest of all, where was enshrined the famous Tree of Ten Thousand Images, which had appeared in Reting Rinpoche's vision in the sacred lake Lhamoi Latso. He prostrated himself before the golden statue of Tsong Khapa, the great reformer, who many centuries before had ushered in a new epoch of Tibetan history, an epoch which now seemed to be coming to an end. He bowed his head, prostrated himself once more, and left the temple in profound distress.[21]

On the last day of the sixth month of the year of the Iron Tiger (1950), Taktser Rinpoche began his journey to the holy city of Lhasa.

Notes

1. The quotations attributed to Aufschnaiter, and to Richardson and Fox in the following paragraphs, were taken from Lowell Thomas, Jr., *Out of This World: Across the Himalayas to Forbidden Tibet* (New York, 1950).
2. Until the United States government, through Ilia Tolstoy and Brooke Dolan, provided the Tibetans with equipment for three complete radio stations in 1942, the only two radio transmitters in Tibet were at the British and Chinese missions in Lhasa. Robert Ford, *Captured in Tibet* (London, 1957), 20.
3. The stone pillar upon which details of this treaty were inscribed was still standing in Lhasa in 1959. For the full text, see H. E. Richardson, "The Sino-Tibetan Treaty Inscription A.D. 821/823 at Lhasa," *Journal of the Royal Asiatic Society* (1978), 137–162.
4. Phagpa Lodro Gyaltsen (1235–1280) was a devoted missionary, an astute politician, and a brilliant phonetician who invented by far the best alphabet for writing preclassical Mongolian. Of greater importance is the fact that he provided the Mongol emperors with a pseudo-historical theory that incorporated them into the line of Buddhist "universal emperors," and with this in mind developed a theory of theocratic rule beginning with Genghis Khan and continuing through Kublai and his successors.
5. The Sakya lamas were the only Tibetan Buddhists to maintain their position through hereditary succession rather than through reincarnation. Until 1959 the head of the Sakya sect, as a lineal descendant of the first lama king of Tibet, held an official rank equal to that of a regent and was accorded the rare privilege of riding in a palanquin. Lobsang Phuntsok Lhalungpa, "Buddhism in Tibet," in Kenneth W. Morgan, *The Path of the Buddha: Buddhism Interpreted by Buddhists* (New York, 1956), 247–249.
6. "Tibet was a part of the Mongol empire in a very peculiar way," Herbert Franke explains. "*It was definitely not part of China nor one of its provinces.* The greater part of Tibet was ruled by indigenous lamas whose government was sanctioned by the imperial court . . . but they received little or no interference from the emperors." Herbert Franke, "Tibetans in Yüan China," in John D. Langlois, ed., *China under Mongol Rule* (Princeton, 1981), 313. Emphasis added.
7. For a discussion of relations between Tibet and the Mongols during the thirteenth and fourteenth centuries, and a fuller explanation of the patron–lama relationship, see Franke, "Tibetans in Yüan China," 296–328.
8. "To conform to the lofty disdain with which the Chinese regarded the outside world, the practical uses of the tribute system were sublimated into elements in

the mystique of imperial statecraft. China was viewed as the centre of the world and 'barbarians' from the outside came there, dazzled by its greatness, to acknowledge its supremacy. In return, the Emperor had the duty of extending his gracious benevolence. The idea of political relationships on an equal footing had no place in such a framework and the absurdities to which that led can be seen in the well-known letter of the Emperor Ch'ien Lung to King George III at the time of Lord Macartney's mission to China in 1793. The Emperor addressed the King as a humble and devout suppliant and exhorted him reverently to obey the imperial instructions. In the same vein, the Pope appears in a list of tributaries of the Ch'ing Dynasty together with Holland, Portugal, and Russia." Hugh E. Richardson, *A Short History of Tibet* (New York, 1962), 37.

9. The Tungus (pronounced Tun-goose) nomads who invaded China at the beginning of the seventeenth century were given the name Manchus by their leader, and the term *Manchuria* came into vogue after the area had become an object of world conflict two centuries later. Composed of different climatic and topographic conditions and ethnic groups—mainly Mongol, Korean, and Tungus— it was referred to as the Three Eastern Provinces by the Chinese.

10. "The smothering of the Great Wall frontier by the power which China drew from the West resulted finally in one of the most extraordinary situations in all Chinese history: the proclamation of the Chinese republic and the recognition of a Chinese title to sovereignty in Manchuria, Mongolia, Chinese Turkestan, and Tibet. The West, far from realizing the extraordinary character of the situation thus created, took it all as a matter of course: a beautiful example of the application of stock ideas to a radically new problem. International practice from at least the time of the Treaty of Nanking in 1842 had come squarely to the point of treating the Manchu Empire as if it were the Empire of China. This led as a matter of course to the assumption on the part of the Western nations, when the Chinese Revolution of 1911 overthrew the Manchu Empire *in China*, that China stood heir to the Manchus and could claim possession of the Outer Dominions.

"There is no doubt whatever that the Mongols and the Tibetans, the two most solid national groups affected by this historic reversal . . . regarded the fall of the Manchu Empire as the destruction of a framework, which ought simply to have allowed the original component parts of the Empire to resume their own national identities. Nor can there be any doubt that legally and historically they were right. They had never 'belonged' without the intervention of the West. The fall of the Empire would have left a China independent of 'barbarian' control and a group of 'barbarian' nations standing free either of commitments to Manchuria, to each other, or to China." Owen Lattimore, "China and the Barbarians," in Joseph Barnes, ed., *Empire in the East* (New York, 1934), 14–15.

11. The expression appeared in Kay's *History of the War in Afghanistan* (1843) and seems to have been coined by Captain Arthur Conolly, a daring but unlucky player of the Great Game who was beheaded at Bokhara in 1842. Peter Fleming, *Bayonets to Lhasa: The First Full Account of the British Invasion of Tibet in 1904* (London, 1961), 30.

12. Buffers "served as an elastic substance placed between the unyielding fabric of colonial sovereignties. They could bend and bounce in a way that the defined boundaries of colonies could not. They prevented the clash of colonial interests from leading to conflicts which would prove extremely difficult to control once metropolitan public opinion was aroused." Alastair Lamb, *Asian Frontiers: Studies in a Continuing Problem* (New York, 1968), 62–63.

13. Edmund Candler, *The Unveiling of Lhasa* (New York, 1905), 11. Curzon's task was further complicated by the unavailability of suitable messengers to carry his

letters to the Dalai Lama. Such messengers not only had to be trustworthy and discreet, but also had to possess the power to cross the Tibetan border freely and to have connections with the highest government circles in Lhasa. The most sophisticated agent available, Sarat Chandra Das, was unfortunately well known in Tibet as an agent of the British since the 1880s. Another candidate, the adviser on Chinese affairs to the government of Burma, was rejected because "he is very fat, and would probably be unequal to the hardships in a journey to . . . Lhasa." A third, a highly respected Tibetan from Ladakh, had recently become so fond of *chang* that he could no longer be considered reliable. Alastair Lamb, "Some Notes on Russian Intrigue in Tibet," *Journal of the Royal Central Asian Society* 46 (January 1959), 54–56.

14. The Buriats, a tribe of nomadic Mongols whose homelands lie at the end of Lake Baikal, were subdued and absorbed into Russia in the eighteenth century. After the Bolshevik revolution, in 1923, Buriat Mongolia became an autonomous S.S.R.

15. In fairness, it should be pointed out that Younghusband was instructed at first to conduct negotiations just across the Sikkimese border at Khampa Dzong. After six frustrating months there, during which time the Tibetan government sent no one empowered to negotiate on its behalf, Younghusband received permission to advance to Gyantse and arrived there in April 1904. Once again there was no one with whom he could conduct talks, and, somewhat reluctantly, the British government gave him permission to continue on to Lhasa.

16. Richardson, *Short History*, 108.

17. Even if such an action had not been excluded by the terms of the 1907 Anglo-Russian Convention, "the most optimistic imperialist would have shrunk from assuming responsibility for another 2,000 miles or so of frontier enclosing over 500,000 square miles of country, mostly high, severe, and unpopulated and totally lacking in communications." Richardson, *Short History*, 104.

18. Richardson, *Short History*, 103.

19. For details on the establishment of the British Mission in Lhasa, see Richardson, *Short History*, 147–148.

20. Edgar Snow, *Red Star over China* (New York, 1961), 343.

21. A lengthy account of this episode may be found in Thubten Jigme Norbu, *Tibet Is My Country* (London, 1960), 205–238.

Tibetan monastery   *Bylakuppe 1980*

CHAPTER 10

A House Divided

S HORTLY BEFORE HIS DEATH the Thirteenth Dalai Lama issued a warning to his people. Predicting that the growing power of the Chinese Communists would pose a grave threat to Tibet, he admonished both monk and lay officials "to tackle unremittingly . . . the task of maintaining the civil and military structure as it is at this happy time when all power still remains in our hands." If all Tibetans, regardless of class, worked enthusiastically to ensure the unity and welfare of the country, there would be nothing to fear, but if they failed to do so their country was doomed. "When that time comes," he added, "regrets will be useless." No sooner had the People's Liberation Army secured control of the Chinese mainland than preparations were begun to launch an invasion of Tibet. The Communists could hardly have chosen a more propitious time to do so, for despite superficial signs of vitality the country was mired in a state of internal instability inimical to the establishment of unified opposition, unprepared militarily, and secluded diplomatically. Even as Taktser Rinpoche set out for Lhasa to meet with the Dalai Lama, the inevitable attack was being readied and the prophecy of the Great Thirteenth was about to come true.

One of the factors weakening the ability of Tibet to resist the Chinese stemmed from the historical failure of most Dalai Lamas to avail themselves of their full political prerogatives. Although they were acknowledged as the paramount spiritual and temporal rulers of the country, few were effective in the latter role. The first of the line to wield political power had been the Great Fifth, but the Sixth Incarnation had been too preoccupied with affairs of the *coeur* and the *corps* to pay much attention to those of the court. The Seventh and Eighth Dalai Lamas concerned themselves mainly with spiritual activities, and the Ninth through the Twelfth had met unnaturally early deaths. As a result of the ensuing lack of centralized rule, bitter conflicts and rivalries between factions for precedence in the affairs of government sapped the vitality of the nation.

Another factor contributing to the nation's instability was the long-standing latent enmity between the lay aristocratic and monastic hierarchies in their struggle for national leadership, a contest in which the latter had almost always had the upper hand since the time of the Fifth Dalai Lama. That the ascendancy of religion had been won at the expense of the hereditary nobility was the cause of constant friction between the two groups. In general, the nobility was more receptive to innovative ideas and more interested in world affairs, while the monastic community was determined to preserve the status quo. It would be too simplistic to label the one group "progressive" and the other "reactionary"; by twentieth-century criteria both were ultra conservative. To set themselves apart from the firmly entrenched monkhood the nobility had little choice but to project themselves as proponents of innovation; but the reforms they envisioned were hardly progressive and were often motivated more by the hope of augmenting their own political power than of bettering the country. Nor were the groups always opposed to one another. To the contrary, the lay nobility was often divided among itself, and rivalries existed likewise between monasteries of different sects, between monasteries of the same sect, and even between different colleges of a single monastery. Moreover, monastic leaders did not always act in accordance with the wishes of a majority of the monkhood, and on a number of occasions voted with the nobility for measures designed to benefit the nation.

The monastic and aristocratic leadership was not grouped, as has sometimes been suggested, into "pro-Chinese" and "pro-British" camps. While it is true that the Thirteenth Dalai Lama looked for assistance to both these foreign powers at various times during his reign, as well as to other nations such as Russia and Japan, he did so only in terms of the best interests of his country, and not infrequently played one off against the other to the benefit of Tibet. That the Chinese, relentlessly seeking to bring Tibet under Nationalist rule, continued the Manchu policy of making substantial financial contributions to key monasteries with the hope of winning over the ecclesiastical leadership cannot be disputed. Nor can the fact that the British, having no such territorial designs and seeking only a formula to ensure Tibetan autonomy while protecting their economic interests in Tibet without endangering those in China, made proposals ultimately less threatening to the nobility than to the monastic community. But as an English visitor to Lhasa wrote in 1905, "Tibetans had had one definite aim in view for centuries—the preservation of their church and state by the exclusion of all foreign and heretical influences."[1]

During two decades of vigorous autocratic rule following his return from exile, the Thirteenth Dalai Lama succeeded in keeping factional disputes to a minimum, but following his death in 1933 there was a progressive relaxation of centralized controls as the historic conflict between the contending forces burst forth once more. By the eve of the Communist invasion the powerful and unified Tibet he had hoped to create had become so debilitated by the struggle for political leadership between rival factions that it was easy prey for the People's Liberation Army. Rather than attempt to suspend their differences in the national interest they chose to seize on the emergency as an opportunity to strengthen their relative positions. Hoping to recover some of the power they had enjoyed under the Thirteenth Dalai Lama largely because of his attention to secular military preparedness, the aristocracy took a hard line toward the Chinese and urged full-scale armed resistance. In contrast, monastic leaders preached a more conciliatory policy and stressed the need for a peaceful settlement. Fully aware of the atrocities committed against Buddhist monasteries in Amdo and eastern Kham, they could not have been gulled by Chinese promises that their institutions would be respected and undisturbed upon "liberation" but were impelled to hold this position because of inbred mistrust of their traditional opponents, who stood to benefit at their expense in the event of a Sino-Tibetan military confrontation. As already suggested, neither group was particularly sympathetic toward the Chinese. Both, it must be stressed, were pro-Tibetan. Their mutual antipathy left the country exceptionally vulnerable.

Only the emergence of another strong ruler might have prevented this. However, if the main strength of the Gelugpa system of reincarnating Dalai Lamas lay in its prevention of nepotism, its major weakness lay in the long interregnum period during which the new incarnation had to be discovered and trained before he could assume at the age of eighteen the full political powers attendant to his position. With the Chinese poised to "liberate" Tibet, the Fourteenth Dalai Lama was barely into his teens, politically naive, and wholly dependent on his advisers. He was certainly not yet prepared to assume the reins of command in the face of such a major crisis. That a regent, lacking the enormous institutional charisma of a Dalai Lama and ruling by secular selection rather than sacred right, stood little chance of uniting the country may be seen through a series of events that culminated in an attempted coup d'état known as the Reting Conspiracy, which sent shock waves through Tibet.

Reting Rinpoche had been selected regent by lottery soon after the death of the Thirteenth Dalai Lama. Short, fair, and delicate, he was an affable, intense-looking young man who, although somewhat high-strung, is said to have gotten along well with all who knew him. Barely twenty years old when he assumed the regency, Reting was highly intelligent, progressive-minded, and a capable administrator. It was he who had seen the vision in the prophetic waters of Lake Lhamoi Latso that had led to the discovery of the Fourteenth Dalai Lama.[2] The regent was not in the best of health. His principal malady was catarrh, a condition aggravated by his habit of taking snuff, a mixture of strong tobacco diluted with powdered yak dung. At the suggestion of a doctor from the British Mission that his health might improve with some exercise, he had taken to kicking a soccer ball around his garden each day, an activity that came to a sudden halt when a delegation of monastic leaders called on him to protest that such activity was inappropriate for a greatly revered incarnate lama. Thereafter he found it expedient to limit his recreational activities to darts and mah-jongg.[3]

There was also a material side to the young regent's nature. His private quarters in Lhasa were decorated "with the exquisite taste which would do credit to a king," and he was always impeccably dressed in robes of the finest yellow silk. It was an open secret in the holy city that since the arrival of their 1934 "condolence mission" after the death of the Thirteenth Dalai Lama, the Nationalist government had been making generous contributions to him and other government officials in the hope of eliciting support for measures that could undermine Tibetan independence; forestalled from moving militarily against Tibet first by civil war with the Communists and later by the Japanese invasion, it was the only course available to them at the time.[4] Moreover, Reting devoted much of his time to financial pursuits, often sending traders to China to purchase satin and porcelain—some for his personal use and the rest for sale in Lhasa. For an incarnate lama to engage in such worldly activity was not unusual; Tibetan monks were inveterate traders, and regents in particular had commonly worked to enrich their *labrangs* (religious corporations) in terms of both movable wealth and manorial estates. "Having eaten the mountain, there is no satiation," went an old Tibetan adage about regents. "Having drunk the ocean, there is no quenching of thirst."

Reting's activities provided certain officials not included in his immediate circle of favorites with a convenient opportunity to complain that he was more interested in acquiring riches than in running the government, and after gaining the support of key figures from the aristocratic and monastic communities, they began to clamor for his removal from office. That there was truth to some of their contentions is undeniable, but it is also true that the individuals who instigated and stoked the protest were less outraged by Reting's behavior than they were intent on securing political favor and advancement under a new ruler once he was no longer on the scene. Subjected to increasingly great pressure, Reting finally consulted the state oracle at Nechung monastery and was told that unless he devoted himself to prayer and meditation his life would be short—a sensible prophecy, for even if his health improved, political assassinations were not unusual in government circles. Reting accordingly resigned from his post and chose as his successor his spiritual mentor, the elderly lama Taktra Rinpoche, who assumed office in the first month of the Year of the Iron Snake (1941). Judiciously retiring to his monastery some sixty miles north of Lhasa, the former regent immersed himself in spiritual affairs, his only diversion being his stable of fine ponies. Not surprisingly he became a good friend of Gyayab Chenmo, the Dalai Lama's father, like himself a lover of horses. There amid the beautifully landscaped gardens, surrounded by fragrant juniper bushes and Himalayan cedars, matters rested until the beginning of 1947. Shortly thereafter, Reting monastery would prove to have been an impermanent Utopia and the ex-regent's years there only a calm before the storm.

When Reting turned over the regency to Taktra, he apparently did so with the tacit understanding that he would resume the powerful post at some time in the future when Taktra, a quiet and impassive man in his seventies with no prior experience in government, would resign on the grounds of old age. This plan took the pressure off Reting while enabling him to remain in the background as an unofficial but highly influential adviser to Taktra. Moreover, it provided an opportunity for the latter to enrich the coffers of his monastery, a modest and relatively insolvent institution that had never before had the good fortune to provide a regent of Tibet.[5] Unfortunately for Reting, when the time came for Taktra to step down, he declined to do so. Whether the decision was the result of simple misunderstanding or base in-gratitude is difficult to determine, for much of Tibetan history, particularly that of a political nature, remains unwritten. What is certain, however, is that Taktra's refusal to bow out led to a strained relationship between the supporters of the two men, and that a parcel containing a bomb fashioned from a hand grenade was subsequently sent to Taktra's office and exploded when opened by a servant: Reting Rinpoche was arrested on April 15 for having masterminded the deed.

Thereafter events moved swiftly. On the following day monks from Che College of Sera monastery, political supporters of Reting who for some time had been suspected of collusion with the Chinese government,[6] not only declared their support for the ex-regent but also murdered their abbot when he attempted to restrain them from armed rebellion. Barricading themselves in the college buildings, the monks, armed with rifles and home-made cannon, fired on all who approached their vicinity. The government made a number of futile attempts to negotiate and finally launched a full-scale attack that brought the rebellion to an end. From start to finish the affair lasted barely three weeks.

Meanwhile, the trial of Reting and his co-conspirators was being con-ducted before the Tsongdu, and the ex-regent was staunchly denying any complicity in the affair. A full account was not long in emerging. Tibetan custom permitted the flogging of recalcitrant suspects, from which treat-ment one of Reting's closest associates broke down and blurted out details of the plot that were later corroborated by other key witnesses. The pro-Reting conspirators admitted sending the explosive parcel, attempting to overthrow the Taktra government and replace it with one of their own headed by Ret-ing, making a number of attempts on Taktra's life, and attempting to assassi-nate a high-ranking government official named Lhalu (more about whom will be said in the next chapter). The punishment of those found guilty was carried out in the third week of May. Some of the conspirators were flogged and fettered, others given sentences of life imprisonment, still others exiled to remote parts of the country. The monk believed to have fashioned the letter-bomb committed suicide before the trial. As for Reting Rinpoche, he was found dead in one of the dungeons of the Potala on May 8. The government carried out a cursory examination of the body, reported finding no evidence of foul play, and solemnly declared that the former regent had "willed himself out of his present incarnation." A convenient explanation under the circumstances, and not as improbable as it might sound, but it is far more likely that he was murdered.[7]

There still exists a great deal of controversy over the precise role played in the conspiracy by the unfortunate Reting. Some maintain that he was an essentially good man who fell victim to the wiles of his advisers and was thrust unwillingly into the thick of the plot. Others have been less generous in their assessment and claim that he had gone so far as writing to Chiang Kai-shek in Nanking requesting that the Kuomintang leader send an aircraft over Lhasa to drop leaflets supporting his coup and to threaten the bombing of the holy city if his plans were resisted. Perhaps the most balanced account of the former regent is that of Hugh Richardson, who was in Lhasa during the abortive uprising. "He was generally believed to favor the Chinese and they certainly looked on him as well-disposed towards their ambitions," he concedes. "But his inclination was probably influenced by the generous payments he received and it is improbable that, in the long run, he would either have wanted or been able to do anything fatally compromising to the Tibetan position."[8] Reting's death, while concluding one of the most unfortunate and tragic episodes of recent Tibetan history, did not succeed in bringing to an end the factional strife that had caused it, and a legacy of bitterness endured.

Compounding Tibet's difficulties was the fact that the country was woefully unprepared militarily, a situation that had persisted since the return of the Thirteenth Dalai Lama in 1912. Having been forced into exile by the British in 1904 and the Manchus in 1910, the Tibetan hierarch needed no further proof that a modernized army would be essential to the preservation of his country's newly regained independence, and he entrusted the task of organizing it to his most capable adviser, a brave and adventuresome individual named Chensal Namgang, the Horatio Alger of Tibet.

Chensal Namgang ("Clear Eye") had been born in 1885 to a peasant family in a village just north of Lhasa. His father was an arrowmaker, a lowly occupation on a par with butchering, blacksmithing, and disposing of the dead. As a child he was initiated into the monkhood and sent to live at Drepung monastery, which he left several years later to become a servant at the monk-officials' school in the Potala. There his keen mind and boundless energy came to the attention of the Dalai Lama, who made him his personal attendant.

When the Manchus sent an occupation force into Lhasa in 1910, Chensal Namgang took command of a small band of soldiers and civilians and held at bay a vastly superior enemy force while the Dalai Lama made good his escape into India, as a result of which he was made commander-in-chief of the Tibetan army and sent back into Tibet in disguise with orders to incite the populace to rise against the invaders. The strategy paid off in 1911 when revolution broke out in Peking and Manchu garrisons were massacred in both Tibet and China. By the time the Dalai Lama returned to Lhasa, Chensal Namgang had become his most trusted and influential aide.

All, however, was not well in the holy city. During the Dalai Lama's exile a group of ambitious officials had begun a whispering campaign against the Kashag, the import of which was that its four Kalons were quislings. This was followed by rumors that the ministers were planning to betray the Dalai Lama upon his return, and demands that they be arrested.

Three of the Kalons had been appointed by the Manchus, but the fourth, patriarch of one of the country's oldest and wealthiest noble families, had been selected prior to the invasion by the Dalai Lama himself and ordered to remain in Lhasa. When the innuendos were brought to his attention he refused to flee. "White blood will flow," he said, professing his innocence, "if ever my head is chopped off." The conspirators were not impressed. In March 1912 he was seized at the Kashag office in the Potala, dragged down a long, steep flight of stone steps to the grounds of the magistrate's building, and murdered. His name was Tsarong.

There is no way of ascertaining what role, if any, Chensal Namgang played in the affair. But shortly afterward the Dalai Lama rewarded him for his services to the country by making him a Kalon and elevating him to the nobility as new head of the Tsarong family. He married the widow of the deceased Tsarong's eldest son (who had been murdered on the same day as his father) and, to continue the ancestral line, one of Tsarong's daughters as well. Within a decade he had become the richest man in Tibet.

As commander-in-chief of Tibetan military forces, the new Tsarong had at his disposal perhaps six thousand soldiers scattered throughout the country whose weapons consisted of old-fashioned matchlocks, spears, swords, slings, axes, and a handful of crudely made rifles. The Chinese refusal to come to terms at Simla in 1914 prompted Britain to send some five thousand modern bolt rifles with the stipulation that they be used only for Tibet's defense. But in 1916 the British, deeply involved in the First World War, not only placed an embargo on further such shipments but also prevented the Tibetans from obtaining munitions from Japan. It was a bitter blow to Tsarong and to the Dalai Lama, who when war broke out had offered a thousand Tibetan soldiers to fight with the British.

Tsarong was frustrated. Campaigns against the Chinese on the eastern frontier in 1917 and 1918 had proved to him that with modern rifles his troops were more than a match for their enemy. Finally he turned to Mongolia, which was surfeited with a variety of inexpensive arms and ammunition originating in Japan. Plans were made to import some fifteen thousand rifles by camel caravan over the well-established Urga–Lhasa trade route across the Chang Tang, Tibet's northern plains, over which a substantial number of rifles had been sent by the Russian government before the war.[9] To economize on time and expense it was decided to import only the barrels, of which each camel would carry twenty to thirty, and to fashion new stocks of walnut in Tibet. To what extent the Tibetan government carried out this plan is difficult to ascertain, but that its implications were ominous to the British could not have been overlooked by the Dalai Lama. Certainly Charles Bell, who seems to have been privy to all its details, would not likely have possessed this knowledge without the latter's consent; and he not only exhorted his government to resume its shipments but also urged that it do so before Japanese military instructors followed in the wake of their weapons. Shipments of military matériel were renewed but with less frequency and in smaller quantities than before; from 1921 onward Britain committed itself to a policy of preserving peace in Tibet and discovering a solution to the Sino-Tibetan impasse, and was fearful lest the Tibetans become as aggressive as the Chinese. Moreover, the British were mindful of the fact that by providing military assistance to the Dalai Lama's government they would anger the Nationalist Government and endanger their substantial economic concessions in China. The problem of securing a regular supply of arms and ammunition was one that the Tibetan government never solved to its satisfaction.

Due in no small measure to monastic opposition, Tsarong also found it difficult to increase the size of the army. Before he assumed its command the overwhelming numerical superiority of the monks in Lhasa's three great monasteries and their unquestioning obedience to their abbots had relegated the military to an inferior position. The vast majority of the 20,000 to 25,000 denizens of these institutions (of whom some 2,000 were the volatile *dob-dobs* discussed in Chapter 4) were nonscholarly worker monks physically and emotionally capable of resorting to violence when mobilized under the banner of defending the Dharma, a situation which gave the monasteries *de facto* veto power over the government. Not until 1921 was Tsarong able, through the offices of the Dalai Lama, to persuade the monk-dominated Tsongdu (National Assembly) to approve the recruitment of 500 to 1,000 soldiers annually until the army's total strength reached 17,000. ("A small force indeed for a country with an area of 500,000 square miles," commented a concerned Charles Bell, who pointed out that while only one-tenth the size of Tibet, Nepal boasted an army of 35,000.)

Tsarong found it no less difficult to secure competent officers for his forces, a situation that reflected both the conspicuous absence of military traditions in Tibet and an anachronistic military organization. The highest field officers were the Depöns ("Lords of the Arrows"), who held a rank more or less equivalent to that of general and whose primary responsibility was commanding regiments of 500 men. The post, which required no prior military experience, was reserved for members of the upper nobility and regarded merely as a stepping stone to some superior, nonmilitary position. Bereft of capable supervision, most Depöns had neither the ability, the inclination, nor, with virtually no chance at advancement within the military, the incentive to coordinate their activities with each other. Moreover, they tended to look on military service as a degradation and avoided it whenever possible.

Not until the rank of Rupön ("Master of the Banner"), or colonel, were there to be found truly experienced military men. Senior professional officers, two of whom were assigned to each Depön, they were low in the official hierarchy with little hope of advancement and had worked themselves up from the ranks, making the army their career. But although they commanded the respect of their men, they lacked the authority to question the decisions and tactics of their superiors and were never utilized to full potential.

Thus, in 1913, when the Dalai Lama arranged to send four young Tibetans to be educated in England in the care of a brilliant, mercurial lay official by the name of Lungshar, Tsarong urged that at least one of them be provided with military training. It was an inspired idea, but one that ended in failure.

Sixteen-year-old Gongkar, like the other boys a scion of the lesser nobility, served with the 10th Yorkshires and the artillery at Woolwich before returning to Tibet and being dispatched to a frontier post in Kham, where he died in 1917. Rumor has it that he had fallen in love with an Englishwoman but was forbidden to marry her by the Dalai Lama, and that his death was caused by a broken heart. On the other hand it was common knowledge in court circles that while in England he had carried on a clandestine affair with Lungshar's wife; and even today it is whispered that the cuckolded official may have had something to do with his early demise. The official cause of death was pneumonia.

Closer to home, Tsarong managed to persuade the British to provide rudimentary training for a few young nobles in India and at Gyantse, the site of their trade mission in western Tibet. More help might have been forthcoming had Britain not been involved with the Great War, but even that which they had already provided was, according to Hugh Richardson, "done in a spirit of grudging circumspection."

From 1914 to 1917 Tsarong employed Yajima Yasujiro, a Japanese trader living in Lhasa, as drill instructor for 200 Tibetan soldiers. A veteran of the Russo-Japanese War of 1904–1905 and an assistant at the Toyama Military College until his release from military service in 1907, Yajima also supervised the construction of Japanese-style barracks for the Kusung Magar (the Dalai Lama's personal bodyguard) before returning to Japan with his Tibetan wife and their son in 1920. The British suspected him of being a spy for the Japanese government.

Despite these obstacles Tsarong was successful in reorganizing and strengthening the Tibetan army; but in doing so he came to be regarded by the gentry with jealousy and resentment. "His manner is somewhat ponderous as compared with the quiet and dignified courtesy of the blue-blooded Tibetan nobles," observed Charles Bell. "But he brings a vigour to the lay nobility which is lacking in many of them." He also brought new taxes to bear on their hereditary estates to help meet the expense of maintaining a standing army.

Of considerably greater significance was the fact that many of Tsarong's actions as commander-in-chief brought him into direct opposition with the monkhood, which resented the increased taxation of monastic properties and suspected that the army would, in time, move to abridge its traditional influence and power. These fears were realized first in 1923, when the Dalai Lama ordered that Tsarong's troops be used to suppress a threatened revolt by the monks of Drepung, and again in the following year, when Tsarong and a group of his young generals made the unprecedented request of the Tsongdu that a military representative be admitted. Although the request was denied, the incident was utilized by Tsarong's enemies in their intrigues against him. Several of the officers were dismissed from their posts, and the condition of the army was permitted to deteriorate until it was no longer considered a threat to monastic supremacy. A year later Tsarong was relieved of his command. It was only by virtue of his friendship with the Dalai Lama and the vigilance of loyal bodyguards that he was not relieved of his life as well.

On the diplomatic front the situation was equally bleak. While enjoying *de facto* independence since the overthrow of the Manchus, the Tibetan government had made no attempt after the unsuccessful negotiations at Simla in 1914 to seek international recognition of this status. "It never occurred to us that our independence, so obvious a fact to us, needed any legal proof to the outside world," the Dalai Lama explains. "When we won it, we were quite content to retire into isolation." It was a critical mistake. The failure to seek international acknowledgment of its sovereign status in the face of persistent and well-publicized Chinese allegations that Tibet was an integral part of China made it possible for the other members of the world community, being under no compulsion to pronounce themselves on the issue, either to assume a posture of neutrality or to ignore it altogether. "If only we had applied to join the League of Nations or the United Nations or even appointed ambassadors to a few of the leading powers before the crisis came," says the Dalai Lama, "I am sure these signs of sovereignty would have been accepted without any question." Perhaps. But it is highly unlikely that the Chinese would have acquiesced quietly, that the British would have provided encouragement, or that the monolithic, ultraconservative Tibetan government would have considered taking such steps.[10]

Nevertheless the government made a series of belated attempts to demonstrate Tibetan independence. A Bureau of Foreign Affairs was created under the Kashag in 1942 in response to the group of Chinese officials in Lhasa whose 1934 "condolence mission" had grown first into a liaison office and later into a branch of a Chinese Nationalist creation called the Commission for Mongolian and Tibetan Affairs. While the British made use of the new bureau, the Chinese refused to acknowledge it, for to do so would be to admit their status as representatives of a foreign nation in Tibet, and they were thus manipulated into a position of practical isolation.

The desire to maintain an international posture distinct from that of China also prompted Tibet's declaration of neutrality in the Second World War. The government refused to permit proposed supply roads from India to China to cross its borders even after Chiang Kai-shek attempted to force the issue by ordering the warlords of western China, including Ma Pu-feng, to whom the Generalissimo reputedly sent some fourteen truckloads of arms and ammunition for the purpose, to invade Tibet. Only the fear of losing the support of the British, who had allied with China in the wake of Japan's entry into the war, induced the Tibetans to change their policy. Even so, the transport of military supplies was forbidden and no Chinese officials were permitted to enter the country.

It was during this same period that the United States government, while arranging the visit to Tibet of Ilia Tolstoy and Brooke Dolan, was unable to obtain permission to enter the country through the Chinese government, but forced instead to secure it from the Tibetan government through the government of India. Documents have been subsequently brought to light which indicate that despite this fact, the United States held the position that Tibet was a suzerain state of China (there seems, however, to be no record of any U.S. official questioning how a suzerain state could prohibit rights of transit through its territory to its overlord). Yet when an American airplane crashed in southern Tibet in 1944 and its crew was rescued and escorted to the Indian border, the U.S. government sent a message of thanks to Lhasa together with the assurance that in the future no American aircraft would fly over Tibetan territory, certainly a tacit admission of Tibet's neutrality and *de facto* independence.

Further efforts were made in the spring of 1947 when the Tibetan government, responding to an invitation from the government of India, sent a delegation to the Asian Relations Conference in Delhi, where the Tibetan flag flew among the flags of other nations to the discomfiture of the Chinese delegation. After an indignant protest by the latter, a map of Asia that showed Tibet outside China's borders was removed. Later in the year the government sent a trade delegation headed by Tsepon Shakabpa to visit India, Great Britain, the United States, and China. Although its ostensible purpose was economic, the trip was also politically motivated, for the delegates carried Tibetan passports, which were recognized by all countries on their itinerary, with the predictable exception of China, and set another precedent supporting the claim of Tibetan independence.

Two years later it had become apparent that Mao Tse-tung's Communist forces would prevail over those of the demoralized Kuomintang. Fearing that with the fall of the Nationalist government the staff at the Chinese mission in Lhasa might transfer their allegiance to the People's Republic, which would thus gain a most unwelcome foothold in Tibet, the Tibetan government, in July, requested them to leave the country within two weeks. Despite the deadline, traditional Eastern courtesies were observed. The Chinese officials and their families were entertained lavishly, a traditional escort party bade them farewell, and a band provided music to speed them on their way. Although a strong manifestation of Tibetan independence, the wholesale eviction did not solve the problem of how to prevent the Communists from entering the country.

As the last of the ousted diplomats made their way to the Indian border (to have attempted a more direct journey eastward and overland through Kham would have been most unwise, for the locals were not particularly enamored of the Chinese), they were met on the trail by the CBS radio commentator Lowell Thomas and his son Lowell Jr. An intrepid globetrotter who had visited some of the most remote places on earth, the elder Thomas had since childhood nurtured a desire to visit Tibet but had never been able to do so. His most recent request had been made at an opportune time, since the Tibetan trade delegation had just returned to Lhasa and its delegates were shocked at how little the world knew about their country. "Some people thought all Tibetans lived either in tents or in monasteries," recalls Tsepon Shakabpa. "When I showed them a picture of the Potala, they stared at it in disbelief. Others asked me about a place they called Shangri-la, where, they said, people lived forever. Then it was my turn to look at *them* in disbelief. It was very discouraging." Hoping to publicize the plight of their country to the world, the Tibetan government welcomed the Thomases to Lhasa, where they met with the Dalai Lama, the regent Taktra, the Kashag, and the Foreign Bureau, and transmitted a series of sympathetic broadcasts back to America.[11]

Shortly after the Thomases' return to the United States, the Communists drove the last of Chiang Kai-shek's forces from the mainland and announced their intention to "liberate" Tibet. The international response to this threat proved that all the Tibetan government's diplomatic efforts had been made in vain. The Kashag appointed delegations to visit the United States, Great Britain, India, and Nepal and ask for help, and sent telegrams to these governments requesting they be officially received. "The replies were terribly disheartening," remembers the Dalai Lama. "The British government expressed their deepest sympathy for the people of Tibet, and regretted that owing to Tibet's geographical position, since India had been granted independence, they could not offer help. The government of the United States replied in the same sense and declined to receive our delegation. The Indian government also made clear that they would not give us military help, and advised us not to offer any armed resistance, but rather to open negotiations for a peaceful settlement on the basis of the Simla agreement of 1914." Tibet stood alone.

On August 15, 1950, a violent earthquake rumbled across Tibet, leaving damage and terror in its wake. Its epicenter was in the southeast, where mountains and valleys were displaced and the mighty Brahmaputra River, blocked by a falling mountain, changed its course and inundated hundreds of villages. Thousands of lives were lost in what is said to have been one of the five largest earthquakes ever recorded. Apart from mourning her dead, the country was heavy with gloom, for the monkhood believed it to be an evil omen for Tibet. There were other baleful portents.[12] A great comet blazed in the sky for several nights, and Tibetans reminded each other that the last comet had been the precursor of war with China. Grotesque births were reported, and the top of an ancient column at the foot of the Potala was found one morning lying on the ground in fragments. One of the gilded gargoyles adorning the Jokhang temple began each day to drip water despite blazing summer weather during which no rain fell. The Nechung oracle made dire predictions, rumors of disaster abounded, and fortunetellers enjoyed an unprecedented business.

Although divided on the issue of appropriate military and diplomatic responses to the Communists, the Tibetan government was unanimous in its belief that the spiritual force of religion, by far the most powerful element in the life of the country, should be mobilized at this most critical time in Tibetan history. New ordinances were passed and large sums of money made available. Monks were ordered to read aloud from the scriptures at daily public services, and religious festivals were held that surpassed in pomp and splendor anything in recent memory. New prayer flags replaced tattered ones; holy walks were crowded with prostrating pilgrims murmuring sacred mantras; in temples and at family altars offerings abounded. On mountain peaks throughout the land incense fires smoldered and prayer wheels revolved with the wind in supplication to the protective deities above.

On October 7, 1950, while a delegation of Tibetans was engaged in a series of desperate negotiations with Chinese officials in India, the Communists launched an attack on eastern Tibet from eight different directions.

Notes

1. Edmund Candler, *The Unveiling of Lhasa* (New York, 1905), 79.
2. The circumstances surrounding Reting's own discovery as an incarnate lama in the village of Dakpo southeast of Lhasa are worthy of note. It is said that when

he was three years old he had hammered a wooden peg into a large rock near his parents' house, and when asked why he had done so replied that he was expecting a caravan of wealthy guests from afar to take him home and that they would need the peg to tether their horses. That evening a caravan composed of high monastic dignitaries searching for the reincarnation of the late Reting Rinpoche arrived in Dakpo, discovered the child to be the one they were looking for, and escorted him and his peasant parents to the Reting monastery.

3. "He revealed a very frail physique, which harbors a delicate spiritual personality with a very sensitive nature," wrote an American student of Buddhism who had several audiences with the regent in the late 1930s. "He was the sort of selfless, sympathetic character with whom you might spend hours without feeling a strain. And the radiance about him was such that no matter how you felt on coming to him you were sure to feel the stronger for having been in his company. A singularly spiritual individual, certainly, yet at the same time with a keen mind, full of wisdom and understanding, and alive with ideas." Theos Bernard, *Penthouse of the Gods: A Pilgrimage into the Heart of Tibet and the Sacred City of Lhasa* (New York, 1939), 164.

4. This practice, which also accompanied the settling of criminal disputes and attaining of political advancement, should not be confused with the Western concept of bribery. Gifts were given not for any specific service but rather to curry favor generally, and their acceptance imposed no obligation on the recipient and attached no stigma to either party in the transaction. In criminal cases it was not unusual for both disputants to bestow gifts of approximately equal value on the presiding magistrate. The Tibetan word for bribery means "secret push."

5. High incarnate lamas from a small group of Gelugpa monasteries monopolized the regency. From 1757 to 1940, for instance, the ten Tulkus who held this highly coveted post represented just five such institutions.

6. Each regent had traditional ties with one or more of the nine monastic colleges within the Three Pillars, from which he had received a substantial part of his education and to which he could turn for political support when necessary.

7. In their 1959 diatribe written in response to the Dalai Lama's flight into exile, the Chinese claimed that beause of his friendship with Reting the Dalai Lama's father was poisoned "for his patriotic ideas by reactionaries who had connections with foreign powers in order to facilitate their control over the Dalai Lama." *Concerning the Question of Tibet* (Peking, 1959), 201, 247. If in fact Choekyong Tsering was murdered—and, as in the case of Reting Rinpoche, there is no way to verify such an action since there were no post-mortems in Tibet—the motive would have been less that "he had the interests of the Motherland at heart" and more that he might have been opposed to the corrupt regime of the Taktra faction.

8. Former finance minister T. W. Shakabpa asserts that he read all the letters exchanged by Reting and his advisers—almost all of whom were relatives—and that Reting made clear his opposition to any actions designed to restore him to the regency by force. Interview with T. W. Shakabpa, Kalimpong, India, April 10, 1980.

9. The caravan, described by the Russians as a "scientific expedition," reached Lhasa in the autumn of 1902. Another such caravan, led by an intelligence officer named Tserempil (alias Bogdanovitch), who, like Dorjieff, was a Buriat Mongol monk, left at the same time and reached the holy city in November. Wilhelm Filcher, *Sturm über Asien* (Berlin, 1926), 364–365, quoted in P. L. Mehra, "Tibet and Russian Intrigue," *Journal of the Royal Central Asian Society* 45 (January 1958), 34–35.

10. The Thirteenth Dalai Lama gave serious consideration to Tibet's joining the League of Nations. "We should have to make the league understand," he told Charles Bell, "that we are an independent nation; that China has claimed suzerainty over us, but we have never admitted this; that in 1912 we fought the Chinese and drove them all out . . . and since then we have governed the larger part of our own country." But he decided against applying for membership because he feared that "travellers of other nations may wish to penetrate our country," particularly missionaries, who "in trying to spread Christianity may speak against our religion. We could not tolerate that."

11. Later the Chinese branded Thomas "a top special agent" who had been "directly dispatched" to Lhasa "to carry out conspiratorial activity there," and asserted that his son's book, *Out of This World*, "exposed before the whole world the criminal activities of the U.S. imperialists in instigating the Tibetan reactionaries to oppose the Motherland and undermine the solidarity between the Han and Tibetan people." Within a year of its publication, the Communists imposed that solidarity at gunpoint. *Concerning the Question of Tibet*, 205–206.

12. "The appearance of an unknown bird—in fact a painted stork driven far off course from the Indian plains—caused serious headshakings," writes Hugh Richardson. "The bird's body was . . . eventually burned ritually at a great ceremony for the averting of evil, when Communist attacks seemed imminent. I was present at the ceremony, which ended most impressively with a tremendous dust-storm out of a clear blue sky. About the same time another great ceremony was held at Sakya, and there the onlookers clearly saw a white dog rush from the burning pyre; this was a sure sign of the success of the exorcism." David Snellgrove and Hugh Richardson, *A Cultural History of Tibet* (New York, 1968), 265.

Kalon T. T. Liushar   *Dharamsala 1980*

· CHAPTER II ·

Blueprint for Conquest

"T HE CHINESE WAY is to say or do something mild at first, then to wait a bit, and, if it passes without objection, to say or do something stronger," the Thirteenth Dalai Lama once remarked to his friend Charles Bell. "If this is objected to, they reply that what they said or did has been misinterpreted and really meant nothing." How well the Great Thirteenth understood his belligerent neighbors to the east was demonstrated by the strategy adopted by the Chinese Communists for their invasion of Tibet sixteen years after his death. Comforming precisely to this pattern, it was a well-orchestrated symphony of subjugation in three movements with China wielding the baton and Tibet an unwilling performer.

The Chinese invasion of Tibet was launched in 1949 with a noisy propaganda campaign designed to provoke and assess the reactions of Tibet and the international community.[1] Chu Teh, commander-in-chief of the People's Liberation Army, began by announcing over Radio Peking his intention to liberate Tibet from British and American imperialists. No reply was forthcoming from the Tibetan government. Several weeks later, Radio Peking reported that the Panchen Lama, the second highest Tibetan Buddhist incarnation, who had been "discovered" and accorded "official recognition" by the Kuomintang, was in Communist hands and had given his wholehearted support to the liberation. Rather than denounce the Chinese Panchen as a fraud, the Tibetan response was conciliatory in tone. An anonymous announcer commented over Radio Lhasa that there were in fact two candidates for recognition as the Seventh Panchen, that it was not known for certain which was the true reincarnation since neither had passed the traditional tests, and that in his opinion—he carefully stressed that he was not speaking for the Tibetan government—the candidate in Lhasa would prove to be the true one. In November a message from Mao Tse-tung on Radio Peking encouraged the people of Tibet to rise up and overthrow the rule of the Dalai Lama, but even this elicited no response from the government. According to Robert Ford, the British radio operator stationed by the Tibetan government in Chamdo, this state of affairs persisted until the eve of the Communist invasion: "I had listened to every news bulletin and talk that had been broadcast. I had still not heard a single reply to Peking. No one had said that Tibet did not want to be liberated. There had not even been a denial that Tibet was controlled by American and British imperialists."[2]

Whereas it is possible that this consistent lack of response to the unending stream of Communist fulminations reflected an official policy of the Tibetan government, it is more likely that the latter, unable to agree on what measures to take because of its persistent factional in-fighting, took none at all. Whether it was active or passive, the practical effect of that lack of response was to place Tibet in the position of playing for time in the vain hope that some other nation would come to its rescue, and to that end refraining from saying or doing anything that might provoke the Chinese into moving up their timetable of invasion. "Either proclaim that you are an independent state and determined to remain so," Ford exhorted is Tibetan friends, "or go to Peking and get the best terms you can. Either would be better than just sitting and waiting to be swallowed up." Tibet waited.

Apart from Tibet itself, the nation that had the most to lose by a Communist occupation of the Roof of the World was India. On the eve of its independence in August 1947, formal declarations had been made informing the Tibetan government of the transfer of power and advising that thereafter the obligations and rights of the British under existing treaties would devolve on the Indians. For several years affairs with the new government gave Tibetans little cause for anxiety: direct diplomatic relations were maintained, Lhasa's British Mission became an Indian Mission, and the Indians even supplied the Tibetan army with arms and ammunition. But as the Communists drew closer to victory on the Chinese mainland, the situation changed.

Indian Prime Minister Pandit Jawaharlal Nehru, although professing to support Tibet's claim to self-government, let it be known in public and on more than one occasion that he recognized the right of China to a "vague and shadowy" suzerainty over Tibet. His words came as a major and unexpected blow to the Lhasa government, for they seemed to indicate to the Chinese that India would be unlikely to oppose the imposition of Communist authority in its territory. Beset with domestic crises resulting from the sudden transition to self-rule, the Indians were more interested in maintaining friendly international relations than in embroiling themselves in the explosive situation developing in Tibet. Without the backing of the Western powers, they were no match for the Communists militarily, and having just shed the humiliating shackles of colonialism, they were constrained from seriously considering requesting such backing. The establishment of friendly and constructive diplomatic relations with the Chinese, they felt, afforded the greatest prospect of keeping the peace. Moreover, one of the major tenets of Indian foreign policy was "Asianism," a strong reaction to the arrogance and racism that had characterized the years of colonial rule, and it was believed that despite political and philosophical differences the future stability of Asia depended upon cooperation between the modern governments of the two great and ancient civilizations. "We, in India, have had two thousand years of friendship with China," Nehru asserted. "We have differences of opinion and even small conflicts, but when we hearken back to that long past something of the wisdom of that past helps us to understand each other."[3] In January 1950 the Indian government became one of the first non-Communist countries to give formal recognition to the new People's Republic and offered to sponsor its admission to the United Nations.

Yet the Communists were also mindful of the fact that for a variety of reasons, including geographical proximity, treaty obligations, and spiritual affinity, India was the nation most likely to interfere with their plans for the future of Tibet. Accordingly, the government of India was accused in the Chinese press of being the tool of Anglo-American imperialism and of aiding imperialist schemes for the annexation of Tibet. "Into his slavish and bourgeois reactionary character," raved Radio Peking about the same Nehru who was making such great efforts to befriend the Chinese, "has now been instilled the beastly ambition of aggression." From the very beginning the Communists had India on the defensive. When reports reached New Delhi in the late summer of 1950 about the Chinese military buildup on the border of eastern Tibet, the Indian government was alarmed. The Indians had only recently responded to a Tibetan appeal for assistance by advising Lhasa to pursue a peaceful settlement on the basis of the 1914 Simla agreement. To the query of the Indian ambassador regarding the troop mobilization, Peking responded that the solution of the "Tibetan question" would be brought about solely through peaceful negotiations. Although evidence indicated that it would be otherwise, the ambassador refrained from pressing the issue. With Tibet unable to mount an effective resistance, India neutralized by the Chinese, and the rest of the world silent owing in no small measure to Tibet's failure to seek and secure legal recognition of its independence, the Communists were free to begin the final stage of their operation.

The military invasion of Tibet was inspired by Mao Tse-tung's oft-repeated conviction that "power grows out of the barrel of a gun." In contrast to the year-long propaganda campaign that preceded it, its duration was less than a month. The response of the Tibetan government on both the military and diplomatic fronts was a reflection of the same disunity that had made it inevitable. In each case the government's policies were vacillating, its hopes unrealistic, and its actions ineffective. Militarily the Chinese invasion on the eastern frontier was a disaster for its Tibetan defenders, for while they fought with extraordinary bravery and died in droves defending their homes, they faced insurmountable obstacles. Poorly trained and under generally inept leadership, they were confronted with seasoned veterans of the Communist army who outnumbered them almost ten to one and were armed with modern automatic weapons, artillery, bazookas, and flamethrowers. In pitiful contrast, Chinese intelligence sources indicated that the entire arsenal of the Tibetan army—half of which would have been retained in central Tibet for the defense of Lhasa—consisted of some 30,000 rifles (many of which were classified by the Chinese as either "antiquated" or "unserviceable"), forty machine guns, twenty trench mortars, twenty field pieces, six mountain guns, and ten infantry cannons. That they fought as long as they did against such overwhelming odds is a testament to their courage.

A great deal of controversy has subsequently attached itself to the nature of the Tibetan response to the Communist invasion, so much so that there are few points of common agreement. The very dearth of these in relation to a national tragedy of such major dimensions makes it essential that they be noted:

1. Barely six weeks before the invasion, the Tibetan government replaced Lhalu Shappé, the governor-general of Kham and commander in chief of the eastern command of the Tibetan army stationed in Chamdo, with another Kashag minister named Ngabo Ngawang Jigme.
2. Lhalu's three-year tour of duty in Kham had ended several months before he was relieved by Ngabo.
3. The Tibetan army and local Khampa levies put up a fierce resistance and suffered as many as 4,000 casualties between them.
4. After learning that Communist forces had battled their way over the Upper Yangtse River, Ngabo decided to retreat from Chamdo and strike westward toward Lhasa.
5. Finding his escape route blocked by Communist troops, Ngabo chose to surrender rather than to fight.

The common denominator in all but one of the foregoing events was Ngabo Ngawang Jigme, surely the most popularly despised, secretly admired, and controversial figure in the last half century of Tibetan history. The bastard son of a well-born nun, Ngabo had married the beautiful young widow of a prominent aristocrat and taken the latter's name, a common practice not limited to offspring born out of wedlock, by which the hereditary nobility ensured the continuity of family name and fortune.[4] It is generally acknowledged that his subsequent political career, like that of many government officials during the strife-ridden interregnum period, was furthered more by efficacious pecuniary contributions and family connections than by recognition of his accomplishments and personal qualities. Although strict and punctual in the discharge of his official duties, Ngabo, like many other aristocrats, was addicted to ballroom dancing, Scotch whiskey, and week-long parties. He was also an inveterate gambler who is said to have bet, during a particularly riveting game of mah-jongg, his entire key ring, which he assured his opponent included everything in his household "from the flag on the rooftop to the broom at the gate"; when asked if his wife was included, he uttered a solemn "Yes."[5]

After a short-lived military career as a regimental officer, Ngabo completed a tour of duty as Tsepon in eastern Tibet, and had just turned forty when he was appointed to the Kashag in 1950 and posted to Chamdo. In this way, too, he followed in the elder Ngabo's footsteps: during the last years of the Thirteenth Dalai Lama's reign, the latter had also been a Kalon and governor-general of Kham.

Ngabo's credentials for assuming the governor-generalship of Kham and the command of some 4,000 Tibetan troops stationed there were, if not imposing, certainly more than adequate. He possessed both a basic grasp of military tactics and an invaluable firsthand knowledge of the country. Moreover, according to Robert Ford, "he was said to be brave and resolute and to have no love for the Chinese." Yet the nagging question persists, especially in light of subsequent events: why should Ngabo have been sent to replace Lhalu at such a critical time? Certainly Lhalu's bravery was never in question, nor was his commitment to fighting the Chinese. Ford, who spent a great deal of time with him during the first nine months of 1950, calls him "the man of action—cool, practical, decisive, and completely unafraid." Neither did the manner in which Lhalu administered the provincial government militate against him. To the contrary, he had not only carried out the orders of the central government but had done so in such a manner as to command an unusually high degree of respect from the Khampas, whom he later recruited into an auxiliary corps of invaluable albeit somewhat undisciplined fighting men.

Lhalu's military judgment was equally sound. He realized that under the circumstances (a garrison of 500 men, another 250 in his personal bodyguard, and an indeterminate number of Khampa levies whose heavy arms consisted of four Lewis automatic rifles and three pieces of mountain artillery, which because of a lack of shells were fired only once a year to amuse the locals), it would be impossible to hold Chamdo against a sustained Chinese attack. He decided to move his forces several days' march westward to Lho Dzong, directly across the Salween River on the route to Lhasa, where his troops could not be outflanked. If his men could not prevent the Communists from crossing the single bridge over the wide, swiftly flowing river, Lhalu concluded, they could fade into the mountains behind them. From Lho Dzong to Lhasa the land was wild and rugged, with an average altitude of 12,000 feet and snowbound passes up to 17,000 feet—an ideal place, Lhalu knew, from which to wage a devastating guerrilla war. But he was also aware that he could not move his forces from Chamdo too soon, for to do so would be to leave its people and the largest monastery in Kham at the mercy of the Chinese. "Lhalu was a realist," explains Robert Ford. "He knew that the longer he stayed, the more favorably impressed the Khampas would be. He did not think they would expect the Lhasa troops to stay and fight to the last man when by retreating they could live to fight another day. The plan, therefore, was to hold Chamdo until the track to Lhasa was almost within reach of the Chinese. Then we would evacuate and, if necessary, fight our way out." So why was Lhalu replaced? Ford maintains that Lhalu told him it was a decision of the Kashag, and most former Tibetan government officials agree that Lhalu was recalled simply because his three-year tour of duty was completed. "There was no ulterior motive," says Kungo Liushar, the high-ranking monk official in the Foreign Office in 1950 and later Tibet's foreign minister. "When the replacement orders went through, the situation in the east was not yet critical." But Ford points out that the terms of all Lhasa officials in Chamdo had expired at the same time as Lhalu's and that the central government had asked them to remain at their posts for the duration of the crisis; only Lhalu and his personal staff were called back to Lhasa.

Many Tibetans believe Lhalu was replaced at his own request. Ford disagrees, and argues that "he was not the sort of man to run away from danger." Those holding that Lhalu left of his own accord do not question his courage; rather they feel his decision was motivated by reasons related to factional in-fighting at the seat of government. Either explanation is plausible, and for that matter the two are not entirely incompatible. Lhalu might have requested to be relieved, and the Kashag, in order to present a united front and to save face, might well have acceded to this request but done so in the form of a directive. One thing is certain: Lhalu's departure ended any possibility of effective Tibetan resistance on the eastern frontier.

Ngabo's demeanor upon his arrival in Chamdo as Lhalu's replacement was comforting to apprehensive Tibetan officials, who were surprised at the change of command and doubtful it should have been made at such a critical time. "He seemed to have everything under control," says Robert Ford. "He gave me the impression of being cool and efficient and quietly confident." When the first reports of the Chinese invasion reached the provincial capital, Ford adds, the new governor "looked as cool and unruffled as ever." Ngabo's impassive mien lasted precisely four days longer. "The Chinese had only begun to cross the Drichu [Upper Yangtse River, the *de facto* Sino-Tibetan border] and a Communist agent to run through the streets of Chamdo shouting 'The Chinese are coming! The Chinese are coming!'" remembers one Tibetan bitterly, "and Ngabo took off like a frightened rabbit."

Frightened rabbit or not, Ngabo had little choice but to leave Chamdo; even the resolute Lhalu had recognized the futility of attempting to defend it. But his hasty plan of departure made no provision for the transport of the Khampa soldiers so assiduously recruited by his predecessor, although he was aware that such a move would result in their feeling betrayed. Even if the ethical implications of such an action did not enter into Ngabo's decision, strategic considerations should have dictated that he accommodate as many of the Khampas as possible. In the end many of those left behind laid down their arms rather than defend a government whose representative, they felt, had deserted them, and a few even acted as guides for the enemy forces.

If this ill-advised treatment of the Khampas seems an inexpedient way of mounting an effective resistance, subsequent events indicate that even though Ngabo had been sent to Kham with express orders to fight the Chinese, he never seriously intended doing so once the invasion became a reality. Barely a day's march from Lho Dzong when informed by runners that some Communist troops had marched south from Amdo and stood between his retreating forces and the Salween River, he elected not to fight his way to safety despite the fact that his officers and men were more than willing to do so. "Ngabo came to the conclusion that the Communists knew where we were and would attack us," says Thupten Thonyo, then a forty-five-year-old high-ranking monk official (Khenchun) and one of Lhalu's two primary assistants who had stayed on after the latter's departure to ease the transition of leadership. "He did not want to fight and die without making an attempt at a peaceful settlement, so he headed southward toward the Drogu monastery rather than toward Lhasa."

A day later Ngabo surrendered. "Only six weeks before, he had ridden into Chamdo with all the pomp of an emperor, in brilliant-colored silks and brocades," comments Robert Ford. "Now he looked frightened and miserable in a drab robe of dark-gray serge." If there is a trace of bitterness in these words it is excusable, for Ngabo later worked for the Communists, whereas Ford spent four years in Chinese jails undergoing an intensive program of "thought reform." Not until his release from prison did Ford discover that one of the coded messages he had transmitted to Lhasa just before leaving Chamdo had been a request from Ngabo for permission to surrender, and that the permission had been refused.

The transfer of power in Kham and Ngabo's subsequent refusal to engage the enemy have since become subjects of much controversy. There is little evidence to support assertions of conspiracy; indeed, the fact that Lhalu and Ngabo came from almost identical backgrounds and had similar political sentiments suggests to the contrary that the first of these episodes, while calamitous in its consequences, was honorably motivated, and that the second could well have been more a matter of personal cowardice than of premeditation. The alacrity with which Ngabo capitulated to the Chinese is better explained by the "frightened rabbit" theory than by conjectures of a hypothetical plot. Robert Ford, who left Chamdo several hours after Ngabo and his entourage, perceived when catching up with them the day before the surrender that the phlegmatic governor had been transformed during his flight into "a fugitive, fearful and wretched." In contrast, Thupten Thonyo remembers that on the day after the surrender Ngabo seemed calm, unfrightened, and apparently relieved. The nightmare might have been over for him, but for Tibet it was just beginning. "Ngabo ferociously went to surrender Chamdo," went a Lhasa street song. "Lhalu has run back to surrender Lhasa."

Finally, it should be pointed out that although critically divided over the proper response to Communist threats of "liberation," the Tibetan government had no intention of surrendering and would hardly have approved the replacement of Lhalu with Ngabo if not confident that the latter would carry out its orders. That its confidence was misplaced is unfortunate and even tragic, but as ensuing events demonstrated, the decision had been in no way conspiratorial.

It was obvious from the start of the invasion that despite a surprising victory at Dengko the Tibetan army could not have prevailed in a conventional war against the vastly superior Communist forces. "Even if Lhalu had remained, it would not likely have made much difference," says Kungo Liushar. "The Chinese army has a saying: 'When we attack, we do so like a fish going into the water.' If they encounter resistance in one place, they simply retreat and then probe again elsewhere. When Muja Depön's regiment repelled them at Dengko, therefore, they regrouped and crossed the Yangtse farther north; then they quickly moved south again and almost succeeded in trapping Muja's men between themselves and the river. Against such tactics and such an overwhelming number of enemy troops, Ngabo must have felt that resistance would have been futile. Lhalu may have made other decisions and adopted other tactics, but the result, inevitably, would have been the same."

Liushar's argument is convincing. But the appalling and iniquitous nature of subsequent Communist rule in Tibet, coupled with the well-publicized resistance of Afghani guerrillas since the end of 1979 against a larger, more mobile, better-equipped, and more sophisticated Soviet invading force, has led many Tibetans to believe differently. "The Chinese invasion could have been handled far more effectively had Lhalu remained in charge," states Dorjee Tashi-Para, a former regimental commander. "Despite the fact that our men were greatly outnumbered by the P.L.A. [People's Liberation Army], an effective resistance could have been mounted had Ngabo not run off and surrendered."[6] He is not alone in this conviction.

Theoretically, a formidable guerrilla war could have been waged against the Communists. Although the total strength of the Tibetan army probably did not exceed 8,000 men, they are described by Robert Ford as "tough as nails, incredibly brave, well disciplined, and fanatically loyal" to the Dalai Lama. Had Lhalu's recruitment of the Khampas been practiced on a larger scale and alliances made with some of the powerful Khampa chieftains, the number of fighters could easily have been doubled. Additional military assistance might also have been realized from thousands of troops deserted by the Muslim warlord Ma Pu-feng when he fled from Amdo to Saudi Arabia in a treasure-packed airplane in 1949; many were waging their own guerrilla war against the Communists as late as 1952 and 1953.

The country was also a military paradise for defensive tactics. In Kham and Sikang (the former Chinese province incorporating that area of Kham on the eastern side of the Yangtse), the mountain ranges and rivers run from north to south and would have been made invasion from the east a difficult proposition when complicated with guerrilla activity. Small groups of defenders could have held the narrow mountain passes against far more numerous forces and inflicted substantial losses on the invaders; in the past Tibetans had enjoyed a great measure of success in repelling the Chinese by rolling boulders down these defiles, and there is no reason to believe they could not have been at least as successful in 1950. The fact that there were no motorable roads in Tibet would have precluded the use of armored cars, tanks, or any form of motorized transport. Airplanes would have been likewise useless. There were no landing strips, and attempts to parachute troops into the country would have been exceptionally dangerous from both a topographical and a military standpoint. Because of the long distances involved and the barren nature of much of the land, moreover, Chinese supply lines would have been severely strained.

Finally, there is evidence that the best Communist troops and equipment were being deployed in Korea and that the majority of men sent into Tibet were not acclimatized to the unusually high altitudes on the Roof of the World. Tashi-Para Depön remembers that the unaccustomed lack of oxygen caused many cases of extreme fatigue and altitude sickness among the invading forces. "When they eventually entered Lhasa after Ngabo's capitulation had put an end to Tibetan military resistance," he says, "it was obvious how poor their condition was. Their lips were blue and they seemed ready to collapse with exhaustion. Had they been given the word, I am certain that the Tibetan people would have overcome them."

There can be little doubt that an organized resistance movement would have resulted in enormous losses being inflicted on the invaders. Furthermore, such an action would have forced the Communists to fight on two fronts simultaneously: against guerrillas in Tibet and United Nations forces in Korea. There is, of course, no way to estimate how long such tactics might have proven effective, especially in light of the fact that at the same time they were breaking through in such strength in Kham, the Communists had also sent a small force through the barren uplands of northwestern Tibet on a route used only once before by an invading force, the Dzungar Mongols in 1716. One thing is certain, however: whatever its duration, an organized guerrilla movement would have demonstrated to the world that Tibetans were willing to fight and die to maintain their independence, making it difficult for most of the international community to feign confusion over Tibet's status when news of the invasion was brought to their attention. Unfortunately, the unanimity necessary for the organization of such a movement was not forthcoming from the Tibetan government.

On the diplomatic front, Lhasa reacted at first to news of the invasion—which because of poor communications it did not learn of until some four days after it had begun—just as it had to the Chinese propaganda campaign that preceded it: it did nothing. "The actions of the Lhasa government would have been easier to understand if it had intended to offer only a token resistance to the Chinese and then sue for peace," observes Robert Ford, "but it was not doing anything of the kind. The resistance was real, and Tibet's subsequent appeals to the United Nations showed that there was never any question of surrender. I could only think it was a matter of habit. The government was so used to the policy of saying nothing that might offend or provoke the Chinese that it kept on after provocation had become irrelevant. It was still trying to avert a war that had already broken out."

Only after Ngabo's surrender on October 20 had ended any chance of effective military resistance, and Radio Peking had announced five days later that "People's Army units have been ordered to advance into Tibet to free three million Tibetans from imperialist oppression and to consolidate national defenses on the western borders of China," did the Tibetan government respond. The *Manifesto by Tibetan Leaders*, transmitted by telegram on November 11 from Tsepon Shakabpa's home in Kalimpong, was an appeal to the United Nations. It stated in part:

> The armed invasion of Tibet for the incorporation of Tibet in Communist China through sheer physical force is a clear case of aggression. As long as the people of Tibet are compelled by force to become a part of China against their will and consent, the present invasion of Tibet will be the grossest instance of the violation of the weak by the strong. We therefore appeal through you to the nations of the world to intercede on our behalf and restrain Chinese aggression.

The Tibetan appeal provided the cue for the Chinese to shift the gears of their invasion from direct action to a period of pause and evaluation. They suspended their advance into Tibet and, in order to give themselves time to assess world reaction, hinted that they were settling the matter through direct negotiation with the Tibetans. It was an impeccable strategy.

Only El Salvador had the courage to make a motion condemning the unprovoked aggression of the Chinese Communists, and the two members of the United Nations who might have been expected to support the Tibetan appeal instead played a leading role in obstructing it. Despite the fact that his country had implied recognition of Tibet's *de facto* independence by concluding treaties with it as a sovereign power ever since the fall of the Manchus in 1912, the delegate from the United Kingdom claimed rather ingenuously that the British government found the legal status of Tibet confusing. To this transparent excuse the delegate from India added his assurances that the Chinese and Tibetans would no doubt soon arrive at an agreement by which the latter's autonomy would be ensured. If the British statement was a flagrant evasion of ethical and moral responsibility, the Indian assertion was an outright lie.

In response to delicately worded suggestions by the Indian government in notes of October 21, October 28, and November 1 that instead of military action the Chinese might consider employing the "slower and more enduring method of peaceful approaches" for solving the "Tibetan question," the Chinese replied on November 16 that "Regardless of whether the local authorities of Tibet wish to proceed with peace negotiations, and regardless of whatever results may be achieved by negotiations, no foreign interference will be permitted." Moreover, they added, China wished to make clear that it regarded India's attitude as "deplorable" and noted with "deep regret" that this attitude had been motivated by "foreign influences hostile to China." The Indian government was so intimidated by the Chinese that it even refused Tibet's request to sponsor the appeal on the grounds that since Tibet was not a member of the United Nations it should do so itself. The Soviet Union and Nationalist China claimed that Tibet had always been an integral part of China and opposed any discussion of the issue, and the United States delegate, basing his decision on the spurious Indian assertion, agreed to an adjournment.

Though not so callous as the conduct of the British and Indian delegates nor so smugly self-assured as that of the representatives from the Soviet Union and Nationalist China, the response of the U.S. ambassador was hardly guileless since the United States government was no more "confused" by the legal status of Tibet than was that of the United Kingdom. It will be recalled that when Ilia Tolstoy and Brooke Dolan visited Lhasa in late 1942 they brought with them a letter dated July 3 of that year from Franklin Roosevelt to the Dalai Lama. The manner in which it was addressed:

> His Holiness
> The Dalai Lama
> Supreme Pontiff of the Lama Church
> Lhasa

might not appear significant at first glance, nor might the president's apparently innocent request that its bearers be permitted by the Dalai Lama to visit his "Pontificate and the historic and widely famed city of Lhasa." But it has since been brought to light that the letter was written not by Roosevelt but rather by Secretary of State Cordell Hull, who forwarded it in draft form to the chief executive accompanied by a note, also dated July 3, which advised that "the letter is addressed to the Dalai Lama in his capacity of religious leader of Tibet, *rather than in his capacity of secular leader of Tibet* [italics added], thus avoiding giving any possible offense to the Chinese government which includes Tibet in the territory of the Republic of China." That the subtle implications of Hull's carefully worded missive were not overlooked by the Tibetan government is evident by the Dalai Lama's response to the White House, which made clear that Tibet "values her freedom and independence enjoyed from time immemorial."

Lest there be any doubt that the secretary of state was not only aware of Tibet's *de facto* independence but also reluctant to admit it publicly, his memorandum to the U.S. ambassador in Chungking sent at 10:00 P.M. the same day will put it to rest: the British Foreign Office, Hull informed Ambassador Clarence E. Gauss, had "informally" supplied the State Department with a copy of a telegram concerning the Tibetan refusal to permit passage of supplies to China, which stated that the British government was prepared to threaten Tibet with economic sanctions, but prior to doing so felt the Chinese should also do their part "to facilitate Tibetan acquiescence, as Tibet's reluctance is believed to be largely due to fear of Chinese penetration." Accordingly they had instructed their ambassador to China, Sir Horace James Seymour, to "suggest to the Chinese Government that it give a definite and public undertaking of intention to respect Tibet's autonomy and to refrain from interfering in Tibet's internal administration" before such cooperation would be forthcoming. "For your information," Hull continued, "it may be added that the telegram refers in two instances to Tibetan 'independence' and in another instance to Tibetan 'autonomy.' It is not clear whether these words are used interchangeably or not." In closing, the secretary of state cautioned that "the Chinese Government has long claimed suzerainty over Tibet, the Chinese constitution lists Tibet among areas constituting the territory of the Republic of China, and this Government has at no time raised questions regarding either of these claims."[7]

Much as it would have desired to halt the invasion of the Chinese Communists in Tibet, the U.S. government was constrained from doing so for two major considerations, the more obvious of which was that it had already committed thousands of its troops to fight the Communists in Korea. The other reason was of a more practical nature. "My father and I have discussed the Tibetan problem with our government heads," wrote Lowell Thomas, Jr., before the invasion had started. "If the U.S. offers any kind of military assistance to Tibet, our country must assume the responsibility of maintaining Tibetan independence. But if the Chinese Reds call our bluff, how could we move an army over the Himalayas? How could we supply it? In the final analysis, the U.S. is not the nation to undertake the task." A compelling argument, and one with which it is difficult to find fault. One question, however, does suggest itself: how could the United States, whose foreign policy was still firmly wedded to Chiang Kai-shek, have moved to help the

Tibetans maintain their independence in the face of Nationalist assertions that Tibet was an integral part of China? By agreeing to an adjournment, they successfully evaded having to answer that question.

The news that the General Assembly had declined to consider the question of Tibet came as a tremendous blow to the Tibetan government. "This filled us with consternation," says the Dalai Lama. "We had put our faith in the United Nations as a source of justice, and we were astonished to hear that it was on Britain's initiative that the question had been shelved." The conduct of the governments of both Britain and India, asserts Hugh Richardson, "amounted to an evasion of their moral duty to make plain what they alone had special reason to know—that there was no legal justification for the Chinese invasion of Tibet." The Tibetan government sent two more impassioned telegrams to the United Nations, to which they received no reply. The question of Tibet would not be debated again before that august body until 1959. Tibet's isolation from the rest of the world was no longer self-imposed.

Notes

1. It would appear that in pursuing this course of action, Mao was heeding the advice of Sun-tzu, one of China's greatest military strategists, whom he was fond of quoting. "The truly great general," wrote Sun-tzu in *Ping Fa* (*The Art of War*) some 2,500 years ago, "will serve his emperor best by mastering the art of conquering hostile territory without bloodshed, of capturing cities without entering them, and of vanquishing the enemy without going into battle."

2. For this and subsequent comments, see Robert Ford, *Captured in Tibet* (London, 1957).

3. Lest the prime minister's words be regarded as somewhat optimistic, if not ingenuous, it should be noted that the coexistence of conflicting religions and ideologies is inherent in the Indian mental and spiritual makeup; the inclination is rather toward philosophical relativity and intellectual equivocation than toward absolutes.

4. Ngabo's mother, Ani (Nun) Champala, came from the prestigious Horkhang family whose main estate was Gyama-Trikhang, birthplace of the thirty-third Tibetan king, Songtsen Gampo. His father was a monk official from another ranking noble family who had lived in a flat in Horkhang House, one of Lhasa's largest residences, while his own house was being built.

5. Fortunately for young Tseten Dolkar, her husband won and they went on to have twelve children, four boys and eight girls.

6. Interview with Dorjee Tseten Tashi-Para, Dharamsala, India, May 14, 1980.

7. *Tibet and the Chinese People's Republic: A Report to the International Commission of Jurists by Its Legal Inquiry Committee on Tibet* (Geneva, 1960), 318–326.

Tibetan family   *Darjeeling 1980*

· CHAPTER 12 ·

Seventeen Steps to Subjugation

W HILE ANXIOUSLY AWAITING the reaction of the United Nations General
Assembly to its appeal, the Tibetan government assembled the country's most famous oracles at the Norbulingka palace. Monastic leaders and
government officials entreated the gathering to stand by them in their hour
of need. "In the presence of the Dalai Lama the old men threw themselves at
the feet of the prophetic monks, begging them for once to give them wise
counsel," Heinrich Harrer wrote. "At the climax of his trance the state oracle
reared up and then fell down before the Dalai Lama, crying, 'Make him
king!' The other oracles said much the same thing, and as it was felt that the
voice of the gods ought to be listened to, preparations for the Dalai Lama's
accession to the throne were at once put in hand." To the people of Lhasa,
who for some time had not only been saying openly that the majority of the
Dalai Lama should officially be declared before he had reached the customary age, but had also been taking the unprecedented action of posting no-
tices to this effect around the holy city, the decision was long overdue.

The solemn request by the Kashag that the fifteen-year-old Kündün assume the reins of government came at a most unpropitious time and filled
him with anxiety. "I was far from having finished my religious education,"
he recalls. "I knew nothing about the world and had no experience of politics, and yet I was old enough to know how ignorant I was and how much I
had still to learn. I protested at first that I was too young, for eighteen was
the accepted age for a Dalai Lama to take over active control from his regent." He was neither too young nor too ignorant, however, to realize why
his country had turned to him: "During my minority, there had been dis-
sensions between separate factions in our government, and the administration of the country had deteriorated. We had reached a state in which most
people were anxious to avoid responsibility rather than to accept it. We were
more in need of unity than ever before, and I, as Dalai Lama, was the only
person whom everybody in the country would unanimously follow." On
the eleventh day of the tenth month of the Iron Tiger Year (November 17,

1950) Kündün, already the supreme spiritual leader of Tibet, became his country's supreme temporal ruler as well.

In the meantime Taktser Rinpoche had arrived in Lhasa after a three-month caravan journey from Kumbum and reported at once to the Dalai Lama. He had first heard the tragic news of the invasion, he told his younger brother excitedly, when the Chinese radio operator assigned by the Communists to accompany him, upon being refused entry into Tibet by frontier guards, had blurted out that he had just received word that Chamdo had fallen. He went on to relate in some detail what life had been like under the Communist regime in Amdo, but hesitated before disclosing the reason he had been dispatched to Lhasa by the Chinese. Finally he revealed the truth. "When I had at last finished my story, the Dalai Lama remained silent for a long time, sunk in thought," he remembered. "I looked at him anxiously. What thoughts must have been going through his mind! With a movement of his hand as though to dismiss an evil specter, he indicated that I should rise. We looked into each other's eyes for a moment or two, and behind those thick lenses I saw nothing but sympathy, love, and concern for me." Taktser Rinpoche descended the time-worn steps of the Potala and, relieved that part of the burden had been lifted from his shoulders, wearily mounted his horse and headed for the family home. He rode only a short distance before abruptly bringing his mount to a halt. Looking up at the window of the room in which the young ruler of his country sat pondering the implications of the ominous report, he felt a pang of remorse that the alleviation of his own anxieties had been realized at such a cost.

The news several days later that the United Nations had declined to debate the question of Tibet distressed the Dalai Lama even more than the chilling revelations of his eldest brother. "Our friends would not even help us to present our plea for justice," he remembers. "We felt abandoned to the hordes of the Chinese army."

Under the circumstances Tibet had no alternative but to make an attempt, from a position of conspicuous weakness, to salvage a modicum of its autonomy at the bargaining table. Accordingly one of the officials sent to Lhasa by Ngabo with news of the surrender and a request for authority to negotiate a settlement with the Chinese was sent overland with another official to Chamdo, where they joined Ngabo before eventually leaving for Peking. Two other government officers subsequently made their way to the Chinese capital by sea via Calcutta and Hong Kong. The Tsongdu was reconvened and after much deliberation announced that it believed the Dalai Lama should emulate the actions of his predecessor in response to the Manchu invasion of 1910 and flee from Lhasa. After his return from two years of exile the Great Thirteenth had proven himself one of the finest rulers in the history of Tibet, and it was hoped that the country might later benefit from a similar response to the current crisis. More realistically, the government was aware that by keeping the Dalai Lama from falling into Communist hands it would retain an invaluable, if solitary, bargaining chip for future negotiations.

It was decided to set up a provisional government in Yatung, a village in the Chumbi Valley a day's journey from the Indian border. "I did not want to go at all, but instead to stay where I was and do what I could to help my people," the Dalai Lama says. "But the National Assembly and the Cabinet asked me to go, and in the end I had to give in. As a young and able-bodied man, my instinct was to share whatever risks my people were undergoing, but to Tibetans, the person of the Dalai Lama is supremely precious, and whenever conflict came I had to allow my people to take far more care of me than I would have thought of taking of myself." Before leaving he appointed two prime ministers, a high monk official named Lobsang Tashi and an experienced lay administrator named Lukhangwa, gave them full authority, and made them jointly responsible in his absence for all affairs of state with the need to refer to him only "matters of the very highest importance."

While awaiting the astrologically auspicious day selected for the Dalai Lama's departure from Lhasa, the Tibetan government began sending well-guarded caravans of mules laden with some of the young ruler's personal treasures to the Chumbi Valley. Although it hoped the operation could be kept secret, news of it inevitably leaked out and many nobles began moving their families and most valuable possessions to more secure places. With the exception of Lobsang Samden, who was seriously ill, the holy family preceded the Dalai Lama by several weeks. The sadness felt by the Gyayum Chenmo at leaving Lhasa was tempered by the belief that the move was essential to her son's safety. "I was unable to relax until he, too, had arrived at Yatung. Because of this the details of my trip are vague; I remember only being exhausted from spending so many hours on horseback." Late in the evening of December 18 the high officials who were to accompany the Dalai Lama gathered together with him at the Potala for a final cup of butter tea. They drank in silence, then left their cups standing refilled in symbolic anticipation of a speedy return. About 2:00 A.M. they quietly started their journey, stopping first at the Norbulingka, where the Dalai Lama offered a ceremonial scarf at the altar as a symbol of farewell. Then the young ruler and his ailing brother Lobsang, carried in a litter to avoid the possibility of capture by the Chinese, accompanied by an entourage of some 40 nobles, 200 soldiers, a cluster of cooks and servants, and a train of 1,500 pack animals, headed southward into the night.

News of the flight spread swiftly throughout the land, and before the end of the first day's march thousands of monks from monasteries along the route swarmed out to meet the Dalai Lama. "They flung themselves before the horses' hooves and begged him not to leave them," Heinrich Harrer recalls, "and cried that if he went away they would be left without a leader, at the mercy of the Chinese." It was a delicate situation that caught the officials by surprise. None seemed to know how to make the alarmed throng disperse, but just when it seemed they might not be able to continue their journey, the Dalai Lama took control. The monks fell silent as he explained calmly that he could do more for his country if he did not fall into the hands of the enemy and that he would return as soon as an agreement with them had been reached. Soon the sea of red robes parted, permitting the caravan to proceed, and on January 4, 1951, sixteen days after leaving the holy city, it arrived at its destination.

The Dalai Lama took up residence first in the headquarters of the district governor (Dzongpon) of Chumbi and later in the little Dungkhar monastery, while his officials found quarters in peasant cottages and farmsteads in surrounding villages. An acute shortage of accommodation forced their families to continue on to Kalimpong, Darjeeling, and other points across the Indian border. For the same reason most of the soldiers were sent back to Lhasa, but only after all approaches to the valley had been manned. Since there was at least one representative of every government office in the retinue, a provisional government was established that kept in close contact with Lhasa by relays of special couriers who could complete the 500-mile round trip through the mountains inside of nine days. Communications were later improved by the arrival of Reggie Fox. Nearly crippled with rheumatoid arthritis, the Lhasa-based Londoner had gone to Calcutta on sick leave the previous year after the Lowell Thomases had arranged, upon their return to the United States, for a supply of a new drug, cortisone, to be flown there for his treatment. Although hardly a well man—he would die less than two years later in Kalimpong—Fox had headed for Yatung when informed that the Dalai Lama had arrived there, and set up a radio station.

Despite the presence of Chinese troops in eastern Tibet, the seven months spent by the Dalai Lama in the Chumbi Valley were perhaps the happiest of his life. With Ngabo authorized to negotiate on his behalf in Peking, there was little for the provisional government to do and even less that required his personal attention. The flight at first forced him to forgo his religious studies altogether, and even after settling in Yatung his formerly rigid tutorial schedule was modified and left him more free time than he had enjoyed since his early days in the Potala. Moreover, the dispersion of the official entourage and his relative isolation at the tiny monastery resulted in a relaxation of Lhasa protocol.

For the first time in years the Dalai Lama was free to act his age. With his brother Lobsang, whose health had improved greatly by springtime, he went for long treks into the surrounding hills. In Lhasa there had been little opportunity for physical exercise, and now he made full use of his pent-up energies, much to the chagrin of his attendants. "Wherever we went, they had to follow," said Lobsang Samden with an impish grin. "His Holiness strode over those trails so resolutely that they fell behind constantly, but we could always tell where they were by the sound of their panting." Heinrich Harrer, who remained in the Chumbi Valley until he left for India at the end of March, remembers that in order to keep pace with the brothers the monks were forced to give up snuff and the soldiers tobacco and spirits. "We must have visited every monastery, shrine, and temple in the entire area," recalled Lobsang Samden. "But we also chased butterflies, waded up to our knees in incredibly cold mountain streams, and played tag. His Holiness was particularly interested in the beautiful wildflowers, of all colors and descriptions, which seemed to grow in blankets on the hillsides. I don't think I have ever seen him so gay and carefree."

The young ruler's merriment was not destined to last long, for by the time he and his entourage left Lhasa the Chinese had already begun to consolidate their hold on Kham by building roads and bringing in additional troops and supplies, despite sporadic attacks by marauding bands of Khampas to whom Ngabo's surrender of their ancestral lands was an irrelevancy. Their unexpectedly swift victory in both eastern and western Tibet and the studied manner in which the United Nations divested itself of any responsibility for Tibetan freedom indicated that they might have simply pressed on to Lhasa with little fear of effective opposition once the winter snows had stopped and the mountain passes were again traversable. Instead they chose to follow Bismarck's advice to "settle everything by discussions, but keep a million bayonets behind."[1]

The Sino-Tibetan negotiations that began in Peking on April 29, 1951, were a series of one-sided sparring sessions whose ostensible purpose was to give the adversaries a chance to probe each other's weaknesses, but which was in reality a face-saving device that provided the underdogs an opportunity to demonstrate their diplomatic footwork before prudently succumbing. The fight was fixed long before the Tibetans arrived at the negotiating arena, and although they held up well at the outset and managed to land some telling blows, they were eventually overwhelmed. At the initial meeting the Communist delegation set forth a ready-made draft treaty consisting of ten articles so unconscionable as to make a mockery of the proceedings, to which the five-man Tibetan delegation headed by Ngabo countered with a well-documented claim that Tibet was an independent country—a defiant gesture in the face of such overwhelming odds. After several days of inconclusive in-fighting from these antithetical stances, the Chinese suddenly shifted their attack, abandoning the pretense of negotiation for the reality of ultimatum. "They expanded the scope of the agreement to seventeen points which we were compelled to recognize," the delegate Dzasa Khemey reported later.[2] "The Chinese threatened that if His Holiness and the Tibetan people, monk and lay, did not accept the terms of the agreement, they would be dealt with accordingly." Under such duress the Dalai Lama's representatives had no choice but to affix their signatures to the *Agreement on Measures for the Peaceful Liberation of Tibet* on May 23, 1951.

The Seventeen-Point Agreement, as this document is more commonly known, was the first Sino-Tibetan treaty since that of A.D. 821. Its rambling, tendentious preamble began with the assertion that Tibet was but one of many nationalities within the boundaries of the "Great Motherland," which had during the past century been "penetrated" by "imperialist forces" carrying out "all kinds of deceptions and provocations." The Dalai Lama's government was accused not only of failing to oppose the "imperialistic deception and provocation," but also of adopting "an unpatriotic attitude toward the Great Motherland," which had resulted in the Tibetan people's being "plunged into the depths of enslavement and sufferings." The People's Liberation Army, it went on to explain, had been ordered to "march into Tibet" so that Tibetans could be freed from "the influences of aggressive imperialist forces" and enabled to "return to the Big Family of the Chinese People's Republic."

While the wording of the ensuing clauses was precise with reference to the rights guaranteed the "Great Motherland" in the future administration of Tibet, it was deliberately vague and ambiguous when it specified those to be preserved for the "Tibetan nationality." Particularly clear, for example, were those passages which effectively negated any Tibetan claims of independence as long as the document remained in effect. Article 1 directed that Tibet "unite and drive out imperialist aggressive forces" and "return to the Big Family of the Motherland," Article 2 that the "local government" actively assist the P.L.A. "to enter Tibet and consolidate the national defense," Article 8 that the Tibetan Army "be reorganized by stages into the P.L.A.," and Article 14 that "the centralized handling of all existing affairs of the area of Tibet" be vested in Peking.

Another group of skillfully contrived provisions, while purportedly indicating a Chinese commitment to maintain the existing social, political, and economic structure of Tibet, was intermingled with articles whose conditions, if enforced, would be contradictory in nature. Article 3 granted to Tibetans the right of "exercising national regional autonomy," Article 4 that of retaining their political system, government officials, and in particular the "established status, functions, and powers of the Dalai Lama," Article 7 freedom to pursue traditional "religious beliefs, customs, and habits" together with the assurance that their monasteries would be protected; and Article 13 promised that upon entering Tibet the P.L.A. would be fair "in all buying and selling and not arbitrarily take a needle or thread from the people."

As clear as they seemed, however, the above promises of regional autonomy were simultaneously qualified, either tacitly or directly, by companion clauses. Article 5 stipulated that the "established status, functions, and powers" of the Panchen Lama be restored; and Article 6 specified that what was meant thereby was the resumption of the amicable relations that had existed between the Thirteenth Dalai Lama and the Seventh Panchen Lama (erroneously identified in the document as the Ninth Incarnation) before the latter's flight from Tibet in 1923. Moreover, Article 9 asserted that "step by step in accordance with the actual conditions" in Tibet "the spoken and written language and school education should be developed," and Article 10 that in similar circumstances "Tibetan agriculture, livestock raising, industry, and commerce" were to be encouraged and "the people's livelihood" improved. Yet all four of these were seemingly qualified in turn by Article 11, whose provisions were of vital importance to the perpetuation of Tibetan civilization since they stated that there was to be "no compulsion" for reform on the part of the Chinese, that the "local government of Tibet" was "to carry out reforms of its own accord," and that "when the people raise demands for reform" they were to be settled "by means of consultation with the leading personnel of Tibet."

This purposely equivocal pattern is also evident when one compares provisions for the prospective revision of the internal administration of Tibet. Article 12 declared generously that "insofar as former pro-imperialist and pro-Kuomintang officials resolutely sever relations with imperialism and the K.M.T. [Kuomintang] and do not engage in sabotage or resistance, they may continue to hold office irrespective of their past." These concessions, such as they were, were largely offset by the provisions of Article 15, which envisioned the establishment by Peking of a military area headquarters as well as a military and administrative committee in Tibet "to ensure the implementation" of the agreement. While the first agency was to be manned solely by Chinese, the latter would in addition "absorb as many local Tibetan personnel as possible to take part in the work," to be selected from "patriotic elements from the local government of Tibet, various districts, and various principal monasteries." The candidates were to be chosen from a roster drawn up "after consultation between the representatives designated by the Chinese People's Government and various quarters concerned and . . . submitted to the C.P.G. for appointment."

The two final provisions were less ambiguous. Declaring that the funds necessary for the maintenance of all Chinese personnel in Tibet were to be provided by the C.P.G., Article 16 ensured the cooperation of the local populace by requiring the Tibetan government to "assist the P.L.A. in the purchase and transport of food, fodder, and other daily necessities." In conclusion, Article 17 affirmed that the agreement would come into force "immediately after signature and seals are affixed to it." On the surface, the relationship between Peking and Lhasa as defined in the Seventeen-Point Agreement closely resembled those of the Yüan and Ch'ing dynasties. Tibet's external affairs were placed in the hands of the C.P.G., and her internal affairs remained the responsibility of the "local government of Tibet." Thus, while it was to be nominally a sovereign, Peking seemed willing to limit its role to that of a suzerain. There were, however, several major differences. First of all, although tacitly admitting the overlordship of the Mongol (1279–1350) and Manchu (1720–1911) emperors, never before had the Tibetans been forced to sign a treaty to that effect. Secondly, the patron–lama relationship that had existed between the Mongol emperors and Sakya lamas and later between the Manchu emperors and Dalai Lamas was conspicuously absent since the new overlords derived their spiritual guidance from the teachings of Marx and Mao. Last, never had provision been made for nearly so great a military presence.

In order to appreciate the nature of subsequent Chinese rule in Tibet, it is essential that three factors regarding the enactment of the Seventeen-Point Agreement be understood clearly. To begin with, rather than herald Tibet's return to the "Big Family of the Motherland" through the affirmation of mutually beneficial terms and principles, the document instead conveyed the impression of a magnanimous gesture by the Chinese to a subject minority. While clearly divesting Tibet of her independence, it provided in return only vague and conflicting promises to respect Tibetan regional autonomy.

Moreover, the deliberate ambiguity of the apparent concessions indicates that the Chinese never intended Tibet to enjoy any real measure of regional autonomy and worded the document in this manner so as to give themselves license to institute future unilateral reforms without flagrantly violating its provisions. Certainly a revolutionary government like that of the Chinese Communists would hardly have sanctioned the perpetuation within the newly enlarged boundaries of the "Great Motherland" of a civilization whose values were so contrary to its own. The provisions that promised not to alter Tibet's social, economic, and political systems were dictated not by a sincere Chinese commitment to protect the regional autonomy of "national minorities" within the People's Republic, but rather by a pair of strategic considerations.

The first of these considerations was the desire of the Chinese to complete their conquest of Tibet through negotiation and political pressure rather than by the more expensive and embittering method of warfare, and the inclusion of these concessions, despite their equivocal nature, was intended to mollify the Tibetan delegation. Second, the Chinese were aware that their chances of successfully effecting a peaceful domination of Tibet would be greatly enhanced if they could control the Dalai Lama. They realized that if military action was renewed or the terms of the agreement were too harsh, there was nothing to prevent him from simply crossing the border into India.

Finally, it is apparent that despite Ngabo's subsequent allegation that the Seventeen-Point Agreement was signed only after "detailed discussions on an intimate and friendly basis with the plenipotentiary delegates of the Central [i.e., Chinese] Government, which arrived at unanimous opinions satisfactory to both parties," the facts indicate otherwise. On the other hand, it is difficult to corroborate claims by the Tibetan government that its delegates in Peking had been threatened with personal violence if they failed to comply and prevented from reporting back to them before the agreement was finalized. However, there is an abundance of evidence to substantiate assertions that the Dalai Lama's representatives acceded to the terms set before them only under duress.

The preamble to the Seventeen-Point Agreement made clear that the P.L.A. had been ordered to "march into Tibet" to force the Tibetan government to "conduct talks" which would lead to the "peaceful liberation" of their country—a curious manner in which to begin "intimate and friendly" discussions. It might be well to remember also that not until some 4,000 Tibetans had died defending their homeland, not until Ngabo's surrender to the P.L.A. had ended Tibetan military resistance, and not until the Tibetan government had made several unsuccessful appeals to the U.N. General Assembly and Security Council did the Tibetans agree to begin "peaceful negotiations" at all. Furthermore, one of the Tibetan team later reported that once the meetings were under way he and his fellow delegates had been threatened with the resumption of military operations against Tibet if they refused to comply with demands that they sign the Chinese-dictated document, which purportedly reflected the "unanimous opinions satisfactory to both parties." Of course there are no transcripts of these proceedings, but considering the Chinese invasion and subsequent military occupation of eastern Tibet, the unflagging Chinese commitment to "liberate" the remainder of the country, and the distinctly one-sided nature of the document in question, the implications are obvious.[3]

The Tibetan government was well aware that once in Peking its delegates might be pressured by the Chinese into making greater concessions than it was willing to accept; and to counteract such a possibility, as well as to continue playing for time during which it was hoped its bargaining position might somehow improve, it engaged in a bit of diplomatic subterfuge. While empowering the group to negotiate and perhaps even to sign an agreement, the government made its ratification subject to the ceremonial affixing of the Dalai Lama's official seal. Although prior knowledge of these arrangements would not have troubled the Chinese, who had stipulated in Article 17 that the agreement would become effective "immediately after signature and seals are affixed to it," they were understandably furious when not advised until the eve of the document's enactment that the Dalai Lama's seal was with him in Yatung. The importance of the seal transcended its ceremonial use, because without it the Seventeen-Point Agreement would be in the eyes of the Tibetan people a worthless document and the Chinese still an enemy and invader. Rather than acquiesce to the request of the Tibetan delegation that they be permitted to report to Yatung with the professed intention of securing the approval of the Dalai Lama and his government, Peking instead decided to fabricate counterfeit seals and get on with its occupation of Tibet.

May 23 had been a balmy spring day, but as darkness crept stealthily over the Chumbi Valley it grew suddenly chilly. The Dalai Lama, his brother

Lobsang, and his closest advisers gathered around Reggie Fox's radio as they had done each evening for the past month while anxiously awaiting news of the negotiations. The group fell silent as the time drew near for Radio Peking to come on the air, and listened intently once the broadcast had begun. The announcer had a familiar voice. Incredulously, they heard it calmly spell out in seventeen steps the bitter fact that Tibet had ceased to exist as a nation. The voice belonged to Ngabo.

The arrival a few days later of a telegram from Ngabo advising that the Chinese were dispatching via Yatung a general named Chang Ching-wu to represent them at Lhasa made a prompt Tibetan response imperative. Would the government return to Lhasa and attempt to coexist with the Chinese under the terms of the Seventeen-Point Agreement, or would it flee into India with its young ruler? The final decision rested with the Dalai Lama, and it is likely that the fifteen-year-old hierarch was strongly tempted to choose the latter course. He had agreed only with reluctance to the premature assumption of his temporal powers because of the crisis facing his country, and just as reluctantly had left Lhasa only when it had been made clear to him how important he was to both the Tibetan people and the Chinese government. But that had been six months earlier, with the P.L.A. far from the holy city and the Communist occupation of Tibet only a cloud, albeit an ominous one, on the horizon. With the Seventeen-Point Agreement in effect, however illegitimately, and with General Chang en route to meet him on the way to Lhasa, the cloud had proliferated into a gray canopy over the entire land that threatened to inundate Tibet with an unwelcome and untimely rain. Ngabo's broadcast brought to the fore a plethora of conflicting forces that converged, inevitably, on the person of the Dalai Lama. For the first time in his life he began to feel the full weight of the formidable responsibilities accorded him, and he suspected that in the future they would grow ever more burdensome.

Peking quite naturally wanted the Dalai Lama to return to Lhasa, and an important part of General Chang's mission was to convince him to do so. The young ruler was aware of the fact that because of his age and lack of political experience the Chinese hoped to mold him into a puppet through whom they might exert more effective control over the Tibetan people, and he could hardly have been enthusiastic at the prospect. On the other hand, it has been suggested that the United States might have chosen this time, via coded radio contact between Kalimpong and Yatung, to urge him to flee. According to this theory, admittedly difficult to substantiate but certainly plausible, in return for the Dalai Lama's public renunciation of the Seventeen-Point Agreement and subsequent flight to India, the American government would have taken up the matter of Tibetan independence and Chinese aggression at the United Nations. Such a move would have provided a dramatic opportunity to remind the international community that the spread of Communism was a constant threat to world peace; however, military assistance would have been out of the question, owing to a combination of American public opinion and the bitter lessons of Korea. To the Tibetan people, who would have suffered thereby the loss of their beloved leader in return for Western expressions of outrage, it would have been a national tragedy.

Nor were foreign pressures the only ones confronting the Dalai Lama during his sojourn in Yatung. He realized that the factionalism pervading the Lhasa court during his minority had neither died nor been left behind in the holy city. Most of the country's noble families had fled in his wake, and many, unable to find accommodation in the Chumbi Valley, had continued on across the border. The majority of them were fearful lest the Communists appropriate their estates and divest them of their privileges despite the vaguely reassuring terms of the Seventeen-Point Agreement, and implored the young ruler to seek exile in India. The majority of monastic leaders, to the contrary, urged the Dalai Lama to return. They reminded him that he had been reborn to provide spiritual and temporal leadership to the Tibetan people and that it would be impossible for him to fulfill either role if he left the country. As long as his physical well-being was assured, they felt strongly that he should devote his life to helping his people live under the rule of the godless invader. Not even within his own cabinet was he able to find unanimity of agreement as to the course he should take.

During the entirety of his stay in Yatung, moreover, delegations drawn from all classes of the population and from all areas of the country kept flocking there to beg him to return to Lhasa and help guide the nation's destiny. "The whole of Tibet was sunk in depression," remembers Heinrich Harrer. "Not until then did I realize how closely the people and their king were bound to one another. Without the blessing of his presence, the country could never prosper." At last the Dalai Lama decided to await the visit of General Chang Ching-wu before he made a final decision. "I was not looking forward to meeting him," he says. "I had never seen a Chinese general, and it was a rather forbidding prospect. Nobody could know how he would behave—whether he would be sympathetic, or arrive as a conqueror." General Chang arrived in Yatung on July 14 and after consulting with Tibetan officials agreed to meet the Dalai Lama two days later on the rooftop pavilion of the Dungkhar monastery. "When the time came," recalls the Dalai Lama, "I was peering out of a window to see what he looked like. I do not know exactly what I expected, but what I saw was three men in gray suits and peaked caps who looked extremely drab and insignificant among the splendid figures of my officials in their red and golden robes. Had I but known, the drabness was the state to which China was to reduce us all before the end, and the insignificance was certainly an illusion."

A short, slight man in his mid-forties, the representative of the Central People's Government in Tibet proved to be friendly and informal despite his stern visage. He insisted that the meeting be conducted on equal terms, so chairs were provided to replace the cushions normally dictated by Tibetan protocol. "Later I got to know him quite well," says the Dalai Lama. "He was, I think, a decent man, a man of good heart. But very short-tempered. Without warning his face would suddenly turn bright red and his voice would rise, then moments later he would be so calm it was difficult to believe he was the same person. A true Chinese. Unfortunately he later suffered very much during the Cultural Revolution, and now he is no more." During this initial meeting, the general kept his temper under control. Stressing that his government was sincerely committed to the preservation of Tibetan regional autonomy under the terms of the Seventeen-Point Agreement, he exhorted the Dalai Lama to return to Lhasa.

At last the young ruler gave in. "We were helpless," he explains. "Without friends there was nothing else we could do but acquiesce, submit to the Chinese dictates in spite of our strong opposition, and swallow our resentment. We could only hope that the Chinese would keep their side of this forced, one-sided bargain." On August 17, 1951, exactly six weeks after his sixteenth birthday, he returned to Lhasa to lead his people.

Notes

1. The following analysis is based to a large extent upon Werner Levi, "Tibet under Chinese Communist Rule," *Far Eastern Survey* 23 (January 1954), 1–9, and George Ginsburgs and Michael Mathos, *Communist China and Tibet: The First Dozen Years* (The Hague, 1964).

2. Dzasa Khemey Sonam Wangdu was one of the three attendants in Kyitsang Rinpoche's search party which discovered the Fourteenth Dalai Lama. Of Mongolian origin, *Dzasa* was a title of high honor awarded to senior government officials, both lay and monk. In 1638, Gusri Khan of the Qośot Mongols came to Lhasa and received religious instruction from the Fifth Dalai Lama, who bestowed titles on him and his officers. In return the Khan gave titles to the Dalai Lama's subordinates, which included *Dzasa*, *Theji*, *Ta Lama*, and *Dayan*, all of which were used by high-ranking Tibetan officials through 1959. The two heads of the Bureau of Foreign Affairs held the rank of Dzasa, as did the two commanders-in-chief of the Military Department—of whom Khemey was one.

3. This does not necessarily indicate that because it was signed under duress the Seventeen-Point Agreement was invalid, because the law on the effect of duress is the subject of conflicting opinions. See International Commission of Jurists, *The Question of Tibet and the Rule of Law* (Geneva, 1960), 96–97.

The Sixth Panchen Lama   *Peking 1934*

· CHAPTER 13 ·

Divide and Rule

E VEN WHILE THE DALAI LAMA and General Chang were meeting in the Chumbi Valley, a 3,000-man P.L.A. vanguard was marching westward from Kham under the command of General Wang Ching-ming, the "Hero of Chamdo" and commander of the Second Field Army, which reached the outskirts of Lhasa on the evening of September 8 and encamped there overnight. Early the next morning an advance guard entered the city and patrolled the route of march, keeping back the curious Tibetans who had begun to gather and ensuring that those carrying swords remained far to the rear. Over 20,000 Tibetans turned out to witness the arrival of what they called Tenda Gyamar, "Red Chinese Enemies of Religion." Most of the spectators were sullenly quiet, gazing at the long gray line of foreigners with apparent indifference. Some wept. Others spat and clapped—Tibetans clap to drive out scapegoats—and a few children threw stones. A number of young monks knotted the ends of their shawls and used them to hit the soldiers riding past. But the well-disciplined Chinese refused to be goaded, although an ugly incident was almost provoked when the large framed portraits of Mao Tse-tung, Chou En-lai, and Chu Teh borne proudly aloft at the head of the procession were smashed by a sudden gust of wind to the accompaniment of gleeful Tibetan applause. On October 26 another 5,000 troops under Generals Chang Kuo-hua and Tan Kuan-sen arrived in the holy city, and by the end of November substantial numbers of P.L.A. soldiers had entered both Gyantse and Shigatse.

From the beginning, Peking authorities adopted a policy of restraint and tolerance toward the Tibetans. Each day loudspeakers assured them that the terms of the Seventeen-Point Agreement would be honored, that the P.L.A. had come as friends and helpers, and that the Tibetan way of life would not be interfered with in any way. The Great Mao Tse-tung, the people were reminded over and over again, wanted to free Tibet from the grip of imperialists and make all Tibetans happy. The first of Mao's aims, of course, had been accomplished long before the loudspeakers ever arrived in central Tibet. Hugh Richardson had been gone for a year, Heinrich Harrer and Peter Aufschnaiter almost six months. Reggie Fox had gone to Kalimpong upon the return of the Dalai Lama to the capital, and Robert Ford had already spent close to a year in Chinese prisons. Mao's second aim would prove somewhat more difficult to fulfill.

The scenes Robert Ford describes in Kham during the two days following Ngabo's surrender, during which the Communists attempted to win over the Tibetan people by peaceful means, were duplicated all over Tibet. Such tactics have since been corroborated by the testimony of thousands of Tibetans. After being filmed "surrendering" their arms for the second time, Ngabo's troops were addressed by a Chinese political officer who explained that the P.L.A. had come to bring peace to Tibet and to liberate the country from "foreign devils" who had been sitting on the necks of the people and keeping them apart from the Great Motherland. "They were completely bewildered," remembers Ford, "for I was the only foreign devil most of them had ever seen, and they could not imagine where all the other foreigners were that needed such a large army to turn them out." The Chinese promised to respect the Tibetan religion and customs. Moreover, Ford notes sardonically, "There was no appeal to the workers of the world to unite. The masses were not invited to throw off their chains. Ngabo and Company were evidently going to keep their jobs as long as they played ball with the Chinese."

More significantly, the Chinese made clear they would honor their word. They treated the monks, soldiers, and civilians with respect and refrained from confiscating private property; not only did the advance troops abstain from living off the land, but they even brought meat and rice with them. Brotherhood was the keynote, and the contemptuous word *mantze* (barbarian) was forbidden. Prisoners of war were provided with safe-conduct passes and money and told to return to their homes. ("They are strange people," said one prisoner incredulously. "I cut off eight of their heads with my sword and they just let me go!") Impressed and relieved—never before had Chinese troops in Tibet behaved so well—many returned to their villages convinced that the Communists meant them no harm and reassured their families and friends that there was nothing to fear. Similar treatment was accorded the captured Tibetan officials with the exception of Ford, who was detained as a spy. At a meeting two days after the surrender at Ngabo's former Chamdo headquarters, they were told by General Wang of the great benefits the Communists would bring to Tibet: hospitals, schools, roads, improvements in agriculture and industry. The general spoke enthusiastically about Soviet wheat farming in the Arctic and predicted even better results for Tibet, whose standard of living, he added, had been kept down artificially by unscrupulous British and American imperialists and would improve dramatically under Chinese supervision. Then the general changed his tone. "Not all the Tibetan people are aware of this," he conceded, "and we rely on you to teach them and explain our policy to them. You are their leaders, and they look up to you. We shall help you to use your prestige and influence for the people's good."

"There it was," remembers Ford. "Not a word about land reform or the rights of peasants and the working class. The Chinese were backing the officials"—those, that is, who "played ball." It was an efficacious strategy but one that depended ultimately on the cooperation of the most important "official" of them all, the Dalai Lama himself, who manifested no inclination to play games. While the young ruler's lack of tractability was a disappointment to the Communists, it was hardly a disaster. A master strategist like Mao Tse-tung would not have permitted his plan to transform Tibet into a socialist state indistinguishable from any other part of the People's Republic to hinge on the acquiescence of a single individual, even one in whom reposed such substantial and far-reaching powers. To the contrary, well before the Dalai Lama returned from Yatung, Mao had decided to promote Chinese control over Tibet by an expedient application of the classical principle of divide and rule. It was a technique that had played a major role in relations between China and the Central Asian peoples to her north and west for over two thousand years.

Chinese dynasties were popularly believed to have come into existence through a "mandate of heaven," which vested in the emperor sole authority to guide the destinies of his people. In practice, however, the emperor and his hereditary successors within each dynasty could rule only through a firmly entrenched administrative organization, and his real power depended on the degree of control he was able to exercise over the bureaucracy and over the scholar-gentry, the ruling social group possessing great influence and authority at the local level. Consequently, civil and military officials were held directly accountable to the central government and their authority was not only limited but also designed to overlap and conflict with that of their colleagues, thus giving the emperor frequent opportunities to manipulate and play them off against each other. Similarly, the ability of the emperors to keep the powerful nomad chieftains on their borders from uniting to attack Chinese territory, or to incorporate their extensive domains into the Imperial Empire, depended in large measure on provoking them to war among themselves. This was possible only when the government was strong and military garrisons were established in nomad territory on the other side of the Great Wall, which by itself had often proven an ineffective barrier to the constant threat of invasion. When the government was in decline, on the other hand, a weakened China risked invasion and often conquest by the nomads, who on a number of occasions replaced the Chinese dynasties with their own. The most notable of these were the Yüan (1279–1368), by steppe nomads from Mongolia, and the Ch'ing (1644–1911), by forest nomads from Manchuria. These conquests were more than mere military affairs, however, for a country as large and complex as China could hardly be governed like a nomad tribe. "You can conquer China on horseback," it was said, "but you have to dismount to rule." Accordingly whoever ruled China, whether native or "barbarian," did so from Peking and through traditional Chinese bureaucratic patterns.

The system of divide and rule reached its greatest refinement during the last dynasty of China, the Ch'ing. In addition to the intricate system of administrative checks and balances previously mentioned, the Manchus appointed their own people to most of the top positions and placed a Manchu official at the side of the Chinese in the most important agencies of the central government. To prevent the concentration of power in the hands of a few great khans, they grouped tribes together under Mongol leaders whom they nominated and controlled partly by bribery, partly by threats, and partly by providing a number of them with Chinese princesses as wives. The same formula of ruling by division was adapted to suit the unique situation in Tibet. There the Manchus made substantial contributions to the monasteries, in the hope of exerting political control through influence on the monastic community while simultaneously tempering the authority of an aristocratic leadership less liable to be receptive to their plans and more liable to provide a military threat if in the ascendancy. More directly, they actively promoted internal discord by playing off against each other Tibet's two most important incarnations, the Dalai Lama and the Panchen Lama.

Mao's plan in 1951 to transform Tibet from a theocratic to a socialist state commenced with a series of measures designed to disperse regional political power, rekindle factional dissension, weaken the Lhasa government, and undermine both the temporal and spiritual authority of the Dalai Lama. The measures, while seemingly consistent with the reassuring language of the Seventeen-Point Agreement, either circumvented the document by the application of casuistic Chinese interpretations or violated it altogether.[1]

The first of these was to redefine what was meant by the "Local Government of Tibet." To the Tibetans the phrase implied no less than the administration by Lhasa of the entire territory independent of Chinese rule since the fall of the Manchus.[2] From the very outset Peking, though nominally in agreement, dealt with the country as if it were composed of three separate and distinct parts: the Dalai Lama's domain of central Tibet, the Panchen Lama's less extensive jurisdiction southwest of Lhasa near the city of Shigatse, and the region of Kham surrounding Chamdo, the provincial capital. There was no historical basis for this action whatsoever, since each had always been under Lhasa's rule. Nor was there any provision for it in the Seventeen-Point Agreement; to the contrary, Article 3 stated clearly that "the Tibetan people have the right of exercising national regional autonomy" and Article 4 that "the central authorities will not alter the existing political system in Tibet." Nevertheless the Communists eventually succeeded not only in partitioning Tibet but also in relegating the Lhasa government to a position of equality with the administrations of Shigatse and

Chamdo. Once this had been accomplished they made it clear that the provisions of the 1951 treaty applied only to territory remaining under the Dalai Lama's dominion—that is, the newly defined "Local Government of Tibet"—and denied to the Dalai Lama the right to protest the initiation of reforms in the other districts where his temporal authority and the protective "guarantees" of the document were no longer applicable.

Peking extended its control over each of these *de facto* entities in a manner befitting their unique social and political situations and did so most directly in Chamdo, which from the very outset was singled out for much closer integration into the People's Republic than the rest of Tibet. One reason for this was the proximity of the region to China and its strategic importance as the natural gateway to Lhasa and central Tibet. Another had to do with the nature of the Khampas themselves. A proud, warlike, feuding people, they were, despite a deep and abiding spiritual loyalty to the Dalai Lama, traditionally resistant to Lhasa's political control. The distance of their land from the capital stimulated a state of semi-independence in which loyalty was extended to local clans rather than to the secular administrators posted in Chamdo by the central government.

In the wake of the Communist invasion many Khampas were taken in by Chinese propaganda, which began virtually upon Ngabo's surrender. Moreover, disaffected Khampas on both sides of the Yangtse were promised independence from Lhasa in return for cooperation. In early 1951, before the Tibetan delegation had signed the Seventeen-Point Agreement, a "People's Liberation Committee" was begun in Chamdo. Empowered to administer the area without reference to the Lhasa government, it was headed by Ngabo, who, although still a Kalon in the Dalai Lama's administration, was working for the Communists through the local Chinese military headquarters.

The Communists deemed it expedient to exercise their authority less directly in Shigatse than in Chamdo. They did so through their control of the Panchen Lama, whom they hastened to transform into an incarnation equal in stature to the Dalai Lama by according him secular powers that neither he nor his six predecessors had ever enjoyed. The motive underlying the action was threefold: to rekindle traditional Chinese-provoked hostility between the two incarnations and especially between their respective entourages; to weaken the supreme authority of the Dalai Lama; and to promote the Panchen as an alternative to the latter if they were unable to bend the Lhasa government to their will. While the return to Tibet by the Panchen Lama and the resumption of his traditional status were stipulated in the Seventeen-Point Agreement despite Tibetan awareness that his presence in the country would be exploited by the Chinese for divisive purposes, there was no historical precedent for his assumption of any temporal authority. To the contrary, the very nature of his incarnation logically precluded his participation in the political arena.

The conflict between the entourages of the two great lamas had begun in the early eighteenth century when the Manchus, shortly after establishing their protectorate over Tibet, initiated tactics designed to create an enduring rivalry between the incarnations and to build up the Second Panchen, and therefore his successive reincarnations, as a tool to further their interests in the country. The Manchus maintained that as the reincarnation of a purely meditative being the Panchen was spiritually "superior" to the Dalai Lama, whose spiritual purity was sullied by contact with the mundane world. Notwithstanding this tenuous metaphysical declaration, they did not feel constrained from granting the Panchen temporal authority over several districts in the vicinity of Shigatse. The recognition of this authority by Lhasa would presumably have caused Tibetans either to lose faith in their newly defiled Panchen or to question the validity of his incarnation, but the government never acknowledged its validity and viewed the Panchen's rights over the districts no differently than they did those exercised by any monastic or aristocratic feudal lord—that is, subject to the central control of Lhasa.

The Manchus had even gone so far as to attempt to invest the line of Panchens with a spurious numerical "equality" with the Dalai Lamas by insisting that there had been three Panchen incarnations before the Fifth Dalai Lama had designated his tutor as first of the line. Here, too, their designs were frustrated, for not only did all but a handful of Tibetans ignore the attempt (which in any event would neither have elevated the stature of the one nor diminished that of the other), but the successive Panchens enjoyed a far greater longevity than the Dalai Lamas and thus continued to lose ground numerically. The Manchu effort was not all in vain, however. Once it took root, the rivalry between the courts of Tashilhunpo and Lhasa represented a constant device for promoting internal dissension, as the tragic story of the Sixth Panchen Lama will attest.

Short in stature and with a fair complexion, Chökyi Nyima (1883–1937) was a charming and gentle man seven years younger than the Thirteenth Dalai Lama. "The smile with which he regards you is touched with the quiet saintliness of one who prays and works for all mankind," wrote Charles Bell after meeting him at Tashilhunpo in 1906, "but it is at the same time the smile of a friend who takes a personal and sympathetic interest in your own concerns. It is not surprising that he should be loved by his people. It is good that there is such a man in Tibet; it is good that there are such men in the world." The same cannot be said for the Panchen's circle of advisers. After the Dalai Lama fled to India in the wake of the 1910 invasion, the Panchen was wooed by the Manchus but refused to cooperate. Members of his court proved more tractable, and when the Great Thirteenth returned in 1913, relations between the respective entourages were even less friendly and more suspicious than usual. Although tensions eased somewhat when the two lamas held a friendly meeting in 1918—it is said that when they parted the Dalai Lama had taken a lantern from one of his attendants and personally escorted the Panchen to the front gate—the situation continued to be a difficult one.

Matters came to a head in 1922 when Lhasa demanded a contribution from Tashilhunpo to help meet the cost of the growing Tibetan army. Believing that the new taxes were being imposed on them as punishment for consorting with the Manchus and fearing further reprisals, the Panchen's officials fled to China, taking him with them. The Panchen left behind a letter in which he protested what he believed were machinations of evil people misleading the Dalai Lama and promised to return when someone could be found to mediate between himself and the latter. After reading it, the Great Thirteenth remarked scornfully that the Panchen should have consulted his "father and teacher" instead of "wandering away into uninhabited places, to his great peril, like a moth attracted by the candlelight."[3] All of Tibet was saddened by the flight of the Panchen and hoped for his speedy return, for it was common knowledge that the two great lamas were untouched by the feelings of antagonism kept alive by their subordinates. But this was not to be, for the Nationalist government insisted that the Panchen and his entourage be accompanied back to Shigatse by a large contingent of Chinese troops, a stipulation to which the Tibetans would not agree. The Sixth Panchen Lama never again set foot in his country, and died at Sining in 1937.

With the aid of the Tibetan government, a traditional search was made for the new incarnation by officials at Shigatse and Sining, and in 1944 three candidates emerged. The Sining authorities—that is, those attendants of the late Panchen Lama who had fled with him to China in 1923—refused to bring their candidate to Tashilhunpo for testing unless he was first accorded recognition as the true rebirth. Lhasa quite naturally refused, and matters remained at an impasse until August 1949, when the Nationalist government sent a representative to Kumbum monastery where the child was living and, without resorting to any of the official tests, "recognized" him as the Seventh Panchen Lama. Since the selection of the Panchen incarnations was the duty of the Dalai Lama or regent and the Tsongdu, Lhasa declined to recognize the validity of the claimant. Several weeks later the Communists captured Amdo, and the child, who like the Dalai Lama had been born there, fell into their hands, a ready-made puppet for use against Tibet.

Mao Tse-tung lost no time in making use of this opportunity. It will be recalled that Articles 5 and 6 of the Seventeen-Point Agreement had provided that the "established status, functions, and powers" enjoyed by the Sixth Panchen Lama when he was in "friendly and amicable relations" with the Thirteenth Dalai Lama were to be restored to his successor. In fact, Mao and the Communists went far beyond these provisions and attempted to elevate the Panchen's position to a level of equality with that of the Dalai Lama. The Panchen Lama's circle of advisers was fashioned into a counterpart of the Dalai Lama's council of ministers, which the Chinese assiduously represented as being the Shigatse equivalent to the Lhasa government, and claims were made that the Panchen's "sovereign" status entitled him to a private army—and that his predecessors had traditionally exercised that right, despite there being no historical precedent whatsoever. To Shigatse, consequently, were attracted various native elements hostile to Lhasa: followers of the late Reting Rinpoche, enemies of the recently retired regent Taktra, lower-echelon aristocrats with little or no political influence, and a plethora of other dissatisfied individuals and groups.

Having secured political mastery of Chamdo directly through the collaboration of Ngabo Shappé, and of Shigatse indirectly from behind the robes of the Panchen Lama, the Chinese next turned their attention to Lhasa and central Tibet, where, not contented with having thereby reduced considerably the political domain of the Dalai Lama, they engaged in a series of machinations designed both to diminish his spiritual status and undermine his government.

As the earthly manifestation of the bodhisattva Chenresi, deity of compassion, and Dharma Raja (Religious King) of Tibet, the Dalai Lama's every public movement was prescribed by ritual. To enhance the dignity of formal processions, protocol dictated that despite his youth he had to walk supported on either side by two senior Kashag ministers, his hands resting on their shoulders, to symbolize the aged and enlightened Buddha. ("I always felt sorry for them," remembers the Dalai Lama, laughing heartily. "Both were quite old, and the Kalon lama, whose name was Rampa, was also quite fat. My legs were stronger than theirs, and I pushed them along at a pace to which they were not accustomed. The Potala had many steps, and I could hear them panting in front of me. Later I tried to go more slowly, but my legs seemed to have a mind of their own and inevitably picked up speed. I'm afraid I caused those old men a great deal of difficulty.") Etiquette demanded a threefold prostration from anyone ushered into his presence, and it was considered a rare privilege to be allowed to gaze at him directly. Few were permitted to address the God-King, and even those who were had to do so while simultaneously drawing in the breath with a gasping sound.

To destroy this aura of divinity the Chinese attempted to "humanize" the Dalai Lama by securing his increased involvement in mundane affairs, and less than two years after they entered Lhasa it was announced that he would be accessible to any Tibetan wishing to petition him directly. While there is little doubt that the unprecedented action represented a concession to Chinese pressures, it should not be thought that the young ruler agreed to it under duress, for had he been firmly opposed to such an infringement on his private rights, the Chinese could not have forced the issue without provoking a serious confrontation. To the contrary, the decision was made by the Dalai Lama himself, who for some time had recognized the compelling need for Tibet to modernize her political practices and wished not only to play a greater role in governing his country but also to enjoy closer contact with his people. Since the age of seven he had spent the first three weeks of each year, during the Monlam festival, in residence at the Jokhang Temple, occasions to which he had looked forward with great anticipation because they gave him the opportunity to talk for hours with the gyepas, uneducated sweepers who spoke as freely to him as they did to each other. "On the one hand they gave me the traditional respect because I was the Dalai Lama," he remembers, "but on the other hand they felt they could tell me anything because I was just a child." From the gyepas the young ruler learned a great deal about his land and his people, including fascinating bits of gossip about members of the nobility and the monastic community. It seemed to him a far different Tibet from that which he observed from behind the curtains of his gilded palanquin or which had been described to him by his tutors, advisers, and attendants. There was no doubt in his mind that fundamental reforms were essential to the well-being of his country.

The Chinese also made certain that the Dalai Lama would play a far greater role in affairs of state by securing the dismissal of the two Silons (prime ministers) he had appointed on the eve of his flight to the Chumbi Valley in November 1950. Resolute champions of Tibetan liberty, Lukhangwa and Lobsang Tashi had been thorns in the side of the Chinese ever since the P.L.A. arrived in Lhasa, and had infuriated the generals by their firm opposition to endless Chinese attempts to infringe on the rights of the Dalai Lama. Matters came to a head in the spring of 1952 when, for the first time in memory, the people of Lhasa found themselves on the verge of famine. Although explaining that they had come as friends and helpers, the Chinese occupation forces brought with them in addition to their arms only "chopsticks and empty rice bowls." Their presence in the holy city swelled its population by over 50 percent and to feed them Peking demanded from the Tibetan government a "loan" of 2,000 tons of barley, an amount so great it could not be met by the state granaries, forcing the government to borrow from the monasteries and private owners. As a result the price of all food grains suddenly shot up to astronomical levels, as did that of butter and other necessities. Meeting in their homes and temples and in the market stalls of the Barkhor, Lhasans asked each other bitterly when the incessant procession of Chinese troops into their city would bring with it food instead of more weapons, loudspeakers, and printing presses.

Complaints poured into the Kashag, which was helpless to alleviate the situation without cooperation from the Chinese authorities. This was not forthcoming and the latter soon demanded the "loan" of a further 2,000 tons of barley, to be repaid by investing its value in the development of new industries in Tibet, a face-saving promise that was never fulfilled. Meanwhile, hostility toward the Chinese was surfacing with increasing regularity. "Children began to go about shouting slogans and throwing stones at the Chinese soldiers," the Dalai Lama remembers, "a sign that the adults were barely keeping their own bitterness in check." As the situation continued to worsen, he appointed his lay Silon, Lukhangwa, to mediate between the needs of the Tibetan people and the demands of the occupation forces.

Tibetan food production, Lukhangwa explained to Chinese officials at the first of a series of tension-filled meetings, was geared to meet only the basic needs of the people. Surpluses in government and monastic store-rooms had taken years to accumulate and were vital safeguards against the ever-present threat of crop failure. Once the Chinese troops had exhausted them, as would be the case in another few months if something were not done immediately, another surplus could not be created suddenly. There was no reason, he suggested, for such an enormous concentration of military personnel to be stationed in Lhasa; if necessary to the defense of the country, they should be employed on the frontiers. The Chinese replied that the P.L.A. had come only to help Tibet develop her resources and resist imperialist domination. Since the Seventeen-Point Agreement directed that Chinese forces be stationed in Tibet, explained General Chang Ching-wu, it was the responsibility of the Tibetan government to ensure they were provided with adequate supplies and accommodation. In any event, once Tibet showed evidence of being able to administer her own affairs and protect her frontiers, the troops would be withdrawn. "When you can stand on your own two feet," he added, "we will not stay here even if you ask us to." To Lukhangwa, who commented sardonically that the only threat to his country's frontiers had come from the Chinese themselves, the meeting was an exercise in frustration.

In subsequent meetings the Chinese complained bitterly about the mounting hostility of the people toward them. They had come to Tibet as benefactors, they said, but the people of Lhasa had responded ungratefully by pasting up wall posters and circulating pamphlets demanding they go back to China. Even worse, they were regularly vilified in public meetings and lampooned in satirical street songs. Chang Ching-wu pressured the Ka-shag into banning public assemblies, but the ban was ignored by the people of Lhasa. Then he suggested that the Tibetan government issue a proclamation calling for friendly relations with the Chinese and presented it in draft form to Lukhangwa. "When Lukhangwa read it, he found it was an order putting a ban on singing in the streets," the Dalai Lama says. "Rather than issue anything so ludicrous, he rewrote it in a somewhat more dignified form. I do not think the Chinese ever forgave him for that." In fact, the generals were already conspiring to remove him from the scene.[4]

The incident which led to the dismissal of the two prime ministers arose at a high-level meeting between Tibetan and Chinese officials in early 1952 at which Chang Ching-wu announced that the time had come for Tibetan troops to be absorbed into the P.L.A. as stipulated in Article 8 of the Seventeen-Point Agreement. It was absurd to refer to that document, Lukhangwa retorted hotly, because Tibetans did not accept it and the Chinese had repeatedly broken its terms. Why did the P.L.A. attack Tibet while peaceful negotiations were going on? he demanded. Why was the P.L.A. still in occupation of eastern Tibet? How could the general move unilaterally to absorb Tibetan troops into the Chinese army when the agreement had stated that the Tibetans would not be compelled to accept reforms? Not only would the people of Tibet resent such a move very strongly, he added, but he, as prime minister, would not approve it. General Chang seemed perplexed. How, he wondered aloud, could the Tibetan government be so incensed at such a minor matter? Changing his tack, he proposed that it would suffice if the Tibetan flag was hauled down from all Tibetan barracks and replaced with the Red Star of China. If that were to happen, Lukhangwa responded, the Tibetans would only pull the Chinese flags down again and cause embarrassment for the Chinese. Furthermore, it was absurd for the Chinese, after violating the integrity of Tibet, to expect to have friendly relations with the Tibetans. "If you hit a man on the head and break his skull," he added, "you can hardly expect him to be friendly."[5]

With passions running high on both sides, the Chinese adjourned the meeting and arranged another one three days hence. This time their spokesman was General Fan Ming, who began by asking Lukhangwa if he had not been mistaken in his earlier statements. The prime minister not only reiterated all that he had said before but also warned that all Tibetans, soldiers and civilians alike, would undoubtedly rise up if Chinese pressure did not abate. Fan Ming accused Lukhangwa of having "clandestine relations" with "foreign imperialist powers" and shouted that he would ask the Dalai Lama to remove him from his post. "If His Holiness believes I have done wrong," replied the prime minister, "I will gladly give up not only my office but also my life." The meeting ground to a sudden halt.

The next day the Dalai Lama received a communication from Chang Ching-wu which insisted that Lukhangwa was bent on impeding rather than improving relations between Tibet and China and suggesting that he should be removed from office. The Kashag received a similar communication and advised him that it would be better if both prime ministers were asked to resign. "So the crisis was brought to a head, and I was faced with a very difficult decision," the Dalai Lama remembers. "I greatly admired Lukhangwa's courage in standing up to the Chinese, but now I had to decide whether to let him continue or whether to bow yet again to a Chinese demand. There were two considerations: Lukhangwa's personal safety, and the future of our country as a whole. On the first, I had no doubt. Lukhangwa had already put his own life in danger. If I refused to relieve him of office, there was every chance that the Chinese would get rid of him in ways of their own."[6] As for the second consideration, the Dalai Lama had no training in international politics and could only apply his religious training and common sense. "I reasoned that if we continued to oppose the Chinese authorities, it could only lead us further along the vicious circle of repression and popular resentment. In the end, it was certain to lead to outbreaks of physical violence. Yet violence was useless; we could not possibly get rid of the Chinese by violent means. They would always win, and our own unarmed and unorganized people would be the victims. Our only hope was to persuade the Chinese peacefully to fulfill the promises they had made in their agreement. Nonviolence was the only course which might win us back a degree of freedom in the end, perhaps after years of patience. That meant cooperation whenever it was possible and passive resistance whenever it was not." Nonviolence, he realized, was the only moral course. "This was not only my own profound belief, it was also clearly in accordance with the teaching of Lord Buddha, and as the religious leader of Tibet I was bound to uphold it. We might be humiliated, and our most cherished inheritances might seem to be lost for a period, but if so, humility must be our position. I was certain of that."

Sadly he asked Lukhangwa and Lobsang Tashi to resign and decided not to appoint any successors. "It was no use having prime ministers if they were merely to be scapegoats for the Chinese. It was better that I should accept the responsibilities myself, because my position was unassailable in the eyes of all Tibetans." It was April 27, 1952. At not quite seventeen years of age, the Dalai Lama's childhood was over.

Notes

1. See George Ginsburgs and Michael Mathos, *Communist China and Tibet: The First Dozen Years* (The Hague, 1964), and Werner Levi, "Tibet Under Chinese Communist Rule," *Far Eastern Survey* 23 (January 1954), 1–9.
2. Not a few former officials of the Tibetan government who were privy to the details of the 1951 Peking negotiations, in fact, insist that the Chinese made a firm verbal commitment to deal with all of Tibet, including that which had been outside the Dalai Lama's political (but not spiritual) domain in recent history, as a single unit.
3. Tibetans refer to the Panchen Lama as the spiritual son and the Dalai Lama as the spiritual father because from the religious point of view the Dalai Lama is the master and the Panchen his disciple.
4. Satiric verse was almost always composed by government officials and then passed on surreptitiously to the common people to be sung in the streets. In a society possessing a rigid code of interpersonal deference behavior which restricted the overt expression of animosity or hostility, it was an acceptable mode of attacking political opponents and releasing pent-up frustrations. The Chinese were not unaware of this tradition and, smarting from a series of exceptionally witty and allusive songs that scathingly derided their every move in Lhasa, suspected Lukhangwa to have been their composer. See Melvyn C. Goldstein, "An Anthropological Study of the Tibetan Political System," unpublished Ph.D. dissertation, University of Washington, 1963, 225–227.
5. That the Chinese paid heed to Lukhangwa's warnings is demonstrable by the fact that not until after the Dalai Lama's flight to India in 1959 did the Chinese flag fly over Tibetan army barracks. Although the Chinese announced in February 1952 that the integration of Tibetan troops into the P.L.A. had been com-

pleted successfully, moreover, the Dalai Lama's troops never merged with the Chinese garrison and, except for adopting Chinese uniforms and weapons, maintained a separate identity under their own officers.

6. "Lukhangwa was always a very straightforward man," said former Foreign Minister Liushar. "He was incorruptible but did not believe in negotiation. He had a sincere feeling for the people and government of Tibet. . . . The balance of power was, of course, in the hands of the Chinese. They might not have killed him, but his active opposition made things very difficult for the government." Interview with Kungo Liushar, Dharamsala, India, May 17, 1980.

Trijang Rinpoche   *Dharamsala 1980*

· CHAPTER 14 ·

Reform and Resentment

L ong ago in Tibet lived a king named Muni Tsenpo. He was a kind-
hearted man, who in an effort to reduce the wide disparity between the
rich and the poor in his country introduced land reform and appointed ministers to supervise the equitable redistribution of property. After some time
he inquired how his reforms were progressing and was informed that the
rich had become richer and the poor poorer. Twice more all were forced to
share and share alike, and each time it was found that the poor, who had
become indolent during their time of ease, had lost the habit of working and
become poorer than ever. Saddened by the failure of his plan, the king consulted the celebrated sage Padmasambhava, who told him that it was beyond
man's power to close the gap between the wealthy and the indigent. The law
of karma, he explained, ordained that as we sow so shall we reap, both in
this and future lives. Since each of us must begin where the good and bad
deeds of our previous life have placed us, how can there be equal opportunities for all? Before he could make another attempt, Muni Tsenpo was poisoned by his mother, and economic reforms in Tibet were laid to rest for
1,200 years.

Although the Dalai Lama was no Muni Tsenpo, his childhood conversations with palace guards and sweepers and his observations, during the
long journey to and from the Chumbi Valley, of the impoverished conditions
in which the majority of Tibetan peasants lived had convinced him that
something must be done to better the lives of his people. Upon his return to
Lhasa in the summer of 1951, he created a Reforms Committee (Lekche)
made up of fifty lay and monk officials whose responsibility was to report to
him the findings of a smaller standing committee on areas in which economic reforms were felt to be needed most urgently.

The first reform recommended by the Lekche revised the system of
local taxation. Each of Tibet's dzongs (districts) was administered by one or
two Dzongpons, unsalaried officials endowed with extensive powers who,

like the robber barons of the European Middle Ages, were subject to only loose control from the central government at Lhasa.[1]

Dzongpons fulfilled two primary functions. As collectors of taxes they were, in essence, contractors, being obligated to send a fixed annual amount of revenue to Lhasa and operating with the tacit understanding that they could collect as much extra as they were able for their own profit. As dispensers of justice they exercised a large measure of discretion in such matters as fines and punishment (flogging and fettering were most common) and consequently had virtually unlimited powers of extortion.[2] The Dalai Lama's reforms stipulated that the Dzongpons would thereafter be paid a fixed salary and required them to submit all revenues to Lhasa but, because of the difficulty of enforcement, deferred action on the Dzongpons' real or potential abuse of their judicial authority.

The Dalai Lama's committee also gave top priority to devising a method of easing the repayment by peasants of loans from the government. No effort had been made to reclaim the loans, many of which had been outstanding for years, and with the addition of interest they had grown so large that in most cases it would have been unrealistic to expect them to be repaid in full. It was decided to group the peasants into three categories according to their ability to discharge their obligations. Members of the first category were economically solvent and therefore required to pay back both capital and interest in installments. Those of the second, who were not so well off but had nevertheless managed to accumulate a small savings, were permitted to repay only the capital, also in installments. Peasants in the third category, whose circumstances were such that they were unable to meet any of the payments, were freed from the debt entirely. The measure took the pressure off the peasants, who had stood to lose their heritable lands.

The reform proposed by the Lekche that was felt to be most urgently needed was in the larger manorial estates vested in the hereditary nobility and the monasteries. In twentieth-century Tibet, as in medieval Europe, one of the most common symptoms of feudal disintegration was the rise of absentee landlordism. The tendency of manorial lords to move with their families to Lhasa, the center not only of the Buddhist faith but also of political power, economic enterprise, and social diversion, left many of the ancestral estates in the hands of salaried stewards. Not a few of these were unscrupulous men who exacted from the estate, and thus from the peasants, more than the customary profits and pocketed the difference. Somewhat less frequently the lords themselves, when burdened by either business reverses or gambling losses at Lhasa's busy mah-jongg tables, instructed their retainers to bail them out by making increasingly greater demands on the peasantry. The Tibetan government had no control over the conditions of these estates, a situation the Dalai Lama planned to remedy by ruling that the estates of the lay nobility would revert to the state upon payment of compensation.

In return for hereditary land grants it had long been the custom for each aristocratic family to provide at least one male heir per generation to serve the government, and it was now proposed to pay these officials cash salaries instead. The land that had been obtained in this manner would be distributed among the peasants who already worked it, thereby putting them on an equal footing as tenants of the state and making possible the uniform administration of justice.

That the Dalai Lama was able to propose such radical reforms, and that he was able, moreover, to muster the support of his ministers and advisers in doing so, was due in large measure to the Chinese military presence in Lhasa. Up to that time even the powerful Tsarong had, despite his close relationship to the Thirteenth Dalai Lama, "quailed at the idea of attacking such a citadel of privilege." There is little doubt that, given time, these and other reforms would have been implemented had it not been for determined Chinese opposition. Peking's representatives had no intention of allowing the Tibetan government to usurp their self-styled role as saviors of the working class.

Quickly they set in motion a program of their own, which was successful mainly because it derived an aura of legitimacy from the early steps taken by the Dalai Lama's administration and because they were able to proceed with less concern for the wishes of the vested interests in the Tibetan power structure. The Dalai Lama's reforms had affected only government lands, but the Chinese extended them to include manorial estates of the nobility and monasteries. Taxes were lowered, interest rates were reduced, the dispossessing of tenants from the land for nonpayment of debts was forbidden, and those holdings already surrendered were returned to their owners. Whereas the Dalai Lama's reforms were designed to provide the basis for a more equitable economic system, those of the Chinese, while undeniably relieving the peasants of an oppressive financial burden, were motivated by the desire to win over the Tibetan masses and manipulate them into opposition to the Lhasa government. In so doing the Chinese hoped to provide the groundwork for the transformation of Tibet into a socialist state when the time was ripe.

With this in mind, the Chinese initiated a campaign of public indoctrination designed to prepare Tibetans to welcome the revolutionary changes projected for their way of life. Loudspeakers blaring Marxist propaganda could be heard every day on the streets of Lhasa, and Chinese presses cranked out crudely printed handouts that extolled the virtues of state socialism. The Communists also disseminated their philosophy by creating a plethora of "patriotic," "social," and "cultural" organizations such as the New Democratic Youth Federation of China (May 4, 1952), the Cultural Association of Patriotic Youth (February 23, 1953), and the Women's Patriotic Federation (founded March 8, 1954, headed by the wives of General Chang Ching-wu and Ngabo Shappé). Attendance at the regularly scheduled meetings of these and similar groups, which took the form of lectures geared to reorient the Tibetan public toward socialism, was voluntary at the outset but later became compulsory.

Additionally, the Chinese made available a substantial sum of money for interest-free loans to agricultural tenants who were seeking to acquire an adequate supply of seed grain. When harvests were poor, most peasants were unable to retain enough seed grain from their share of the crop to resow the fields and were forced to borrow from their landlords at usurious rates of interest. The ostensible purpose of the loan program was to relieve the financial burden of the Tibetan peasantry, but its underlying intentions were to encourage larger crops, which could be used to feed their army of occupation; to drive a wedge between lord and serf; and to win over the peasants to the side of the Chinese.

Soon after their arrival in Tibet, the Chinese built several hospitals in Lhasa, Shigatse, and Chamdo, an event of great significance since the quality of medical care available to most Tibetans was poor. Before the Communist invasion the only modern facilities were located at British trade marts that had been established at Gartok, Gyantse, and Yatung shortly after the Younghusband expedition, and in 1936 at the British Mission in Lhasa. Before that time progressive-minded Tibetans like Tsarong had to import Western medicines from India, an experiment with mixed results: when a British visitor to Lhasa in 1923 was taken ill, Tsarong sent along his entire supply of pharmaceuticals, which consisted of a dozen boxes of "very moldy" Beecham's Pills and three pounds of Epsom salts.

A handful of monasteries, most notably the Chakpori on a hilltop opposite the Potala, specialized in the memorization of ancient medical scriptures and the preparation of remedies derived from the Ayurvedic system of India. The few medical practitioners available to the public were most likely to be laymen who purchased the herbal concoctions made by the monks and, after testing the urine and pulse of a patient by traditional methods, dispensed them in the manner of an apothecary of the Middle Ages. This system often worked to great effect, but the practice of surgery was poor and many serious illnesses like pneumonia, tuberculosis, venereal disease (which the Tibetans referred to as *gyasa*, the "Chinese affliction"), and smallpox were usually beyond treatment.

In the villages and countryside, where the majority of Tibetans lived, a medical practitioner was rarely available and the people relied upon prayers and incantations, charms and amulets, and the taking of *rilbu*, holy pills made up of barley flour and powdered relics of past or present saints and incarnations (a system described by a visiting Westerner as one dependent on "mud, manure, and muttered mantras"). To reach the more remote regions the Chinese set up mobile medical units based in the three major cities.

The Chinese also opened a number of elementary schools in Lhasa. While higher education was all but unknown in Tibet, the people were, for the most part, literate. "In respect to ordinary education," reported Frederick O'Connor, a British officer who arrived in the country as a member of the Younghusband expedition and remained as trade agent in Gyantse, "it is surprising to find how many of the commonality can read and write—far more, certainly, than was the case of our own lower orders one hundred or even fifty years ago." O'Connor, who spoke Tibetan fluently, discovered that in each village he visited, the headman and at least one or two members of almost every family were "tolerably well-educated."

All monks were able to read and write, as were all the children of noble families. Most towns had schools that were open to all upon payment of a small fee (Lhasa alone had over twenty), and in the country manorial lords brought in teachers for their children and invited the offspring of their servants, village headmen, and better-off peasants to participate. Those Lhasans who attended the new Chinese schools found them to be little more than agencies for Communist, anti-Tibetan propaganda.

During the pivotal years of 1951–1954 the Chinese engaged in a series of measures whose purpose was plainly to strengthen Peking's domination of Tibet with little or no regard for the needs or desires of the Tibetan people. By far the most dramatic of these was the road-building program. Prior to the 1950 "liberation" there had been no motorable roads in Tibet, just time-worn caravan tracks suitable only for pack animals that linked the major trading centers with each other and with Lhasa.

Even before the signing of the Seventeen-Point Agreement, P.L.A. forces had begun large-scale highway and bridge construction, a process given further impetus by the ratification of the controversial treaty in May 1951. By November 1954 the 2,255-kilometer Sikang–Tibet highway linked Lhasa with Chamdo and western China, and less than a month later the first vehicles reached the holy city from Sining over the 2,100-kilometer Tsinghai (Amdo)–Tibet highway, which followed almost exactly the route taken by Kyitsang Rinpoche and his search party when they returned to Lhasa with the four-year-old Dalai Lama a quarter-century earlier. The Lhasa–Shigatse and Shigatse–Gyantse highways, which stretched 428 kilometers over central Tibet, were completed by the end of the following year. "Over 3,000 Tibetan workers of both sexes, grateful for the deep concern shown by the Central Government, participated," boasted the New China News Agency. "They were encouraged by the prospect of building a happy land. These two newly opened roads yet again indicate the concern and care which the Chinese Communist party and Chairman Mao have for the Tibetan people." In fact the road-building program was motivated primarily by military considerations, and once completed the arteries enabled the Chinese to move ever-larger quantities of armament and military personnel into the interior of Tibet. The simultaneous development of postal, telegraph, and telephone connections completed the communications link between the two countries.

The road-building program also made possible the intensification of Peking's domination of Tibet through greater control over local finances and economic resources. While the roads were under construction the Chinese relied upon supplies secured by Tibetan traders through India, but upon their completion Tibetans were urged to trade with China instead. Shortly after the occupation, branches of the People's Bank of China were opened in Lhasa, Shigatse, and Gyantse that refused to accept Tibetan currency for remittances to India. As a result, only traders who could prove legitimate possession of Chinese silver were permitted to secure drafts for further purchases. Private trade was discouraged, and by the end of 1952 Tibet's foreign trade was monopolized by a Sino-Tibetan syndicate and her trade with China was in the hands of a Peking-controlled General Tibetan Commercial Corporation.

The Chinese also altered the traditional Tibetan trading pattern. For over a thousand years traders had gathered just after harvest time at outdoor markets, sprawling tent-cities that sprang up overnight at predesignated spots in the wilderness. The markets were trading posts where the majority of business was conducted by barter, and they were also social centers where old friends met and exchanged news of their lands and regions—an especially important consideration for Tibetans, because aside from the pages of Tharchin's Kalimpong-based *Tibet Mirror* there was little other way for the news of the world to reach them. Gradually the markets were shut down. Many Tibetans were forced out of business, and much of the free trade still permitted fell into the hands of Chinese settlers sent by Mao to colonize Tibet—the first of a projected seven or eight million who would turn Tibetans into a minority in their own land.[3]

The Chinese also began making inroads on the entrenched position of the monasteries. Propaganda aimed mainly at Tibetan youth extolled the virtues of state socialism and disparaged the austere monastic life. Why join the monkhood? suggested some of the leaflets distributed on the streets of Lhasa. Why spend your life poring over boring, musty scriptures? Marry, raise a family, feel some silver jingling in the fold of your *chuba*, contribute to the progress of Marxist Tibet! Toward the end of 1953, moreover, Chinese authorities announced that, beginning the following year, monks from Drepung monastery would no longer be permitted to maintain law and order in Lhasa for the first three weeks of each year during the Monlam festival, a tradition begun by the Fifth Dalai Lama to symbolize the primacy of the monastic community in the governance of Tibet.

Finally, several changes were wrought by the Chinese in the Tibetan government. The Dzongpons, whose tenures had long been determined by the will of the Dalai Lama, were now limited to a fixed term of three years, and they were cautioned to perform their duties "only after consultation with and advice from the local Chinese military commander." Even the Dalai Lama's Council of Ministers was subjected to a significant reorganization. A special commission of three ministers, headed by Ngabo, was appointed to act as a liaison between the Kashag and the Chinese authorities, and individual Kalons were made responsible for specific tasks. Traditionally the Kashag had reached its decisions collectively, but the new system made it easy for the Chinese to exert pressure on those ministers hesitant to carry out the duties assigned them.

The reaction of the Tibetan peasantry to this chain of events was mixed. Chinese innovations in the fields of medicine and health care were generally welcomed, as were the lowering of taxes and the interest ceiling on loans, but, as later became evident, without being accompanied by a feeling of gratitude. Many of those who had taken advantage of interest-free seed loans, moreover, not only continued to view the Chinese as invaders in their midst but also attempted to avoid repayment by claiming poverty and either hiding their surpluses or donating them to local monasteries. Nor did the Communist propaganda campaign win many converts, for rather than demanding reform, the vast majority of the masses were passively resisting it. "Beware of the sweet honey," they reminded each other in the face of glowing Chinese enticements, "offered on the blade of a knife." At one Chinese-sponsored meeting in Lhasa, workers responded to Chang Ching-wu's request to air their grievances by stating it was their hope that the people of Tibet would continue to be guided by the teachings of Lord Buddha and that His Holiness the Dalai Lama and the great monasteries would continue to occupy their sacred position as guardians of the faith.[4]

The Chinese highway construction program produced an even more negative effect. Remembering their proverb "Enemies on the outside are like the snow, but on the inside like a blizzard," Tibetans at first viewed it with alarm and resisted efforts to lure them to work as road laborers. Gradually, however, the determination with which Chinese labor battalions pursued their task, the inevitability of the result, and the promise of high wages persuaded many to change their minds. The arrival of large numbers of troops shortly thereafter depressed the wage scale dramatically, and the Tibetans quit en masse, refusing to go back to their jobs until paid what they had been promised. In response the Chinese resorted to conscript labor, a system they were simultaneously attacking as a barbarous relic of feudalism and "a drain on the blood and sweat of the Tibetan working people." This apparent discrepancy caused them no embarrassment, and soon tens of thousands of Tibetan peasants were laboring on highways, fortifications, and airfields all over the country.[5] Chinese insensitivity in plotting the course of the highways, which frequently resulted in the destruction of farmhouses, the ruin of cultivated fields, and the appropriation of prime farmland, likewise left a legacy of bitterness.

Peking's domination of Tibetan commerce also provoked a great deal of hostility. Members of the small but relatively affluent merchant and trading class witnessed helplessly the collapse of their businesses but, although angry and resentful toward the Chinese, considered themselves fortunate to secure employment as salaried middlemen in Chinese trade monopolies. Even worse, indiscriminate purchasing by Chinese authorities and the ever-growing number of occupation forces in Tibet drove prices of local products steadily upward and resulted in a disastrous inflation, which a series of makeshift measures dictated by Peking was unable to curb. Coupled with the Chinese appropriation of grain reserves from state and private store-houses, which Silon Lukhangwa had complained about to Chang Ching-wu, this created severe shortages and placed the cost of all but the most basic items beyond the reach of the majority of peasants.

One result of these developments was the spontaneous appearance of a mass protest movement that came to be known as the Mimang Tshogpa, or "People's Party," which took its name from a group of Tibetan noblemen who, at the end of the nineteenth century, had banded together to prevent the Manchu Ambans from murdering the Thirteenth Dalai Lama before he reached his majority and assumed full powers. The Mimang was too loosely organized to be considered a formal political party in the modern sense; there was, after all, no precedent for such a phenomenon in the Tibetan tra-dition. It lacked both regular leadership and a consistent platform other than unswerving and often emotional opposition to the Chinese presence in Lhasa and the rest of the country. Moreover, although many of its complaints and demands fell on sympathetic ears in the Tibetan government, the latter lacked authority to have them seriously considered. While not particularly effective or efficient, the Mimang gave frustrated Tibetans the opportunity to join together in adversity and air their grievances, and its members were largely responsible for the anti-Chinese leaflets and posters circulated in and around Lhasa as well as a provocative memorandum addressed to both the Kashag and the Chinese authorities demanding that all P.L.A. troops be withdrawn from the city. Given its inherent weaknesses, it is unlikely that it would have developed into an effective revolutionary group, but the Chinese regarded it as the greatest single threat to their supremacy in Tibet. After failing to subvert it through innuendo, bribery, infiltration, harassment, and arrest, they brought pressure to bear on the Tibetan government, and on May 1, 1952 the Dalai Lama announced the Mimang's disbandment. There-after its operation went underground, to surface at a later date.

Despite concerted Chinese efforts to undermine the paramount position of the monasteries in the eyes of the people, most Tibetans reacted to the occupation and its aftermath by drawing closer to their religious leaders, whom they looked to for reassurance and guidance. Although disturbed that Chinese trade regulations had siphoned off an important source of subsidi-ary financial support for their institutions and that their young monks were preferred targets for Communist propaganda, the monastic authorities counseled all Tibetans to proceed with patience and caution.

Their advice was not always heeded. On the fifth night of 1954, the first year the Chinese ban on the traditional right of monks from Drepung to civil and criminal jurisdiction in Lhasa went into effect, two Chinese patrols were set upon and hacked to pieces with swords; and the next morning a grim, haughty procession of giant warrior monks marched defiantly through the city wielding staves and swords. A major clash was averted only because P.L.A. officers ordered their troops to let the *dob-dob*s pass without interference, and monastic officials realized with apprehension that the time was rapidly approaching when prayers would not be enough to keep the people from rising up against the invaders.

Officials of the Tibetan government found themselves in an equally difficult position. At the local level, the Dzongpons, now required to govern with the "advice" of Chinese military authorities, were pressured into enforcing directives that, like the conscription of laborers for road building, were often extremely unpopular with the Tibetan people. If they proved too lenient in the discharge of their duties, they were likely to be dismissed by the Chinese; if too firm, they risked bodily harm from the exasperated peasantry. Similarly the Dalai Lama's Council of Ministers, chastened by the abrupt dismissal of Lukhangwa and Lobsang Tashi, found it expedient to proceed with caution. Instead of overt opposition to Chinese "suggestions," it employed delaying tactics when compromise proved impossible or unsatisfactory. The Chinese-dictated assumption of specific duties by each minister soon put an end to the collective anonymity that had made possible such subterfuge. Moreover, Kashag members were often divided among themselves, a situation the Chinese exploited to their advantage by wooing ministers like Ngabo and isolating or threatening others. Some Kalons believed that no good would come from the Chinese despite their protestations to the contrary, and adopted the traditional Tibetan posture in the face of such adversity by vacillating and temporizing.[6] Others, more progressive and bowing to a clearly superior force, hoped to ameliorate Chinese measures by maintaining good relations with the military authorities.

For the Dalai Lama the period 1951–1954 was one in which both his religious convictions and strength of character were put to the test. Although Tibet had twice before experienced periods of foreign overlordship, on neither occasion had it been subject to direct control. During the Ch'ing dynasty the Manchu Ambans stationed in Lhasa had functioned as observers and advisers, but played no role in the governing of the country. ("We were able at last to estimate the authority of the Chinese suzerains and the influence of the Amban himself," wrote a member of the Younghusband expedition. "Neither existed.")[7] While it is true that before initiating a new internal policy the Tibetan government had been expected to secure the approval of the emperor in Peking, in practice the petition would be dispatched and the policy begun simultaneously. This was done with the connivance of the Ambans, who, endowed with no real power and protected by only a small military garrison, were satisfied that formalities were observed and that neither they nor the Tibetans lost face.[8] During the first years of Communist occupation, the situation was visibly different. Chinese authorities endowed with far-reaching authority and backed by tens of thousands of well-equipped troops could, despite the "guarantees" of the Seventeen-Point Agreement, pursue vigorously whatever course Peking desired; and the only figure in all of Tibet able to exert a restraining influence on their designs was the Dalai Lama.

Not yet twenty years of age and far less self-confident than his predecessor, the young man had been subjected to intense pressure by the Chinese from the very beginning. Even before engineering the dismissal of Lukhangwa and Lobsang Tashi, the generals had bypassed the Kashag and met with him alone on several occasions, an intentionally insulting violation of protocol that had since become more frequent. Yet they found that despite his youth and lack of political experience they were unable to persuade him to do their bidding. Not that he was either inflexible or uncompromising; to the contrary, he was committed to bettering the lives of his people and unafraid to participate in Tibet's transformation from a medieval to a modern state. But he persevered determinedly in his attempts to convince the Chinese to honor the conditions of the Seventeen-Point Agreement, and yielded to them, as when dismissing his two prime ministers, only to avoid bloodshed. The 1954 outburst of the *dob-dobs* distressed him, not only because as a Buddhist he believed in the sanctity of life, but also because he knew that open defiance of Peking's directives was highly dangerous. Similarly he acquiesced in the "disbandment" of the Mimang to avoid certain imprisonment for its leading members, and the Tibetans, aware that he did so for their benefit, went through the charade of dispersing and quietly reorganized underground.

It would have been a sufficiently difficult situation had the Dalai Lama been able to count on united support from his government, but the factional strife that had permeated Tibet's body politic since the death of the Great Thirteenth was still very much in evidence and he was too young and unaccustomed to handling the reins of authority to restrain it. Even without this debilitating phenomenon it is likely that a combination of Tibetan isolationism, Chinese megalomania, and Western indifference would have made the Communist invasion inevitable, but now more than ever, when unanimity was absolutely essential, it was not forthcoming.

Traditional cleavages were partially responsible for this lamentable state of affairs, as was the infiltration by the Chinese of Communist sympathizers into the Tibetan government. Appointees of the Taktra regency could not be summarily dismissed from their posts, so the Dalai Lama was able to make appointments of men upon whose support he felt he could count only when vacancies occurred through death or retirement. Consequently he proceeded with caution and took few into his confidence. There are indications that he relied most heavily upon his spiritual adviser and junior tutor, Trijang Rinpoche; and he placed his brother Lobsang Samden in the key position of Chikyap Khenpo (lord chamberlain), the official liaison between himself and the monastic branch of government, as well as between himself and Peking's military commanders in Lhasa.

Never before had the Dalai Lama felt so isolated and alone. His family was scattered: his mother had remained in Kalimpong with his two sisters and youngest brother, Ngari Rinpoche; and Taktser Rinpoche was afraid to return to Tibet lest he be punished by the Chinese for disobeying them. The dismissal of his two prime ministers required an increasingly great involvement in temporal affairs, and just when he felt the need for deeper religious training there was little time for it. There were few government officials he felt he could trust, and the precarious Tibetan economy was in shambles. The Chinese regularly impeded his reforms, attempted to discredit him by seeking to identify him with unpopular causes, and instituted measures designed to diminish his personal authority and limit his spiritual authority. His country was rapidly becoming a vast military camp, and it was Mao's professed intention to bring in four Chinese settlers for every Tibetan. The Chinese looked to him to validate their actions, the Tibetans to protect and guide them. A less energetic, determined, and selfless man would have crumbled under the pressure.

The Dalai Lama could have disengaged himself from the mundane world and withdrawn into a life of meditation like his predecessor, the Eighth Incarnation. But that course of action would have made it easy for Peking to control the Kashag by default, and he could not permit that to happen. He could have cooperated fully with the Chinese, but that would have been repugnant to his intelligence and moral principles. He was fully aware that he was all that stood between his people and the Chinese, and he resolved to remain there as long as he was able.

Notes

1. In the fourteenth century the original division of Tibet known as Trikhor Chuksum (*Trikhor* refers to 10,000 family units, *Chuksum* to the number thirteen) was replaced by the organization of the country into numerous *dzongs*, or districts. Each district had its headquarters in the shape of a *dzong*, a strongly built fort situated on a rocky hill.

2. The farther away their districts were from Lhasa, the more likely Dzongpons would be to impose larger fines and greater punishments. In remote areas they would not hesitate to lop off the hand or foot of a habitual offender or decree that a miscreant's eyes be gouged out, despite the fact that such measures had been forbidden by the Thirteenth Dalai Lama. It is little wonder, then, that upon completing the customary three-year term of office, most Dzongpons had become enormously wealthy.

3. "In the past, the reactionary rulers, from the emperors of the Ch'ing dynasty to Chiang Kai-shek, have oppressed and exploited you. Imperialism has done the same to you. As a result you are weak economically, backward culturally, and

your population is small," stated Mao Tse-tung to a group of Tibetan officials in Peking on October 8, 1952. "Tibet covers a large area but is thinly populated," he continued. "Its population should be increased from the present two or three million to five or six million, and then to over ten million."

4. Thus Mao Tse-tung was simply accepting reality when in October 1952 he reassured a delegation of Tibetan officials visiting Peking at his invitation that "Whether land should be divided in minority nationality districts is a matter for the minority nationalities to decide. In the Tibet region, the problem of the division of land does not exist now. Whether or not land should be redistributed in the future the Tibetans will have to decide by themselves; we cannot do it for you."

5. For example, the New China News Agency reported in November 1954 that some 20,000 Tibetans worked on the western sector of the Sikang–Tibet highway, and in October of the following year that more than 3,000 Tibetans completed the ninety-one-kilometer Shigatse–Gyantse highway in 102 days.

6. A Manchu Amban complained to a British officer who had arrived in Lhasa with the Younghusband expedition of 1903–1904 that the Tibetans were "dark and cunning adepts at prevarication" and that he had met with nothing but "shuffling" from the "barbarians" during his entire term of office. Edmund Candler, *The Unveiling of Lhasa* (New York, 1905), 290.

7. Perceval Landon, *The Opening of Tibet* (New York, 1905), 153.

8. An amusing example of this relationship occurred at the beginning of the twentieth century when the Ambans appointed an aristocrat named Rampa to the Kashag, a duty reserved for the Dalai Lama or regent. Shortly thereafter the Thirteenth Dalai Lama sent for Rampa and said to him: "The Ambans have made you a Kalon, but you are not one of my Kalons." Upon hearing this the Kashag reported to the Ambans that Rampa had died, and although they knew perfectly well that Rampa was alive, the Ambans reported similarly to the emperor. Rampa retired quietly to his estate a short distance from the capital and remained there for about a year, and in due course the Great Thirteenth appointed a Kalon of his own choosing. So many false reports were sent by the Ambans to Peking that to the people of Lhasa the Manchu emperor became known as "the Bag of Lies."

Lobsang Samden   *Dharamsala 1980*

CHAPTER 15

Meetings with Mao

A LTHOUGH THEY WOULD LATER tell the world that "a tiny collection of the biggest serf-owners" in the Tibetan government had been imposing their will on the Dalai Lama from the moment he assumed full temporal authority in 1950 until he fled into exile nine years later, the Chinese Communists were not averse to attempting to do so themselves when they felt it suited their purposes. At first they chose to pursue a moderate course, hoping that a combination of time and circumstances would eventually win him over. But it soon became evident that he showed no inclination to become their puppet, that he stalled and temporized whenever possible and acceded to their wishes only under pressure, and that while agreeing wholeheartedly that his country's social and economic system was in need of reform, he insisted that this be accomplished without Chinese compulsion as stipulated by the Seventeen-Point Agreement. Less than two years after they had marched into Lhasa, therefore, they decided to invite him for an extended visit to the Great Motherland. Despite his keen intelligence and genuine devotion to his people, he was, after all, only a boy, and an impressionable one at that. They could not help being aware of his fascination with mechanical things and his thirst for knowledge of the outside world, and considered it an ideal opportunity to awe him by exposure to carefully selected glittering achievements "in the political, economic, and cultural fields and the blissful life of all the people." Away from time-consuming official and religious duties and the cloistered confines of his palaces, and thrown into contact with foreigners for the first time, he could not fail to be persuaded to abandon his passive resistance to Mao Tse-tung's program for the transformation of Tibet. The historic visit was timed to coincide with the framing of the Chinese constitution, and the Dalai Lama was to lead the Tibetan delegation to the National Assembly.

Concerned lest his prolonged absence from Tibet might prompt Chinese authorities there to initiate more repressive measures, the Dalai Lama weighed the invitation carefully. On the one hand, he realized that the Chinese would spare no effort to "educate" him properly and that he would be shown only those things which would reflect favorably on Communist rule. At their suggestion he had sent a "goodwill delegation" of government officials, monastic leaders, and influential traders to China in August 1952, whose broadcasts back to Lhasa offered reassurances to every segment of the population. The delegation head, monk official Kungo Liushar, had reported from the Central People's Radio Broadcasting Station in Peking that since the Communist takeover the people of another "national minority area" had "fully enjoyed the right of being their own masters and have begun to live a happy life;" that "not only has private capital not been confiscated but, on the contrary, it has been restored and developed with the help of the Communist party;" that land belonging to monasteries was not divided during the land reform, and that monks "were living a bountiful life." Upon his return to Lhasa in the summer of 1953, however, Liushar advised the Dalai Lama that the glowing reports had been dictated to him by the Chinese and should be construed as Communist propaganda, and that Mao's personal "guarantees" to the delegation in October of the previous year that religion would be protected and land reform postponed until sought by the Tibetans themselves were highly suspect. Liushar's sentiments were echoed by fellow delegate Trijang Rinpoche, the Dalai Lama's spiritual adviser. The Dalai Lama was also aware that his presence in China would be used by the Chinese to justify to the world their claim that Tibet was an integral part of the "great family of fraternal nations voluntarily associated" within the People's Republic, and that they would miss no opportunity to make it appear that he and the Panchen Lama were equals.

On the other hand, the Dalai Lama did not wish to jeopardize his government's relations with the Chinese, which had improved slightly since the dismissal of Lukhangwa and Lobsang Tashi and the "disbandment" of the Mimang; while greatly disappointed by their utter disregard for the interests and welfare of his people, he still believed that a policy of nominally amicable relations was preferable to one of confrontation. He was aware, too, that the trip would give him an opportunity to meet with Chinese leaders and urge them to honor the terms of the Seventeen-Point Agreement. Thus he decided to go.

The decision was greeted with despair by the people of Tibet. Many believed that the Dalai Lama's absence from the country would leave them defenseless in the hands of the hated invaders from the east. Others recalled that when his predecessor visited Peking in 1908 he was treated with disrespect, and that the Sixth Dalai Lama, en route to China two centuries earlier after being deposed by Lhazang Khan with the connivance of the Manchu emperor, had died suddenly—and might have been murdered. Would a similar fate befall the Fourteenth Incarnation? Delegations began arriving in Lhasa from every corner of the land, seeking audiences with the young ruler to entreat him not to go. Fearing widespread rioting and bloodshed, Tibetan officials borrowed Chinese loudspeakers, pleaded for patience, and promised that the Dalai Lama would return within a year. The God-King himself issued a declaration indicating he was going voluntarily, but the people, aware that several of his public statements had been made under Chinese coercion, took this to mean that the opposite was true. As the date for his departure drew near, thousands descended on the holy city to catch what they felt might be a last glimpse of their beloved leader.

On July 11, 1954, the Dalai Lama left the Norbulingka to begin the journey to Peking, his entourage including personal servants, high government officials, senior tutor Ling Rinpoche and junior tutor Trijang Rinpoche, and important lamas. Members of his family were also in attendance: Lobsang Samden, elder sister Tsering Dolma and her husband P. T. Takla, eight-year-old brother Tendzin Choegyal (who, having been recognized at birth as the most recent incarnation of a famous lama, was more commonly known as Ngari Rinpoche),[1] and the Gyayum Chenmo. The Dalai Lama's mother had only recently returned to Lhasa after spending nearly three years in India, where she had gone in February 1951 after accompanying him to the Chumbi Valley in the wake of the Chinese invasion. She had made a religious pilgrimage to India and Nepal, before the heat of the plains forced her to cut short her journey and return to the comparative coolness of Kalimpong. There she had taken up residence in a house lent her by a wealthy trader of the Pangdatsang clan from eastern Kham and kept in touch with Lhasa by weekly cables sent by her host from Gangtok, the capital of Sikkim, some two hours distant. "I was so worried about the future of my country and the safety of His Holiness that I was unable to eat or sleep properly and lost a great deal of weight," she remembered. "Since none of the local doctors seemed able to help, I finally arranged for a Tibetan doctor to be sent from Lhasa with a supply of herbal medicines, and in less than six months I was fully recovered and able to return. I was so happy when I saw the Potala again. Its golden turrets glowed in the sunlight. I felt as if a weight had been lifted from my shoulders, and went straight to the Jokhang Temple to make prostrations to the statue of Jowo Rinpoche."

A tremendous outpouring of grief accompanied the Dalai Lama's departure from the holy city. Thousands thronged the route along which he was carried in his golden palanquin, and all wept unashamedly. "He was so young and had undertaken such a great responsibility," remembers Amala Yuthok, a member of the nobility who witnessed the procession as it passed the walls of her family's home near the Norbulingka. "What would become of him in that alien, godless land? We thought the Chinese would prevent him from ever returning to us. For many weeks after he left, Lhasa was sunk in gloom."[2] Leaving his palanquin behind, the Dalai Lama, his shaven head sheltered from the sun by a large red umbrella carried by one of his attendants, crossed the Kyichu River in a yak-hide coracle. As he joined Lobsang Samden in his resurrected 1931 Dodge, he saw what seemed to be all of

Lhasa standing on the opposite bank, silently turning prayer wheels and waving religious banners, their dejection negating any pleasure or excitement he might have felt at his first journey out of Tibet.[3]

The roads were motorable only for the first ninety miles, after which travel by horseback became necessary. The Dalai Lama had two teams of attendants, one of which always rode a day's journey ahead and pitched camp before his arrival, to which local monks and peasants flocked to pay him homage. At Ngabo Shappé's estate in Gyamda he was given a great reception, after which Ngabo and his wife joined the entourage. Twelve days out of Lhasa the route became dangerous. Heavy rains had washed away whole sections of the new road, and from the surrounding mountainsides landslides hurtled huge boulders across the road and into the river hundreds of feet below. Large stretches of roadway were so steep that the party was forced to dismount and walk in mud up to nine inches deep; little Ngari Rinpoche, exempted from this exhausting activity by virtue of his age, laughed merrily as he watched his elders slog their way through the mire. Many mules and horses fell to their deaths in the river, or over precipices onto rocks, and three people lost their lives in similar mishaps.

Finally a group of concerned Tibetan officials approached General Chang Ching-wu and asked that the party be permitted to return to Lhasa and proceed from there over the ancient caravan route to Chamdo. While sincerely wishing to protect the Dalai Lama and ease the suffering of the party's elder members, they were also aware that the request could not be granted without causing the Chinese to suffer a great loss of face. The general refused and in a fury accused the officials of gravely insulting the Chinese people and their road-building capabilities. He alone, Chang added heatedly, was responsible for the safety of the Dalai Lama; if any others wished to divert their route, they were welcome to do so. The matter was resolved by the Dalai Lama himself, who, after reassuring the general that the officials had intended no offense, opted to press on along what he called the "new Chinese road." Not until a fortnight later were they able to travel by jeep again. After a short stop in Chamdo, they arrived at Tachienlu, a sleepy village nestled in a peaceful, verdant valley near the ancient border between Tibet and China. At Chengtu, the provincial capital of Szechuan, the Dalai Lama was flown to Sian, where he boarded a special train to Peking. "Only a few years before, when mechanical things so interested me, flying or traveling by train would have seemed like a glorious dream," he says. "But now that I was doing them both for the first time, my mind was much too full of our political misfortunes and my responsibility for me to enjoy these new experiences."

At Sian the Dalai Lama was joined by the Panchen Lama. They had met once before, when the Panchen and his advisers, the Chinese-inspired counterpart of the Kashag called the Panchen Khenpo Lija, had arrived in Lhasa the day after the dismissal of Lukhangwa and Lobsang Tashi in April 1952. Fourteen years old at the time, he had never been in Tibet before. Nor had he undergone the traditional tests, but when Ngabo wired the Dalai Lama from Peking in 1951 that the negotiations which culminated in the Seventeen-Point Agreement would be hindered unless the Tibetan government extended formal recognition, the latter felt it had no choice but to acquiesce. "He was formally presented to me in the traditional ceremonial way, as my junior not only in age but in position," the Dalai Lama says, "but I could see at that very first meeting that the Chinese and some of his own officials were not happy with our ancient customs. They would like to see the Panchen Lama seated on a level with myself. So that first meeting was constrained and not very successful. But on the same day we met again informally and had lunch together alone, and I must say that we got on well together. He showed a genuine respect for my position, as the custom of Buddhism requires toward a senior monk. He was correct and pleasant in his manners—a true Tibetan—and I had a firm impression of unforced goodwill. I felt sure that left to himself he would have wholeheartedly supported Tibet against the inroads of China." The people of Tibet were not so generous in their assessment. Chinese posters announcing the Panchen's arrival in Lhasa were smeared with dung, and uncomplimentary verses were sung about him in the streets. And, although forced to accept him as an ecclesiastical figure, Tibetan officials refused to accept him as anything more than that despite Chinese attempts to vest him with temporal authority.

A large, enthusiastic crowd greeted the Dalai Lama and Panchen Lama at the railway station in Peking. "Most of them looked like students or members of youth leagues, and they clapped and cheered loudly," the Dalai Lama recalls. "But I had a cynical feeling that they would have shown hostility just as readily if that had been what they had been told to do." The two lamas offered ceremonial scarves (which the *New York Times* erroneously identified as "white silk handkerchiefs") to Prime Minister Chou En-lai and Communist party vice-chairman Chu Teh, and were driven to separate residences specially prepared for their visit. That evening a banquet was given in their honor by Chu Teh, a new experience for the Dalai Lama, who was accustomed to dining alone and never with alcoholic beverages present.

Two days after his arrival in Peking, the Dalai Lama, accompanied by a small group of advisers, met Mao Tse-tung for the first time at a brief session in the House of Reception, which began with the Communist party chairman making a predictable statement: "He was glad Tibet had come back to the motherland and that I had agreed to take part in the National Assembly. He said it was the mission of China to bring progress to all Tibet by developing its natural resources, and that the generals who were in Lhasa were there as representatives of China to help me and the people of Tibet. They had not gone there to exercise any kind of authority over the Tibetan government or people." The Dalai Lama paid these sentiments little attention, but when Mao asked suddenly if the Chinese representatives in Lhasa had done anything against his wishes, he was placed in a difficult position.

Although sorely tempted to complain that the generals had been violating the terms of the Seventeen-Point Agreement with impunity, he knew that unless he could maintain friendly relations his country would suffer more than it had already. Choosing his words carefully, he replied that it was only because the people of Tibet had such great hopes for their future under Mao's leadership that they had not hesitated to air their grievances when they believed his directives were not being implemented properly. Under the circumstances there could have been no better rejoinder, and Mao, nodding silently, seemed content to let the matter drop.

Subsequent meetings, held in private with only an interpreter present, were of a more substantive nature. Unlike other Chinese officials, whom the Dalai Lama found to be stiff, formal, and indirect, Mao seemed to him both frank and open, "a simple man of dignity and authority" who never hesitated to speak his mind. "I met him many times on social occasions, apart from our private meetings. His appearance gave no sign of his intellectual power. He did not look healthy, and was always panting and breathing heavily. His dress was of just the same style as everybody else's, although it was usually a different color; but he did not pay much attention to his clothes, and once I noticed that the cuffs of his shirt were torn. His shoes looked as though they had never been polished. He was slow in his movements and slower still in speech. He was sparing of words and spoke in short sentences, each full of meaning and usually clear and precise; and he smoked incessantly while he talked. Yet his manner of speech certainly captured the minds and imaginations of his listeners, and gave the impression of kindness and sincerity. I was sure he believed what he said, and that he was confident of achieving whatever object he had in view."

The Chinese leader let it be known that he was not entirely pleased with the receptivity of the Tibetan people to the imposition of Communist rule or with the temporizing role played by the Tibetan government in setting what he felt was a poor example to them. The P.L.A. had come only as benefactors, he explained, but the people had been responding without gratitude; Tibet had returned to the Great Motherland and it was time they began accepting that fact. Given time and patience, the Dalai Lama replied, his people would most certainly come to accept the intended reforms. But they would never do so under pressure; popular resentment could not be repressed for long by force without growing stronger and eventually fomenting a potentially violent confrontation. His words were not intended as a threat, for both men were aware that in the event of such a confrontation the Tibetans would not stand a chance. Nor was he playing for time. "I was still convinced that we could not get rid of the Chinese rule simply by uncompromising opposition to it. We could only hope to alleviate it and try patiently to make it evolve into something tolerable." Rather, through a personal account of the recent events in Tibet he was trying to convince Mao to pursue a more practical course. "Mao seemed very pleased with what I told him and said that at one stage the Chinese government had decided to set up a committee of political and military members to govern Tibet directly under the Chinese government, but now he did not think that would be necessary."[4] Instead of that, the Chinese leader added, they had now decided to set up a Preparatory Committee for the Autonomous Region of Tibet, the details of which would be forthcoming.

The two men also spoke of religion. Soon after his arrival in Peking, the Dalai Lama had received a message that Mao would be coming to see him in an hour's time. "When he arrived he said he had merely come to call," the Dalai Lama remembers. "Then something made him say that Buddhism was quite a good religion, and Lord Buddha, although he was a prince, had given a good deal of thought to the question of improving the conditions of the people. He also observed that the goddess Tara was a kindhearted woman. After a very few minutes, he left. I was quite bewildered by these remarks and did not know what to make of them." His surprise was understandable, since the Communists had already begun a systematic attack on the religion of Tibet. "The founder of Buddhism was Sakyamuni," began a typical diatribe. "His kingdom was very aggressive among all the Indian kingdoms of his time. It always used to invade the small kingdoms. It was during the reign of Sakyamuni that his subjects revolted against him and later also other small kingdoms also rose against him simultaneously. As they attacked Sakyamuni, he accepted defeat and escaped amid the fighting. Since there was no other way out for him, he wandered into the forests. Having founded Buddhism, he brought about pessimism and idleness in the minds of the people, weakening their courage, and thus reached his goal of redomination over them. This fact was clearly recorded in history." Shortly before the Dalai Lama's departure from China, Mao expressed to him his conviction that religion was like a poison that undermined the race and retarded the development of countries like Tibet and Mongolia in which it had taken hold. "I was thoroughly startled; what did he mean to imply?" the Dalai Lama recalls. "I tried to compose myself, but I did not know how to take him. I tried to explain that these things were not the fault of religion, but he seemed unwilling to discuss the matter further. He came out to the car with me, and his parting advice was merely that I should take care of my health."

The strained relations between the Panchen Lama and what Mao insisted on calling the "Local Government of Tibet" was another topic of discussion. "He suggested that as we were both in Peking we should take the opportunity to settle our differences," says the Dalai Lama. "I told him these differences were a legacy of the past and that personally I had no differences with the Panchen Lama. If there were any lingering misunderstandings, I would be able to clear them up." To the people of Tibet there were no misunderstandings, lingering or otherwise. Even the mighty Communist Chinese could not alter Buddhist scriptural doctrine by vesting in the Panchen

Lama spiritual "superiority" to the Dalai Lama, any more than they could alter historical fact by granting him political authority. Nevertheless the Chinese prevailed upon the two of them to reach an official agreement in January 1955 bringing an end to all their "historic and unsettled problems."

Despite the Panchen's spurious "recognition," conceded by the Tibetan government only under pressure, the Dalai Lama insisted on treating him as a true incarnate. Perhaps he was simply yielding to the inevitable, perhaps sensing that he and his unfortunate rival shared a similar fate. Both were young and politically inexperienced and had come to occupy their exalted positions through no active volition of their own. When he wrote of the Panchen that "the Chinese have made use of him for their own political ends, knowing that he was too young to protest," he might almost have been writing about himself and the Tibetan government. It is hardly surprising, then, that at the conclusion of their first meeting the Dalai Lama "reminded him how important it was for him, as it was for me, to pursue religious studies," for only in the Buddha's teachings could be found the strength to enable them to persevere. A decade after that meeting, he wrote from exile: "The Panchen Lama cannot be personally blamed. No boy who grew up under such concentrated, constant alien influence could possibly retain his own free will. And in spite of this influence, I do not believe he will ever quite abandon our religion in favor of Communism."

In the meantime, the Dalai Lama found himself treated as an equal to the Panchen Lama, while the Chinese circulated false statements to Western journalists about their relationship. Thus in November 1954 a London newspaper described the Panchen Lama as "the political side of the mysterious Tibetan diarchy," and credited him with organizing the Chinese occupation of Lhasa. The *New York Times* reported three months later that "a triumvirate of the Dalai Lama, the Panchen Lama, and a Chinese general instruct the *Kashag*" and captioned a photograph of the two lamas at the Peking railway station with Chu Teh and Chou En-lai: "The Dalai Lama and Panchen Lama, spiritual and political heads of Tibet." The Chinese also continued to rewrite the history of Tibet and Tibetan Buddhism to suit their own purposes. The Communist Hong Kong daily *Ta Kung Pao* declared that after the death of the great reformer Tsong Khapa, "two of his disciples ruled over Inner and Outer Tibet respectively in accordance with his will. The elder disciple, the Dalai Lama, became ruler of Inner Tibet and the younger disciple, the Panchen Lama, ruler of Outer Tibet." It did not trouble them that the first Dalai Lama to be recognized as such was not born until well over a century after Tsong Khapa's death, that the first Panchen Lama was not identified until yet another century had passed, that the Panchen Lamas never had political authority other than that exercised by any other feudal lord, and that "Inner Tibet" and "Outer Tibet" had existed only on paper as part of the British proposal at Simla in 1914—a proposal, it will be recalled, that the Chinese refused to sign.

At a reception given by Chou En-lai in honor of the Indian prime minister Nehru at the end of October 1954, the Dalai Lama was approached by a British journalist who asked for his autograph. As he wrote his name, another hand appeared. It belonged to the Panchen Lama, who had been pushed forward by his Chinese attendants to add his signature. The reception was one of several occasions on which the Dalai Lama and Nehru were thrown together in Peking, but each time the Indian prime minister went out of his way to avoid substantive conversation. "I was introduced to him by Chou En-lai at a cocktail party," the Dalai Lama says. "He seemed to be absorbed in thought, and for a little while he did not say anything. I told him his name and reputation as a leading statesman of the world had reached us in our isolation in Tibet and that I had been looking forward to meeting him. He smiled but only said he was glad to have met me." When they met on another occasion, a Western journalist noted that "Mr. Nehru appeared to do a swift double-take, then embarked on a most animated conversation to which the Dalai Lama replied with bemused nods." Nehru's evasiveness came as a great disappointment to the Dalai Lama, for he "very much wanted his help and advice."

There was good reason for Nehru's discomfort. In April he had successfully urged the Indian Parliament to approve a controversial treaty with China that included his personal formula for world peace, the Panch Sheela (Five Principles of Peaceful Coexistence), and, by frequent reference to "the Tibet Region of China," deliberately ignored the fact that India and Tibet had been bound by treaty obligations for half a century. The Panch Sheela was apostrophized by opposition spokesman Acharya Kripalani as a document "born in sin,"[5] but however Nehru might have sympathized personally with the plight of the Tibetan people, he was ever fearful of Chinese military power and committed to a policy of avoiding conflict with them at virtually any cost. It had been said, the prime minister replied to the charges of his critics in words doubtless intended to reassure Peking of his good intentions, "that we have committed the mistake of admitting that China has full authority over Tibet. . . . In my opinion, we have done no better thing than this since we became independent. I have no doubt about this." Nehru had no intention of undermining what appeared to be a constructive relationship with the Chinese by involving himself in the problems of Tibet.

His meetings with other foreign dignitaries proved no more rewarding, and after several futile attempts to initiate anything more than polite conversation, the Dalai Lama began to realize that the Chinese did not want him to have a chance to speak frankly to foreigners. He was introduced to Soviet Communist party head Nikita Khrushchev and Defense Minister Nikolai Bulganin when they arrived in Peking to attend the celebration of Chinese National Day, but was given no opportunity to exchange views with them. The Chinese reluctantly permitted him to meet with the Indian ambassador but put a damper on the interview by insisting on replacing his interpreter, who could translate directly from Tibetan into English, with two of their own: one to translate Tibetan into Chinese, and the other Chinese into English. "There were two other extremely grave and pompous Chinese officials present," he recalls. "During the meeting a large bowl of fruit was upset, and my main memory of the occasion is seeing these two very dignified gentlemen on their hands and knees under the table looking for oranges and bananas."

His infrequent and largely happenstance meetings with members of the press were even more constrained, for one or two Chinese attendants were attached to him like shadows, following him wherever he went in public, taking down notes of all he said, and ending prematurely all but the most cursory interviews.

Subtle efforts were also made to indoctrinate the Dalai Lama. A high-ranking official from the Committee of Nationalities Affairs, a Chinese Muslim named Liu Kei-ping, was appointed to accompany him on his tour of China. "Whenever there was leisure time he came to my room and we would discuss the Chinese revolution and Communist ideology," the Dalai Lama says. "I learned a great deal from him and we became good friends."

He was invited to sit in on meetings of high officials, one of which was held at the home of Mao Tse-tung. "I sat next to him and could feel the impact of his personality. The subject of the meeting was the standard of living of the Chinese peasants. He spoke bluntly and, I thought, with great sincerity, saying that he was not yet satisfied with what was being done in this respect. He quoted letters from his own village saying that the Communist officials were not doing all they should to help the people. After a while, he turned to me and said that the Tibetans were firm, or stubborn, in their ideas, but that after twenty years Tibet would be strong. Now China was helping Tibet, but after twenty years Tibet would be helping China. Then Mao spoke of the famous Chinese military leader Shi Ring-gnow who, he said, had led his armies to many victories but had finally met his match in the Tibetans." The story took the Dalai Lama by surprise, for he did not know what was meant by it. Might the Chinese leader have been trying to win him over by flattery? Might he have been threatening to employ harsher methods if Tibetans did not become more receptive to Communist rule? The story would prove a prophetic one both in the near future and during the next quarter-century of Sino-Tibetan relations.

The Dalai Lama was also encouraged to attend meetings of the Chinese National Assembly. "These were my first experience of political meetings, and what struck me v s that so many members showed so little interest in what was going on. I admit I could not take much interest myself. I was too tired after the long journey to China, and the proceedings were in Chinese, which I could not follow. I would have expected the Chinese themselves to be more alert, but I was sitting near some elderly representatives, and they seemed even more tired and bored than I was. The expressions of their faces showed that they could not follow what the discussions were about. They were always watching the clock for the tea break, and when the break was shorter than usual, they complained." He attended many other such conferences during his visit and came away with the same impression of each: "When speeches were made from the floor, they were often irrelevant and usually mere echoes of Communist achievements. When members did express views of their own, it made no difference. A senior member of the party would get up and state the official view, and the chairman would accept it without allowing more discussions. There were genuine discussions in committees, but not even these affected the party's decisions. In short, the long meetings and conferences were empty formalities, because no mere delegate had the power to bring about changes even if he were interested enough to do so."

Accustomed to the clarity of expression in the Buddha's teachings, the Dalai Lama was astounded at the duration of the rambling, monotonous speeches made by the Chinese officialdom. "All the leaders seemed to be passionately devoted to oratory, and they never missed a chance to express their views. I especially remember the speech which Chou En-lai gave after he returned from the Bandung Conference. It was while I was on my way back to Tibet and was held up at Chengtu because there had been an earthquake on the road ahead. Chou En-lai and Marshal Chen Yi, a vice-chairman of the party, also stopped there on their way from the conference back to China. I was told they were coming, and went to the airfield to meet them. Chou En-lai came to the house where I was staying and we had a few minutes' talk, and then we went on to the local army hall. There were about three or four hundred people there, and he started a speech about the success of the Chinese delegation at the conference. He spoke of the importance of studying foreign affairs and told the audience that when he was at the conference he had met representatives of states he had never heard of, so that he had to look them up in an atlas. That speech went on for five solid hours before we came to the usual ending in the glorification of the achievements of the Communist regime. But Chen Yi probably held the record for speeches. When he started, he usually did not stop for seven hours. Listening to this verbosity, I often wondered what was going on in the minds of the audiences. But these were mostly younger Communists, not the few remaining representatives of the older way of life whom I had seen at the National Assembly; and looking around, I hardly ever saw any sign of boredom or weariness. The patience of most of these people seemed to me to show that their minds had already been reformed and reshaped in the pattern of Communism."

This same strong impression of a uniform mass mind was evident during the Dalai Lama's three-month tour of the Chinese provinces. Accompanied by his Chinese tutor and entourage of Tibetan officials, he visited monasteries, industrial plants, workers' organizations, cooperative farms, schools, and universities. "I must say that the whole country had an air of efficiency," he says. "I met many officials, and I still have very happy recollections of some of them. The best were capable and courteous and well trained in diplomacy. Government departments were well organized and worked promptly. I must also say that the ignorant workers seemed to be satisfied, and the general conditions of their life seemed, at that time, to be adequate. It was only among the literate people that one ever had a sense of hidden dissatisfaction. Nor could anyone deny the enormous industrial progress which China had made under Communism.

"But even the merits of efficiency and progress must be balanced against their cost, and it seemed to me that in China the cost was formidable. Progress had cost the people all their individuality. They were becoming a mere homogeneous mass of humanity. Everywhere I went, I found them strictly organized, disciplined, and controlled, so that they not only all dressed the same but all spoke and behaved the same, and, I believe, all thought the same. They could hardly do otherwise, because they had only one source of information—the newspapers and radio published only the government's version of the news. Foreign papers and radio were prohibited. Once, when I was going through a village near Peking with a Chinese officer, I was pleasantly surprised to hear European music, which sounded like the music broadcast by the BBC before its news bulletins. And the startled expression on my escort's face was most revealing. The people even seemed to have lost the habit of laughing spontaneously; they only seemed to laugh when they were supposed to laugh, and to sing when they were told to sing. Certainly some of the young Communists were clever and well educated, in their fashion, but they never expressed original opinions. It was always the same story of the greatness of China and her glorious achievements."

Not even in Sining, near his birthplace on the borders of Tibet, was the Dalai Lama free from such rhetoric. "One of the leaders of the local party gave me a long lecture which was exactly the same thing I had heard so often in Peking. But he did make one original remark: 'Except for Russia,' he said, 'China is the greatest country in the world. It is the only country so great that you have to travel all day and night to cross it.' Even today, a train trip across northern India takes four days, I think. And four nights. It seems he did not know this. At the time, of course, the Chinese could not find words to praise the Russians highly enough! In one of the Manchurian cities I visited there was a museum exhibiting a pictorial history of World War II. An official there explained to me how a combination of Soviet and Chinese Communist forces had defeated the Japanese Imperial Empire. One of the most prominent photographs showed General Douglas MacArthur accepting the Japanese surrender on the battleship *Missouri*. The official bypassed it without comment, but I asked him about it and he told me it was the picture of a famous Russian general."[6]

For the duration of the Dalai Lama's visit to the Chinese People's Republic, the people of Tibet prayed unremittingly for his return. Within two weeks of his departure from Lhasa unusually heavy rains had fallen, causing lakes, streams, and rivers to overflow their banks and inundate the countryside; several thousand perished in the wrathful waters and many more lost their homes, crops, and possessions. "The gods are displeased that His Holiness has left us," they told each other. "If he does not return we shall all be destroyed." The gods, it seems, were selective, reserving their greatest fury for the area of Gyantse and Shigatse, where they took the greatest toll of life and destroyed one of the Panchen Lama's palaces. Upon hearing that Prime Minister Nehru was planning a visit to Peking, some three thousand Tibetans converged on New Delhi to ask him to help bring about the early return of their leader; and many made use of the recently completed Chinese communications system to send telegrams to Peking begging the Dalai Lama to come back to them. Finally their prayers and entreaties were answered, and on March 12, 1955, he left the Chinese capital for the long trip home.

In six fascinating months the Dalai Lama had traveled from one end of the People's Republic to the other, abandoning the traditional Tibetan horse, coracle, and palanquin in favor of the modern jeep, limousine, steamboat, train, and airplane. He had met world leaders Mao Tse-tung, Chou En-lai, Chu Teh, Liu Shao-chi, Khrushchev, Bulganin, Nehru and the Indian prime minister's thirty-six-year-old daughter, Indira Gandhi, as well as ambassadors, journalists, minor functionaries, workers, and peasants, all of whom had treated him with respect—but the kind of respect accorded an ordinary human being rather than a living buddha and God-King. Smiles and handshakes had replaced lowered eyes and prostrations, and conversation had been sought rather than blessings. Such behavior would have shocked and grievously offended the Tibetan people but was found by the Dalai Lama, after years of rigid formality, to be remarkably refreshing. He had learned a great deal about the history of China and particularly about the rise of the Chinese Communist party, committed to memory several hundred Chinese characters so he could read local newspapers, and, with the aid of a tutor from East Turkestan, even begun to study the Russian language. Subjected to a steady diet of propaganda and indoctrination, he had survived it by following Mao Tse-tung's classic advice on the absorption of foreign influence, which the Chinese leader likened to food "first chewed, introduced into the stomach, digested, and separated into essence and residue so the essence becomes our nourishment and the residue is rejected." He had openly admired much of what he had seen, which confirmed in him his belief in the potential benefits of modernization, but discovered that in the People's Republic Communism had provided precious little nourishment and a great deal of residue. Efficiency and material progress had been accompanied by "a gray fog of humorless uniformity, through which the traditional charm and courtesy of old China occasionally shone in a surprising and welcome gleam." He did not think it possible "that the Chinese would ever succeed in reducing Tibetans to such a slavish state of mind. Religion, humor, and individuality are the breath of life to Tibetans, and no Tibetan would ever willingly exchange these qualities for mere material progress, even if the exchange did not also involve subjection to an alien race." Whether he would be proven right or wrong, only time would tell.

As he prepared for his journey back to Lhasa, the Dalai Lama still had hopes of saving his people from the worst consequences of Chinese domination. "I thought my visit to China had helped in two ways. It had certainly shown me exactly what we were up against, and, which was more important, it seemed to have persuaded the Chinese not to go ahead with the original plan, which Mao Tse-tung had admitted, of governing us directly from Peking through a military and political committee. Instead, we seemed to have been left with some authority over our own internal affairs, and we seemed to have a firm promise of autonomy." He would soon discover that Mao's promises were as worthless as the "guarantees" of the Seventeen-Point Agreement.

Notes

1. The Gyayum Chenmo had given birth to a male child in 1943, who died two years later. "It was a grief only too familiar to my parents, because so many of their children had already died," the Dalai Lama says. "But a curious thing happened on the death of the baby. It is the custom in Tibet to consult the lamas and astrologers before a funeral, and sometimes the oracles too. The advice which was given was that the body should not be buried but be preserved, and he would then be reborn in the same house. As proof, a small mark was to be made on the body with a smear of butter. This was done, and in due course my mother had another baby boy—her last child. And when he was reborn, the pale mark was seen on the spot of his body where the butter had been smeared. He was the same being, born again in a new body to start his life afresh."

2. Interview with Amala Yuthok, New York City, July 10, 1981.

3. One of the two Austins had also been put in working order and carried the Gyayum Chenmo, Tsering Dolma, and Ngari Rinpoche. P. T. Takla opted to ride a motorcycle, and the Dalai Lama remembers that upon removing his dust mask and protective goggles several hours later he was surprised to find that Takla had a beet-red, sunburned nose.

4. Mao may have been pleased, but he was conceding nothing. Beginning in May 1952, Chinese officials in Lhasa had been pressuring the Dalai Lama to accept the chairmanship of such a body but had met with his stubborn refusal. In October, Peking abolished military and administrative committees in the rest of the People's Republic, and none ever came into existence in Tibet despite being sanctioned by Article 15 of the Seventeen-Point Agreement.

5. "That is the point where the conduct of the Indian Government is most open to criticism," says Hugh Richardson, "that the enunciation of those high-sounding principles should be based on Indian acquiescence in the extinction of Tibetan freedom and territorial integrity and that the long-standing treaty connection between India and a *de facto* independent Tibet—officially acknowledged only 5

years before—should be allowed to be wiped out without its existence ever being mentioned." Hugh E. Richardson, *A Short History of Tibet* (New York, 1962), 198.

6. "Here is a people with a 3,000-year-old tradition of artistic excellence," remarked a Western journalist in Peking during the Dalai Lama's visit, "queuing for miles to see an exhibition of chocolate box lids, because they are Russian."

Tibetan boy   *Darjeeling 1980*

· CHAPTER 16 ·

Nightmare in the East

"I HAVE HEARD CHAIRMAN MAO talk on different matters and I received instruction from him," said the Dalai Lama shortly after his return from Peking in June 1955 to Alan Winnington, a British reporter for a Communist newspaper who had been invited to Tibet by the Chinese. "I have come to the firm conviction that the brilliant prospects for the people of China as a whole are also prospects for us Tibetan people; the path of our entire country is our path and not any other. New China's economic construction is going ahead quickly. Tibet is still backward economically and educationally, but we know definitely that the central authorities and the people and public servants of the more advanced Han nationality will give every possible help to such backwards nationalities as ourselves." Adjusting his horn-rimmed spectacles—hours of studying the scriptures by the uneven light of the Potala's oil lamps had long since taken its toll of his eyesight—he took a sip of butter tea from a Chinese porcelain cup, which he then returned to its ornate golden stand on the low table in front of him. Before the Seventeen-Point Agreement, he continued, his country had seen no way ahead, but since it had come into effect "Tibet has left the old way that led to darkness and has taken a new way leading to a bright future of development." He smiled gently and rose, indicating that the audience was over. Taking a flowing white *khata* from an official standing at his side, he draped it around the journalist's neck and shook his hand with a surprisingly firm grip. Then, amid a hushed flurry of officials, bodyguards, and attendants, he was gone.

Winnington was clearly impressed. "Here . . . was the ultimate product of Tibetan society, and there was no gainsaying its quality," he wrote shortly afterward. "It was incredible that he was only twenty years old, for he carried himself not only as His Holiness but as a 20th-century Holiness in horn-rimmed spectacles and representing an ancient society meeting the modern world."[1] Throughout the audience, he noted, the God-King had spoken "with ease and assurance, without even a glance at the galaxy of advisers around him, on any subject that came up, sometimes leaning forward

to stir his tea, or gently lift the cup and appear to take a sip, sometimes leaning back, but still appearing to stop just before the moment of relaxation,
fingertips together, smiling, shrewd, and composed beyond his years."
Upon leaving the reception room he was shown around the lush gardens of
the Jewel Park by Lobsang Samden, the Dalai Lama's elder brother and
Chikyap Khenpo, or lord chamberlain. "I was most impressed with His Holiness's manifest ability and strength of character," Winnington commented.
Lobsang smiled wryly. His younger brother, he knew, had told the journalist only what he wished to hear and had done so in the Communist
rhetoric, which alternately amused and appalled him; to have spoken the
truth, to have expressed his sincere convictions regarding the state of his
country, would have been both futile and provocative. "When he went to
Peking he was no more than a boy," he replied. "He learned many things
there and when he came back he could take decisions for himself." And so
he could. But as wheels were put in motion to launch the Preparatory Committee for the Formation of a Tibetan Autonomous Region, it became increasingly obvious that the Chinese would no longer provide him with the
opportunity to do so.

For almost five years the Chinese plan to transform Tibet into a socialist
state had been frustrated. By refraining from land reform and not meddling
in monastic affairs, they had avoided incurring overt opposition from the
nobility and monkhood but had won few friends. Measures designed to
curry favor with the masses had failed to entice the peasants to rise up and
demand that they be freed from the shackles of serfdom. The Tibetan government in general and the Dalai Lama in particular continued to pursue a
policy of passive resistance to their requests and directives, and when the
Tibetan people heard their Precious Protector advocate unity with the Chinese and speak in praise of Chairman Mao, they knew the words came from
his mouth but not from his heart. The Chinese constitution for which the
Dalai Lama had cast his vote in Peking provided regional autonomy for all
"national minorities," but although this status would soon be conferred on
Inner Mongolia and East Turkestan (Sinkiang), Tibet, whose feudal social
and political system had proved stubbornly resistant to Chinese schemes of
modernization, was not deemed ready for similar dispensation. The task of
the Preparatory Committee, therefore, was to lay the groundwork for Tibet's eventual transition to such a stage.

As privately described to the Dalai Lama by Mao Tse-tung in Peking,
the Preparatory Committee was to consist of fifty-one delegates: fifteen
from the "Local Government of Tibet" (the Dalai Lama's government); ten
from the Panchen Khenpo Lija; ten from the "People's Liberation Committee of Chamdo"; eleven from major monasteries, religious sects, public organizations, and prominent individuals; and five from Chinese officials stationed in Lhasa. The Dalai Lama was to be its chairman, General Chang
Kuo-ha and the Panchen Lama the two vice-chairmen, and Kalon Ngabo the

secretary-general. By providing membership to the newly invented "regions" of Shigatse and Chamdo, and by reducing the role of the Dalai Lama from sole authority in Tibet to that of a mere chairman whose vote would count no more heavily that that of any other delegate, the plan was clearly an abrogation of Article 14 of the Seventeen-Point Agreement, which stated that Peking would alter neither the existing political system of Tibet nor the established status, functions, and powers of its leader. "But people in desperate situations are always ready to cling to the slightest hope," the Dalai Lama says, "and I hoped—in spite of my gloomy experience of Chinese political committees—that a committee with forty-six Tibetan members and only five Chinese could be made to work."

That the situation was indeed desperate had become obvious to the Dalai Lama during his three-month journey back to Lhasa through eastern Tibet, areas of his spiritual realm where Chinese reforms had already been begun. "All the way through these border areas, I found the same heavy air of foreboding," he says. "Among the Tibetans, I saw mounting bitterness and hatred of the Chinese; and among the Chinese I saw the mounting ruthlessness and resolution which is born of fear and lack of understanding. To the Chinese I urged moderation with all the emphasis I could; and to Tibetans I often spoke at meetings, telling them that they should remain united, try to improve things by all peaceful means, and accept whatever was good in Chinese methods." In this advice, he felt, lay the only hope of averting violence. But now that he had seen how mutual enmity had grown in the year since he had passed that way, he had to admit to himself that the hope was slender.

This was brought home with painful clarity during a short and bittersweet visit to the village of Taktser where he had been born twenty years earlier. "I was proud and thankful that I had been born in a humble and truly Tibetan family," he remembers, "and I enjoyed reviving my faint memories of the places I had left when I was four." When he spoke to the villagers, he was abruptly brought back to the present. "I asked them if they were happy, and they answered that they were 'very happy and prosperous under the guidance of the Chinese Communist party and Chairman Mao Tse-tung.'" But even while they said it, he saw tears in their eyes and realized "with a shock that even to me they were afraid to answer the question except by this Chinese Communist formula."

Lamas in one of the neighboring monasteries were more outspoken. "I managed to have some long talks with them," says the Dalai Lama, "and found them very anxious. The Chinese had already started to enforce collective farming, and the peasants bitterly resented it. The lamas foresaw that the Chinese would take more and more drastic action to compel the peasants to accept their schemes." He spoke also to a number of lay leaders, who told him that this and other reforms had increased tensions and that the Chinese were becoming more oppressive and suspicious. "I made a point of meeting the Chinese officials and told them that although reforms were necessary, they should not be the same reforms as in China and should not be enforced but only introduced by degrees, with consideration for the local circumstances and the wishes and habits of the people." He found that unlike the Chinese he had met in Peking, the local officials were "rude and completely unsympathetic." They made it clear that the people's needs were of no consequence to them, and one Chinese general went so far as to tell the Dalai Lama that he was calling up extra troops in order to enforce the reforms and that he would not hesitate to make use of them if the Tibetans remained obdurate. Similar reports were brought to the God-King's attention by three high incarnate lamas among his Peking entourage whom he sent to visit those monasteries he could not reach by car during his return journey to the capital. His junior tutor, Trijang Rinpoche, represented the Gelugpa sect, Chung Rinpoche the Nyingmapa sect, and Karmapa Rinpoche (the most recent embodiment of the same Karmapa whose fourth reincarnation had founded the hermitage on the mountain overlooking Taktser) the Kagyupa sect, which had a great many followers in the area.[2]

Nevertheless the Dalai Lama felt he had no alternative but to make a sincere effort to guide his country's destiny through the framework of the Preparatory Committee, and made this clear to his own people and to the Chinese at its inauguration in April 1956. Acting against the advice of the Kashag, he made a point of going to greet Peking's representative to the event, Marshal Chen Yi, when the latter arrived in the holy city. He described the committee as "another brilliant achievement of the Chinese Communist party's nationalities policy" which "not only shows the greater unity within Tibet but also marks the increasing consolidation and growth of unity and cooperation among the peoples of all the fraternal nationalities in the country," declaring it to be "an unprecedentedly happy event of great historical significance to the political life of the Tibetan people" and emphasizing that "the earnest implementation of the various provisions of the Agreement is our sacred and glorious task."

On the surface the new constitutional scheme was attractive and seemed sound. It brought Lhasa, Shigatse, and Chamdo together under a single administration once again and, with such a high proportion of Tibetan members on the committee, seemed to the Dalai Lama "as though it could evolve into a more efficient form of government not too unlike our own." Moreover, he felt, it might provide an opportunity for Tibetan officials to learn from the Chinese the modern administration of government. But it soon became apparent that rather than protect regional autonomy and ensure the survival of a modicum of Tibet's ancient individuality, the Preparatory Committee was going to be used to subvert his government and substitute for it a system completely subordinate to the direct control of Peking under the guise of legitimate authority.

To begin with, twenty of the members were representatives of the

Chamdo Liberation Committee and the Panchen Khenpo Lija, purely Chinese creations whose members owed their positions mainly to Chinese support and voted accordingly. Together with this block of controlled votes were those of the five Chinese members, a combination just one short of a majority. When the regulations were adopted in final form in September 1956, moreover, the committee's size had been increased to fifty-five members and Lhasa's representation reduced from fifteen to ten, the same as that of Shigatse and Chamdo. Peking was no longer willing to acknowledge Lhasa's primacy by assigning it a few extra votes; to the contrary, it was indicating that the time of its ascendancy had come to an end.

Just as the overwhelming numerical superiority of Tibetans to Chinese on the committee was meaningless, so, too, were the relative numbers of pro-Tibetans and pro-Chinese because all basic policy was decided by another body called the Committee of the Chinese Communist Party in Tibet—a group that had no Tibetan members. "We were allowed to discuss the minor points but could never make any changes," the Dalai Lama says. "Although I was nominally chairman, there was nothing much I could do. Sometimes it was almost laughable to see how the proceedings were controlled and regulated, so that plans already completed in the other committee received a pointless and empty discussion and then were passed." Additionally, substantive decisions by the Preparatory Committee had first to be submitted to the State Council before being put into effect, a stipulation giving Peking the power to veto any measure it did not find to its liking, and a negation of both the spirit of the Chinese constitution and the concept of regional autonomy. The Dalai Lama was hardly unaware that the Chinese had made him chairman only to provide a further semblance of Tibetan authority to the scheme.

As the humiliating details of the Preparatory Committee gradually leaked out to the Tibetan people, the situation in Lhasa grew tense. While the Dalai Lama was in Peking they had repressed overt expression of their hostility toward the Chinese for fear he might be held hostage, but upon his safe return to the holy city, tempers flared anew. A public meeting was held in Lhasa to protest the new organization and a resolution sent to the Chinese authorities which stated that Tibetans neither needed nor wanted a new form of government because they were happy with their own. In response the Chinese forced the Kashag to draft a new proclamation banning public meetings, which the Dalai Lama signed unwillingly and with the awareness that the suppression of such assemblages would not succeed in suppressing public indignation.

The Dalai Lama's fears were confirmed during the Monlam festival at the beginning of 1956, when incendiary pamphlets and posters appeared all over Lhasa declaring that "the Tibetan nation is facing as grave a danger as a candlelight in a severe storm," demanding the Chinese leave Tibet, and vowing to "shed our blood and sacrifice our lives to oppose the Communists." Furious, the Chinese called in the Kashag. Berating the ministers for not controlling the people, they produced the names of three of the popular leaders and demanded they be arrested at once; if the Kashag refused to do so, the Chinese made clear that they would arrest and interrogate them. The Dalai Lama was in a quandary. "These were the men who organized and led the Lhasan population," he says. "On the whole, the anger they felt and expressed on behalf of the people had its normal reaction—they wanted to hit back. Inevitably that brought them into conflict sometimes with my cabinet, who saw as I did the futility of trying to hit back against the Chinese army. The cabinet had to restrain them from a policy which was patriotic but suicidal. On the other hand, they naturally thought the cabinet went too far in appeasing the invaders." Sometimes he found it necessary "to intervene and oppose their violent instincts for the sake of the very people they represented. They might have resented that, but to the bitter end they remained passionately loyal to me. I do not flatter myself that I earned this loyalty by personal qualities of my own. It was the concept of the Dalai Lama which held their loyalty, as it did and does all Tibetans. I was a symbol of what they were fighting for." Reluctantly he gave his assent to the arrest of the three men.

Despite being forced to make such unpleasant and unpopular decisions, the Dalai Lama was hardly a willing accomplice of the Chinese. During the course of the same speech in which he described the new Preparatory Committee as a "brilliant achievement" and "an unprecedentedly happy event" and praised the "wise and correct leadership" of Mao Tse-tung and the Chinese Communist party, he also managed both to reassure the citizens of Lhasa that he was aware of their plight and to urge the Chinese to proceed with caution. While "extremely grateful" for the Chinese road-building program in which thousands of Tibetans had been compelled to work under dangerous and trying conditions, he noted that "many people have sacrificed their valuable lives in the cause of construction" and expressed "my sincere condolences to these martyrs' dependents." Noting that the Chinese had adhered so far to the policy of freedom of religion, he made clear that "the Tibetan people treasure and protect their religious beliefs as they would their life." And although conceding that Tibet "has no alternative but to take up the road of socialism" he emphasized that reforms were to be carried out "step by step" and only "through consultation by the leaders of Tibet and the broad masses of people themselves—and not by others on their behalf." Chairman Mao, he added, had told him repeatedly "that we should carry out reforms slowly and with patience," so there was "no need to be apprehensive or fear reform or worry too much."

To the people of eastern Tibet, who owed their spiritual allegiance to the Dalai Lama but lived ouside his temporal domain, there was a great deal to fear. Even while the God-King was delivering his speech in Lhasa, the people of Kham and Amdo were being brutalized by the Chinese under the banner of reform. Just as they had conquered Tibet in three stages—propaganda, invasion, and treaty—so, too, had they moved to assimilate it into the People's Republic. First they completed road and air communications between the two countries, an act that oriented trade toward China rather than India, facilitated a massive immigration of Chinese settlers to dilute the hostile Tibetan population, and permitted the supply and reinforcement of their substantial military presence in Tibet. Second, through a policy of divide and rule they either subverted the Dalai Lama's government or supplanted it altogether. All that remained was for them to break down local resistance to their scheme by a concerted attack on the very fabric of Tibetan society. The following are but a few examples of atrocities they committed in doing so, the majority of which occurred in areas of Tibet where for various reasons the "guarantees" of the Seventeen-Point Agreement and Preparatory Committee's regulations did not apply. On the other hand, all who fell victim to the Communists were presumably under the protection of the new, and much-vaunted, Constitution of the People's Republic of China.

CONSTITUTION OF THE PEOPLE'S REPUBLIC OF CHINA

ARTICLE 11: *"The state protects the right of citizens to own lawfully earned incomes, savings, houses, and other means of life."*

Kham, 1957

A nomad is promised ten Chinese dollars a month to appear at public meetings and denounce members of the wealthy classes for exploitation. Their elimination, he is told, is the only chance for the poor to better themselves. He is aware that what he is doing is wrong and after attending two such meetings he flees to the hills.

Kham, 1955

After their property has been confiscated, some fifty landowners are first imprisoned and then made to stay in trenches. They are fed once a day and told they must atone in this manner for their love of wealth.

Kham, 1950

A thirty-three-year-old farmer witnesses the execution of his village headman, who was caught by the People's Liberation Army attempting to flee. His servants are shot and he is kept without food for several days and led like a dog with a chain around his neck. The Chinese accuse him of ill-treating the peasants, but the latter deny this and plead for his life. He is not shot, but all his property is confiscated and his four children, aged thirteen and under, are taken to China.

Amdo, 1956

A list of people who have allegedly failed to disclose and surrender their assets is given to the Chinese by the new Tibetan "People's Leaders," former beggars whom the Communists have "reformed" by the simple expedient of a few coins. All are arrested. Some are sent to work on railway construction and the others shot in full view of a large gathering of villagers. One man is shot in stages working up the body, there being nine stages in all. Another is asked whether he would prefer to die standing up or lying down. He prefers standing. A pit is dug and he is placed upright inside it. Then it is filled with mud and compressed, a process which is continued until his eyes protrude from his head and are severed by the Chinese. By then he is already dead.

CONSTITUTION OF THE PEOPLE'S REPUBLIC OF CHINA

ARTICLE 89: *"Freedom of person of citizens of the People's Republic of China is inviolable."*

Kham, 1956

The daughter of a village headman and landowner is accused of being an exploiter of the people and publicly humiliated by the local riffraff, egged on by the Chinese. The woman, about forty years of age, is forced to get down on all fours. She is harnessed and saddled and her mouth stuffed with hay, then "ridden" by her tormenters until they grow tired of the sport.

Kham, 1954

A middle-aged farmer hears a disturbance at his brother's house next door. Peering from his window, he sees his brother's wife, her mouth gagged with a towel, being raped by four Chinese, three soldiers and a civilian. He does not attempt to intervene because they are armed, nor does his brother when told of the incident after returning home from a visit to a nearby nomad encampment. After a series of similar incidents, a group of villagers complain to the local Chinese commander, who tells them he is about to be transferred and that they should bring the matter to the attention of his successor. When they do so, they are instructed to report to the police, who promise to instruct the soldiers to behave themselves. No attempt is made to punish the offenders, and the rapes continue.

Kham, 1955

A man is arrested by the Chinese and taken to a hall where the local villagers have been instructed to assemble. He is accused of failing to turn in all his property to the people, and Tibetan beggars who have recently become soldiers in the P.L.A. beat him with sticks and pour boiling water on his head until he "confesses" that he has nine loads of gold. Then he is trussed and strung up by his thumbs and big toes over a straw fire and ordered to reveal its location. He is unable to answer because he has none. Finally a red-hot copper nail is driven into his forehead. The gold is never found.

Kham, 1950

A district officer runs away when the P.L.A. march into his jurisdiction but is captured and brought back naked. Being a fat man, he has difficulty walking fast enough to suit the Chinese, who prod him with bayonets to make him go faster until his body is covered with wounds. The Chinese tie him to a tree and invite all Tibetans he has mistreated to beat him—but not to beat him to death because he would benefit by this. No one comes forward, so the Chinese beat him themselves for eight days and cut off his lips when he begs to be shot instead of tortured.

CONSTITUTION OF THE PEOPLE'S REPUBLIC OF CHINA

> ARTICLE 96: *"The state protects marriage, the family, and the mother and child."*

Amdo, 1957

At a public assembly the Chinese announce that Tibetan families in which the husband is either dead or away from home must permit a male Chinese immigrant to move in with them. Thirty-five such "attachments" subsequently take place in one village.

Amdo, 1951

Young Tibetans aged fifteen to twenty-five begin to be sent to China for education. When they have been educated, they are told, Tibet can become autonomous. But first they must learn modern agricultural methods, how to drive cars, and Communist ideology so they can join in the fight against the American and British imperialists. Later in the same year children from eight to fifteen begin to be sent as well. The youngest of these are taken to see movies and plays and told they will see many more in China. If the children are willing to go but the parents unwilling, the parents are told by the

Chinese they have no right to interfere. If neither the child nor the parents are willing, the parents are taken before a public meeting and denounced as reactionaries, but no other steps are taken.

Amdo, 1955

Babies are taken away to China, and the reason given is that they are to go to learn Communism and to come back and lead in the development and progress of their country.

Kham, 1954

Forty-eight infants below the age of one are seized by the Chinese, who say they are to be taken to China so their parents can do more work. Fifteen parents who protest are thrown into the river and drown. One commits suicide.

Kham, 1954

Children are encouraged to submit their parents to indignities and to criticize them if they fail to conform to the "wise and correct leadership" of Chairman Mao. Upon seeing his father with a prayer wheel and rosary, a nineteen-year-old youth begins to abuse him and a fight ensues. Several villagers try to intervene but are stopped by three Chinese soldiers, who announce that the boy has a perfect right to act in this manner. Beaten and humiliated, the father commits suicide by jumping into the river.

Kham, 1951

A twelve-year-old girl is told by the Chinese that her father is an imperialist, and is made to shoot him.

Amdo, 1956

A twenty-two-year-old man is told by the Chinese that a blood specimen taken from him the previous day revealed that he is in need of urgent medical treatment. He is undressed and placed on a chair, and his genital organs are examined. A digital rectal examination is carried out and the finger is agitated, causing him to ejaculate a whitish fluid, of which several drops are taken away on a glass slide. A long pointed instrument with scissorlike handles is inserted inside his urethra and he faints with pain; when he regains consciousness he is given a white tablet, which the doctors say will give him strength. He receives an injection at the base of his penis where it joins the scrotum; the needle hurts but the injection does not. After ten days in hospital he is permitted to return home, where he remains in bed for a month. He is given no further medical treatment but is instructed to tell no one what has taken place.

Prior to this treatment he had been in good health; he had suffered no discomfort in his genital organs and had seen no sores. Now he finds that he has no sexual desire at all. Three or four months after the treatment he attempts to have intercourse with his wife, but has no desire and no erection. He is very upset and does not try again: he used to have very strong sexual feelings. He sometimes suffers from giddy spells and his voice, which was formerly a good singing voice, has become higher-pitched; people now tell him he sings like a goat.

Amdo, 1956

The thirty-two-year-old wife of another peasant is sent for by the Chinese and a blood sample taken from her arm. The following day she is called in and told she is suffering from an illness left behind from the birth of her only child, a girl seven years of age. She does not understand this, for she has never suffered a miscarriage and her daughter has always been very healthy. Nevertheless she is strapped to a chair and examined. Something is inserted inside her vagina and she suffers a burning sensation; it seems to grow larger and, at the same time, she feels as if something is being removed. She sees a few drops of blood and experiences severe pain, but is told that others are waiting and that she should dress and go home. Although her menstrual cycle had been normal prior to the treatment, she now ceases to menstruate entirely.

CONSTITUTION OF THE PEOPLE'S REPUBLIC OF CHINA

ARTICLE 88: *"Citizens of the People's Republic of China enjoy freedom of religious belief."*

Amdo, 1954

Two laymen are arrested by the Chinese and accused of setting a bad example by making religious offerings. A board displaying their names is attached to their backs and the local villagers are summoned to witness their humiliation. "Here are two people who have faith in religion and have given all their wealth to the lamas," the Chinese announce. "As such they are useless to the Chinese Communist party, and letting them live will set a bad example for our youth." The men are led to the edge of a trench and shot in the back of the head, and the villagers are told that if they fail to display the proper patriotic feeling by continuing to go to monks, they will be dealt with similarly.

Amdo, 1956

His hands bound by a chain that tightens whenever he moves, an abbot is placed in waist-high cold water and kept there over two weeks after he denies having hidden gold in his monastery. Valuable images are removed, and those of little monetary worth thrown into the river by the monks and lamas on the orders of the Chinese, who explain they are merely trying to discover if the images can swim. When they fail to do so, the Chinese tell the people called to witness the act that the images were meant only to deceive them.

Amdo, 1957

Three high lamas are arrested and accused by the Chinese of being the main obstacles on the road to progress. They are publicly humiliated by Tibetans acting under the threat of death and Chinese women, who pull out their hair and beat them. Forced to kneel on gravel, they are asked, "Since you are great lamas, did you not know you were to be arrested?," a reference to their supposed powers of prophecy. Then they are placed inside a pit and the public is ordered to urinate on them, while the Chinese stand by and invite them to fly out of the pit by means of their supernatural powers.

Kham, 1958

The Chinese begin to press monks to live with women, threatening them with death if they refuse. A mill girl is offered one hundred Chinese dollars for each monk she is able to persuade to have intercourse with her. Soon there are some fifty monks cohabiting with women in one monastery alone.

Kham, 1958

A hermit lama is locked up without food or water for five days. The Chinese accuse him of being an exploiter and tell him that God will provide him with sustenance. After he dies they summon the local people to come and see the corpse, and tell them that if God had helped the man, he would still be alive.

Amdo, 1955

The Chinese use the main temple of a monastery to stable their horses, and bring in groups of women under armed escort. When the monks refuse to take them, two are crucified by nails and left to die. Scriptures are turned into mattresses or used for toilet paper, and when a monk asks the Chinese to desist, they cut off his arm above the elbow. God, they tell him, will give him back his arm.[3]

Herdsmen on the Tsinghai [Amdo] Pastures Advance Bravely with Flying Flags

After the liberation . . . our party adopted the principle of peaceful reform, correctly carrying out the policies of (a) "no struggle, no confiscation, no class-division," (b) protection of benefits for both the herdsmen and their employers, (c) assistance for poor farmers and herdsmen to develop their production, and (d) freedom of religious worship. . . . However, the feudalistic exploiting class has always been reluctant to give up; they have consistently adopted double-dealing methods to undermine the policies of the party and have refused to be reformed.

The diehard faction among them, encouraged by reactionaries from outside, has been engaged in conspiracies for a long time under the camouflage of national minorities and religion. . . . During the high-tide period of socialist reform, they were very active in producing rumors and in sabotage, engaging themselves feverishly in counterrevolutionary activities with the purpose of frustrating the socialist revolution. This became intolerable for the masses; therefore, we adopted the principle of fighting back with firmness, wiping out all counterrevolutionary elements . . . and speeding up the socialist reform; we mobilized the masses in time without restraint, widely and deeply carried out a thunderous socialist education movement, developed the two-way big debate, and thus started the great socialist revolution.

The great socialist revolution . . . has been a very violent class struggle of life and death. After the accusations and exploitations of the vast masses, the reactionary essence and ugly features of the feudalistic exploiting class have been fully revealed. Economically, they have been exploiting the people . . . politically, they have put the vast laboring herdsmen into a constant situation of extraordinary poverty and distress, by various kinds of barbaric lynch laws such as cutting off people's hands, eyes, tongue, or ears. In the places where they lived you could usually find human skulls, human bones, bloody knives, guns, ammunition, fetters, handcuffs, whips, etc. . . . These facts indicate that the feudalistic exploiting class is utterly cruel, venomous, obscene, and shameless.

In this violent class struggle . . . the class consciousness of the vast laboring herdsmen was rapidly promoted. After they perceived the reactionary essence of the feudalistic exploiting class, they were all greatly surprised and rose up with set teeth to accuse the exploiting class of their heinous crimes; and they voluntarily bound the counterrevolutionary elements . . . and handed them over to the government, asking for them to be punished.

After stripping off the religious cloak of the counterrevolutionary elements in religious circles, they exposed their fraud; and the
masses say: "We shall never permit these man-eating wolves to do
evil things while riding on the neck of the people waving religious
banners." At the debate meetings, the masses were so excited that
they shouted continuously: "Long live Chairman Mao! Long live
the Communist party! We are liberated!"[4]

By the end of 1955, armed rebellion had broken out in eastern Tibet.
The Dalai Lama did not learn of it until the spring of the following year
because his government had no representatives there and Peking's officials in
Lhasa preferred he remain ignorant of the situation. Chinese Foreign Minister Chen Yi had in fact barely escaped assassination when he passed through
the volatile area en route to attend the inaugural meeting of the Preparatory
Committee in April 1956 but had neglected to mention it upon his arrival.
Early accounts of the uprising were brought to the holy city first by traders
and pilgrims and later by refugees whose villages had been destroyed by the
Communists in retaliatory raids, and similar reports began leaking out to
the Western press through Kalimpong and the Nepalese capital of Kathmandu. These were so persistent that Peking was obliged finally to concede
that a rebellion was indeed taking place—but claimed it was localized in
western Szechuan rather than in Tibet. According to Premier Liu Shao-chi,
it had been instigated by Kuomintang agents and "a few feudal landlords
hostile to the introduction of even the most elementary reforms in the backward social structure of that region."[5]

To the Dalai Lama the situation seemed desperate and without any
imaginable end. The guerrillas, he knew, could hold out for years in the
vast, impregnable mountains of Kham and Amdo, and the Chinese would
never be able to dislodge them. Equally certain, however, was that they
would never be able to defeat the P.L.A., and for as long as the fighting went
on it would be the people of Tibet, especially women, children, and the elderly, who would suffer. "I was very despondent," he remembers. "The
situation now had become even worse than it had been two years before. The
vicious circle of dictatorial repression and popular resentment, which I
thought I had broken when I allowed Lukhangwa to resign, had enclosed us
again. So far, all my attempts at a peaceful solution of our problems had
come to nothing, and with the Preparatory Committee a mere mockery of
responsible government I could see no better hope of success in the future."
Worst of all, he felt he was losing control of his people. "In the east they
were being driven into barbarism. In central Tibet they were growing more
determined to resort to violence; and I felt I would not be able to stop them
much longer, even though I could not approve of violence and did not believe it could possibly help us."

More than ever he felt buffeted by circumstances beyond his control and torn between two apparently irreconcilable roles. "My dual position as Dalai Lama was becoming almost insupportable. In both my capacities as religious and secular leader, I felt bound to oppose any violence by the people. I knew the Chinese were trying to undermine my political authority; and insofar as I opposed the people's violent instincts, I was helping the Chinese to destroy the people's trust in me. Yet even if the people lost faith in me as their secular leader, they must not lose faith in me as religious leader, which was much more important. I could delegate or abdicate my secular leadership, but the Dalai Lama could never abdicate as religious leader, nor would I ever have dreamed of doing so. Thus I began to think it might be in the best interests of Tibet if I withdrew from all political activities, in order to keep my religious authority intact. Yet while I was in Tibet, I could not escape from politics. To withdraw, I would have to leave the country. Bitterly and desperately I hated that idea."

At that moment, at the depth of his despondency, he received an invitation to visit India.

Notes

1. "And here was something more, which no Dalai Lama had ever been," Winnington continued enthusiastically, "Vice-Chairman of the Standing Committee of the National People's Congress of China." His words were meant to be neither humorous nor ironic. Alan Winnington, *Tibet: Record of a Journey* (New York, 1957), 129–136.
2. Four years later the Chinese would accuse the three lamas of inciting the locals to rise up against them. The charge was sheer nonsense, for such an action would have been completely contrary to the Dalai Lama's wishes.
3. Eyewitness accounts supplied to the Legal Inquiry Committee on Tibet of the International Commission of Jurists by Tibetan refugees in India. The committee found that acts of genocide had been committed by the Chinese occupation forces in Tibet "in an attempt to destroy the Tibetans as a religious group." However, "despite evidence of wide-spread killings and forcible transfer of children," the committee held that the Tibetans' right to exist as a national, ethnic, or racial group was not violated, for although "a Tibetan who would not give up his religion was killed or ran the risk of being killed, he could never give up being a Tibetan." *Tibet and the Chinese People's Republic: A Report to the International Commission of Jurists by Its Legal Inquiry Committee on Tibet* (Geneva, 1960).
4. Liu Tse-hsi, Director, Rural Work Department, C.C.P., Tsinghai Provincial Committee, in *Min-tsu T'uan-chieh*, no. 11, November 6, 1958.
5. The Chinese mistreatment of ethnic Tibetans residing within the borders of the Chinese People's Republic was a major cause of the Tibetan National Uprising in 1959. Although the Khampas "were hostile to the Tibetan Government and in particular to the lay aristocratic ruling elites, their loyalty to the Dalai Lama as an incarnation of the Buddha of Compassion, and as supreme pontiff of Tibetan Buddhism which was operative throughout Buddhist Central Asia, was unquestionable." Dawa Norbu, "The 1959 Tibetan Rebellion: An Interpretation," *China Quarterly* (March 1979), 80.

The Dalai Lama and Jawaharlal Nehru   *New Delhi 1956*

• CHAPTER 17 •

A Special Sort of Gentleness

THE INVITATION for the Dalai Lama to visit India was delivered to him personally in Lhasa by his friend the Maharaj Kumar, crown prince of Sikkim, the Buddhist kingdom in the foothills of the Himalaya which had recently become an Indian protectorate. It was extended by the Mahabodhi Society of India, an institution founded near the end of the nineteenth century to propagate Buddhist teachings and to care for pilgrims and holy shrines in India. The occasion was to be the Buddha Jayanti, the 2,500th anniversary of the birth of Lord Buddha.

Religious, personal, and political considerations prompted him to attend the celebration. Although the Buddha's birthplace had since fallen within the political borders of Nepal, to Tibetans India was still the holy land to which, after Lhasa, they hoped to make a pilgrimage once in their lives. Hundreds of years before, great saints and seers like Atisha, Marpa, and Padmasambhava—Guru Rinpoche, the Precious Protector—had traversed the snowy peaks separating the two ancient lands to bring the Dharma to the Roof of the World; and in many ways Tibet was still a child of Indian civilization. The trip would also provide an opportunity for the young ruler to absent himself, for a short time at least, from the increasingly stressful situation in the holy city and give him a much-needed emotional respite; even for an individual blessed with such determination and strength of character, the close contact with the Chinese and their endless machinations were beginning to take their toll. Moreover, the Dalai Lama hoped to solicit the advice of Jawaharlal Nehru and other Indian political leaders. "I cannot exaggerate our feeling of political solitude in Tibet," he says. "I knew I was still inexperienced in international politics, but so was everyone else in our country. We knew other countries had faced situations like ours, and that a great fund of political wisdom and experience existed in the democratic world; but so far, none of it had been available for us, and we had been forced to act by a kind of untrained instinct. We desperately wanted sympathetic wise advice."

Despite his advocacy of the Panch Sheela, there is little doubt that the Indian prime minister was sympathetic to the plight of the Tibetan people. "Since Tibet is not the same as China," he had asserted during the course of a parliamentary debate shortly after the Communist invasion in 1950, "it should ultimately be the wishes of the Tibetan people that should prevail and not any legal or constitutional arguments." That Nehru's sympathy would not be expressed in political action helpful to the Tibetan people, however, became obvious in his next words. "Whether the people of Tibet are strong enough to assert their rights or not is another matter," he continued. "Whether we are strong enough or any other country is strong enough to see that this is done is also another matter." Because the British government of India had long been the sole Tibetan contact with the Western world—a contact that had faded precipitately after the transfer of power to the Indian government in 1947—the Dalai Lama hoped, despite Nehru's open courtship of Peking, "to renew it and keep it strong as a lifeline to the world of tolerance and freedom." Under the circumstances there was little else he could do.

But before he could accept the invitation, the Dalai Lama had to obtain the approval of the Chinese officials. A few months earlier he had been invited to the coronation of Nepal's King Mahendra but had been obliged to send word that he would be too busy with "constitutional reforms" to attend, and that in any event the heat of Kathmandu would be too great for someone used to the temperate mountain air of the Tibetan plateau—despite the fact that the temperature of the Nepalese capital customarily hovered around seventy degrees at that time of year. Nevertheless he brought this new invitation to the attention of General Fan Ming, a high-ranking official who had been in Lhasa from the beginning of the occupation and was temporarily replacing General Chang Ching-wu as Peking's senior representative, and asked for the requisite approval. "He started by saying that he could only offer me suggestions," the Dalai Lama remembers. "But he did not really leave me any doubt that they would be the kind of suggestions which have to be accepted, and my heart sank as he spoke. For reasons of security, he said, a visit to India was undesirable. He also thought that as the Preparatory Committee still had much work to do, and as I was its chairman, I ought to stay in Lhasa. And then he added, like a consolation, that after all, the invitation had only come from a religious organization, not from the government of India, so that there was no need for me to accept it, as I could easily send a deputy."

Disappointed, the Dalai Lama put off naming a deputy and did not advise the Mahabodhi Society of his inability to attend. Some four months later, in the middle of October 1956, he was visited by Fan Ming, who suggested again that he choose someone to represent him; the name, explained the general, had to be sent in advance to India. Accordingly he made arrangements for a delegation to go on his behalf, but less than two weeks later the general was back again. "He admitted that on the first of October the Chinese government had received a telegram from the Indian government inviting me and the Panchen Lama as its guests for the celebration, and added that the Chinese government had considered the matter in all aspects and that it would be all right to go if I wanted to. I was delighted, and so were the Lhasan people. And the story went round that the Indian consul general in Lhasa had told several people about the invitation before General Fan Ming told me; and of course everyone inferred that the Chinese had been trying to keep the invitation secret until it was too late for me to accept it, and had been only forced to make up their minds by this disclosure." No doubt the invitation of the Panchen Lama played a part in Peking's decision, as did the desire to promote the notion that Communism and Buddhism stood side by side in their devotion to peace and nonviolence. At a recent Buddhist Congress in Nepal, Chinese and Soviet speakers had glowingly portrayed Karl Marx as another reincarnation of Lord Buddha.[1]

Before leaving Lhasa the Dalai Lama was given a long lecture by General Chang Ching-wu, who had returned as permanent representative of the People's Republic in Tibet. "He said that recently there had been a little trouble in Hungary and Poland which had been engineered by small groups of people under the influence of foreign imperialists," he recalls. "But Soviet Russia had responded immediately to the Hungarian and Polish people's call for help, and had put down the reactionaries without any difficulty." Reactionaries were always looking for chances to create trouble in socialist countries, the general continued, but the solidarity of the socialist powers was so great that they would always combine to meet any threat. "He talked about this so long," the Dalai Lama says, "that I realized it was the hint of a warning that no other country would be allowed to interfere in Tibet."

The general also spoke of the visit to India. "Although the occasion of the Jayanti, he said, was purely religious, it had something to do with UNESCO. The Chinese government was sending a delegation to it, but there was a possibility the Kuomintang would also try to send one from Formosa. If they did, the Chinese would leave the meeting, and they had already told the Indian government so; and I was also to refuse to take part if anyone from Formosa was present." If asked about the situation in Tibet by the press or minor officials, the Dalai Lama was to reply that there had been a little trouble but that everything was back to normal, but Nehru and other high officials of the Indian government could be told that there had been uprisings in some parts of Tibet. Finally it was "suggested" that if he was to make any speeches during the celebration, they be prepared in advance in Lhasa, and he was given the draft of one to be delivered at the Buddha Jayanti which had been written by Kalon Ngabo, as secretary-general of the Preparatory Committee, in consultation with the Chinese. He rewrote it entirely after arriving in India.

The route taken by the Dalai Lama was almost the same as the one he had taken when he had fled to the Chumbi Valley six years earlier when the Chinese invaded eastern Tibet. A new highway now reached to within two days' march of the border, and he was driven to Yatung in two days, stopping along the way at Shigatse for the Panchen Lama. In 1950 the same trip had taken two weeks. On horseback he ascended the steep track leading to Nathu-la,[2] the snowy mountain pass high above the treeline. Behind him lay the familiar barren scenery of Tibet, before him the beautiful wooded gorges of Sikkim and the flat steaming plains of India; and for a moment, freed from the burdensome presence of his Chinese watchdogs and the turmoil of his homeland, he surrendered himself to a reverie of pleasant anticipation and excitement he had not experienced since he was a child.

At the top of Nathu-la the Dalai Lama was greeted by a guard of honor led by the Maharaj Kumar and the Indian political officer of Sikkim, who extended the welcome of his government and presented him with a *khata*, the traditional symbol of greeting in Tibet, and a garland of flowers, the corresponding symbol in India. The party moved down to a resthouse at Tsongo, where hundreds of Tibetans, turning prayer wheels and telling rosaries, had braved sleet and freezing winds to await their leader. Their presence made him feel "almost as if I were not in a foreign country at all," he says. "I felt at home." Early the next morning the caravan, swollen in size to some two thousand horsemen, proceeded down the steep, winding trail into the heart of the little country, no larger than Yellowstone National Park. At the tenth mile a motorable road began and they took to scores of jeeps, light trucks, and Land Rovers that had been sent for them. On the outskirts of Gangtok, the capital, the Dalai Lama changed from his jeep into the Maharaj's car, a brand-new Buick flying a Sikkimese flag on one side and a Tibetan flag on the other. "There was a comic incident with that car," says the Dalai Lama. "We had stopped for a little while on the way into town. A great crowd of people was throwing scarves and flowers in greeting, when I was surprised to see a solitary Chinese gentleman, who turned out to be the ambassador's interpreter, furtively removing the Tibetan flag and tying on a Chinese flag instead. My Indian friends noticed him too, and I was delighted to find that they also saw the funny side of it." An estimated 10,000 people turned out to greet him.

After spending the night at the monastery of the Maharaj's palace, the Dalai Lama was driven down the narrow, winding roads of the Himalaya to the airport of Baghdogra on the Indian plain some five hours distant and boarded a chartered aircraft for New Delhi. There he was welcomed by Prime Minister Nehru, Indian Vice-President Radhakrishnan, and a huge throng of excited Tibetans. Nehru's daughter, Indira Gandhi, presented him with a bouquet of red roses, but Indian officials thought it wise not to garland him with the customary floral wreath. "Everything he touches becomes holy," explained one to a confused Western journalist. "When he casts them off there might be a riot among his followers clutching for one of the flowers." Newsmen were stunned by the reception accorded the Tibetan leader. One described it as "something strange and different, a blend of reverence, tenderness and affection." When the Dalai Lama stepped off the airplane, Nehru and Radhakrishnan "each took him by the hand and gently, almost lovingly, led him to a reviewing stand." That "special sort of gentleness" toward the young ruler was felt during his entire visit. "This is something no reporter can demonstrate quantitatively, or even prove at all," conceded the writer, "but can only report as something he knew existed." By way of contrast, despite persistent Chinese efforts to get equal publicity for the Panchen Lama, to Indians and reporters alike "he seemed to be just somebody who came along."[3]

The Dalai Lama arose before dawn the next morning and visited the Rajghat, site of Mahatma Gandhi's cremation nine years earlier. As he prayed there on the green lawns that sloped down to the banks of the Jamuna River, he was deeply moved. "I felt I was in the presence of a noble soul—the soul of the man who in his life was perhaps the greatest of our age, the man who had contended till death itself to preserve the spirit of India and mankind—a true disciple of Lord Buddha and a true believer in peace and harmony among men. As I stood there I wondered what wise counsel the Mahatma would have given me if he had been alive. I felt sure he would have thrown all his strength of will and character into a peaceful campaign for the freedom of the people of Tibet. I wished fervently that I had had the privilege of meeting him in this world. But, standing there, I felt I had come in close touch with him, and I felt his advice would always be that I should follow the path of peace. I had and still have unshaken faith in the doctrine of nonviolence which he preached and practiced. Now I made up my mind more firmly to follow his lead whatever difficulties might confront me. I determined more strongly than ever that I could never associate myself with acts of violence."

Despite his involvement with the Buddha Jayanti celebrations, the Dalai Lama made himself available to his people. Every morning at nine the gates of Hyderabad House, the palace in which he and his entourage were living, were opened to admit huge crowds of Tibetans eager to receive his blessing: barefooted monks spinning prayer wheels, women in brightly striped aprons, some with infants tied to their backs, traders in fur-trimmed hats, and merchants with turquoise earrings. Creeping forward one by one past his modest pavilion in the palace gardens, they placed small offerings at his feet—a few rupees, perhaps, or some flowers—and received the rare blessing of being touched directly on the head by their Precious Protector; in the holy city of Lhasa protocol would have dictated that he touch them only with a tassel. Then they backed away, showing their tongues as proof that, unlike the apostate King Lang Darma, they had no sins on their consciences.

After the first day or two, more and more non-Tibetans lined the street leading to the palace: a great many Hindus, bearded Sikhs, turbaned Muslims, all there for *darshan*, the blessing that arises from the touch or even the sight of a man of great eminence or holiness. "The young, spectacled, close-cropped man on the dais had that rare gift of being able to project his personality to people with whom he never spoke," wrote A. M. Rosenthal, the New Delhi correspondent of the *New York Times*. "It was not austerity or remoteness or religious power that he projected, but gentleness, almost overwhelming gentleness. Even when he was not smiling, and he smiled a great deal, he seemed to be smiling. This was not just a reaction felt by the devout or the believing. Every day there were a few newspapermen, devoutly non-believing, in the crowd and they, too, after a while lost their embarrassment over their feeling that they were in the presence of a young man who had a special quality of goodness and kindness."

The Dalai Lama's address to a symposium of Buddhist scholars in New Delhi radiated these qualities. Expressing his wish that the celebration would help spread the knowledge of the path of enlightenment not only in Asia but also among the people of the Western world, he predicted that "even in our present life, hatred, exploitation of one by another, and the ways of violence will disappear, and the time will come when all will live in friendship and love." The salvation of humanity, he added, could be found in the principles of Buddhism; for the Buddha's teachings "could lead not only to contented and peaceful lives for individuals but also to an end of hostility between nations." He had wanted to include the statement that "the salvation of humanity lies in the religious instinct latent in all men, whatever their creed; it is the forcible repression of this instinct which is the enemy of peace," but refrained from doing so for political considerations. He ended his talk with a gentle appeal: "I am glad to have had an opportunity of expressing my humble appreciation of the efforts which many peace-loving great countries make day and night toward the freedom of small countries and the elimination of aggression and war."

During those first days in India the Dalai Lama found the air of freedom infectious. The celebrations had given him "just the opportunity I wanted so much to talk to wise men from different parts of the world who were working, free from any immediate oppression, to proclaim the teaching of Lord Buddha for the sake of the peace of the world," and he had come to the conclusion, although not without some misgivings, that he should not return home to Tibet until the Chinese began to honor their commitments there. "Perhaps my feeling of the closeness of Mahatma Gandhi, and my meetings with so many learned sympathetic men, had helped to bring me to this sad decision," he says. "For almost the first time, I had met people who were not Tibetans but felt true sympathy for Tibet. At home, I thought, I could not help my people any more. I could not control their wish to resort to violence; all my peaceful efforts so far had been failures. But from India, I could at least tell people all over the world what was happening in Tibet, and to try to mobilize their moral support for us, and so perhaps bring a change in China's ruthless policy. I had to explain this to Mr. Nehru."

He could not have chosen a less propitious time to do so, for his first substantive meeting with the Indian prime minister took place on the eve of Chou En-lai's arrival in New Delhi. It was the Chinese prime minister's third visit to the subcontinent since the signing of the Sino-Indian agreement in April 1954, and he was still basking in the goodwill enunciated by the popular phrase *Hindi chini bhai bhai*—"Indians and Chinese are brothers." The Indian people in general and Nehru in particular wanted almost desperately to believe the best of the Chinese; the only power likely to disturb the much-needed peace in Asia was China with her irredentist ambitions, and a China befriended by India was thought to be a China more amenable to reason.

As he listened solemnly to the story of deceit and suffering in Tibet, there is little doubt that Nehru, despite his obvious affection for him, wished that the Dalai Lama had remained in Lhasa. "I explained how desperate things had become in eastern Tibet and how we all feared that worse troubles would spread through the rest of the country," the Dalai Lama remembers. "I said I was forced to believe that the Chinese really meant to destroy our religion and customs forever, and so cut off our historic ties with India. And all Tibetans, I told him, now pinned their remaining hopes on the government and people of India. And then I explained why I wanted to stay in India until we could win back our freedom by peaceful means."

The prime minister listened patiently, but made clear his firm conviction that nothing could be done for Tibet at that time. "He said that nobody had ever formally recognized our country's independence. He agreed with me that it was useless to try to fight against the Chinese. If we tried, they could easily bring in more forces to crush us completely. And he advised me to go back to Tibet and work peacefully to try to carry out the Seventeen-Point Agreement. I said I had done all I possibly could to carry it out, but however hard I tried, the Chinese refused to honor their side of the agreement, and I could not see any sign of a change of heart among them." The interview ended with Nehru promising to discuss the matter with Chou En-lai, a situation he doubtless would rather have avoided.

In fact the Dalai Lama was able to speak with Chou first, at a long meeting on the evening of his arrival in New Delhi. At their first encounter in Peking two years earlier, he had found the Chinese leader "clever and shrewd" and had come away with the impression that he would be "ruthless in carrying out whatever projects he had in mind," but felt nevertheless that he had no choice but to make an appeal on behalf of his people. "I told him that in our eastern provinces the situation was getting worse and worse. The Chinese were enforcing changes without any thought for local conditions or the wishes or interests of the people." Chou commented sympathetically that the local Chinese officials must have been making "mistakes" and agreed to report what the Dalai Lama had told him to Mao Tsetung. He would not, however, commit himself to any definite promise of improvement.

Several days later the Chinese prime minister invited the Dalai Lama's elder brothers Thupten Jigme Norbu and Gyalo Thondup to dinner at the Chinese embassy. Since they were no longer living in Tibet and had no official position in the Tibetan government, they were unafraid of direct repercussions and spoke out boldly in criticism of Peking's policies in their homeland. "They told Chou En-lai that for centuries Tibet had respected China as an important and friendly neighbor," says the Dalai Lama. "Yet now the Chinese in Tibet were treating Tibetans as if they were deadly enemies. They were making deliberate use of the worst types of Tibetans, the misfits of Tibetan society, to stir up discord, and they were ignoring the many patriotic Tibetans who might have been able to improve relations between Tibetans and Chinese. They were supporting the Panchen Lama in secular matters, in order to reopen the old rift between his predecessor and mine, and so undermine the authority of our government. And they were keeping such vast unnecessary armies in Tibet, especially in Lhasa, that our economy was ruined and prices had risen to the point where Tibetans were facing starvation. It was not the ruling classes of Tibet but the mass of people who were most bitter against the Chinese occupation. It was they who were demanding that the armies should withdraw and a new agreement, as between equal partners, should be signed; but the Chinese in Lhasa would not listen to popular opinion."

Although he could not have been pleased with this criticism, Chou lost neither his charm nor his temper. "He assured my brothers that the Chinese government had no thought of using undesirable Tibetans, or the Panchen Lama, to undermine my authority or cause dissension. They did not want to interfere in Tibet's affairs or to be an economic burden. He agreed that perhaps some difficulties had been caused by lack of understanding among local Chinese officials; and he promised to improve the food supplies in Lhasa and to begin gradual withdrawal of Chinese troops as soon as Tibet could manage her own affairs. And he also said he would report their complaints to Mao Tse-tung and would see that the causes of them were removed. These promises were not mere words, he said; my brothers could stay in India if they liked to see whether his promises were fulfilled, and if they were not, they would be perfectly free to criticize the Chinese government."

The brothers were surprised by the prime minister's conciliatory response to their list of grievances. They had accepted his invitation not because they believed their complaints on behalf of the Tibetan people would persuade Peking to change its course of action, but rather to demonstrate their solidarity and to indicate that, even though they were living in exile, they would work for the Tibetan cause. At the end of the interview the probable explanation for Chou's helpful attitude became evident. He had heard, he advised them, that the Dalai Lama had been thinking of staying in India and wanted them to persuade him to go back to Tibet. It could only harm their younger brother and the people of their homeland, he cautioned, if he did not return.

On this somber note the Dalai Lama began a tour of India. He was taken to several new industrial projects, such as the huge hydroelectric station at Nangal, and was impressed by "the great difference between the ways that such things are organized under Communism and under a free democracy—the whole difference of atmosphere and spirit between conscripted labor and voluntary labor." A visit to the Indian Parliament provided another contrast to his Peking trip a year earlier; he found it "a very pleasant surprise to hear the ordinary Indian members of parliament speaking frankly and freely, and criticizing the government in the strongest terms." The main object of his tour, however, was to make a pilgrimage to historic religious sites, and he visited Sanchi, Ajanta, Benares, Sarnath, and Bodh Gaya. "I was lost in admiration of masterpieces of Indian religious art, with their evidence both of creative genius and of fervent faith," he says. "I reflected how sectarianism and communal hatred had harmed this heritage in the past, and how hatred had been changed to calm and peace by the assurance of religious freedom in the Indian constitution." At Bodh Gaya and Benares he was welcomed by thousands of Tibetan pilgrims, to whom he spoke of the Buddha's doctrines, stressing always the path of peace. He later came to consider the trip one of the most moving and memorable experiences of his life.

"The Dalai Lama was not simply a high priest on a pilgrimage," wrote A. M. Rosenthal in the *New York Times*. "He was a young man seeing for the first time what life was like outside Tibet or China. Everything seemed to shine with interest for him—from the long conversations about the world in general with Mr. Nehru to the power-driven windows of the Maharaja of Sikkim's car and the photographer's electronic flash equipment." He had, moreover, the ability to transfer this sense of excitement to the people around him. "The Prime Minister of India, a man who makes every minute of the day account for itself, took almost four hours off one day to show the Dalai Lama the glory of the Moghul Gardens in the President's palace, and to ride with him on Udaygiri, President Prasad's magnificent tusker. That afternoon, in the President's banquet room, the usual formal table was gone and the President and Prime Minister sat with the Dalai Lama on chocolate-covered pillows and ate with him from silver bowls." Everywhere the Dalai Lama went in India there was "the same sort of eagerly personal reaction to him. This was not a triumphal tour, and it was not meant to be. But certainly of all the kings and princes and prime ministers and dictators who have come to India these past two years, no man was received with more warm joy or gave as much in return." The pilgrimage was interrupted by a telegram from General Chang Ching-wu in Lhasa. The situation at home was deteriorating rapidly, it said. A huge revolt was imminent, and it was imperative that the Dalai Lama return as soon as possible. Almost simultaneously came word from Chou En-lai, who had just returned prematurely to New Delhi from a goodwill tour of Southeast Asia, that he was most anxious to speak with the Dalai Lama. "So after a few more days," remembers the object of these compelling missives, "I had to drag myself back to the world of politics, hostility, and mistrust." He would know no other world for the next two years.

Back in New Delhi the Dalai Lama was told by Chou En-lai that the situation in Tibet was reaching critical proportions and that he was prepared to suppress any popular uprising by force. "I remember him saying that the Tibetans who were living in India were bent on making trouble, and that I must make up my mind what course I would take myself. I told him I was not ready yet to say what I would do, and I repeated all I had told him before of our grievances against the Chinese occupation. And I said we were willing to forget whatever wrongs had been done to us in the past, but the inhuman treatment and oppression must be stopped." Chou replied with the shopworn explanation that reforms would be introduced only in accordance with the interests of the Tibetan people, and the Dalai Lama found it remarkable that "he spoke as though he could still not understand why Tibetans did not welcome the Chinese." The next morning he was visited by another senior Chinese official, Marshal Ho Lung, who repeated Chou's advice to return at once to Lhasa. "The snow lion looks dignified if he stays in his Chinese abode," said the marshal, quoting a Chinese proverb, "but if he comes down to the valleys, he is treated like a dog." By then the Dalai Lama had made up his mind to return.

It could not have been an easy decision. The Kashag ministers who had accompanied him to India—Ngabo, Surkhang, and Ragashar—felt that there was no point in his returning. They had been hopeful that the trouble in eastern Tibet would incline the Chinese to adopt a more conciliatory posture, and at his instruction had made four requests of them: (1) the withdrawal of Chinese troops from Tibet, (2) the restoration of the status quo at the death of the Thirteenth Dalai Lama, (3) the reinstatement of the dismissed prime ministers Lukhangwa and Lobsang Tashi, and (4) the abandonment of Communist reforms. Their response had been disappointing, and the Kalons hoped that the Dalai Lama's prolonged absence from Tibet might strengthen their bargaining position in future talks with Peking's representatives in Lhasa.

Nor did the Dalai Lama's family wish him to return. The Gyayum Chenmo had made a number of friends during her year in China who had spoken candidly to her about life in the People's Republic. "I do not remember anyone trying to convince me that Communism was a good system," she said. "Those who ventured opinions indicated to the contrary that they felt the Tibetans were lucky to be free. Some told me that the Communists had killed or imprisoned their fathers and said that if Communist rule came to Tibet the same would happen to us. These conversations made me fear for the future of my country." Now, some two years later, their prediction seemed to be coming true, and she believed her son should seek asylum in India and await further developments. Thupten Jigme Norbu and Gyalo Thondup agreed with their mother. They felt that despite his promises Chou En-lai could not be trusted, and urged the Dalai Lama to join them in exile; and Lobsang Samden, in poor health and a state of nervous exhaustion from acting as his younger brother's liaison with the Chinese in Lhasa, decided to relinquish the post of Chikyap Khenpo and remain in India. The Gyayum Chenmo voiced her family's concern to the Dalai Lama. "But he replied, 'What good would be remaining here in safety while all the people of Tibet are left at the mercy of the Chinese?' He always seemed calm, and reassured us that everything would turn out all right in the end."[4]

Finally, practical considerations made the Dalai Lama's remaining outside Tibet a logical move. The remarkable outpouring of warmth and enthusiasm with which he had been welcomed in India gave him hope that voluntary exile might focus world attention on the Tibetan situation and bring about the amelioration of conditions there; perhaps the United Nations might even be persuaded through his efforts to intervene in Tibet as they had in Korea. Financially he would experience no difficulty, for a substantial amount of his personal fortune had been removed from his private treasury in the Potala and deposited in India when the P.L.A. invaded Tibet six years earlier, and despite appeals by Mao Tse-tung and other Chinese officials that he bring it back to Tibet, he had refrained from doing so. Being in exile would also provide him an opportunity to resume the religious studies he had found so satisfying and which he believed had instilled in him the strength to sustain the onerous burden thrust upon him, studies that had been interrupted less by his assumption of temporal power than by Chinese efforts to involve him in time-consuming mundane duties.

Before leaving New Delhi, the Dalai Lama had a final meeting with Jawaharlal Nehru. He was returning to Tibet, he explained, for two reasons: because of Chou En-lai's promises that steps would be taken to ease the situation there and because Nehru himself had advised him to do so on the basis of these assurances. He might have added that there was a third, and more compeling, reason: he was unwilling to abandon his people in what was rapidly becoming their time of greatest need. There was no doubt in his mind that without his presence in Tibet rebellion would engulf the entire land, and that sooner or later the Chinese would exterminate every last spark of resistance. There seemed to him to be no choice but to go back and do whatever he could to prevent that from happening.

Despite his apparent unwillingness to aid the Tibetan cause, the Indian prime minister had impressed the Dalai Lama greatly. "Although the mantle of Mahatma Gandhi had fallen on him, I could not catch any glimpse of spiritual fervor in him," he concedes. "But I saw him as a brilliant practical statesman, with a masterly grasp of international politics, and he showed me that he had a profound love for his country and faith in his people. For their welfare and progress, he was firm in the pursuit of peace." Unlike Nehru, the Dalai Lama believed firmly that one did not compromise with morality. To the Tibetan leader a people who suspended their principles in favor of security would lose far more than they could possibly gain.

On January 22, 1957, the Dalai Lama flew to Baghdogra and proceeded from there to the Darjeeling–Kalimpong area of Bengal where a great many Tibetan exiles and refugees had settled, including most recently former prime minister Lukhangwa. Chou En-lai, who had been reported by the *Times of India* some three weeks earlier to have complained of the use of Kalimpong "as an international base by the United States and others to undermine Chinese influence in Tibet," had asked him not to go. But as his presence there "was not entirely a political matter," he went anyway, because of "a spiritual duty to visit my countrymen, on which Chou En-lai could certainly not advise me."

The Dalai Lama was weary of politics. "Political talks had taken up most of my time in New Delhi and cut short my pilgrimage. I had begun to detest them, and would gladly have retired from politics altogether if I had not had a duty to my people in Tibet. So I was happy to find that in Kalimpong and Gangtok I had time for meditation and for religious discourses to the people who had gathered there to hear me."

It was snowing hard in the mountains. He had to wait nearly a month before the way to Tibet, across the Nathu-la, was clear. As he walked across the top of the pass, scores of little prayer flags fluttered in the breeze with an incantation to the heavens for peace and love. On the Tibetan side they were obscured by portraits of Mao Tse-tung and the huge red flags of the Chinese People's Republic.

Notes

1. Dr. Bhimrao R. Ambedkar, the leader of India's Untouchables, who died in December 1956, replied that "Marx was thought by a large number of Asians, particularly students, to be the only modern prophet. They were quick to follow the rising star of Communism rather than the slow path of religion. . . . What would be Buddha's reaction to modern problems? . . . He spoke of salvation through the conquest of *Dukha* [poverty], really meaning the abolition of poverty. This happy state could be achieved by the personal conquest of evil. Here lies the difference between Communism and Buddhism. While one conquers with fear, the other conquers with love." *Time*, December 17, 1956, 68.

2. There are a variety of tones in the Tibetan language. *La* in a low tone means a pass over a mountain range. In a higher tone it refers to the wages of a laborer.
3. A. M. Rosenthal, "Chou and the Lama: An Asian Drama," *New York Times Magazine*, January 13, 1957.
4. Interview with the Gyayum Chenmo, Dharamsala, India, May 16, 1980.

*Ratuk Ngawang with portrait
of Gompo Tashi Andrugtsang*

Dharamsala 1980

· CHAPTER 18 ·

Four Rivers, Six Ranges

F OR SOME TWO THOUSAND YEARS before the coming of Mao, the people
inhabiting China's lush agricultural lands had referred to their neighbors on the barren steppes and rugged mountain ranges of the Inner Asian
borderland as "barbarians." Had there been a Frederick Jackson Turner observing the region at that time, he doubtless would have described the Great
Wall just as he did the frontier of the American West: "the meeting point
between savagery and civilization."

The meeting point between China and Tibet fell in eastern Kham and
Amdo. Unlike the American frontier, this one remained static rather than
moving relentlessly westward, and there was as little social mobility as there
was shifting of population. No Great Wall was needed there to repel invaders, for once Buddhism had taken root on the Roof of the World, the days of
Tibetan militarism ended. Uninterested in territorial expansion, the people
of eastern Tibet wanted only to be left alone to cultivate their fields, tend
their herds, and practice the Dharma. For over three hundred years spiritual
leadership of the region had been reposed in the Dalai Lamas, Precious Protectors of the Tibetan people. Political control had proven somewhat more
transitory and had passed back and forth between Lhasa, Peking, and local
Tibetan feudal lords.

Like Turner's American frontier, Tibet's had developed a primitive social
organization shaped by the wilderness, based on clan rather than immediate
family. Likewise the frontier had produced a people with a strong antipathy
to control, and they looked upon tax collectors, whether Chinese or Tibetan, as agents of oppression. In many ways, too, the area had served as "a
military training school, keeping alive the resistance to aggression and developing the stalwart and rugged qualities of the frontiersman." To a Khampa
his rifle was his most precious possession, for when he was not involved in
an internecine feud there were always Chinese to be fought. "A blow on the
nose of an enemy," went a familiar Khampa adage, "is more satisfying than
listening to the advice of mediators." Khampas and Amdoas alike were

proud, resourceful, independent peoples who were more truculent and more demonstrative than their central Tibetan neighbors. As recently as 1934 there had been an abortive attempt led by the Pangdatsang family to organize all of Kham—part of which was subject to the Lhasa government and part to that of Peking—into an independent state, albeit one under the spiritual guidance of the Dalai Lama; and it has been said that another such movement was afoot just prior to the Chinese invasion.

One of the ancient semi-independent districts of Kham, which until the Communist occupation had been ruled by a succession of hereditary chieftains, was Lithang, located in a remote and beautiful valley to the southeast of Chamdo not far from the border of Szechuan. It was from Lithang that the Sixth Dalai Lama, in the now-famous poem given to one of his lady friends as he was being escorted into exile in 1706, had prophesied his return to Lhasa; and he had in fact done so on two occasions, as the Seventh and Tenth Incarnations. The Lithang monastery was one of the largest in all of Kham and had been founded by the Third Dalai Lama in 1580.

The people of Lithang had no love for the Chinese, whatever their political persuasion. During the waning years of the Manchu dynasty the Szechuanese General Chao Erh-feng, known to Tibetans as Chao the Butcher because of his wholesale slaughter of monks and laymen alike, had ravaged much of Kham and looted villages and monasteries. A decade later, Lithang's priceless copy of the *Tengyur*, commentaries on the Buddhist scriptures, was destroyed by Chinese soldiers. Written by hand on lacquered parchment with liquid gold and silver, it was described by an American medical missionary and Tibetan scholar as "one of the most perfect pieces of work I have ever seen." In 1934 the ragged Communist armies of Mao Tse-tung had passed through the area on their heroic Long March, a march whose ramifications were anything but heroic to the Tibetan peasants from whom crops and livestock were seized to fuel a revolution of which they wanted no part.

With such a recent history, it is hardly surprising that when the P.L.A. invaded Kham in 1950 the people of Lithang prepared to fight. In the beginning the Chinese averted violence by dispatching a group of officials to confer with the village headmen and monastic leaders, assuring them that they had come only to help the people and would leave as soon as the Tibetans were able to govern themselves. The vision of an independent Kham free from external taxation but spiritually subject to the guidance and protection of the Dalai Lama was hardly unwelcome, and local oracles were consulted who proclaimed that cooperation with the Communists was the proper course of action. Accordingly, the chief abbot of Lithang monastery sent the Chinese authorities a letter indicating that although he was advising the populace to accept the Chinese presence without resistance, if they did not live up to their word, bloodshed would be unavoidable.

For several years all was peaceful, but by 1955 Peking had moved in many more troops. Without warning the Chinese began to levy steep taxes on traders returning from India and to demand from all but the poorest families a detailed list of property holdings and household possessions. Although taxation was purportedly the motivation for these inventories, what ensued was confiscation of lands, valuables, and weapons. At first the Lithang monastery was exempted from the new regulations, a sensible decision considering that within its ancient walls resided some 5,600 monks together with a collection of weapons that, while hardly of recent vintage, were sufficient to arm all of them in rudimentary fashion. By the end of 1955, however, the Chinese delivered an ultimatum to the institution's eight abbots: "There are two roads leading to liberation, a white road and a black road. If you choose the white road you will have nothing to fear, but if you choose the black road we will not hesitate to use force." The white road, they went on to explain, consisted of handing over an inventory of the monastery's possessions to be assessed for taxation. In response the abbots did not bother to point out that such a procedure was a glaring violation of Article 7 of the Seventeen-Point Agreement, which stated in part that "the central authorities will not effect a change in the income of the monasteries." Instead, one of them calmly drew a pistol from the folds of his robe and pointed it at the Chinese military commander.

During the Monlam festival at the end of February 1956 the people of Lithang launched a surprise attack on the local Chinese garrison and succeeded in capturing a small quantity of weapons before they were driven back and forced to take refuge behind the walls of Lithang monastery. Called upon to surrender, they replied that they would rather die. Two monk brothers, however, slipped out and gave themselves up. Taken to a village below the monastery, they suddenly drew pistols from their robes and killed the two officers who had come to interrogate them. The elder monk was shot down instantly, but his younger brother, although gravely wounded, managed to get back to the monastery, where he died a few days later. The Chinese thereupon laid siege to Lithang monastery for sixty-four days, then approached its defenders with a proposal: in return for surrender they would promise to postpone reforms for a minimum of three years, but if their offer was rejected they would bomb the monastery into the ground. Although a few of the monks might have heard of airplanes, none had ever seen one or had any idea of the destruction they could cause. Their refusal to budge prompted the Chinese to send aircraft to bomb the buildings along the monastery's periphery and to follow this by strafing the area with machine-gun fire. The demonstration succeeded in thoroughly cowing the monks, who that night tried to fight their way out through Chinese lines. Over 800 were killed and some 2,000 captured.

Shortly after seizing the monastery, the Chinese brought two elderly lamas, former abbots, before the other captives. It was obvious, they announced, that the lamas were charlatans, for they had been unable to save the lives of their friends and relatives, and the time had come to see if they possessed the ability to save even their own lives. Boiling water was poured over the head of one of them, and then he was strangled; the other was stoned and then clubbed on the head with an ax. During the next few weeks other lamas were crucified, incinerated, disemboweled, or buried alive in full view of groups of horrified Tibetans. A few were simply locked up and left to starve to death. After being questioned closely, the other captives were released with a warning. In the mountains surrounding Lithang there remained over a thousand Tibetans committed to avenging the deaths of their people and ridding their country of the godless Chinese.

In Chamdo the Communists adopted a more conciliatory posture. Calling together some 350 Tibetan officials from the various districts of the local administrative area, General Wang Chi-mei informed them, "The Dalai Lama has stated that Tibet is not yet ready for democratic reforms, and that these must be introduced gradually and not until a majority of Tibetans approve them. The Panchen Lama, on the other hand, has demanded that the reforms be introduced immediately. Now you must decide what will be done here in Chamdo." After many days of deliberation, the Tibetans reported back. About a hundred voted to have reforms only when they were accepted by the Dalai Lama and the rest of Tibet. Another forty voted to have them right away. But a third group, totaling about two hundred, voted never to have reforms at all, although that had not been offered as an alternative. The general thanked them all, then announced ambiguously that it had been decided to introduce reforms "as finally desired by the Dalai Lama and Panchen Lama." Presenting each of the representatives with a picture book, pen, ink, paper, and some toilet articles, he dismissed them.

Barely a month later the officials were summoned to Jomda Dzong, an ancient fortress to the east of Chamdo and hub of the most important town on the motor road between the provincial capital and the Drichu River. It was occupied by some 3,000 Chinese troops. "The Chinese told us that since the region of Jomda Dzong was adjacent to the border of Szechuan, it had been decided to initiate democratic reforms there," says Gyakar Gompo Namgyal, a legendary resistance fighter now living in Sikkim. "When we protested that we had seen the misery caused by reforms on the other side of the Drichu and wanted no part of them, we found ourselves surrounded by more than two thousand troops brought in as reinforcements. They built barracks and dug trenches on the hills and, with this show of force, compelled us to concede, at least verbally, to their plans." Namgyal and the others were told they would be sent back to their districts to explain the reforms to the people, but not until they had been given a course of instruction themselves. The guards surrounding the fort relaxed, and the night before the course of indoctrination was due to start, all the officials broke out and escaped into the mountains. From there they began to launch periodic guerrilla raids on Chinese encampments.

Soon all of eastern Tibet had erupted against the Chinese. In one engagement the pugnacious Golok nomads of Amdo, armed with swords and muzzle loaders, massacred a Chinese garrison of over 800 men before being routed by a punitive expedition and chased into the mountains. Thousands of monks offered back their vows and lived thereafter only to kill Chinese. The much-vaunted Lhasa–Sikang road, via Chamdo, became so unsafe that only heavily armed convoys were able to make use of it, and even these were not immune from attack. To Chinese truck drivers it became known as the Route of Death.

The Chinese were stunned by the extent and ferocity of the resistance. Fearful that the rebellion would spread to Lhasa and central Tibet and conscious that their garrisons were inadequate to suppress an all-out popular uprising, they appealed to the Dalai Lama to appoint a peace delegation to eastern Tibet to urge the population to lay down their arms. He agreed to consider the proposal but took no action. The Chinese then approached his junior tutor, Trijang Rinpoche, who replied that as a man of religion he had little understanding of such worldly affairs as warfare. Next the abbots of Lhasa's Three Pillars were requested to appoint well-known lamas of Khampa origin to go and ask their people to discontinue the rebellion, but they, too, refused. Finally the Chinese were forced to operate through their recently inaugurated Preparatory Committee for the Formation of a Tibetan Autonomous Region, which dispatched Karmapa Rinpoche, head of the Kagyupa sect which had a great many adherents in Kham, and the ubiquitous Kalon Ngabo to Chamdo in July 1956. "The Chinese tried to do anything of a controversial nature in my name so as to give it a better chance of winning popular acceptance," says the Dalai Lama. "It was as if I had one head and two bodies: the Dalai Lama as chairman of the Preparatory Committee and the Gyalwa Rinpoche [Precious Protector] as head of the Tibetan government. When they could not have their way with one, they simply dealt with the other." Despite the efforts of Ngabo and the Karmapa Lama, the rebellion continued.

At the same time Peking launched a *mea culpa* propaganda campaign designed to allay the fears of the people of Lhasa and the rest of Ü-Tsang, who had given sanctuary to thousands of Khampas and Amdoas and had heard from them terrifying accounts of Communist atrocities committed in the name of democratic reforms. Addressing the Eighth Congress of the Chinese Communist Party on September 20, 1956, General Chang Kuo-ha, vice-chairman of the Preparatory Committee, admitted that "in terms of the demands of the Tibetan people, we have done very little" and declared that reforms were to be postponed in Tibet until "demanded by the laboring people and wholeheartedly supported by the upper strata of society," and even then only "after a set of reform measures based on scientific investigation of the social and economic conditions of Tibet and agreed to by the representatives of all strata of the people." Premature reforms, he warned, would "certainly affect unity within the Tibetan nationality as well as that between the Tibetans and other nationalities and will only create difficulties for a smooth progress in peaceful reforms."

While acknowledging that "upper-strata Tibetans must . . . realize that it is only through reform that the Tibetan nationality can have a broad future," the general explained that the Chinese Communist party was giving them special consideration because they had "intimate relations with the broad mass of the Tibetan people" and because they had "contributed much during the past several years to the unification of the motherland and the unity and progress of Tibet." Neither their political status nor living standards, he emphasized, were to be lowered under the reforms. Noting that Buddhism "still has a deeply rooted influence upon the Tibetan people of all strata," he asserted that "in every aspect of our work . . . we have been treating the question of religion with the utmost care, and hereafter we will continue to observe the policy of freedom of religion in order to strengthen the work of uniting the religious circles." As for reform within these circles, he added, "it should be studied and undertaken by the religious people themselves; the party will never interfere." Similar sentiments were aired in the *Tibet Daily News*, a Communist news sheet published in Lhasa, and in the *People's Daily* of Peking. "Although the policy of the Central Government cannot be erroneous," stated the latter, "the cadres carrying out the policy erred, and since the reform was badly done, it caused consternation in the whole area, and rich and poor alike fled to the western side of the [Drichu] river and many fled to Lhasa. That is why the Tibetan people think of reform with terror and anxiety."

The culmination of this campaign of self-flagellation was Mao Tse-tung's speech on "contradictions" of February 27, 1957, an edited version of which was not released until June 18, which declared that conditions in Tibet were "not ripe" for "democratic reforms" and that the latter would be postponed for at least five years. According to some of those who heard a tape-recorded version of the original speech, Mao severely condemned the mistakes his cadres had been making in Tibet and disclosed that had it not been for the intervention of Chou En-lai, the Dalai Lama, then in Sikkim waiting for the Nathu-la to clear, would not be returning to Lhasa. Peking soon announced that in view of the postponement 91.6 percent of its officials were being withdrawn from Tibet.

While in Sikkim the Dalai Lama had decided "to see what the Chinese reaction would be to a little plain speaking in Tibet." In speeches at Yatung, Gyantse, and Shigatse, he "repeated emphatically what I had always told my people, and the Chinese and Tibetan officials, since my return from China in 1955: that the Chinese were not our rulers, and we were not their subjects. We had been promised autonomous government, and everyone should do his best to make it work. Our duty should always be to right wrongs, whether they were committed by Chinese or Tibetans. The rulers of China had assured me, I said, that the Chinese were only in Tibet to help the Tibetans, and therefore any Chinese who failed to be helpful to us was disobeying his own central government." He did not have long to wait before assessing the Chinese reaction to his "plain speaking." On the night before he was to leave Shigatse for Lhasa, there was a farewell banquet attended by both Tibetans and Chinese. The next morning Kalon Ragashar, the Tibetan defense minister who had presented his country's demands to Chou En-lai in New Delhi and who had cleverly thwarted several Chinese demands of the Kashag, was dead. Chinese newspapers reported he had died from "bad circulation," and Western sources indicated that "the unexpected and unexplained" death of the Kashag's "outstanding personality" was due presumably to heart failure. Tibetans knew better. Only fifty-four years of age and reportedly in excellent health at the time he left India, Ragashar was undoubtedly poisoned as a warning to the Dalai Lama and the people of Tibet that despite Chou En-lai's assurances of fair treatment and Mao Tse-tung's talk of "contradictions," the situation in their country was not likely to improve.

That the situation was in fact worsening became evident to the Dalai Lama upon his return to Lhasa on April 1, 1957. During his absence the Chinese authorities had been at first "as courteous to my ministers as only Chinese can be" and advised them that in response to the people's wishes, reforms would be postponed for six years. But shortly afterward they had announced at a public meeting—convened without the prior knowledge of the Kashag—that revolt had broken out in eastern Tibet and that they were fully prepared to crush it by force of arms. The announcement had come as a shock to the Kalons, who, while they knew that the Khampas and Amdoas had risen against the Communists, had no idea that the fighting had become serious enough to make the Chinese admit its existence in public. Peking had also launched its "Reclaim the Wastelands" program, whose underlying intention was not only to reduce threats of revolt through intermarriage with countless thousands of resettled Han Chinese but also to scatter and destroy the effectiveness of "counterrevolutionary" groups in Kham and Amdo.

With the Dalai Lama safely back in Tibet and no longer able to appeal for help to the outside world, Peking apparently felt the time had come to drop its mask of conciliation. When the decision to postpone reforms was announced in Lhasa three weeks after his return, speakers trotted out the old theme of "imperialist intrigue," which they had discarded upon their occupation of Tibet some six years earlier. General Chang Kuo-hua called for "constant vigilance against the subversive activities of imperialist elements and the rebellious activities of separatists," while the *Tibet Daily News* appealed for vigilance against the activities of the "imperialists and the criminal and traitorous activities of the separatists." On August 1, 1957, General

Tan Kuan-sen, political commissar of the P.L.A., was more specific. "The American imperialists," he wrote in the *Tibet Daily News*, "are engaged in carrying out subversive activities through some refugees from Tibet." It was the first public statement that recognized that a number of political refugees had fled Tibet and found local support, mainly in Kalimpong and Darjeeling, for their demand for independence from the tyranny of Chinese rule in their homeland. While announcing that the vast majority of its officials had been withdrawn from Tibet, Peking failed to point out that the cadres had merely been transferred from western Tibet, where they could be observed by trade agents of the Indian government, to eastern Tibet, where they could assist a newly reinforced Chinese army in "disciplining" the recalcitrant Khampas and Amdoas. "The only way to settle questions of an ideological nature or controversial issues among the people," Mao Tse-tung had proclaimed in his "contradictions" speech, "is by the democratic method of discussion, of criticism, of persuasion and education, and not by the method of coercion or repression." In Tibet, Peking followed precisely the opposite course.

In Lhasa during this critical period there lived a man named Gompo Tashi Andrugtsang.[1] Powerfully built and sporting a thin black mustache, he had come from a village in the Lithang Valley where he had been born in the Fire Horse Year of 1905. His father had been a successful trader, his uncle a monk at Drepung monastery, and his family generous contributors to religious institutions both locally and in Lhasa. At the age of seventeen he had joined a citizen's posse from his village to rid the area of a large force of mounted bandits, an experience from which he emerged with a fondness for firearms and a love of hunting and shooting. "Although I was conscious that it was morally wrong to destroy living creatures, I did not in the beginning lose much sleep over it," he remembers. "But my mother condemned my behavior strongly. She pointed out that it was sinful for one who had been educated in Lord Buddha's doctrine, with its reverence for all forms of life, to regard hunting as a pastime."

Like his father, who had died when he was a boy of eight, Gompo Tashi tried his hand at trade. An initial venture in wool, deer horns, and musk met with little success, but when he added tea and silver to his merchandise he began to prosper. By 1942 he was able to make a pilgrimage to the holy places of eastern Tibet, India, and Nepal, making at each shrine substantial offerings to the monks and lighting thousands of butter lamps in memory of his departed family members. As the years passed he continued to prosper. He took up residence in Lhasa, where he conducted his business through 120 highly trained agents, a substantial number of whom lived in and around Kalimpong and reported to him in person each year to present their accounts. After having evaluated his wealth and power, the Chinese authorities deemed it wise not to interfere in his affairs. "Gompo Tashi loved laughter, singing, sitting around drinking *chang* with his friends," says Nyima, a former monk from the Dayab region of Kham who became his private secretary in 1954. "But like all Khampas he had an inbred sense of what was right and what was wrong, and despite his easygoing nature he always tried to see that justice was done."

By the end of 1954 Gompo Tashi had begun to receive reports of Communist oppression in eastern Tibet. He was not surprised, for he had been one of the Tibetans "invited," in the wake of the dismissal of Lukhangwa and Lobsang Tashi, to tour China in the summer of 1952. Rather than accept what he felt was an "odious" invitation, he had sent one of his employees in his place. Upon his return the agent told him that the Chinese claims and promises were "simply a long list of lies." Although away from Lhasa on business when the three Mimang leaders were arrested after the Monlam festival in February 1956, he worked hard to secure their release upon his return. The generals were well aware of the danger of bringing the men to trial in the tense months that followed, and finally agreed to grant them their freedom after the abbots of the Three Pillars stood surety for their good behavior. By then one of the men had died. Of the remaining two, Gompo Tashi was most impressed with his fellow Khampa Alo Chondze. "I thought he might be useful in furthering Tibet's cause if he could go to India," he says. "So I provided him with two horses and a forty-caliber pistol with a fully loaded magazine, and he proceeded to India via Bhutan."

The time had come, Gompo Tashi believed, for organized resistance; while the Khampas and Amdoas had enjoyed moderate success in constantly harassing the Chinese with hit-and-run raids and ambuscades, they would be more effective if they could unite and synchronize their operations. In December 1956 he sent three of his men, on the pretense of taking a business trip, to Kham with a message to be delivered personally to village headmen, monastic leaders, and other nationalistic elements. "The time has arrived," it read in part, "to muster all your courage and put your bravery to the test. I know you are prepared to risk your lives and exert all your strength to defend Tibet. . . . In this hour of peril I appeal to all people, including government officials, who value their freedom and religion, to unite in the common struggle against the Chinese." Similar messages were sent to India to explain that the Tibetans had no alternative but to take up arms against the Communists.

Gompo Tashi also met with the abbots of the Three Pillars and convinced them to affix their seals to a document describing the plight of the Tibetan people that was to be sent to Prime Minister Nehru and to the World Buddhist Society and which would presumably arrive in India during the Dalai Lama's visit. A draft was drawn up but in the end it could not be sent because a number of influential monks and government officials felt it would accomplish nothing but infuriate the Chinese; and it was made clear to him that "they were against any secret meetings to discuss such moves." The response to his message to the people's leaders in eastern Tibet was far more

promising. Meeting with the treasurer of Lithang monastery and other monastic representatives in early 1957, he was given hundreds of letters from
the people of Kham declaring their intention to carry on their resistance and
welcoming the organization of unified leadership.

Gompo Tashi then approached the Kashag and stated that he and several
other wealthy merchants wished to launch a nationwide appeal for gold,
silver, and jewelry for the purpose of constructing a golden throne for the
Dalai Lama in the hope that this would assuage the evil omens that had been
afflicting Tibet, and that they would like to present it as an offering to their
Precious Protector at a special religious ritual known as the *tenshuk shapten.*
Permission received, the task of collecting contributions began in earnest all
over the country. Monasteries and manorial estates gave generously, women
willingly parted with their personal ornaments, and even beggars made small
donations. So great was the outpouring that it required the labors of forty-
nine goldsmiths, five silversmiths, nineteen engravers, six painters, eight
tailors, six carpenters, three blacksmiths, three welders, and thirty laborers
to complete the throne; and while the work was going on the scriptures were
read out loud, prayers were conducted, new prayer flags were hoisted, and
incense was burned.

The throne was a work of exquisite beauty, consuming over eighty
pounds of pure gold and studded with diamonds, pearls, onyx, coral, and
turquoise; the *dorje,* or spiritual thunderbolt and scepter of the gods, in front
of it accounted for another five pounds of gold, and was embedded with
diamonds and turquoise carved into the shape of lions. Other items included
a gold Dharma wheel containing the eight auspicious signs; a gold table; a
massive gold butter lamp engraved with symbols of the deities; three sets of
golden offering bowls, seven in each set; a gold pitcher inlaid with turquoise; and a collection of smaller lamps, bowls, cups, and pitchers. Between 150 and 200 pounds of pure gold went into the construction of the
throne and its accoutrements, which were offered to the Dalai Lama as an
expression of the people's loyalty and confidence in his leadership and in
confirmation of his earthly sovereign powers, at a magnificent ceremony at
the Norbulingka on July 4, 1957. So splendid was the event, for which virtually the entire population of Lhasa turned out, that it was decided to repeat
it each year, when the Dalai Lama would sit on the throne and receive his
people in audience.

The Chinese authorities were amused that the people of Tibet should
still think it possible, after six years of military occupation and the P.L.A.'s
recent display of strength in eastern Tibet, that mere religious offerings
would spare them the inevitable "democratic" reforms. Western sympathizers to whom news of the golden throne had leaked out were bewildered that,
in the face of such severe Chinese repression, the people could rely on a traditional religious approach to a military and political problem. Both underestimated the depth of the Tibetans' faith; and neither was aware that the

sponsors of the national appeal, while devout believers, were motivated by a further consideration. "Until the Khampas and Amdoas were pushed into Lhasa by the Chinese, the guerrilla movement was largely disorganized," says one of its original leaders, now living in India. "The throne was an excuse to gather together the leaders of these disparate forces without arousing the suspicion of the Chinese. Gompo Tashi explained to the Lhasa government and to the Chinese authorities that they were undertaking the project in order to pay homage to their dead comrades in the east. What he omitted to tell them is that while externally they were paying homage, internally they were plotting."[2]

Approximately three dozen resistance leaders, all of them private businessmen, gathered together regularly in July 1957 in Gompo Tashi's Lhasa home. Among them were such stalwart fighters as Rakra, Baba Yeshi, Amdo Jimpa, Para Shisok, and Ratuk Ngawang. "The thing that kept us together was our desire to fight back," one of them recalls. "There was no thought of whether we would win or lose. We just wanted to kill Chinese and get our country back."[3] They called themselves the Chushi Gangdrug (Four Rivers, Six Ranges) after the rivers and mountains of eastern Tibet.

In the meantime, through his agents in Kalimpong, Gompo Tashi had gotten in touch with Gyalo Thondup, the Dalai Lama's elder brother, who with the assistance of his Chinese wife had already enlisted the aid of Taiwan in parachuting a limited quantity of arms and supplies to the guerrilla forces of eastern Tibet. Subsequently he appears to have been approached by the United States Central Intelligence Agency, which pointed out that since his requests for Taiwanese aid were always passed on to them, he might as well deal directly with the United States. As a result of this liaison, a group of six Khampas were selected by Gompo Tashi to be trained by the Americans in guerrilla warfare and then to be parachuted back into Tibet. One of them was Gompo Tashi's nephew, Gyatso Wangdu.

The six Tibetans were taken to an unidentified island somewhere in the North Pacific—most likely Okinawa, Saipan, or Guam—and trained for four months in map reading and radio transmission. During the last month they were flown to another island, which they believed was in the Philippines, for cursory parachute training. Then in late 1957 they were loaded into a small black four-engined airplane probably belonging to C.A.T., a commercial airline and CIA proprietary based on Taiwan, and parachuted back into Tibet.[4] Each man carried with him a pistol, a small machine gun, an old Japanese radio, $132 in Tibetan currency, and a bracelet containing vials of poison to be taken in the event of capture. Two men were dropped in southern Tibet and made their way to Lhasa, where they contacted Gompo Tashi. The others were dropped into Lithang. Of the four men who went into the heartland of Kham, only one came out again—Gompo Tashi's nephew Wangdu.[5]

As the Year of the Fire Bird drew to a close, the stage was being readied for the inevitable confrontation. The resistance forces were thirsting for blood, vengeance, and freedom, the Chinese for blood, retaliation, and "reform." Sensing the impending disaster, the Dalai Lama wanted only to protect the lives of his people and to preserve whatever he could of their civilization.

Notes

1. See Gompo Tashi Andrugtsang, *Four Rivers, Six Ranges* (Dharamsala, India, 1973).
2. Interview with a former member of the Chushi Gangdrug, Dharamsala, India, May 26, 1980.
3. Ibid. There were fifteen or sixteen of these meetings, which started at 3:00 P.M. and lasted an hour or more.
4. *Pentagon Papers* (Gravel Edition) II, 648–649.
5. Chris Mullin, "Tibetan Conspiracy," *Far Eastern Economic Review*, September 5, 1975, 30–34.

The Dalai Lama and family (l. to r.):
The Gyayum Chenmo (1900–1981),
Tsering Dolma (1919–1964),
Thuben Jigme Norbu (1922–   ),
Gyalo Dhondup (1928–   ),
Lobsang Samden (1933–1985),
His Holiness the Dalai Lama (1935–   ),
Jetsun Pema Gyalpo (1941–   ),
Ngari Rinpoche (1946–   )

New Delhi 1956

CHAPTER 19

End of an Era

N GARI RINPOCHE LOVED GUNS. At the age of six he was given a German air rifle by a Tibetan businessman who traveled frequently between Lhasa and India. He pestered the soldiers of the Kusung Regiment, the Dalai Lama's Royal Bodyguard, to teach him to shoot. Since his uncle Takla was its Depön, or regimental commander, and his elder brother was the Precious Protector himself, they complied good-naturedly despite their amusement that an incarnate lama could take a keen interest in such worldly activity. He practiced diligently and became a crack shot. Later he acquired a Webley air pistol, which he took with him when he entered Drepung as a novice. On windy days he would often slip outside and fire at the bells hanging from the corners of the monastery buildings. The puzzled expressions on the faces of the monks and lamas as they wondered what had caused the bells to ring doubled him over with laughter. When he grew tired of this sport he would go out into the countryside and fire at birds and small animals.

One day Ngari Rinpoche shot a sparrow. Walking over to where it had fallen, he saw that it was still alive. It was lying on its side, a tiny brown mound of fluff with blood trickling from the wound and one eye staring, unblinking, at the sky. He was gripped by a sudden pang of remorse. Although he knew that the taking of life was a sin, he had killed before, and attributed his difficulty in mastering Tibetan grammar to having done so. But this time was different. The bird struggled to stand, but he could not bring himself to shoot it again, even though he knew that doing so would put an end to its suffering. He stood there, immobile, as it died. Wrapping his robes securely about him, he vowed silently never to engage in such gratuitous violence again. Inanimate objects became his targets thereafter, but the intricacies of grammatical Tibetan continued to elude him.

In the autumn of 1958 Ngari Rinpoche was spending a few days at Yabshi Sarpa (New Father's House), the stately home built for his family by the Tibetan government a decade earlier near the foot of the Potala. One afternoon he was outside, practicing shooting at a row of tins perched on a ledge with a .22-caliber rifle given him two years before by his brother Lobsang just before Lobsang left for India. Now that he was no longer firing at living creatures, the Gyayum Chenmo seemed not to mind her youngest child's curious preoccupation. As dusk approached he began to experience difficulty sighting the targets, and a number of shots passed over them and landed in the grounds of Chinese military headquarters at Yuthok House. Deeply engrossed in correcting his aim, he was startled when two jeeploads of Chinese soldiers screeched to a halt in a cloud of dust just outside the main gate and spilled out of the vehicles with rifles at the ready. When they saw that their presumed sniper was only a slight twelve-year-old monk and brother of the Dalai Lama, they were relieved but not amused, and they cautioned him sternly either to shoot more carefully or to aim in another direction. Such was the atmosphere of the holy city during the Year of the Earth Dog. Outwardly life went on as usual, but with an undercurrent of tension that needed only a spark to set Tibetans and Chinese at each other's throats.

In January of that fateful year Gompo Tashi Andrugtsang had arranged a meeting between the two Khampas who had been parachuted into southern Tibet and the Dalai Lama's lord chamberlain, Thupten Woyden Phala. A tall, imposing nobleman with close-cropped graying hair and a warm, infectious smile, Phala had replaced Lobsang Samden in the sensitive post when the latter had opted to remain in India the year before. Despite his legendary sense of humor, Phala was not at all amused by the request of the two men for the help of the Tibetan government in overt resistance of the Chinese. He explained to them that this would be out of the question for a number of reasons, not the least of which was the fact that the Kashag was divided over the proper course of action to pursue and that one or more of the Kalons were certain to report such a request to the Chinese authorities.

Moreover, the Dalai Lama was still firmly opposed to armed opposition to the occupation forces. During those troubled days he thought often of his visit to the Rajghat "and wondered afresh what advice Mahatma Gandhi would have given me in the changing circumstances. Would he still have advised nonviolence? I could only believe he would. However great the violence against us, it could never become right to use violence in reply." On the practical side he viewed the Chinese atrocities in Kham and Amdo "as a dreadful example of what the Chinese could do so easily all over Tibet if we fought them" and so could not give his consent to the request of the freedom fighters.

Having been apprised of Phala's response, Gompo Tashi sent a message to the CIA through the two radio operators asking if the Chushi Gangdrug could count on American support if fighting broke out. The reply was disheartening: help would be given only if requested directly by the Tibetan government. He tried to arrange another meeting with Phala in the spring, but by then the Chinese had been made aware of his role in the resistance by paid informants, and the lord chamberlain declined on the grounds of security. Gompo Tashi decided to leave Lhasa. If he remained, his life would be in danger, and with no help forthcoming from either the Tibetan government or the United States it made no sense to remain there any longer. The two radio operators left with him.

Gompo Tashi established Chushi Gangdrug headquarters at Drigu Thang in Lhoka, a region southeast of Lhasa and two days' journey—only one by a really swift horse—from the river Tsangpo. By June over 5,000 resistance fighters had gathered there to celebrate the group's official inauguration. Most brought their own rifles and pistols, and to the others Gompo Tashi distributed arms and ammunition purchased at his own expense. He personally equipped and "armed to the teeth" forty-six of his employees and provided a hundred pack horses and mules as well as large quantities of white canvas and khaki cloth for making tents. On June 16 an impressive cavalry parade was staged, incense burned, and a large framed photograph of the Dalai Lama carried reverently to the main tent. Then the new flag of the Chushi Gangdrug was unfurled. Made in secret by a Lhasa tailor, it bore two crossed swords on a yellow background, their handles made of the *dorje* and lotus flowers. Officers were selected, a twenty-seven point code of conduct was drawn up, and scouts were dispatched to ascertain the location and strength of Chinese forces in the area.

In August 1958 Gompo Tashi and 500 of his volunteers set out on a five-day journey to the Tibetan government arsenal at Shang Ganden Choekor, west of Lhasa. The men were disappointed that this first mission was intended only to secure arms and ammunition. They were eager to fight the Chinese and were granted their wish when ambushed on the third day near the river Nyemo. "They had apparently received advance information about our plans, and they had concealed themselves behind boulders on either side of the track,"[1] says Ratuk Ngawang, a former monk from Lithang monastery who was present at the secret meetings at Gompo Tashi's Lhasa home in July 1957. Tall and powerfully built, he had arrived in Lhoka astride a beautiful dun-colored horse recently purchased in Lhasa for a thousand Chinese silver dollars, carrying a rifle, several pistols, and a thirty-six-inch silver-handled sword engraved with the eight auspicious symbols—the consummate Khampa warrior. The battle lasted for the better part of three days and claimed the lives of some two hundred Chinese and forty guerrillas. It also established a precedent, for the Chushi Gangdrug always exacted a heavy price for each of its own men lost.

When the band finally reached Shang Ganden Choekor, they discovered that the government arsenal had been emptied on orders from the Kashag and its contents distributed among the monks of a nearby monastery. For three days Gompo Tashi negotiated with monastery representatives and local government officials, who had been instructed not to surrender the weapons to the Chushi Gangdrug. "Andrug Gompo Tashi had what we call *wang-thang chempo*," says Loden, his former private secretary, who was by his side during the discussions. "The first of these words indicates someone endowed with natural power, the second means 'great.' In the West such a quality would best be described as charisma. Eventually he won over the officials by the sheer force of his personality, and they turned over the arms and ammunition to us."[2] The Chinese were furious when they learned of Gompo Tashi's success. "They complained bitterly to the Kashag," remembered Kungo Liushar, the Tibetan foreign minister at the time. "Only recently they had been urging us to go and collect the arms, and they intimated that someone had advised the Chushi Gangdrug to act before we did. Whether or not this was true I do not know, but certainly Gompo Tashi was intelligent enough to have done so on his own. I, for one, was not surprised when told of it."[3]

Neither were the Chinese, who had already begun to move large numbers of troops into the area and had deployed them in such a manner as to prevent the guerrillas from crossing the Tsangpo and rejoining their main body in Lhoka. A dozen bloody battles and skirmishes were fought to the west and northwest of Lhasa during the next few months as they tried to kill or capture Gompo Tashi. But whenever he seemed just within their grasp, he and his men would vanish suddenly into the surrounding mountains, only to emerge a day or two later with swords drawn and rifles blazing and descend on isolated Chinese encampments, storehouses, and convoys. While continuing their pursuit of the Khampa commander the Chinese opted to deal with the guerrilla stronghold south of the Tsangpo in a different manner by utilizing perhaps their most potent weapon: time. "While in Lhoka the Chushi Gangdrug rarely had enough food and had to rely on the nomads and villagers," Kungo Liushar remembered. "But the local people were short of supplies themselves, and once their resources became exhausted it would probably have been necessary to shift the base of operations westward into Tsang. The Chinese policy was simply to permit them to live off the local population in the hope that this would provoke animosity. Then, in the guise of supporting the peasants, they could move in and destroy the Chushi Gangdrug."[4]

In the same spirit the Chinese also sent out roving bands of disloyal Tibetans in their pay masquerading as freedom fighters to plunder villages and nomad encampments, but reprisals by the Chushi Gangdrug were swift and brutal. In October 1958, for instance, a group of deserters who had been engaging in widespread looting were captured by 400 of Gompo Tashi's men. The group's leaders were tried, found guilty, and executed, and the followers given the option of paying a fine or receiving fifty lashes. Then their right arms were cut off. When news of this got around, few outlaw bands had the courage to continue their activities.

The Chinese also brought pressure to bear on the Tibetan government, demanding that it order the Chushi Gangdrug to disband and give themselves up. A series of eight messages was sent to Lhoka, the last of which was delivered by a delegation of five government officials headed by Tsepon Namseling and bore the official seal of the Dalai Lama. "In it I called the guerrillas 'reactionaries' and stated that the Tibetan people should not support them," the Dalai Lama says. "At the same time the delegation was instructed to tell the guerrillas to go on fighting. We spoke in two tongues, the official and the unofficial. Officially we regarded their acts as rebellion, and unofficially we thought of them as heroes and told them so." The dual message was in keeping with a time-honored Tibetan tradition commonly practiced by government officials to ensure the confidentiality of important communications. During a visit to Shigatse in 1906, Charles Bell had noted that letters to him from the Panchen Lama were always accompanied by verbal messages that were invariably the most important part of the communication and not infrequently modified their contents. According to Bell, the practice had arisen for "fear that the letter may be seen by the Chinese or other unfriendly persons."

Having delivered the messages, Namseling and the four other delegates chose not to return to Lhasa. Instead, they joined the Chushi Gangdrug. As for the Dalai Lama, the continuing atrocities in eastern Tibet and the stubborn intransigence of the Chinese leadership in Lhasa had convinced him that armed resistance was the only course left. "Part of me greatly admired the guerrilla fighters," he remembers. "They were brave people, men and women, and they were putting their lives and their children's lives at stake to try to save our religion and country in the only remaining way that they could see. When one heard of the terrible deeds of the Chinese in the east, it was a natural human reaction to seek revenge. And moreover, I knew they regarded themselves as fighting in loyalty to me as Dalai Lama: the Dalai Lama was the core of what they were trying to defend."

In late 1958 the Chinese caught up with Gompo Tashi and his band near their recently completed airfield at Dhamshung, north of Lhasa on the Tibet–Chinghai (Amdo) highway. "It was a beautiful sunny day," Loden remembers. "Earlier we had met a nomad who warned us that the Chinese were waiting in ambush, but we didn't believe him. While we were discussing what to do, they lobbed a mortar at us. This was followed by a hail of cannon and machine-gun fire that seemed to be coming from all directions at once. We had no idea of its origin or where we could hide. Our rifles were useless." Within moments two men were dead and twenty-one injured, among them Gompo Tashi. "He was bleeding profusely from a series of wounds—he had caught over a hundred bits of shrapnel—down his right side from his face past his knee," says Loden. "He was unable to speak, and I did not think it possible he would live. We bandaged him up as best we could with supplies taken from the bodies of Chinese soldiers we had killed, since we had none of our own. Then we strapped him to his saddle and retreated into the hills. It was a miracle more of us were not killed."[5]

Gompo Tashi's retreat was covered by Ratuk Ngawang, who, with his friend Tsenphel, was cut off from the others. "Although we were both wounded, Tsenphel very badly, we knew we were still alive only because we had been protected by the blessings of the lamas," he remembers. "I carried him to a wooded area to avoid detection by Chinese aircraft. Our food and horses were gone but we still had our weapons. On the third day I managed to walk about three kilometers carrying Tsenphel over my shoulders; fortunately there seemed to be no Chinese in the area. Then we met two nomad families who provided us with food and shelter and dressed our wounds." A month later the two men obtained monks' robes and, concealing their pistols beneath them, made their way to Lhasa. There they got in touch with Tashi-Para Depön, commander of the second regiment of the Tibetan army at Thupchi Margar four miles north of the capital near Sera monastery.[6]

A tall, slender aristocrat in his mid-forties, Dorjee Tseten Tashi-Para had been an army officer for more than a decade and had taken part in suppressing the revolt of Sera's Che College in the wake of the ill-fated Reting Conspiracy in the spring of 1947. Since the beginning of the occupation he had attempted to maintain amicable relations with the Chinese military leadership in Lhasa, but after a series of incidents with the P.L.A. garrison at Chakrong a half mile away from his own—one in which four of his men had been machine-gunned in cold blood on the flimsiest of provocations and another in which three of his four junior officers had been poisoned by the Chinese at a "fraternal" dinner party given for them—he had become bitterly anti-Chinese.[7]

Some six months earlier Tashi-Para had accepted the surrender of a Chinese artillery commander by the name of Chang Ho-ther, who had appeared at Thupchi Margar one night seeking asylum. Chang, who held the rank of captain in the P.L.A., explained that he had fallen in love with the daughter of the gardener at the Lingka Sarpa (New Park) on the north bank of the Kyichu, and, after being granted permission to marry her by his superior officer, was advised later that this would be out of the question because she was Tibetan. Tashi-Para, a former magistrate, was a cautious man. "I interrogated him closely for three days," he remembers, "after which I told him that I still could not be certain he was not a spy planted in our midst and that I had no choice but to send him back to his regiment. When he heard this he told me quite calmly that I might just as well have him shot, for he was certain to be executed if he returned. I felt he was telling the truth, so I contacted Andrug Gompo Tashi, who was preparing to leave for Lhoka at that time. Gompo Tashi took a liking to him and realized that he had a far greater knowledge of military tactics than any other member of the Chushi Gangdrug. So he gave him the Tibetan name Lobsang Tashi and took him to Drigu Thang."[8]

Ratuk Ngawang sent word through Tashi-Para to Lord Chamberlain Phala that although Gompo Tashi was in Kham recuperating from his wounds, the guerrilla leader would be returning soon to Lhoka. "Tashi-Para

Depön then asked me what kind of assistance they might expect from the Chushi Gangdrug if trouble broke out unexpectedly," he says. "I told him that if he would protect the Dalai Lama in Lhasa, we would provide for His Holiness's safety if he were to leave the city." In January 1959 he and sixty-two other freedom fighters who had filtered into the holy city slipped through Chinese lines and rejoined the main force at A-Lhagyari. "Upon my return we held a large meeting. I explained that the situation in Lhasa was becoming very dangerous and suggested we consider seriously the problem of His Holiness's safety if he were to leave the capital. All of us agreed to station our best troops along possible escape routes leading through Chushul, Nyathang, Samye, Kongpo, Dakpo, Potamo, and Tsethang."[9]

It is said that when the monkey and the mountain ogress met and married in the Land of Snows sometime in remote antiquity, they produced six offspring from whom the Tibetan race descended. The monkey then led his children to a fertile plain in south-central Tibet where barley grew in abundance, and there he fed them and taught them to play games. Many centuries later the principal village of the area became known as Tsethang, a combination of *tse* (to play) and *thang* (a plain). By January 1959 Tsethang had become the site of a sprawling military garrison, the main base of the Chinese army in central Tibet with over ten thousand troops. "We decided we must attack and destroy it," says Ratuk Ngawang, "or at least disrupt it so the Chinese would be unable to pursue His Holiness if he should decide to leave." On February 8, 1959, the four thousand men under his command began a march to Tsethang. At dawn on February 11 they attacked the P.L.A. stronghold from four different directions but discovered that the Chinese were too well dug in for them to inflict much damage. Some had even fortified themselves in caves where the Tibetans' monkey ancestors were still to be seen. It was decided to lay siege to the camp, and some of the guerrillas were billeted in peasant cottages, others in a nearby monastery, still others in tents. "We were very near to the Chinese," Ratuk Ngawang recalls, "and could see them cooking and brewing tea. We exchanged fire with them, and there were a few casualties on each side almost every day." His forces were reinforced by monks from Sera, Ganden, and Drepung, and by the Lhokapa (people of Lhoka). Ratuk Ngawang sent two of his men, a monk and a soldier disguised as a monk, to Lhasa to report to Tashi-Para that all points from the capital to the Tsangpo were under Chushi Gangdrug control and that, with Tsethang surrounded, all of Lhoka was free.[10]

It was at about this time that the CIA decided to deliver its first consignment of weapons to the guerrilla forces. Furious that Gompo Tashi and the two radio operators had left Lhasa the previous summer, they had adamantly refused to act unless requested to do so by the Tibetan government itself. As the year drew to a close it began to dawn on them that, as Gompo Tashi had informed them, no such request would be forthcoming. With the situation in Lhasa deteriorating every day, they reluctantly decided to deal instead with the Chushi Gangdrug, and announced somewhat precipitately that the first arms drop would take place on a Lhoka plateau. When it was pointed out that this was directly over a nomad encampment, they refused to alter the arrangement. Moreover, they sent word that the guerrillas should assign a single man with thirty mules to await the shipment; the fact that it was impossible for one man to control so many of these obstreperous animals had apparently not occurred to them. The arms themselves—a hundred rifles of British manufacture, twenty submachine guns, sixty hand grenades, a pair of fifty-five-millimeter mortars, and three hundred rounds of ammunition per gun—fell far short of what the freedom fighters had been led to expect. They did not realize it at the time, but it was the last shipment they would receive.[11]

Back in Lhasa the situation was grave. Well over ten thousand refugees from eastern Tibet, Khampas, Amdoas, Goloks, and others, had converged on the holy city. Tempers were flaring, food supplies were strained almost to the breaking point, resistance leaders stealing in and out of the city under cover of darkness. Tibetan soldiers trained Bren guns on Chinese residences, itching for confrontation. The Gyayum Chenmo had not returned from India until August 1958 because of her belief that trouble could erupt at any time. "No one could speak in peace because someone might be listening. Many people, especially those known to hold anti-Chinese views and those capable of resisting Chinese intentions, disappeared, never to be seen again. The Chinese were kidnapping and murdering them, and blaming the murders on the Khampa guerrillas. I visited His Holiness every week and brought him a loaf of the Amdo bread he liked so much. He kept reassuring me that everything would be all right and that I should not worry. Finally I asked him *why* I shouldn't worry. 'What could happen?' he asked me. 'They will kill you,' I replied. 'What good would *that* do them?' he said, laughing. 'And if they try to take me to China against my will, I won't go.'"[12]

The Chinese authorities did nothing to alleviate this volatile state of affairs; to the contrary, their actions fanned the flames of discontent. Their response to the refugee problem in Lhasa was to conduct a door-to-door census in the capital, a course of action thought of as a prelude to wholesale arrests that prompted group after group to take to the mountains and join the resistance forces.[13] Next they insisted that the Kashag send the Tibetan army to suppress the Chushi Gangdrug, a directive manifesting either exceptional stupidity or deliberate provocation. The idea of pitting Tibetan against Tibetan to protect the Chinese army of occupation was as unthinkable as it was ridiculous, and there is little doubt that, like the officials who bore the Kashag's message to Lhoka some months before, the Tibetan soldiers would have joined forces with the freedom fighters. For the first time in some eight years of uneasy coexistence, the Kashag refused to comply with a major Chinese order.

The generals also announced that any resistance fighter who agreed to surrender his arms and return home would not be punished, a statement greeted by bitter laughter on the part of the Tibetans. A Khampa willingly give up his rifle? To the same Chinese who had destroyed and looted his temples and monasteries and killed his mother and father, his sisters and brothers, his wife and children, his lamas and oracles? How could a man return home when his village had been leveled in savage reprisals? After years of broken promises under the banner of "national liberation" and "democratic reforms," who in his right mind could trust or believe anything the Chinese said?

The breaking point had finally been reached. The breach between the Kashag and the Chinese was open, and growing wider every day. The Chinese were arming their civilian population and reinforcing barricades in Lhasa, and declaring publicly that in the event of violence they would protect only their own people and communications network; everything else was the responsibility of the Tibetan government. "They summoned more meetings in schools and other places," the Dalai Lama remembers, "and told the people that the Kashag was in league with the reactionaries and that its members would be dealt with accordingly—not merely shot, they sometimes went on to explain, but executed slowly and publicly. General Tan Kuan-sen, addressing a women's meeting in Lhasa, said that where there was rotten meat, the flies gathered; but if you got rid of the meat, the flies were no more trouble. The flies, I suppose, were the guerrilla fighters. The rotten meat was either the Kashag or myself."

As the Year of the Earth Dog drew to a close, the holy city began to fill with pilgrims and other visitors who had come to share in the festivities, their black yak-hair tents clustered like colonies of mushrooms on the plain. Thronging the streets day and night, they were joined by merchants, laborers, and government officials, for all work had ceased for the duration of the holiday period. The influx of celebrants swelled the capital's population to twice its normal number. It was a time of new beginnings, of prayers and offerings to the gods, of the driving out of evil; and great care was taken to do or say nothing that might give rise to bad luck in the coming year.

For weeks the people of Tibet had been busy making preparations. Given a short but welcome respite from their strict monastic routines, monks scoured their rooms, then polished the stone floors by attaching woolen rags to their shoes and gliding back and forth over them until they shone. Fresh white curtains were hung on the windows, and over them brightly colored valences. Hundreds of *torma* sculptures of dough, many in the form of tiny robed monks, were made and meticulously painted for ritual use, and scores of butter lamps were lighted. Pots of earth sown a few weeks earlier with barley seeds were placed on altars as an offering, ready to burst forth with silky green sprouts at the beginning of the new year.

In private Lhasan households similar scenes were enacted. Special holiday dishes were prepared, but only after kitchens had been subjected to a relentless scrubbing to appease the hearth gods. Family altars were carefully dusted and the tables on which they rested polished, as were the gleaming silver offering bowls arranged in a row along their fronts. Tables were covered with white cloths, placed before the altars, and filled with stacks of large, flat biscuits decorated with the eight auspicious symbols, as well as bowls of dates, nuts, butter, and brick tea; and the whole was illuminated by the flickering light thrown off by silver butter lamps set down in their midst.

The Losar festival began on the evening of the twenty-ninth day of the twelfth and final month of the Tibetan year. In monasteries and private homes people partook eagerly of a traditional stew of meat, rice, and vegetables to which a number of small wheat dumplings, each containing a tiny nonedible item, had been added. The person serving the stew was often blindfolded, and there was much laughter and teasing among old and young alike when they discovered what their dumplings contained. A lump of charcoal meant that the person who found it had a black mind. Wood signified a new house, porcelain procrastination, a pea frugality, cotton tractability. Dumplings shaped like the sun and moon were considered auspicious signs, while one containing a figure of a mother and child meant its recipient would be certain to give birth in the new year. To the great amusement of all, this figure was invariably discovered by either a man or an elderly woman.

Later the same evening, monks from the Namgyal monastery performed the Black Hat dance for the Dalai Lama at the Potala. Clad in costumes of the same color as their headgear, which represented the world of demons, and draped in long amber chains fashioned from human bones, which rattled eerily with their every gesture, they moved in ritual steps to the haunting music of drums and horns around a large sheet of rice paper on the courtyard floor, which had been painted with a figure representing the old year. Dancing faster and faster to the strident tempo of the drums and symbolically throwing onto the paper all the misfortunes and evils of the past year, they climaxed the breathtaking spectacle by seizing the sheet and cramming it into a large cauldron of boiling oil and in so doing created a fresh start for the coming year.

The Year of the Earth Hog dawned crisp and clear in Lhasa, but so great had been the revelry that few had slept the night before and the streets were already crowded. Pilgrims, beggars, and Lhasans colorfully dressed in their finest clothing rubbed elbows with wandering minstrels called *drekar*s, whose songs were considered good luck to all who heard them on this particular morning. Carrying a box of *tsampa* and a bottle of *chang*, children paid visits to the homes of friends and relations and enacted a sort of Tibetan trick-or-treat: in exchange for three sips of *chang* and three pinches of *tsampa* tossed in the air for the gods, they received holiday delicacies and perhaps a few coins.

On the third day of the new year began the Monlam festival. Some twenty thousand monks from nearby monasteries suddenly appeared in the holy city, swarming in their claret-colored robes over the already overcrowded streets and lanes, which miraculously accommodated them. According to tradition, the civic administration of the city was now turned over to the monastic authorities from Drepung, and the capital was transformed from a place of drinking, gambling, dancing, and singing to one of solemn religious observance. Order was maintained by a group of brawny *dob-dob*s, who had smeared their faces with soot to enhance their ferocious appearance and carried long wooden staves, which they were not reluctant to use. Although it had originally lasted for fifteen days so as to culminate with the first full moon of the year, the festival had later been extended to last three full weeks.

On the evening of the fifteenth day came the ritual known as Offerings of the Fifteenth. Lining the Barkhor, Lhasa's main business street that encircled the ancient Jokhang Temple, was a succession of wooden scaffolds on which rested enormous cakes of dough, as much as forty feet high and covered with intricately sculpted and painted butter. The sculptures had been fashioned by monk artists in icy water during the weeks immediately prior to the ceremonies, and retained their intricate forms in the wintry air.

As darkness descended on the holy city, thousands of butter lamps were lighted, their rays casting a mystical glow over the exquisite spectacle. At the sound of approaching drumbeats the crowd immediately became silent and bowed low as the gilded palanquin bearing the Dalai Lama was borne slowly past the magnificent creations, followed by a solemn procession of monastic and lay officials resplendent in finery of silk and brocade and golden jewelry encrusted with gemstones. After they had passed, the festivities took on a less formal tone. People mingled freely, strolling arm in arm to study the sculptures, and groups of villagers sang to each other all night long. By morning all the elaborate works were gone, melted down into oil for holy lamps.

The final days of the Monlam festival were marked by a series of symbolic processions and athletic events, including wrestling, weight lifting, sprinting, and horse racing. For a few short hours an enormous banner called the *goku*, several hundred feet in length and half that in width, elaborately appliqued and embroidered with gold thread and gems by the Lhasa Tailors' Union, was unfurled on a wall of the Potala. Last came the ceremony known as Togyek, or "*torma* destruction." To the beating of drums and the clash of cymbals, two enormous and ornately decorated dough figures were consigned to the flames of a massive bonfire.

By the end of the third week of the Year of the Earth Hog, all traces of the elaborate ritual artwork had been destroyed, symbolizing the Buddhist belief in the impermanence of life. Monks returned to the structured life of their monasteries and pilgrims packed up their tents and began the long journey home. Still glowing from the intoxicating events in which they had participated so thoroughly, the people of Lhasa returned to the routines of their everyday life and looked ahead eagerly to the festivities that would begin anew in a year's time. In a few short weeks, thousands of them would lie dead in the very streets in which their merrymaking had taken place. Life was, as Lord Buddha had taught, impermanent indeed.

Notes

1. Interview with Ratuk Ngawang, Dharamsala, India, May 11, 1980.
2. The haul of arms included two eighty-millimeter mortars with eighteen lots of shells, each containing six shells; two sixty-millimeter mortars with sixteen lots of shells, each containing eighteen shells; ten Bren guns with five packets of shells, each containing 2,660 shells; eighteen Sten guns; 385 British .303 rifles; 378 bayonets; and sixty boxes of shells, each containing 1,000 shells.
3. Interview with T. T. Liushar, Dharamsala, India, May 17, 1980.
4. Ibid.
5. Interview with Loden, Dharamsala, India, May 20, 1980.
6. Interview with Ratuk Ngawang, Dharamsala, India, May 11, 1980.
7. Interview with Dorjee Tseten Tashi-Para, Dharamsala, India, May 14, 1980.
8. Interview with Dorjee Tseten Tashi-Para, Dharamsala, India, June 8, 1980.
9. Interview with Ratuk Ngawang, Dharamsala, India, May 13, 1980.
10. Ibid.
11. Chris Mullin, "Tibetan Conspiracy," *Far Eastern Economic Review*, September 5, 1975.
12. Interview with the Gyayum Chenmo, Dharamsala, India, May 16, 1980.
13. George N. Patterson, "China and Tibet: Background to the Revolt," *China Quarterly* (January–March 1960), 98.

The Dalai Lama in his garden   *Dharamsala 1980*

· CHAPTER 20 ·

Playing for Time

I T WAS DURING the final joyous days of the Monlam festival that the act
which triggered the sequence of events leading directly to this tragedy
was carried out, although no one except perhaps the Chinese were aware of
this at the time. The date was March 1, 1959, the place the private apartments of the Dalai Lama in the Jokhang Temple. Assisted by a battery of six
tutors, the twenty-three-year-old ruler was deeply engrossed in preparations
for the final and most rigorous scholarly examination of his life, the *geshe
lharampa*, or doctor of metaphysics, to be administered the following day,
when two Chinese junior officers sent by General Tan Kuan-sen appeared
without prior notice and demanded to see him at once. The purpose of their
call, they explained to him, was to extend an invitation to a theatrical performance at the Chinese military camp at Silling-Bhuk and to ask him to
specify the precise date on which he would attend.

In what must be regarded as either an intentional understatement or a
remarkable display of equanimity, the Dalai Lama has said that he thought
the surprising visit "curious." Protocol demanded that all communications
intended for him be directed through either his lord chamberlain or the chief
official abbot, yet here were a pair of junior officers not only deliberately
flouting this convention but also having the audacity to insist upon an immediate commitment. "I was entirely preoccupied at that moment with religious questions," he remembers, "so I told the officers I would arrange a
date as soon as the ceremonies were finished." To his surprise they refused to
accept this decision and "kept on pressing me to decide on a date at once."
Displaying admirable patience, the Dalai Lama repeated that he could only
specify the date when the ceremonies had been completed, and finally convinced them to leave.

There is no doubt that this rash gesture, more of a command than an
invitation, was designed to insult and provoke the Dalai Lama and through
him the Tibetan people. "It had been our painful experience under the Chinese regime that I did not have the option even to decline a social invitation if

it did not suit me, except at the risk of incurring the displeasure of the Chinese and causing unpleasant repercussions," he says. "Their annoyance in such a case always found vent in some other direction, and so we thought it wiser, in the interest of the country, to suffer such minor humiliations in silence rather than risk a further stiffening of the general Chinese policy of relegating me and my government to a position of subordination."

Arriving at the Jokhang for his final examination on March 2, the Dalai Lama betrayed no sign of emotion over the events of the previous day. To the contrary, he smiled warmly at the vast throng of monks in attendance and seemed completely at ease. Yellow hat in hand, he listened carefully to each question and then, putting the hat upon his head, responded without hesitation to even the most profound and difficult of them; and at the end of the day he appeared as relaxed and cheerful as he had been at its start. "He was able to answer every one of our questions correctly and with clarity, precision, and even elegance," recalls Khyongla Rinpoche, a learned *geshe* who was one of the Dalai Lama's debating partners on that important day. "For an ordinary man to have responded that way would have been impossible. We were convinced that he was truly the incarnation of Chenresi."

Three days later, on March 5, the Dalai Lama, borne in his golden palanquin, made his way from Lhasa to the Norbulingka in a glittering state procession to which General Tan and his aides had been invited but were conspicuous only by their absence, yet another deliberate affront to the Tibetan people and their leader. Begun by the Eighth Dalai Lama in 1783 and enlarged by the Great Thirteenth over a century later, the Jewel Park was a square walled garden, each side a quarter of a mile in length, containing, in addition to well-tended flowers and trees, the Dalai Lama's tiny zoo, an arsenal for the Kusung Regiment (Royal Bodyguard), and residences for a few high-ranking government officials. In the middle of the park stood the Precious Protector's private garden and summer residence, surrounded by high yellow walls, its two gates guarded by members of the bodyguard and a pair of mastiffs. Away from the drafty confines of the Potala and the dust and smells of the holy city, it was the Dalai Lama's favorite place of residence.

On the 7th of March, General Tan again contacted the Dalai Lama, this time through proper channels, and was informed that His Holiness would be pleased to attend the theatrical performance at the Chinese camp in three days' time. While this exchange was taking place, Khyongla Rinpoche was on his way to the Norbulingka to hear the Dalai Lama deliver a series of teachings on Tantric themes. Provided with accommodation at Lord Chamberlain Phala's quarters, he remained at the Jewel Park for three days and after the final sermon on the evening of March 9 walked tranquilly back to Lhasa, "meditating, as I strolled, upon all that I had heard and learned." It was, he remembers, "the last event and stroll of that kind in my life." The events of that fateful day had placed Tibet on an irreversible collision course with the Chinese forces of occupation.

P. T. Takla, the Kusung Depön, or commander of the Dalai Lama's bodyguard, and husband of the Precious Protector's elder sister, was having breakfast at eight o'clock that morning in his residence, a few minutes' walk from the main gate of the Norbulingka, when he was interrupted by two officers sent by Brigadier Fu, the Chinese military adviser, who, they informed him, wished to see him at once. Pointing to his unfinished meal, Takla told them he would appear at the Chinese headquarters at ten. They left, but returned an hour later to tell him that he must come at once because the brigadier was waiting impatiently. He rose with a sigh and followed them to Fu's office.

The brigadier was in a foul humor and came straight to the point. "The Dalai Lama is coming here tomorrow to see a dramatic show," he stated flatly. "There are some things to settle. That is why I have sent for you."

"Has the date been fixed?" asked Kusung Depön.

"Don't you know?" snapped Fu. "The Dalai Lama has accepted the general's invitation and he is coming on the tenth." He paused a moment, then continued in carefully measured tones. "I want to make this clear to you. There will be none of the ceremony you usually have. None of your armed men are to come with him. No Tibetan soldier is to come beyond the Stone Bridge."

Kusung Depön was stunned. The Stone Bridge marked the outer limits of the Chinese army camp, whose existence barely two miles from the gates of the Norbulingka had always rankled the Tibetans. The very idea of their leader entering it for any purpose was extraordinary. Furthermore, the Dalai Lama was accompanied wherever he went by an armed escort of twenty-five guards, and armed troops were always posted along his route. Similar arrangements had been made for every Dalai Lama in Tibetan history. Recovering his composure, he asked Fu the reason for such a plan.

The brigadier flew into a rage. "Will you be responsible if somebody pulls the trigger?" he screamed. "We don't want trouble. We shall have our own troops unarmed when the Dalai Lama comes. You can post your men on the road as far as the Stone Bridge if you like, but none of them are to come beyond it under any circumstances. And," he added ominously, "the whole thing is to be kept secret."[1]

As the bellicose brigadier must have known, this last command was absurd. "It would have been quite impossible to keep any journey I made outside the Norbulingka a secret, unless a total curfew had been enforced," the Dalai Lama points out. "The moment I prepared to go out, the word always went round and the whole of Lhasa turned up and lined the route to see me." He and his advisers felt the Chinese invitation to be highly suspicious, and the order to keep the visit secret further fueled their fears.

The Chinese had purposely placed the Dalai Lama on the horns of a dilemma. For him to agree to their terms would constitute a profound personal humiliation and strike a severe blow to the political prestige of his government. Yet this is precisely what he chose to do, for the alternative of potential reprisals he found even more distasteful. There can be no doubt that the Chinese felt they had successfully maneuvered themselves into a situation that would benefit them regardless of the course of action taken by the Tibetans, but they greatly underestimated the strength of Tibetan nationalism and the intensity of devotion to the Dalai Lama. That both sides had been heading for a major confrontation cannot be doubted, but it is highly unlikely that either would have chosen that particular time and place to make a stand.

Having resolved to attend the performance and realizing the futility of attempting to do so secretly, the Dalai Lama was concerned lest some of his countrymen attempt to follow him into the Chinese camp and provoke an outburst of violence, a likely prospect considering the bitter recrimination, constant tension, and mutual suspicion that had marked the years of occupation. It was thus decided to issue orders forbidding Tibetans to cross the Stone Bridge on the following day, a precaution taken in good faith to prevent "tragic consequences" which unfortunately backfired.

Within hours of the announcement of this edict, rumors swept through the holy city that the Chinese were planning to kidnap the Dalai Lama, and there can be no denying that it looked that way considering the curious events of the past nine days. Intensifying these fears was the fact that the Dalai Lama had been urged repeatedly by the Chinese to attend a meeting of the Chinese National Assembly in Peking the following month but, "knowing the mood of the people," had avoided accepting the invitation; yet Radio Peking had broadcast to Lhasa just a week earlier the news that the Dalai Lama would be making the trip. "That announcement without my consent had already made people in Lhasa very angry," he recalls, "and naturally they concluded that the strange new invitation was simply a ruse to fly me out against my will to China." By sunset thousands of Tibetan men, women, and children had begun to gather outside the walls of the Norbulingka. They had come together to protect the living symbol of their land.

The Dalai Lama slept poorly that night, and on the morning of March 10, a day he has called "the most momentous Lhasa has ever seen," he arose at five and went as usual to the peaceful, familiar confines of his prayer room. Butter lamps in front of the altar cast a warm glow over the chamber, offering bowls of gold and silver sparkled with aromatic saffron water, and the fragrance of incense filled the air. After offering prayers and meditating, he went downstairs for what had become a ritual stroll in the lush gardens surrounding his summer palace. Preoccupied at first with the unsettling events of the previous day, he soon forgot them in the beauty of the crisp spring morning. In a cloudless sky the sun was rising over the mountains behind the city and casting its first beams on the Jewel Park. A faint breeze stirred the air, and all, it seemed, was green: the tiny poplar and willow buds, the unfolding lotus leaves in the lake, the new grass, even the Dalai

Lama's personal prayer flags fluttering on the roof of his residence. Later he realized that this was "the last brief moment of peace of mind I was to know."

A barrage of angry shouts from outside the high walls of the Nor-bulingka roused the Dalai Lama from his reverie and, hastening indoors, he sent some of his officials to investigate. Mounting a platform near the gates, they were stunned by the spectacle that confronted them. A sea of faces, fed by a seemingly endless stream of people all the way back to Lhasa, had sur-rounded the park, and from their cries it was apparent that they had come to prevent the Precious Protector from going to the Chinese camp. By nine o'clock the crowd had grown to such proportions that Kalons Liushar and Shasur experienced difficulty reaching the gates when they arrived in their Chinese army jeep. Moments later, violence erupted when a recently ap-pointed minister named Samdup Phodrang arrived but was not recognized by the crowd. Thinking that he and his Chinese driver had come to take the Dalai Lama away, the crowd lost control. A barrage of stones was hurled at the car, one of them striking Samdup Phodrang in the temple and knocking him unconscious. When Kalon Surkhang arrived later, he found it expedi-ent to leave his vehicle some distance away and complete the trip on foot.

It was apparent to the Kashag that something must be done quickly if further violence was to be avoided, for the mood of the people was growing increasingly ugly and there was the distinct possibility that it would lead to an attack on the Chinese camp. After waiting in vain for the appearance of their colleague Ngabo, they went to the Dalai Lama and advised him to can-cel his visit. If he entertained any thoughts of disregarding this advice, they were dispelled when he was informed of a bloody incident that took place just outside the gates of the Jewel Park a short time later.

Just before midday, a monk official named Phakpala approached the gates on a motorcycle. Widely known to be a collaborationist, he was wear-ing instead of his monk's robes a Chinese quilted jacket, dark glasses, and a dust mask that concealed the lower half of his face. Uncertain as to his iden-tity, someone tore the mask from his face and a man standing nearby recog-nized him and shouted, "It's Phakpala the traitor!" When the crowd surged forward and began jostling him, the monk panicked and pulled from his belt a small pistol, which he fired twice. It was the last conscious act of his life. "The enraged crowd swarmed upon him, hitting him with stones, sticks, and knives until he lay dead," recalls an eyewitness. "He took a long time to die." A fellow monk from Sera monastery remembers: "The crowd had gone mad with hysterical religious ecstasy. The body was roped around the legs and dragged along head down, while the crowd ran along yelling and cheering. It was terrible, especially when I thought of the times we had prayed together."[2]

Upon learning of this, the Dalai Lama had Lord Chamberlain Phala telephone General Tan's interpreter and convey the message that he would not attend the theatrical performance, and sent Surkhang, the senior Kalon, to inform the crowd of his decision. The announcement was greeted with cheers of jubilation, but the Tibetans made no move to disperse. "The people were in an angry mood," recalls P. T. Takla. "They berated Surkhang and the other members of the Kashag. 'You people are responsible for this!' they shouted. 'Even now you are being too friendly with the Chinese. From this day on *we* will attend to the security of His Holiness, and the Tibetan government should not attempt to interfere.'"[3]

The tension outside the walls of the Jewel Park was temporarily defused, but within those same walls the situation was quite the opposite. "The mental stress of that morning was something I had not experienced before," says the Dalai Lama of those harrowing moments. "I felt as if I were standing between two volcanoes, each likely to erupt at any moment. On one side, there was the vehement, unequivocal, unanimous protest of my people against the Chinese regime; on the other, there was the armed might of a powerful and aggressive occupation force. If there was a clash between the two, the result was a foregone conclusion. The Lhasan people would be ruthlessly massacred in thousands, and Lhasa and the rest of Tibet would see a full-scale military rule with all its persecution and tyranny." To mollify the Chinese, he sent his ministers to see General Tan and explain in person what had been transmitted to him earlier by telephone. The crowd outside the gates was reluctant to permit them to leave, and did so only after searching their cars to ensure that the Dalai Lama had not been secreted there.

When Liushar, Shasur, and Surkhang entered the conference room, they discovered that their colleague Ngabo was, as they had suspected, already in attendance and seated on the Chinese side of the table. Although Ngabo's pro-Chinese sympathies were hardly a secret to the trio, they were, to say the least, distressed when he chose not to get up and join them. This quietly defiant gesture indicated to them that the time for pretense had passed and that Sino-Tibetan relations had reached an extremely perilous state. These fears were not allayed by the demeanor of General Tan, who strode into the room some ten minutes later.

A short, stocky man about sixty years old, the political commissar of the Tibet Military District was literally speechless with rage and sat for several minutes in total silence, unable even to greet his visitors. First Surkhang and then the other two Kalons gave detailed explanations of what had transpired, and by the time the interpreter had finished translating their comments, Tan was red in the face. He paced up and down the room in an effort to control his emotions, then sat down and began to harangue the ministers about "Tibetan reactionaries." In a barrage of deliberately foul-mouthed invective he accused the Tibetan government of secretly arming the Chushi Gangdrug and other guerrillas to fight the Chinese. "How many guerrillas are there at most?" asked another general. "A thousand? Ten thousand? For the People's Liberation Army these numbers are meaningless; we can bring in as many troops as we wish to destroy them. If you believe the Khampas will save you, you are fools." The time had come, added a third general, to crush the "reactionaries" once and for all. "Our government has been tolerant so far," he warned, "but this is rebellion. This is the breaking point. We shall act now, so be prepared!"

The Kalons took these words as an ultimatum that if the popular uprising did not cease at once, military force would be used to suppress it, and tried to counsel patience. Referring to *so-pa*, the Buddhist concept of refraining from drastic action through proper understanding, Shasur suggested that the Chinese try to understand the ordinary Tibetan people and, even though they might be irritated, try not to react in anger. "There is a limit to *so-pa*," said one of the generals who spoke Tibetan. "For Tibetans practicing Mahayana," replied Shasur, "there is no such limit." "All of us laughed," Liushar recalled, "and the tension eased somewhat. For a while it seemed we would be detained or arrested, but soon the meeting broke up and we were able to report to His Holiness." Ngabo remained behind.[4]

Under the circumstances there was little for the Dalai Lama to do but play for time, "time for anger to cool on both sides, and time for me to urge moderation on the Lhasan people." To this end he exchanged over the following week a series of letters with General Tan Kuan-sen which were later published by the Chinese, who claimed they were irrefutable evidence that he was kept in the Norbulingka by a "reactionary clique" and then abducted to India against his will. The Dalai Lama has repeatedly denied these charges, and it is unlikely that even the Chinese believe them any longer, yet he has stressed that "even if I had thought at the time that these letters would have been quoted against me later, I would still have written them, because my most urgent moral duty at that moment was to prevent a totally disastrous clash between my unarmed people and the Chinese army."[5]

General Tan initiated the correspondence within a few hours of his meeting with the three Kalons, and his letter was found by the Dalai Lama to have been "written in friendly terms which would have seemed more sincere if I had not already been told of his rage by my ministers."

10 March 1959

Respected Dalai Lama:

It is very good indeed that you wanted to come to the Military Area Command. You are heartily welcome. Since you have been put into very great difficulties due to the intrigues and provocations of the reactionaries, it may be advisable that you do not come for the time being.

Salutations and best regards,

Tan Kuan-sen

The Dalai Lama replied on the following day:

11 March 1959

Dear Comrade, Political Commissar Tan:

I decided to go to the Military Area Command to see the theatrical performance yesterday, but I was unable to do so owing to the obstruction of the people, both religious and secular, who were instigated by a few evil elements and who did not know the facts. This has put me to indescribable shame. I am greatly upset and worried and at a loss as to what to do. When I received your letter, I was immediately overjoyed because you were not disturbed.

Reactionary, evil elements are carrying out activities endangering me under the pretext of protecting my safety. I am taking measures to calm things down. In a few days when the situation becomes stable, I will certainly meet you. If you have any internal directives for me, please tell me frankly through this messenger.

Dalai Lama, written by my own hand

The general's next letter was minatory in tone and stiffly polite. He threatened the Kashag ministers (except for Ngabo, now openly working on his behalf, and Samdup Phodrang, convalescing from the concussion he had suffered on the previous day) and from addressing the Tibetan leader as "Respected Dalai Lama" changed to a curt "Dalai Lama."

11 March 1959

Dalai Lama:

The reactionaries are now audacious enough to have openly and arrogantly carried out military provocations. They have erected fortifications and set up a large number of machine guns, and armed reactionaries are along the national defense highway, thereby seriously disrupting the security of the national defense communications.

Many times in the past, we have told the Kashag that the People's Liberation Army is duty-bound to defend the country and to protect the security of communication lines related to national defense, and therefore it certainly cannot remain indifferent to this serious act of military provocation. Therefore, the Tibet Military Area Command has sent letters to Surkhang, Liushar, Shasur, and Phala asking them to tell the reactionaries to remove all the fortifications they have established and withdraw from the highway immediately. Otherwise, they themselves will have to bear the responsibility for all the serious consequences. I want to inform you of this. Please let me know what your views are at your earliest convenience.

Salutations and best regards,

Tan Kuan-sen

Although hardly formidable in a military sense, the barricades were a visible symbol of defiance against Chinese authority. Well aware of what the "serious consequences" might be, the Dalai Lama replied:

12 March 1959

Dear Comrade, Political Commissar Tan:

I suppose you have received my letter of yesterday forwarded to you by Ngabo. I have received the letter you sent me this morning. The unlawful actions of the reactionary clique break my heart. Yesterday I told the Kashag to order the immediate dissolution of the illegal people's conference and the immediate withdrawal of the reactionaries who arrogantly moved into the Norbulingka under the pretext of protecting me. As to the incidents of yesterday and the day before, which were created under the pretext of protecting my safety and have seriously estranged relations between the Central Government and the Local Government, I am making every possible effort to deal with them. At 8:30 Peking time this morning a few Tibetan army men suddenly fired several shots near the Tsinghai–Tibet Highway. Fortunately no serious disturbances occurred. As to the questions mentioned in your letter, I am planning to persuade my subordinates and give them instructions. Please tell me frankly any instructions you have for me.

Dalai

The demonstrators were in no mood to listen to the advice or heed the commands of the Kashag and refused either to tear down their barricades or to disperse. By that morning the crowd surrounding the Jewel Park had swelled to some 30,000 and tempers were growing short. Two days later the Dalai Lama took the unprecedented step of meeting publicly with the people's leaders and urging them to discontinue a course of action he believed would lead to an inevitable clash of arms with the Chinese occupation forces. That his fears were justified became evident upon the receipt of Tan's next, and last, letter:

15 March 1959

Respected Dalai Lama:

I have the honor to acknowledge receipt of your two letters dated March 11 and March 12. The traitorous activities of the reactionary clique of the upper strata in Tibet have grown into intolerable proportions. These individuals, in collusion with foreigners, have engaged in reactionary, traitorous activities for quite some time. The Central People's Government has long adopted an attitude of magnaminity and enjoined the Local Government of Tibet to deal with them seriously, but the Local Government of Tibet has all along adopted an attitude of feigning compliance while actually helping them with their activities, with the result that things have now come to such a grave impasse. The Central People's Government still hopes that the Local Government of Tibet will change its erroneous attitude and immediately assume responsibility for putting down the rebellion and mete out severe punishment to the traitors.

Otherwise the Central People's Government will have to act itself to safeguard the solidarity and unification of the Motherland.

In your letter, you said: "As to the incidents which were created under the pretext of protecting my safety and have seriously estranged relations between the Central Government and the Local Government, I am making every possible effort to deal with them."

We warmly welcome this correct attitude on your part.

We are very much concerned about your present position and safety. If you think it necessary and possible to extricate yourself from the present dangerous position of being abducted by the traitors, we cordially welcome you and your entourage to come and stay for a brief period in the Military Area Command. We are willing to assume full responsibility for your safety. As to what is the best course to follow, this is entirely up to you to decide.

In addition, I have much pleasure in informing you that the second National People's Congress had decided to open its first session on April 17.

Salutations and my best regards,

Tan Kuan-sen

In the same envelope was another letter, signed by Ngabo and warning the Dalai Lama not to attempt to leave the Norbulingka because the Chinese had taken strict measures to prevent his escape, and that even if he were successful in the present international situation he would never be able to return to Lhasa. "If Your Holiness with a few trusted officers of the bodyguard can stay within the inner wall," concluded the maverick minister, "and hold a position there, and inform General Tan exactly which building you will occupy, they certainly intend that this building will not be damaged." Neither this letter nor ones similar to it forwarded to the Dalai Lama's council of Kalons were published by the Chinese. Fearing the worst, the Dalai Lama wrote to Tan:

16 March 1959

Dear Comrade, Political Commissar Tan:

Your letter dated the 15th has just been received at three o'clock. I am very glad that you are so concerned about my safety and hereby express my thanks.

The day before yesterday, the fifth day of the second month according to the Tibetan calendar, I made a speech to more than seventy representatives of the government officials, instructing them from various aspects, calling on them to consider seriously present and long-term interests and to calm down, or my life would be in danger. After these severe reproaches, the conditions took a slight turn for the better. Though the conditions here and outside are still very difficult to deal with at present, I am trying skillfully to make a demarcation line between the progressive people and those opposing the revolution among the government officials. A few days from now, when there are enough forces that I can trust, I shall make my way to the Military Area Command secretly. When that time comes, I shall first send you a letter. I request you to adopt reliable measures. What are your views? Please write often.

Dalai

When reading the above letters, it must be kept in mind that once the Norbulingka had been surrounded and the Dalai Lama prevented from attending the theatrical performance, the Chinese were assured of attaining their final goal on the Roof of the World, that of governing Tibet as part of the Great Motherland without interference from either the Dalai Lama or the Kashag. By failing to persuade the demonstrators to disband, the "Local Government" had proven itself incapable of controlling the Tibetan people, and whether the Chinese subsequently induced the crowd to disperse through peaceful negotiations or recourse to arms, there was no longer any chance that even a vestige of Tibetan autonomy would be permitted to remain.

In his communications to the Dalai Lama, Tan Kuan-sen was motivated less by a desire to suppress the uprising peacefully than he was to establish a documentary record to prove to the world that he and his regime had responded with commendable restraint to the "grave impasse" brought about by the "intrigues and provocations" of "reactionary, traitorous" elements, and that finally he had no choice but to take steps "to safeguard the solidarity and unification of the Motherland." Accordingly, he referred to the Dalai Lama's having been "abducted" by the crowds outside the Jewel Park, indicated that the "abduction" was inimical to the safety of the Tibetan leader, and offered to protect him if he chose and was able to deliver himself to the Chinese camp—even while ordering that heavy artillery be trained on the grounds of the Norbulingka.

The Dalai Lama, on the other hand, was preoccupied not with building a record for future publication but only with preventing the wholesale slaughter of his people, and the temporizing tone and content of his replies to the political commissar were dictated by circumstance rather than by conviction. When in his letter of March 15 General Tan charged that the Tibetan government had "all along adopted an attitude of feigning compliance" with Chinese directives while pursuing an independent path, he was not far from the truth. During the benign years of Manchu overlordship, the government had followed precisely the same pattern of passive resistance and thereby managed to retain a large measure of *de facto* authority. The Dalai Lama and his advisers had attempted to emulate the actions of their predecessors, but the presence in Tibet of a vigorous and ruthless Chinese leadership and a massive military machine had doomed their efforts to failure. By March of 1959 there was no room left to maneuver, for Peking had evidently decided that the time had come to achieve the total integration of Tibet into the Chinese People's Republic.

The Dalai Lama's missives to Tan Kuan-sen must be interpreted in this light, especially when the volatile nature of the situation during those fateful days is taken into account. He and the general seem to have vied with each other to see who could use most often the word *reactionaries*, an epithet the Chinese insisted be employed to describe the volunteer soldiers of the Chushi Gangdrug and others who had taken up arms against them, many of whom were involved in the activities outside the Norbulingka and in the ensuing uprising. "The word had a special emotional significance for the Communists," he recalls, "but of course it had none for us. Everybody, in the government and out, began to use it as a synonym for *guerrillas*. To Communists, no doubt, it implied the height of wickedness, but we used it, on the whole, in admiration."

Similarly, the Dalai Lama's letters were replete with exaggerated phrases. One incident put him to "indescribable shame," others broke his heart, and he was "immediately overjoyed" that the general was not disturbed by the actions of "reactionary, evil elements." He signed the latter two simply

"Dalai," and on the last added innocently, "Please write often"; if he could keep the general writing, he might prevent him from deploying Chinese artillery against the Tibetan people. While there is no doubt that he was a very young man to be burdened with such an onerous responsibility, it is also true that as a pragmatic but resolute leader, a brilliant scholar holding the equivalent of a first-rate Western doctoral degree, and an individual in whom long sessions of religious study and meditation had produced a remarkable equanimity, he was perfectly capable of speaking and writing in language other than Communist doggerel and unlikely to be nearly so shaken as his words seem to indicate. With the situation ready to explode at any time, he had no choice but to play B'rer Rabbit to General Tan's B'rer Fox.

As events turned out, the general was even wilier than he suspected.

Notes

1. Interview with P. T. Takla, Dharamsala, India, May 31, 1980.
2. Khyongla Rato Nawang Losang, *My Life and Lives: The Story of a Tibetan Incarnation* (New York, 1977).
3. Interview with P. T. Takla, Dharamsala, India, May 31, 1980.
4. Interview with T. T. Liushar, Dharamsala, India, May 17, 1980.
5. See "How General Tan's First Letter Was Brought to the Dalai Lama," *Peking Review*, 13 (April 3, 1959), 10–11; and "Photocopies of the Originals: The Dalai Lama's Three Letters to General Tan Kuan-san," *Peking Review*, 15 (April 14, 1959), 8–9.

MICHAEL HARRIS GOODMAN

The Gyayum Chenmo   *Dharamsala 1980*

· CHAPTER 21 ·

Into the Night

E ARLY ON THE MORNING of March 10, the Gyayum Chenmo was at home
dyeing some woolen fabric to be made into clothing for the household
staff when a neighbor burst into the room chattering excitedly. "What are
you doing here?" he asked in the Amdo dialect. "Everyone in Lhasa is going
to the Norbulingka with sticks, clubs, knives, and whatever else they can
lay their hands on to prevent the Dalai Lama from going to the Chinese
camp. Even if we have to die, we will stop him from going!" She sat down,
stunned. Her entire family had been invited to attend the theatrical performance, and her youngest child, Ngari Rinpoche, was to have gone there directly from Drepung. She could hear his voice calling to her. "He sounded
frightened, in need of help." An hour later the neighbor returned. "When I
heard that Phakpala had been killed, I felt still worse, that it was all over for
Tibet. My servant left and promised to return with news of anything else
that might happen." Chinese drivers arrived at ten o'clock to take her to the
performance but were informed by the servants that she was too ill to attend,
and left after a brief scuffle in which they were ejected from the doorway.
From behind a curtain in an upstairs bedroom, the Gyayum Chenmo watched
them drive off in a fury.[1]

An hour earlier a light-blue sedan of Soviet manufacture had arrived at
Drepung monastery to collect Ngari Rinpoche and three other monks.
When they reached the main road they could see hundreds of people walking
purposefully in the direction of the Jewel Park. They asked the driver, a
young Chinese wearing a faded blue outfit, what was happening, but his
response was noncommittal. Their first stop was at Lhasa headquarters of
the Tibetan Autonomous Region, where they joined a discussion group
reading the works of Comrade Mao, and they did not arrive at the Chinese
camp until almost two o'clock. Not until then did they know that the Norbulingka had been surrounded, that the Dalai Lama had sent word that he
would not be attending the performance, and that the monk Phakpala had

been stoned. Before they had time to digest this information, General Tan burst into the room.

The political commissar was furious. His face crimson, he pounded his fist on the table behind which he stood shifting his weight from side to side as if trying to adjust an unwieldy load. "Reactionary elements must behave or all will be liquidated!" he announced to the gathering of some one hundred Tibetans. "Up until now we have been patient, but this time the people have gone too far." The harangue lasted an hour. "I had never before seen him so furious," says Ngari Rinpoche. "I did not feel frightened, but I thought something terrible was going to happen. We all listened politely as he raved on, and then watched an abbreviated version of the cultural show." The dinner to which the group had been invited was canceled and cars were sent to take them away. "As I watched them pull up, I thought to myself, 'Things are really getting hot.' First came a troop carrier, then our car, and then a truck full of Chinese soldiers." They had gone only a short distance when they were waved to a halt by one of the Gyayum Chenmo's servants, who explained that his mistress was ill and wanted her son to come home. "I told the driver to go on without me and walked to my mother's house," Ngari Rinpoche remembers. "It was dusk when I arrived, and the gate was locked. 'This is unusual,' I thought. Then I looked up. My mother was peering from her window, and when she saw me she began to clap."[2] When her son walked through the door, the Gyayum Chenmo recalled, she felt as if he had come back from the dead.[3]

Ngari Rinpoche and his mother talked well into the night, interrupted only by a telephone call from P. T. Takla to find out if he was safe. "Don't you think what's happening is great?" he asked his uncle excitedly. The Kusung Depön made no reply; the Chinese might have been monitoring the call. To protect the household in the event of trouble he abandoned his bedroom for the sitting room, but was dismayed when he discovered that he had only one bullet left for his .22 rifle. Carefully he loaded this single shell into the breech, cocked the weapon, and slept with it by his side.

At five the next morning mother and son breakfasted on butter tea and *tsampa* with butter and brown sugar. "We spoke as if the day were no different than any other," Ngari Rinpoche remembers, "but I could tell from her manner that she was very upset." At half past seven a jeep arrived at the main gate, one of the half dozen provided by the Chinese for the Dalai Lama's personal use. Olive-green and bearing the number 67, it had had its windows shattered by the crowd outside the Norbulingka, who thought at first it belonged to the Chinese. "The driver was a former family servant named Lhakpa, an intelligent man of military bearing who bore a striking resemblance to the British actor Richard Attenborough and had joined the Kusung Regiment several years earlier," Ngari Rinpoche says. "He told us that he had been ordered by His Holiness to bring us to the Summer Palace at once."

The route to the Norbulingka was guarded by soldiers of the Chushi Gangdrug. "At first it was impossible to see the walls of the Summer Palace because of the vastness of the crowd surrounding it," Ngari Rinpoche remembers. "Many were carrying rifles, others sticks and staves, still others knives and swords. Everyone was looking alert and aroused. The whole scene was astonishing, and I was completely dazed by it. I was used to seeing soldiers armed—they were my superheroes—but certainly not ordinary people in civilian clothing. The soldiers of the Kusung Regiment had discarded the Chinese uniforms they had been forced to wear and had replaced them with khaki-colored outfits. They looked grim, determined, and fantastic, and I felt a shudder of excitement as I watched them. Everywhere there were little fires burning over which tea was being brewed, and tiny wisps of smoke were rising into the air. Clusters of people were sitting cross-legged around them sipping tea, talking, and trying to keep warm. They seemed to be in good spirits, determined and confident. But I knew they were in for a surprise."

In the meantime demonstrations and processions had begun to spring up all over Lhasa. Urged on by cheering crowds, speaker after speaker proclaimed the need for Tibet to regain her independence, derided Chinese claims of the "peaceful liberation" of their land, and denounced Chinese violations of the Seventeen-Point Agreement. The time had come, they exhorted, for the people of Tibet to rise as one in defense of their Precious Protector and their nation.

With the Dalai Lama publicly committed to a path of nonviolence, there was little unity to the people's uprising, but many Tibetans formed small fighting units. One such group was comprised of members from the Do-Sing Chesa (Association of Masons, Carpenters, and Builders). Five units were formed of fifty persons each, all between twenty and thirty-five years old, with three leaders for each group; older men and younger apprentices were formed into auxiliary bands. "If the need arose," recalls Langdun Gyatso, a carpenter who escaped to India in 1961, "the women were to join in by hurling stones from roofs as the women did years ago when the Chinese were driven out of Lhasa after the fall of the Manchus in China." Some of the older men had taken part in that fighting a half century earlier, and nodded their heads in approval. "Everyone felt that fighting would break out along similar lines, and that by a united and desperate action the Chinese might be driven away."

Since the group could muster only a few pistols, a delegation was sent to the government arsenal to request rifles and ammunition, but it was told that the Dalai Lama was still trying to arrive at a peaceful settlement with the Chinese. If conditions deteriorated, arms would be issued, but in the meantime it was suggested that the group join units like those of the painters, tailors, and leatherworkers to reinforce the city police and protect the Jokhang Temple. "It seemed as if Tibet was indeed free, for no Chinese could be seen in the streets," the carpenter says. "Looking back, the inevitable result was obvious. But in our excitement we had neither doubt nor fear. As one man we knew only one thing. We wanted to be free."

The Chinese wisely kept out of sight, but kept close watch on the turbulent city. "From my window with the help of binoculars I had a clear view of the Potala and the Iron Mountain," one of them wrote. "The sills of innumerable windows of the Potala are usually the favorite playground for doves. Now rifle barrels glint from them. Halfway up the Iron Mountain, Tibetan troops have taken up positions. At its summit in the Medical College there are more signs of military activities. Men are hauling up ammunition and other supplies."[4]

By the time the Dalai Lama's last letter reached General Tan, a vast throng of Tibetans, armed with sticks, spades, knives, a few rifles and machine guns, and a dozen or so antiquated mortars, occupied the area between the outer and inner walls of the Jewel Park. But within the yellow inner walls all was calm and peaceful. The Dalai Lama remembers: "The peacocks strutted about with their plumes held high, unconcerned about the human turmoil; singing birds were flying from tree to tree, mixing their music with that of the fountains near the rock garden; the tame deer, the fish, and the Brahmini ducks and white cranes were as placid as ever. A contingent of my bodyguard, out of uniform, was even watering the lawn and flower beds." That night would be the last he would ever spend in his beloved Summer Palace.

While the Tibetans were readying themselves for the confrontation, the Chinese were also busy. Reports reached the Dalai Lama that four cannon and twenty-eight heavy guns had been moved by several truckloads of soldiers from a construction site to Lhasa, and the district officer from the village of Bomtue fifteen miles to the east reported that twenty heavy guns had been sent to the capital. Two massive military vehicles were seen near the north gate of the Norbulingka with three soldiers in each, apparently taking range-bearing measurements. During the night over a hundred Chinese trucks were seen moving toward the city, and on the morning of the 17th, fifteen to twenty Chinese dressed in civilian clothing were observed perched on telegraph poles, apparently repairing the lines but in all probability taking artillery readings. "Usually we hear temple bells and horns resounding from the Potala calling the lamas to morning scriptures, but things are different today," noted Shan Chao, the Chinese observer. "The bandits are showing their real face more clearly." Later in the day he and his colleagues went to within a discreet distance of the Jewel Park. "We set out in a big armored car, with two smaller ones accompanying us. The rebels were building fortifications and it looks like there is going to be fighting soon. The rebels have been busy day and night deploying troops and bringing up ammunition. We cannot just sit and wait."

Shan Chao's words were prophetic, for even while the Dalai Lama was sending a hasty, coded message to the erstwhile Kalon Ngabo offering to deliver himself to the Chinese in order to avert "the massacre of my people," guns were being trained on the Jewel Park. The messenger returned with Ngabo's brief acknowledgment of the message and a promise to reply in detail later, but the answer did not come until all was over. At four in the afternoon two mortar shells were launched at the Norbulingka, one landing in an ornamental pond inside the grounds and the other just outside the gates. Although there was no further attack, the Dalai Lama remembers that "within the palace everyone felt that the end had come" and that "the first thought on the minds of every official was that I must leave the city at once." It was the only logical course of action.

There can be no doubt that the Dalai Lama's life was in danger. It must be remembered that the Chinese had first tried to persuade him to leave the Summer Palace and, when this became impossible, had then asked him to pinpoint the exact location of his chambers so as to avoid firing in that direction and jeopardizing his life. When this was not forthcoming they fired the two shells, whose purpose was to cow and disperse the crowd rather than to injure the Dalai Lama. Whatever their justification, the action manifested a callous disregard for the safety of the Tibetan leader. Yet the Dalai Lama's decision to flee the palace was not dictated by fear for his own safety. "I was not afraid of being one of the victims of the Chinese attack," he explains. "I honestly believe that my strict religious training has given me enough strength to face the prospect of leaving my present body without any apprehension. I felt then, as I always feel, that I am only a mortal being and an instrument of the never-dying spirit of my Master, and that the end of one mortal frame is not of any great consequence." Rather his intention was to remain as a living symbol to his people, who had not attained his state of enlightenment. "To them the person of the Dalai Lama was supremely precious. They believed the Dalai Lama represented Tibet and the Tibetan way of life, something dearer to them than anything else. They were convinced that if my body perished at the hands of the Chinese, the life of Tibet would also come to an end."

Arrangements for the escape had to be kept secret not only from the Chinese, whose spies were mingling with the crowd surrounding the Norbulingka, but also from the Tibetans, thousands of whom would have followed the Dalai Lama to ensure his safety and in doing so would have provoked a massacre. It was necessary to enlist the aid of the leaders of the people, whose cooperation was vital if the plan was to be successful. The escapees were to leave in four groups. First a twenty-five-man bodyguard would be stationed outside the walls and from there drift inobtrusively into the night. Next would be the members of the Dalai Lama's immediate family still in Tibet: the Gyayum Chenmo, elder sister Tsering Dolma, and thirteen-year-old Ngari Rinpoche. The Dalai Lama was to follow with Lord Chamberlain Phala, Kusung Depön, and the chief official abbot; and finally a much larger group consisting of senior tutor Ling Rinpoche, junior tutor Trijang Rinpoche, Kalons Liushar, Shasur, and Surkhang, and various attendants.

On the evening of March 17 the Gyayum Chenmo put on a man's green fur-lined *chuba* and a maroon hat with gold stitching. A servant was sent to the Barkhor to fetch a pair of boots for her, which she smeared with soot to make them look old. She asked the Dalai Lama where they were going and he replied, "Somewhere safe"; she wondered where in her country they would ever be safe again.

Soon after his arrival at the Norbulingka, Ngari Rinpoche sent for a Luger, inherited from his predecessor, which he had left in his room at Drepung. "I was disappointed to discover that I had only seven rounds for it," he remembers, "so I went around the palace grounds soliciting ammunition from the soldiers and managed to collect about two hundred bullets. Then I felt ready to take on the Chinese." On the evening of the departure he exchanged his monk's robes for a simple *chuba* and covered his shaven head with a stocking cap. Although exhilarated by the events of the past week, he was saddened by the thought of leaving all that was familiar to him, and was on the verge of tears when the sight of his mother and sister, entering the room wearing the clothing of male Khampas, made him burst out laughing.

Leaving the Norbulingka was "like walking on air." It was a starry night but the moon was not visible. A cool breeze was blowing and a few dogs barked in the distance. Ngari Rinpoche, the Gyayum Chenmo, and Tsering Dolma were flanked by four bodyguards from the Kusung Regiment. The lights of the Chinese camp were clearly visible, and they walked in silence, the only sound being the crunching of their boots on the sandy soil. Half an hour later they reached the Kyichu and crossed over in a coracle. "As we waited for horses to be brought for us, I suddenly had the feeling that I wanted to be alone," Ngari Rinpoche remembers. "I walked a short distance into the woods, then turned slowly until I could make out the outlines of Drepung in the moonlight. I stared at it for some time and then prostrated myself three times. 'May I see this place again,' I thought, 'once more before I die.'"

As Ngari Rinpoche stood alone in the moonlight his brother the Dalai Lama left the Mahakala Temple on the grounds of the Jewel Park.[5] "I had always gone there to say goodbye when I went on long journeys. Monks were still there, offering their constant prayers, and they did not know what was about to happen; but I offered a scarf at the altar as a symbol of farewell. I knew they would wonder why I did so, but I also knew they would never express their surprise." Returning to his quarters, he removed his monk's habit and donned the clothes and fur hat of a Tibetan soldier, and in that unfamiliar dress went into his prayer room for one last time. He sat on his throne and opened the book of Buddha's teaching that lay before it, and read until he came to a passage in which Lord Buddha counseled one of his disciples to be of great courage. Then he closed the book, blessed the room, and left as silently as he had entered. "As I went out, my mind was drained of all emotion. I was aware of my own sharp footfalls on the floor of beaten earth, and the ticking of the clock in silence."

At the doorway of his house he took a rifle from one of his guards and slung it over his shoulder to complete the disguise. Outside he met Kusung Depön at the garden gates and Lord Chamberlain Phala and the chief abbot at the gate of the inner wall; as they passed the Mahakala Temple, they bared their heads in homage and farewell. Together the group crossed the park toward the gate on the outer wall, the Dalai Lama having in the meantime taken off his glasses so as better to conceal his identity. Phala went ahead and informed the guards he was going on a tour of inspection, and the gate swung open.

Only once before, when he had fled to the Chumbi Valley nine years earlier, had the Dalai Lama passed through this gate without a ceremonial procession. But no one took notice of the humble soldier who passed, unchallenged, into the dark night.

Notes

1. Interview with the Gyayum Chenmo, Dharamsala, India, May 23, 1980.
2. Interview with Ngari Rinpoche, Dharamsala, India, June 1, 1980.
3. Interview with the Gyayum Chenmo, Dharamsala, India, May 23, 1980.
4. For this and following quotations, see Shan Chao, "Sunshine after Rain," *Peking Review* 18 (May 5, 1959), 21–24.
5. Mahakala (in Tibetan, Gompo Chakdrug, "Six-Armed Protector of the Dharma") is a deity endowed with the power of protection against evil and symbolizes the militant aspect of Chenresi, the bodhisattva each Dalai Lama incarnates.

Tibetan monk in cave   *Dharamsala 1980*

· CHAPTER 22 ·

Flight to Freedom

A N UNEASY AND UNDECLARED TRUCE hung over Lhasa for the next forty-eight hours. No further shells fell on the Jewel Park and no one was attacked. Tension continued to grow as Tibetans wondered when the Chinese would make an attempt to break through their lines and take the Dalai Lama, and why their mortars had been silent. Chinese heavy artillery had been trained on each of the four sides of the Norbulingka, pillboxes erected at strategic points, and the entire area surrounded by trucks and armored cars. The best the Tibetans could offer as resistance was a protective barrier of sandbags inside the palace grounds. Clustered in groups and drinking butter tea to ward off the cold and keep up their spirits, they were still grimly determined to defy the Chinese and protect their leader.

On the morning of March 19 the women of Lhasa held a public meeting denouncing the Chinese occupation forces, then marched in procession through the streets of the city carrying prayer banners. At least one female member from every household is said to have been present, and in many cases all the women from a given family were in attendance. Among these were the wife and twelve-year-old daughter of the carpenter Langdun Gyatso, who with a group of his friends ran ahead of the procession posting anti-Chinese posters proclaiming Tibetan independence. "As on previous occasions there were no incidents," he remembers, "although demonstrators defied the Chinese on rooftops to shoot. But the Chinese were content with shooting with their cameras."

Shan Chao's version, which appears to be the only Chinese firsthand account of events in and around Lhasa during those fateful days, is quite different. The demonstration around the Jewel Park, he wrote, was not at all spontaneous. To substantiate this contention he related a conversation between two Tibetan collaborators: "The rebels ordered it! They said anyone who does not attend the meeting at the Norbulingka will be fined; if he still fails to go, then they will have his head cut off! All the Tibetan cadres and students have been ordered to leave their offices and schools. Orders have been issued to shoot to kill anyone who disobeys. Their families will be shot too! These rebels are devils!"[1]

Collaborators and their families, Shan Chao continued, flocked to the Chinese for protection and soon packed every spare office, conference room, and dormitory; and when there was no more space they declared: "If the houses are full, we won't mind staying in the courtyards. As long as we are with the Communists, nobody will suffer even if the sky falls down." He added that the grateful Tibetans insisted on joining the Chinese in their military preparations: "Don't we have a share to do in fighting the scum of our own people? The reactionaries want to kill us. Why shouldn't we take defensive action?"

Shan Chao seemed amazed that the Tibetans were insisting on their independence. "They are raising such havoc all through the city that it's as if some imperialist invader had entered our land," he commented. He may have taken exception to their convictions but could hardly deny their intentions: "You didn't need to ask what was going to happen. Those who had their ears and eyes open once more began polishing their rifles and bullets. Following their example, I also took out my hand grenades and put them by the side of my pillow." He claimed that at the nunnery in front of the Jokhang Temple, "not a single one of the scores of young nuns escaped being raped" by the "bandits."

"These upper-class reactionaries are always saying that the Tibetans want to drive out the Hans. But what kind of Tibetans do they mean?" Shan Chao continued. "It's certainly not the ordinary folk like the shopkeeper. It's those reactionary nobles and running dogs of imperialism that they mean." On the night of March 19 the carpenter Langdun Gyatso, one of those "ordinary folk," whose wife kept a small tearoom just off the Barkhor, went to bed early but was awakened at 1:00 A.M. by the thunder of artillery fire. Shifting his wife and children to a room on the ground floor for safety, he improvised a rough shelter by placing a large plank from the kitchen against the wall as precaution against falling debris if the house was hit. Outside, the sound of the bombardment continued, coming from the direction of the Norbulingka, and at sporadic intervals the night was turned into day by flares.

At sunrise there was insistent knocking at the carpenter's door. It was a messenger from the Do-Sing Chesa calling all members to a rally at the Jokhang. Langdun Gyatso rushed out into the streets and joined a small crowd that grew larger with each passing moment. Members of the crowd requested arms from the soldiers in their midst but were refused. "To our disappointment they had only one rifle each and a couple of Bren guns and not much ammunition. Those like myself with pistols joined the soldiers in firing a shot every now and then at buildings occupied by the Chinese."

The Tibetans trained their one small field gun at the office of the Preparatory Committee on the Formation of a Tibetan Autonomous Region and fired a first, symbolic shot, which was greeted with loud cheers even though it did no damage. After a few more shots the gun was trained on the Yuthok House, a closer target which served as the Chinese military head-quarters, with similar results. As the Chinese began to train their guns in the direction of the cannon, the men dragged it to another corner of the Jokhang and from there began firing in the direction of the buildings occupied by the Chinese administration. In neighboring houses people began offering in-cense, and the fighters could see clouds of smoke billowing from the roof-tops. "Although there were more than a thousand of us at the Jokhang," recalls Langdun Gyatso, "we could not do much without firearms. Knives and swords were useless since no Chinese could be seen. The nearest Chi-nese were behind protective ramparts guarded with machine guns and auto-matic rifles. Those who attempted to charge at them were mowed down in no time." A few Tibetans managed to set up sandbag shelters on rooftops and succeeded for a time in pinning down the Chinese at a few locations. That night they attempted to set the Yuthok House on fire but were repelled by enemy machine-gun fire.

At the Norbulingka the situation was even worse. A Chinese mortar attack had begun about seven o'clock on the morning of March 20 and showed no sign of abating. As in Lhasa, defenders were unable to return fire effectively because the larger and more modern Chinese guns were en-trenched behind strongly fortified barricades; and the smoke and chaos in-side the grounds reduced visibility to a minimum. "There was tremendous confusion," remembers Lobsang Tenzin, one of the 600 soldiers of the Kusung Regiment who had remained behind to defend the Jewel Park. "People were running in all directions and taking shelter wherever they could. Whole trees were being uprooted and many people killed all around me, and I was certain all of us would die. I was so frustrated I was on the verge of crying. 'If I could only see the Chinese,' I kept thinking, 'I would gladly give up my life if I could just take one of them with me.' But I was not so fortunate."[2]

As the shelling continued, tanks and armored cars crept forward, shel-tering the infantry behind them. Lobsang Tenzin took refuge in a stone water trough inside one of the stables. "I still had my Mauser and a Lee-Enfield rifle with the barrel sawed off," he says. "But they were useless; there was no one to shoot at." Finally he heard shouts from captured Tibetans call-ing on everyone to surrender and saying that the Chinese had promised not to harm anyone who came out of hiding. "An elderly monk official in the trough next to mine suggested we give ourselves up because we were certain to be discovered, so we came out with our hands held high." It was nine o'clock on the evening of March 21.

On the morning of that same day, Langdun Gyatso had returned home to find his house inundated with neighbors, including five Chinese families, who had flocked there for safety. "There were over fifty of us," he says.

"Fortunately we had enough food since we kept a tearoom." Outside, the fighting continued unabated. A shell landed in the courtyard of an adjacent building, killing an elderly man and two mules. The carpenter was appalled: "Men, women, and even children were shouting and urging others to come out and launch human waves at Chinese positions. Many rushed, armed with knives, meat cleavers, stones, and even staves. But they were simply mowed down by machine guns."

By six o'clock on the morning of March 22 the fighting had stopped. Over loudspeakers the Chinese announced that the Norbulingka, the Potala, and the Chakpori hill had been taken and that further resistance would be useless. "The firing was now only sporadic and sounded far away," remembers Langdun Gyatso. "The neighbors who had taken shelter with us returned to their quarters. Loudspeakers continued to announce that other places had fallen into Chinese hands. On roofs and from windows people were holding *khatas* tied to sticks as a token of surrender." For the first time since the fighting had erupted Chinese soldiers were seen in the streets, and they rounded up all who surrendered. "The streets were littered with corpses, some of them heaped in piles. Already street dogs were tearing bits and pieces from the bodies. A few women were rushing frantically from corpse to corpse in search of their menfolk."

From the pen of Shan Chao a different story emerged. A number of his comrades, he wrote during the battle's waning moments, had gone to investigate the scene at the Jewel Park and returned joyously with the news: "All our shells fell right on the fortifications in front of the walls. What shooting! Our men didn't destroy a thing in the Norbulingka. But the rebel bandits, when they were cornered and put up a desperate fight, knocked out the corners of houses and broke down walls." About the Potala a similar tale was told: "We saw shells exploding only on the concealed pillboxes at the foot of the palace. What was the matter? Bad marksmanship? We found out later that the artillerymen had been given orders that no shell should fall either on the Potala or the Jokhang. They could fire only in places of secondary importance, so that no building would be destroyed." The Tibetan and Hui cadres at his office, he stated, were stunned by the restraint displayed by the Han forces. According to Shan Chao, they exclaimed: "What a humane and polite way of fighting a battle!"

On the once-green grounds of the Norbulingka, on the terraced steps of the Potala, in the inner courtyard of the Jokhang Temple, on the rocky slopes of Chakpori hill, and in the cobblestoned streets of Lhasa, between ten and fifteen thousand Tibetans lay dead.

In Lhasa the advent of spring is marked not only by the blooming of flowers, trees, and foliage, but also by powerful sandstorms that sweep in off the plain with great velocity. As they approach the holy city, people scurry for cover, street dogs huddle together in corners, and field animals turn their tails resignedly to the wind. The storms are of such ferocity that people must close their eyes to avoid being blinded.

It was into such a storm that the Dalai Lama walked as he left the grounds of the Jewel Park on the night of March 17. It could not have come at a better time, for as the escape party trudged along the dried-up bed of a stream leading to the Kyichu, it passed within two hundred yards of the Chinese military encampment. Screening the group from both the Chinese and the storm's full fury was a grove of willow trees planted a decade earlier—providentially, it would seem—by Heinrich Harrer. The chief abbot, a large man who elected to carry a sword commensurate with his proportions, adopted a threatening attitude at every bush, but none was found to conceal an enemy.

Waiting at the banks of the Kyichu were about thirty members of the Chushi Gangdrug, who had managed to requisition a group of coracles to ferry the group to the other side. After hurriedly exchanging *khatas* with them, the party crossed over, mounted the ponies tethered there, and quickly rode off. The first few miles were likely to be the most dangerous. The group's first objective was to cross the broad waters of the Tsangpo some forty miles to the south of Lhasa, and to do so they had to begin by negotiating a narrow three-mile track skirting a hill directly above and parallel to the Kyichu. To their right they could see the lights of the Chinese camp, and they were painfully conscious of the sound of their ponies' hooves against the stony path. The storm had subsided and the night was pitch black; several of the party lost their way, including the Dalai Lama, who had to turn his mount around and catch up with the others.

To reach the Tsangpo they could not take either of the main routes leading southwest out of Lhasa for fear of encountering Chinese patrols, so they decided instead to strike out for the lesser-known crossing at a tiny village named Kyeshong, or "Happy Valley." Once across the river they would be in the heart of the Himalaya, an almost impenetrable area controlled by the Chushi Gangdrug, which the Chinese would find difficult to invade in any great strength. Their route led them southeast over roadless mountains to the foot of a 17,000-foot pass named Che-la, or "Sandy Pass," which lay between them and the mighty river. It was eight o'clock in the morning when they stopped there for a cup of steaming hot tea. The first brilliant rays of sunlight were beginning to appear above the peaks and cast their light on the plain they had just crossed. It had been ten hours since they had left the Norbulingka behind them.

The ascent was exhausting and the footing so treacherous that the group had to dismount frequently and lead their mounts along the narrow track. Some of the ponies and mules began to lag behind, but all were cheered by an act of generosity considered highly auspicious: an elderly man materialized suddenly and offered the Dalai Lama a graceful horse as white as the snows surrounding them, which was accepted gratefully. They continued climbing until well above the snowline and stood at last at the summit, which was marked with fluttering prayer flags and cairns of stones. Each of the group added a stone to the piles and looked down at the river, winding like a tiny blue band before them.

Once across the Che-la, the Dalai Lama and his party were confronted with great slopes of sand. They ran down to the level ground of the valley, leaving their mounts to follow in the traditional manner suggested by the old Tibetan proverb:

> If you do not carry him up a hill, you're no horse;
> If you do not walk down the hill, you're no man.

The party hastened to the ferry landing ten miles to the east and were rowed across the Tsangpo. On the southern bank of the river the group was greeted by a large crowd of villagers and freedom fighters, wearing badges of white and yellow indicating their status as volunteer soldiers. It was the first village through which the Dalai Lama passed on the journey, and many of the people were weeping openly, making him feel "even sadder. There, I thought, were the people of Tibet who had lived in the Happy Valley for centuries in perfect peace and harmony, and now grim fear stood over them and threatened all they lived for." After a brief pause for tea, the party pushed on for the monastery of Ra-me, which they reached at half past four. By nine o'clock the rest of the party had caught up with them, and all had their first night's rest twenty-four hours after leaving Lhasa.

By the time it left Ra-me in the morning, the escape party had increased in number to 100 and was escorted by 350 Tibetan regulars commanded by Depöns Takla and Tashi-Para and some 50 members of the Chushi Gang-drug. Their destination was the village of Chenye, a five-day march over narrow, stony tracks deep into the mountains ahead. "The Luger had by now become quite uncomfortable as it pressed into my hipbone," remembers Ngari Rinpoche, "but I had no intention whatsoever of removing it from its place of honor in my belt. I was also carrying a brand-new Mauser rifle, a gift from the Kusung Regiment, with one clip in the breech and an extra one in the folds of my *chuba*. I even had an eighteen-inch dagger thrust under my belt. I looked the perfect soldier that day, except I was a bit too short." He was later forced to relinquish the Mauser because it proved too heavy for him; in its place he carried the Dalai Lama's umbrella.[3]

A hundred-man force was dispatched to the southwest as protection in the event Chinese forces approached from the direction of the main road to India, and the rest split up into groups of fifty so as to make faster time and avoid aerial detection. Although the drone of aircraft caused them to seek shelter from time to time, the weather was fortunately overcast. All the while they were watched over silently by an invisible guerrilla network whose leaders, the Dalai Lama recalls, "came and went, keeping in touch with all the isolated bands who were living in the mountains; and we knew we were surrounded by faithful, determined men whom we never saw."

Up to this point the Dalai Lama knew nothing of the uprising in Lhasa. The plan was to reach the Tibetan stronghold of Lhuntse Dzong near the Indian border and from there attempt to negotiate with the Chinese to prevent the shelling of the holy city. Although the group carried a battery-operated radio receiver, Radio Lhasa was silent, and it was not until they had reached Chenye that the first news emerged over the Voice of America indicating "unrest" in the Tibetan capital and that the whereabouts of the Dalai Lama were unknown.

The story of the bombardment of Lhasa was brought by Tsepon Namseling, one of the officials who had been sent by the Kashag seven months earlier to "persuade" the Chushi Gangdrug to discontinue its armed resistance, but who instead had joined them. Arriving on the same day was a tragic eyewitness account written by the Dalai Lama's private secretary, Khenchun Tara, who before making his escape had remained behind for several days once the shelling had begun despite being wounded by shell splinters. The Dalai Lama was shaken. "From that moment it was inevitable that I should leave my country. There was nothing more I could do for my people if I stayed."

That night at the monastery of Chongay Rewo Dechen he met with leaders of the Chushi Gangdrug, among them Ratuk Ngawang, who had ridden from Tsethang to meet him. "When I first saw His Holiness I burst into tears because he was not wearing his monk's robes but just an ordinary *chuba*," he remembers. "It took several moments before I was able to address him. 'Do you have news of Andrug Gompo Tashi?' he asked. 'He will be arriving shortly,' I answered him. 'And is there any word of Gyalwa Karmapa? Is he safe?' asked His Holiness. 'I know only that he is fleeing from the west of Lhasa,' I replied, 'but other than that I have heard nothing.' 'Take care of him when he arrives,' he told me. Then he asked me if I had heard any news of Shudup Rinpoche. I was unable to answer at first because I was trying not to cry. He had been my guru at the Lithang monastery and I thought he had been killed by the Chinese. 'It was wrong of me to ask,' His Holiness said. 'I am sorry.' Then he changed the subject by asking me about my sword. I told him I never used it in battle but had killed perhaps thirty wounded Chinese with it because we were always short of ammunition. I do not think he was pleased with my reply." Before returning to Tsethang the next day Ratuk Ngawang met one last time with the Dalai Lama. "He examined our rifles and asked us to show him how they worked. We began to do so but were stopped by Phala. 'Don't play with your weapons so close to His Holiness,' he rebuked us. 'There might be an accident!' 'Don't worry,' His Holiness reassured him, 'these men know how to handle them.' Then he took me aside. 'Do not die foolishly,' he said. 'Since you are a *magchi* [military commander], you must be clever.'"[4]

High in the craggy peaks of the Himalaya, the Dalai Lama and his party continued to push southward toward Lhuntse Dzong, a vast fortification built on rock like a miniature Potala, where they hoped to establish a temporary government. The constant travel was exhausting and they were forced to cross a pass every day, some slippery with mud where the snow had melted and others, at altitudes over 19,000 feet, still encrusted with ice and snow. They spent one night at the village of E-Chhudhogang, a motley collection of makeshift dwellings on land so barren that Tibetans had long since coined an adage about it: "It is better to be born an animal in a place where there is grass and water than to be born in E-Chhudhogang." Despite their impoverishment its inhabitants were happy, "for they know how to look poverty in the face," and welcomed the weary travelers to share their humble quarters. The following day the party heard over the radio an announcement from Peking that Chao En-lai had dissolved the Tibetan government and replaced it with the Preparatory Committee for the Formation of a Tibetan Autonomous Region. It came as a severe blow, but hardly an unexpected one.

In contrast to the humble reception accorded the Dalai Lama at E-Chhudhogang, his arrival at Lhuntse Dzong two days later was marked by a colorful spectacle. Local officials awaited the party on the track a mile from the *dzong* and accompanied them the rest of the way. Over a thousand villagers, burning incense and clasping prayer banners, lined both sides of the approach, and as the travelers drew closer they heard the welcome sound of religious music played by an orchestra of monks from a nearby terrace. Over three hours of rituals followed, beginning with a ceremony of thanksgiving for the group's safety. "All of us quite forgot our immediate troubles and tragedies," the Dalai Lama remembers. "We felt we were doing something positive for the future of Tibet." A religious service was held to commemorate the founding of the new temporary government and monks, lay officials, and village headmen joined in, bearing the scriptures and appropriate emblems. The lamas in attendance chanted prayers of enthronement. A proclamation of the establishment of the government was read out to the assemblage, and the Dalai Lama signed copies to be sent to all districts of Tibet. With the staging of the *droshey*, or "dance of propitious fortune," the ceremonies came to an end. They were the last the Dalai Lama would observe in his native land.

Reports of Chinese military movements in the area induced the group to move on the next day; not even the well-fortified *dzong* would be able to withstand an onslaught of modern armament. "By then all of us had admitted the unwelcome truth to ourselves," the Dalai Lama says, "that wherever we tried to stop, the Chinese could hunt us out, and that my presence there would only lead in the end to more fighting, and more deaths of the brave men who would try to defend me." It was decided to send a group of officials ahead to the border to ask the government of India for asylum, since they did not wish to enter that country without permission. The advance party left at midnight with orders to proceed as fast as possible to the nearest Indian outpost, where they were to send a message to Prime Minister Nehru in New Delhi and, upon receiving a reply, return at once to the frontier.

The Dalai Lama and his party followed five hours later and were beset by the worst weather of the entire journey. First they were caught in a heavy snowstorm at the summit of a pass known as the Lagoe-la, in which the Dalai Lama's eyebrows were frozen and Ngari Rinpoche "had a very bad time of it." Since none of the party had extra clothing they were able to keep warm only by dismounting and continuing on foot. "We tried to spare our ponies as much as we could all through the journey," the Dalai Lama says, "not only because Tibetans always do, but especially because they had so far to go and there was so little fodder for them." By midday they were clear of the pass and stopped for a brief meal of bread, hot water, and condensed milk, which despite its humble nature the Dalai Lama found delicious. "I took it upon myself to serve him in a large wooden bowl which used to belong to my brother Lobsang," Ngari Rinpoche remembers. "It looked especially large in my little hands and caused quite a bit of amusement among the members of our party." That night the Dalai Lama caught up with his mother and sister, who had preceded his party on a different and less arduous route, at the village of Jhora.

Conditions were even worse the next day. As they ascended the Karpo-la the weather was fine and clear, but heavy snow, whipped by a strong wind, bit into their faces; and no sooner had the storm abated than brilliant sunshine reflecting off the primeval whiteness threatened them with snow-blindness. Those without protective goggles covered their eyes with strips of colored cloth or with braids of hair many wore around their heads. When they stopped to eat at noon a violent dust storm broke over them and put a hasty end to their meal, and the rest of the day was spent plodding through heavy, blinding snow. Two more days of similarly grueling travel brought the group to Mangmang, the last settlement in Tibet.

Then came the rain, a long torrential downpour that forced the party to erect tents for the first time since leaving Lhasa. The Dalai Lama tried without success to sleep, but his tent leaked so badly that he was forced to sit up shivering all night, and the next morning found him so ill he was unable to ride. Moved by his companions to a tiny house encrusted with grime and black with soot, he spent his last night on Tibetan soil in a second-story room with cattle lowing on the ground floor and roosters crowing in the rafters above. Reports that Chinese troops were drawing closer forced the group to continue their journey on the following day, and the Dalai Lama, still too ill to ride a horse, was placed on the broad back of a *dzo* and on that primitive Tibetan transport embarked on his last journey on native soil.

When the party neared the border, the Chushi Gangdrug escort sought the Dalai Lama's blessing and bade him goodbye, returning in the direction from which they had come to face the Chinese. Of all the government officials, only one chose to follow a similar course: Tashi-Para Depön. "A man like him, he told me, would be of no use in a foreign country," the Dalai Lama says. "After all, he explained, he did not even speak the language. Now that he was assured of my safety, he was returning to lead whichever of his men were still alive. He was a real hero."

Finally they reached the end of their journey. "There was nothing dramatic about our crossing of the frontier," the Dalai Lama remembers. "The country was equally wild on each side of it, and uninhabited. I saw it in a daze of sickness and weariness and unhappiness deeper than I can express."

The date was March 31, 1959. It had been exactly two weeks since the Dalai Lama had left the once-idyllic confines of the Jewel Park behind him. Tibet would never be the same.

Notes

1. Shan Chao, "Sunshine after Rain," *Peking Review* 18 (May 5, 1959), 22.
2. Interview with Lobsang Tenzin, Dharamsala, India, June 8, 1980.
3. Interview with Ngari Rinpoche, Dharamsala, India, June 1, 1980.
4. Interview with Ratuk Ngawang, Dharamsala, India, May 13, 1980.

The Dalai Lama in meditation *Dharamsala 1980*

CHAPTER 23

Exile from the Land of Snows

T O REACH LOWER DHARAMSALA one must begin by making a twelve-hour overnight rail journey from Delhi to Pathankot, a dusty market town in the Kangra Valley, and partake there of an obligatory cup of tea at the dingy, single-roomed dormitory-cum-snack-bar run by a surly but enterprising Tibetan named Tsultrim that serves as the unofficial waystation between Dharamsala and the rest of the world before boarding the local silver-and-blue bus of Himachel Transport, which will strain and rattle its way up the serpentine mountain road at the edge of town for three and a half additional hours until it wheezes to a stop some 450 miles from the Indian capital.

From here Upper Dharamsala, a euphemism for the village of Macleod Ganj, lies perhaps a mile north as the crow flies but almost six by road: past the gates of an Indian army cantonment, where a bronze-skinned Punjabi sentry with proud, dark eyes and a thin mustache stands at attention, the white of his puttees and bandolier and jade-green turban contrasting strikingly with his khaki uniform; past a haphazard cluster of Tibetan-occupied cottages and shops that calls itself Forsythe Ganj; past the tiny Anglican Church of St. John's in the Wilderness, which was well attended during the British Raj but now looks forlorn and abandoned despite a sign promising services on the second and fourth Sundays of each month; past the monument to Lord Elgin, who before assuming the post of viceroy of India in March 1862 commented to a group of friends that "the vast amount of labor devolving on the Governor-General of India, the insalubrity of the climate, and the advance of years, all tend to render the prospect of our meeting again remote and uncertain" and fulfilled his prophecy by dying in Dharamsala eighteen months later at the age of fifty-two; and past a large, squat building bearing the sign "Nowrojee & Sons Inc., General Merchants."

"Macleod Ganj was founded in 1856 when British troops moved up from Jullundur during the Sepoy Mutiny," says Nauzer Nowrojee, a seventy-one-year-old Parsi whose great-great-grandfather opened the store four years later. "It was made district headquarters of the Punjab local government and was named after Sir Donald Macleod, who later became lieutenant-governor." Until Nowrojee's father, Nadirshaw, heralded the age of the automobile by chugging into town in a new Model T Ford toward the end of the First World War, a combination of poor transport and a 1905 earthquake had kept the population low, but during the next three decades it increased to almost 4,000, mostly British on civil and military postings but including local Muslims, wealthy Hindus and Muslims who migrated there in summer to escape the heat of the plains, and a tribe of nomadic shepherds known as the Gaddis. Nowrojee's emporium flourished along with the village, importing and distributing wines and spirits, china and glassware, confectionaries and oil-burning stoves from England, and the finest sugar from Java; "everything from a pin to an elephant," he remembers wistfully. But in 1947 came independence and partition; the British went to Britain, the Muslims to Pakistan, and the wealthy to Delhi, leaving behind them a population of less than 700. Nowrojee tried to entice businesses, government agencies, universities, and religious organizations to relocate there, but not until 1960, when the Indian government was searching for a remote site for the Dalai Lama's residence in exile, were his efforts rewarded. He steps from the gloomy confines of his shop into the bustling marketplace outside. "It is remarkable what these people have accomplished here," he says. From mountain wilderness to outpost of the British empire to ghost town, Macleod Ganj has evolved into a thriving Tibetan community, the focal point of all Tibetans in exile, a veritable Little Lhasa in India.

From the dusty clearing in front of Nowrojee's store where tired buses rest before making their way back down the mountain, a half-dozen narrow roads plunge into the surrounding evergreen-and-rhododendron forest. One of the roads leads to the Tibetan Children's Village, another to the Tibetan Dance and Drama Society, a third to the dispensary of the Tibetan Medical Center. Two others border the congested marketplace and its focal point, the Namgyalma stupa, a massive reliquary shrine flanked by twin rows of bronze prayer wheels, which the villagers revolve as they circumambulate it telling their beads and intoning the mantra *Om Mani Padme Hum*. Surrounding the stupa is a courtyard filled with seated devotees, their heads bowed in silent prayer. In a small adjacent building a gray-haired woman turns a prayer wheel twice her size by leaning against the waist-high handle projecting from it and circling it slowly; a bell clangs reassuringly upon the completion of each revolution.

The lane on the north side of the marketplace begins at a bakery where Tibetan breads are made freshly each day and continues past Tashi's, whose menu includes butter tea, tsampa porridge, and *momo*; past the Tibet Photo Center and a stall in which an old man stencils the sacred mantra onto prayer flags; past the office of Dr. Yeshi Thonden, one of the world's foremost authorities on Tibetan medicine and the Dalai Lama's personal physician; past a pair of tiny eateries named The Yak and Tibet Memory; and down the long hill to Gangchen Kyishong (Snowcapped Happy Valley), a complex that includes the Tibetan Library and Archives and the Tibetan Secretariat.

The lane on the south side of the marketplace begins just past Nowrojee's and passes a row of shops selling offering bowls and rubber sandals, butter lamps and tinned preserves, tea churns and plastic buckets, rosary beads and bidis, before skirting the grounds of the nursery school and the village's solitary beggar and arriving at Thekchen Choling, "Place of Mahayana." There sits the tent of Dorjee, who spends his days chiseling the mantra onto *mani* stones for sale to his fellow believers. There, too, is the School of Buddhist Dialectics, where pairs of monks debate in the traditional manner, one punctuating each question by stamping his right foot forward while smacking the back of his right hand into his left palm and the other endeavoring to respond calmly and correctly from a seated position. There is the Namgyal Temple, its most precious possession fragments of sacred images from Lhasa's Jokhang Temple, destroyed by the Chinese during the Cultural Revolution and smuggled out by devout Tibetans risking beatings, imprisonment, and death. And there, through the gates of the private compound, is the residence of His Holiness the Dalai Lama.

It is dawn. Streaks of sunlight appear over the Dhauladhur spur of the Punjabi Himalaya, its ridges a montage of jagged silhouettes in shades of gray. A solitary figure in monk's robes slowly circles the forested hilltop, the fingers of his left hand telling rosary beads. For the Dalai Lama it is the most relaxing time of the day, one of silent reflection and communion with nature. He usually arises at four and spends at least a half hour in this manner before breakfast. It is a habit acquired in early childhood and his only opportunity for physical exercise.

Returning to his residence, he places a cup of tea on the altar as an offering before sitting down to a meal of toast, cheese, honey or jam, fruit, and tea, which he usually takes without butter owing to a history of liver trouble. At the same time he studies the scriptures, for he is a man who makes the most of every moment. A stack of Western publications sits nearby, among them *Time*, *Newsweek*, the *Far Eastern Economic Review*, and *National Geographic*, of which he has been an avid reader since his early days in the Potala when he discovered back issues belonging to his prior embodiment, the Thirteenth Dalai Lama. He rarely looks at these, or at the daily Indian newspapers—the *Times of India*, the *Indian Express*, the *Hindustan Times*, and the *Statesman*—until evening. After breakfast he retires to the large, dimly lighted interior chamber that serves the dual purpose of bedroom and private chapel. Sitting cross-legged upon a faded orange floor cushion, he assumes the posture of meditation: the right hand, symbolizing discipline, above the left, symbolizing wisdom. "If you would like to take a photograph," he says, "switch on the lamp so you will be able to focus." Without waiting for an answer, he shuts his eyes and takes a few deep breaths. The rosary dangles motionlessly from his fingers and his face assumes an aura of serenity; although his physical form remains, his essence seems to float away into some other level of consciousness.

He opens his eyes an hour later as if awakened by an internal alarm clock and, reaching to his left, removes the dust cover from a short-wave set and switches it on. After a few moments of static, BBC London comes in clearly with a half-hour summary of international news. Occasionally he tunes in the Voice of America, Radio Moscow, or All India Radio, but the BBC has always been his favorite. Radio Lhasa and Radio Peking are monitored and transcribed for him each day at the Secretariat.

At exactly eight he shuts off the radio and moves into the front room, a combination parlor and study with a southern exposure overlooking well-tended flower beds in full blossom with the colors of Tibetan Buddhism: claret and yellow, orange and gold. As was once said of his predecessor, "flowers are an abiding joy to him." Seating himself on a floor cushion behind a low table, he begins a period of private study, the two neat piles of time-worn scriptures before him among those few salvaged from Lhasa and eastern Tibet. The pressure of temporal responsibilities usually limits its duration to an hour, but during the past week he has been preparing for sermons to be given at Tibetan refugee settlements in South India and works without interruption until half past twelve. He is studying the *Prajnaparamita*, the ancient Discourse on Perfect Wisdom, that wisdom which destroys all illusion and guides the individual to the world of liberation, of enlightenment, of buddhahood. It is the same collection of sutras with which he began his spiritual education as a child in the Potala. "After visiting Dharamsala or one of our refugee settlements in South India, many foreigners have come to me and said, 'Despite your suffering, you Tibetans seem to lead honest, happy lives. What is your secret?'" His voice has a melodic, resonant quality, and although his English is limited—due to his own "laziness," he explains with a merry laugh—only rarely does he choose the wrong word; his language is precise and controlled. "There is no secret. Our culture is very much based on compassion. We are used to saying all the time, always, 'All sentient beings are our own fathers and mothers.' Wherever I am I express my feelings about the importance of kindness, a true sense of brotherhood, human harmony. It doesn't matter whether we are believers or nonbelievers, educated or uneducated, Easterners or Westerners, so long as we are the same kind of human beings with the same kind of flesh and the same kind of features. Everyone wants happiness and doesn't want sorrow, and we have every right to be happy." He radiates an extraordinary personal purity, a visible holiness—which has nothing to do with his monk's robes but rather with his manifest gentleness, his utter lack of affectation, his guileless, captivating smile. During a 1967 visit to Japan he was surrounded by a mob of jeering Maoist demonstrators whom the police were unable to control. When he turned to look at them, to try to understand what they were saying and why they were so angry, a hush fell over the crowd and it gave way. Then he smiled at them and walked on. Similarly, television crews waiting for him at New York's Kennedy Airport in September 1979 were transformed suddenly by his appearance from an unruly mob into a gathering of beaming participants in a special event; even network news reporters, who had caught only a glimpse of the Dalai Lama on videotape as he made his way through a joyous throng of Tibetans and Mongolians there to welcome him, reported his arrival with obvious warmth.

Owing in large measure to the logical and systematic nature of its doctrines, Buddhism has proven an appealing philosophy in today's rational and scientific world, and there are an estimated half-million adherents in North America and western Europe. Traditionalists have been concerned lest some of its external forms—rituals, chants, ceremonies, and the like—be transformed in this new environment into something completely different, but not the Dalai Lama. "These things are not so important," he explains. "Certain methods of practice, certain methods of presentation changed when Buddhism was brought from India to Tibet and adjusted to its new environment. What *is* important is that the essence of the Buddha's teachings be unchanged." Yet while he believes that "religion is like food—for everybody a different taste," he advises those interested in Buddhism to approach it through reason rather than through faith. "The Buddha himself said, 'O monks and nuns, you should not accept my teachings just out of respect for me, but should analyze them the way a goldsmith analyzes gold, by rubbing, cutting, and melting.'"

This advice is especially important in the choice of a spiritual guide. "In Buddhism it is said, 'Rely not on the person but on the doctrine.' In other words, when choosing a guru or teacher one must listen carefully to what he is saying and should not rely on whatever fame or popularity he might have." He pauses, deep in thought. "In the past, in our own country, and also in China, Mongolia, and Russia, Buddhist monasteries were originally centers of learning. This was very good. In some cases, due to social influences, these became corrupt. Sometimes they became more like centers of business and moneymaking than religious centers. So in the future we must take care." It saddens him to hear of the handful of gurus in India and elsewhere who seem to be preoccupied with financial endeavors. "This sort of attitude is self-destructive to the teacher and harmful to the followers. The Buddha, and Jesus also, taught that spiritual wealth is much more important than worldly wealth." He refuses to accept payment for sermons delivered in India, Japan, Mongolia, Europe, Canada, and the United States: when informed that the group sponsoring his American visit in the summer of 1981 was considering charging an admission fee for the rare Tantric sermon he was scheduled to give, he advised them that unless they found another way to meet their expenses he would be unable to come because in the Buddhist tradition such teachings were meant to be free. Likewise he graciously declined the offer of some Swiss admirers to give him money for the purchase of an automobile, but accepted contributions for his teachings and placed them in an emergency fund for the use of the 2,000-strong Tibetan community in Switzerland.

His considerable personal fortune, removed from the Potala treasury at the time of the Chinese invasion and shipped to India, is invested in a special trust fund, whose profits are used to aid Tibetan refugees and assist in the preservation of Tibetan cultural institutions: education, religion, and the arts. He has willingly exchanged the trappings of the monarchy for the life of a simple Buddhist monk.

Although a brilliant theologian—despite mirthful protestations that as a boy he studied only when obliged to by his senior tutor, Ling Rinpoche— who takes great delight in mastering the intricacies of Buddhist metaphysics, the Dalai Lama has not lost sight of the essentials of his faith. "My true religion," he says, "is kindness." He rises from the table and gazes at the *thonka* painting on the opposite wall of Manjusri, the bodhisattva of meditation and personification of supreme wisdom, holding a sharp sword used to pierce the cloud of ignorance and cut away human attachment to the illusion of subject and object. It is the only *thonka* he carried with him into exile. "Enlightenment," he says finally, "cannot be obtained merely by living a monastic life or reciting from these pages." His hand caresses the yellowed leaves he has been reading so intently. "Whether such activities, in themselves, should even be called religious is open to question, for religion should be practiced in the mind. If one does not have the right mental attitude, an entire lifetime spent in monasteries reading holy books will achieve nothing. Only if you practice charity, morality, forbearance, and kindness will you find inner peace." His eyes fall once more on the painting of Manjusri. "Without inner peace," he says softly, "it is not possible to have world peace."

Nor does he believe that inner peace is attainable only by following the path of the Buddha. "The purpose of religion is not for arguing," he says. "If we look for differences, we can find many differences. . . . Lord Buddha, Jesus Christ, and others developed their own ideas and teachings with sincere motivation, love, and kindness, and shared them for the benefit of mankind. I do not think these great teachers brought about these differences in order to make trouble in the world. Because I believe in Buddhism, because I believe there is no creator, if I criticize other religions which believe in a creator, then if Lord Buddha was here, he might scold me."

Head tilted back and eyes squeezed shut, he bursts into a gale of laughter at the incongruous picture his words have conjured up. Like most Tibetans he is gifted with a keen sense of humor, and when he laughs his entire body takes part. He has a wonderful, unembarrassed laugh that begins as a deep-throated roar and fades away on a high pitch, as if all his previous thirteen incarnations were joining in with him. That he is able to see the humorous side of any situation, that he is able to laugh in the face of adversity after all he has experienced during the past three decades, suggests that he is a man who has found inner peace. "I make distinctions in order to get peace in your mind, not for criticizing, not for argument or competition. In each religion the ultimate point is that its followers must be moral, honest, and compassionate through that teaching. Whether there is a God or not, whether there is karma or not, the fundamental thing is that the followers must be good human beings. If we understand the oneness of humankind, then we realize these differences are secondary. With an attitude of respect and concern for other people, we can experience an atmosphere of happiness. Only that way can we create real harmony, real brotherhood."

Behind the modest bungalow in which the Dalai Lama has been living for the past eighteen years rise the snowcapped peaks of the Himalaya, the forests teeming with gorillas, leopards, bears, and deer. Woodpeckers, pheasant, orioles, bluejays, scarlet minivets, paradise flycatchers gleam in the dark trees; the shadow of the eagle soars overhead. The cold season is bitter, bringing heavy snow and driving wild animals from the heights, but as the rainy season approaches, scarlet rhododendrons burst into bloom and the entire forest seems to be aflame. The nightingale sings, the hyena wails, monastery horns echo through the stillness, and occasionally, on a soft moonlit night, the glowing eyes of a panther are seen. Far above the banana, palm, sugar cane, and paddy fields of the plain, the mountain in its splendor is a solace to the Dalai Lama and his fellow refugees, a reminder of the grandeur of the homeland that lies on its other side, a reminder of their country, Tibet.

In the early years of his exile he liked to trek deep into the cool, hushed recesses of the mountain forests and encamp there for several days at a time, as if to serve notice that he and his people would never relinquish their right to the land of their ancestors, that their sojourn on the Indian side of the Land of Snows was only temporary. Recently, increased involvement in government affairs has kept him from the slopes, just as it has curtailed the time he has been able to spend gardening in his greenhouse or repairing transistors in his tiny electronics workshop. His fascination with technology is no less strong today than it was when he was tinkering with generators during his boyhood in Lhasa, finding a counterpart to the formalism of ritual in the elegance of circuitry. "There is no contradiction between Buddhism, modern techniques, and science," he says. "Spirit and matter or energy and matter are only two aspects of the same thing. Does not modern physics teach us this? Our lamas have known this for centuries and come to know it again and again. Energy or spirit condenses itself at regular intervals into matter. According to the Buddha Dharma, matter evaporates into energy. Things which we see are only the different transitory phenomena of the same immortal stream from which we originate and into which we all merge again."

A pair of monk attendants serve the Dalai Lama's lunch promptly at half past twelve, a bowl of vegetables and Tibetan-style noodles in mutton broth known as *thukpa*. It is his last meal of the day, for the *Vinaya Sutra* of monastic discipline prohibits monks from taking food after midday. According to the same sutra, it is permissible for a monk to eat meat provided it has been killed neither by nor for him; but during his travels in India the Dalai Lama discovered that animals were being slaughtered and prepared especially for him and in 1965 decided to become a vegetarian. Two years later, however, he contracted hepatitis and was urged by both Tibetan and Western doctors to eat meat again. He prefers beef—rarely available in Dharamsala—and mutton but avoids chicken: the smaller the animal, he feels, the more of its kind must lose their lives to provide human sustenance.

Before descending the hill from his private residence to his office and reception area at 1:30, the Dalai Lama checks on the progress of a baby cuckoo he has been looking after since he found it on the ground with an injured wing while taking one of his morning walks; like his predecessor, he is especially fond of birds. "Many people have expressed sadness that I am forced to spend so much time and devote so much attention to political and mundane affairs." His smile is glowing, his glittering eyes gay behind tinted glasses. "According to the Buddhist tradition, service to others is one of the most important religious practices. Just to sit and pray is not sufficient. For example, a U.N. declaration on human rights is nothing on paper; it must be implemented in the real world. So a good person must be involved in politics. Religion is meant for man, politics is meant for man. All these political systems, economic systems, ideological systems . . . for what? For the benefit of mankind. To control oneself and to serve others: this qualification is highly necessary for a politician too, I think. So, as long as my motivation is correct, my temporal work is an act of religion."

Shortly after his arrival in India the Dalai Lama announced that "Wherever I am, accompanied by my government, the Tibetan people will recognize us as the government of Tibet," and although the international community has refrained from granting this body *de jure* recognition, the fact remains that today, twenty-seven years later, he presides not only over a government-in-exile but also over a nation in exile more truly Tibetan in character than that which is left in Tibet after three decades of Chinese misrule. In Dharamsala he meets at least twice weekly with his five-man Council of Kalons, three of them lay and two monk, each holding a separate portfolio: the Council of Religious and Cultural Affairs, the Home and Rehabilitation Office, the Council for Tibetan Education, the Office of Information and Publicity, and the Office of Security and Personnel. The Kashag also oversees the activities of Offices of Tibet in New York, Tokyo, Winterthur, Switzerland, and the Bureau of His Holiness the Dalai Lama in New Delhi. Ultimate decision-making authority is vested in the seventeen-member Assembly of Tibetan People's Delegates, an elective body consisting of four delegates from each of the three regions of Tibet, one from each of the four major sects of Tibetan Buddhism, and one from practitioners of the ancient Bön faith; but just as the Dalai Lama tends to be guided by majority opinion when approving a given measure, so, too, does the assembly tend to defer to his judgment on matters of a politically sensitive nature. One of his first acts after reaching Dharamsala was to write, with the aid of Indian lawyers, a democratic constitution for Tibet. Dated March 4, 1963—the fourth anniversary of the Tibetan National Uprising—the document contains a bill of rights and provides for representative government, universal suffrage for those over the age of eighteen, free elections, an independent judiciary, and major reforms in land tenure. A radical departure from the former system, it will remain in draft form until approved by the six million Tibetans still living under the Chinese yoke. In the meantime the Dalai Lama and his ministers must govern an estimated 110,000 Tibetan refugees, approximately 88,000 of whom are in India and Sikkim, 15,000 in Nepal, 4,000 in Bhutan, and the rest in western Europe and North America. One of their earliest and most significant moves was to settle the refugees in India, a decision met with widespread and highly emotional opposition. To many Tibetans the act of putting down roots in foreign soil was like making the tacit admission that any return to Tibet was at best a long way off, that many would never again see the land of their ancestors. But as thousands of ragged fugitives poured from the mountain passes into hastily established transit camps, where they died in droves from unaccustomed heat, low altitude, disease, and depression, the only alternative seemed to be migratory road-labor tent encampments where conditions were even worse. If their way of life was to survive the Tibetan diaspora, the Dalai Lama knew, his people would have to become self-supporting as quickly as possible and do so in a community or group of communities where they could band together in the common cause; and he conceived, secured funds for, and supervised the programs and institutions that made this possible.

Founded in 1960 as a haven for children whose parents had died in transit camps and on road gangs, the Tibetan Children's Village in Dharamsala now has an enrollment of more than 1,000 youngsters between the ages of six months and eighteen years and is the prototype for the more than fifty all-Tibetan schools in India. The Tibetan Medical and Astrological Center nearby manufactures and dispenses herbal medicines according to instructions contained in ancient medical scriptures, conducts research, and trains a new generation of Tibetan doctors. The Tibetan Library and Archives, housed in a three-story building of traditional Tibetan design, houses 40 percent of Tibet's literature (the remainder is presumed to have been destroyed by the Chinese) and is considered to be the most complete collection of Mahayana Buddhist literature and liturgy in the world. The students of the Tibetan Dance and Drama Society dedicate themselves to keeping alive traditional regional dances and the *lhamo*, or folk opera; despite bitter protests from Peking they have conducted highly successful tours of the United States, Europe, Australia, and Southeast Asia. Dharamsala also boasts a half-dozen monasteries. The function of Namgyal Dratsang, the Dalai Lama's personal monastery, which was given its name by the Third Dalai Lama and housed in the Potala by the Great Fifth, is to assist the Dalai Lama in his religious ceremonies and rituals. The Nechung monastery is there together with its famous oracle, whose services are still very much in demand, as is the Nyingma monastery with its equally renowned rain-maker, sought after to stop rain and to help with the emotionally disabled.

At Bylakuppe, the first refugee settlement in South India, there are monasteries for each of the four major sects of Tibetan Buddhism. One is a replica in miniature of Lhasa's venerable Sera, built by the monks and settlers from the original plans; another a duplicate of Tashilhunpo, hereditary seat of the Panchen Lamas. The remaining members of Lhasa's Three Pillars, Drepung and Ganden, have been reproduced in other settlements. The most striking evidence of the Tibetan refugee presence on the Indian sub-continent, they seem nevertheless to be in perfect harmony with their surroundings.

Today Bylakuppe is the model for more than thirty other large-scale agricultural settlements in which the majority of the 85,000 Tibetan refugees in India now live. Its 5,000 acres support a population of 10,000, and driving over the network of dirt roads connecting its eighteen villages and six monasteries one can almost believe, in spite of the heat, humidity, and absence of majestic mountains, that one is in Tibet. A group of rosy-cheeked children play barefooted with a makeshift shuttlecock in a small clearing, giggling gleefully. An irregular procession of women, clad in dark *chubas* and brightly striped aprons, black eyes sparkling from weatherbeaten faces and tongues extended in smiles of greeting, passes a cluster of claret-robed monks, some wearing sunglasses, telling their rosaries and wielding large black umbrellas to protect their shaven heads from the tropical sun. Two elderly men, their braided hair tied around their heads with red ribbon, sip tea on a tiny veran-dah with a Lhasa Apso sleeping at their feet.

Yet when the first group of settlers arrived at Bylakuppe after a 2,000-mile train journey from the road camps of the Punjab, such a scenario would have seemed wildly optimistic: for equipped with only axes and machetes, they were confronted with the task of clearing theretofore impenetrable forests despite the threat of attack from the wild animals they were displacing—elephants, boars, cobras. Stunned and frightened, many burst into tears and, when the Dalai Lama visited—he personally inspected the site of each settlement as soon as it had been selected—begged him to send them elsewhere. "Of course I saw how they were suffering," he remembers. "But there was nowhere else for them to go. Over and over again I counseled them to have faith and to persevere. They did, and I am proud of them."

Life in the settlements is not easy. The hours are long, the work hard, the earnings low. Yet the settlers persevere, and a few even prosper. They insist that their children's educational curriculum include Tibetan language, literature, history, and religion. They seek out, when ill, their own medical practitioners who are trained in the ancient art of Tibetan medicine but are able to fall back on modern medical science. They consult their lamas, oracles, and astrologers for advice on personal affairs and the proper path toward spiritual enlightenment. They resist any effort to assimilate them and cling tenaciously to their Tibetan citizenship. They serve in the Indian army, but only in a special Tibetan outfit stationed along the borders of their homeland. They look to the Dalai Lama for spiritual and temporal leadership, paying voluntary taxes to Dharamsala and electing members of the Assembly of Tibetan People's Delegates. Whether Mahayana Buddhists in Mysore, Bön practitioners in the Punjab, or Muslims in Kashmir, all remain, first and foremost, Tibetans.

A large portion of the Dalai Lama's afternoon consists of audiences with foreigners. "It is more important to meet people who might help the Tibetan cause than to be isolated," he says. "We have remained isolated quite long enough." During the early days in Dharamsala his Western visitors were not well screened, but now they consist mainly of journalists, scholars, and students of Buddhism, and have included Coretta King, John Lindsay, and Thomas Merton. A few eccentrics, however, do sometimes manage to inveigle their way into his presence. Several years ago a young American woman who had been studying Buddhism in Dharamsala announced during the course of an audience that she was the true reincarnation of the Panchen Lama and requested that he recognize her as such. "His Holiness replied to her that to be recognized as a Tulku is not important but that the practice of the Dharma is," says Doboom Rinpoche, the Dalai Lama's assistant private secretary. "He further explained that if one practiced well, one could become a Tulku whether others recognize it or not."

Those meeting him for the first time are often surprised to find an affable human being rather than an impassive God-King, a label he does not much care for and which he has taken pains to correct. But is he not, in fact, a god? "There are many different types of reincarnations," he says. "My own has been blessed by Chenresi, and my being has been sent to earth as his representative. So it is true." And is he not a king? He laughs gleefully. "The line of Tibetan kings—Songtsen Gampo and the others—ceased many centuries ago. But in the sense of the Sanskrit term *Dharma Raja*, or Religious King, I am the head of the religious community. So this is true also." He pauses to adjust his robes. "I rather think of myself as a *bhiksu*, a simple Buddhist monk."

Meetings with Westerners give the Dalai Lama an opportunity to practice his English as well as to dispense with what he believes is excessive formality, a feeling he shares with his prior embodiment. "Maybe you noticed that on my visits to the United States, the more formal the occasion the less relaxed I was," he says. "We are, after all, only members of the same human family, and such an atmosphere suppresses our true feelings." Nevertheless, members of his staff still draw in their breath when addressing him and back out of the room when taking their leave, and Tibetans greet him with the traditional threefold prostration. When he issued strict orders to settlement administrators that there were to be no grandiose preparations made for his visits, the people were horrified, for above and beyond his temporal aspect they value him as the living symbol of their country.

The Dalai Lama's working day usually ends at 5:30, although it is not uncommon for pressing matters to keep him in the office an hour or two longer. Returning to his bungalow—which the Tibetans refer to as Phodrang, "the Palace"—he scans the newspapers and journals that have accumulated there or picks up a book on botany, zoology, or astrology; sometimes he is visited by members of his family or old friends like Heinrich Harrer. He rarely watches television, and then only to tune in occasionally to a program named *Animal World*, broadcast on Sunday evenings from a station in Lahore, Pakistan. Always he ponders the plight of his people. "Tibetan history is quite sad, I think. We did not develop and did not grow. I think the main reason for this was the decentralization of the Tibetan government after the assassination of Lang Darma in the ninth century; it was never again that strong. If the central authority had remained, our whole history might have been different. When our great kings Songtsen Gampo and Trisong Detsen ruled Tibet, ours was one of the most powerful nations of Central Asia. The region of Amdo, where I was born, was once ruled by Songtsen Gampo's grandson, King Mangsong Mangtsen, and my ancestors were soldiers sent there by him from central Tibet; not until many years later did it come under Chinese rule. But in Amdo, just as in other areas on the border of Tibet and China, our people lived side by side with the Chinese for over a thousand years. Of course they spoke the Chinese language in addition to their own, but they never accepted the Chinese way of life: Tibetan spirit and traditions never changed. Now, if we look at Buddhism in Tibet from a purely political angle, we may find it had some faults, but we cannot say that because of the Buddha Dharma, Tibet became weak. It was because of Buddhism that Tibet remained one word—Tibet."

The 1940s, he feels, provided a golden opportunity for Tibet. "In China the Communists had not yet come to power and the Nationalists were weak. India had just become independent and many of her leaders, like Mahatma Gandhi, were sympathetic to us. But instead of utilizing that period to further the cause of Tibet as a nation, we fought among ourselves." He sinks back into his chair, as if drained by the memory of the ensuing events. "Suppose that the Chinese had been sincere and helpful," he says, sitting upright once more. "Let's say they had abolished the old system and at the same time pursued *real* liberation, not indoctrination. If they had provided for the people's education—which the Tibetan government never achieved—and for the people's food and health . . . if they had done these things, then the attitude shown by the Tibetans might have been different. Instead they brought suffering." He removes his glasses and gently massages the bridge of his nose; his face is smooth and unlined, and he seems far younger than his years. "The rebellion of our people against the Chinese was inevitable," he says finally. "Many people have the idea that it was initiated by the Americans. This is not true. It was started by the Tibetans themselves, and only later were they offered assistance. The CIA was pursuing a global policy against Communist China, while we were opposing Communist Chinese aggression in our country; our basic aims did not clash, so we accepted it."

But how could a man of religion and a firm believer in nonviolence condone acts of violence? "True violence is more than a rough method," the Dalai Lama explains. "It is bad motivation and hurt. With the proper motivation—to spare the long-term pain and misfortune in this and the next life—rough action is theoretically not violent at all when instead of harming another it actually helps. In one of the Jataka Tales, Lord Buddha's prior incarnation was on a large merchant ship with a staff of 500, among them a man who was contemplating killing all the others and taking their property," he says, closing his eyes. "He warned the man several times that he should refrain from doing such a thing," he continues, reopening them, "but failed to convince him and decided at last to kill the man so that he might spare the lives of 499 people and spare the man the sin that would have come from killing all those people. With that motivation he killed, and according to the scriptures his behavior was just. According to the Buddhist viewpoint, result and motivation are more important than method. Here the violence—the method—was killing, but the motivation was compassion." There is a long silence. "The main difficulty in such cases is determining after serious and careful consideration whether there is any possible alternative to violence." He inclines his head to the right and fixes his eyes on a spot high up on the wall across from him. How many tales of horror were brought to this gentle man before he found he could no longer advise his people to refrain from violent acts of retaliation? "In the case of Tibet, the Chinese have admitted that in the central part of the country alone 87,000 people were killed in military actions between March 1959 and September 1960. On that basis, by the time the large-scale revolt ended in 1963, over 200,000 people had been killed; there are many records of entire villages being wiped out. Also it is now very clearly understood that in 1969 there was another rebellion. Result? Mass public executions. In the same day, in each district of Tibet, fifteen, twenty, thirty, forty people were killed, executed publicly. Thousands were thrown into prison, and sooner or later they faced starvation. What else could the people do but fight back? If there is a clear indication that there is no alternative to violence, then violence is permissible."

However, twenty-six years of exile have not been without some advantage to the Dalai Lama. "What has happened, has happened," he points out. "It is fact. I must live according to that fact—and use what I have learned to the maximum benefit of myself and my people." Freed from the traditional restraints of the old society, he has been able to democratize the Tibetan system of government at a pace and to a degree he might not have been able to attain had the Chinese not invaded his country. "Had it not been for them," he says with a smile, "I might have become a conservative old man." Moreover, refugee life has exposed him to new people and concepts, given him the opportunity to meet and exchange ideas with such disparate peoples as the pope and the archbishop of Canterbury, elders of the Hopi Indians and chiefs from the Iroquois Confederacy, and members of the U.S. Senate Foreign Relations Committee; and helped him mature into an independent, open-minded thinker. "In a way, the Chinese have done us a great service. Until they invaded and occupied our country the political awareness of Tibetans had been poor for several centuries; they were united by the Buddha Dharma and looked to the Dalai Lama for spiritual guidance, but thought more of their own clan or region than they did of our nation as a whole. Now all that has changed. When I receive private letters from central or southern Tibet, the people refer to our country as Bod Chenpo, 'Greater Tibet.' This means the inclusion of Kham and Amdo. When I receive letters from eastern Tibet, they refer to our country as Khawachen, 'the Land of Snows'—also the whole of Tibet. This demonstrates that all Tibetans are clearly conscious that our country is much larger than the 'autonomous region' whose name and borders were given to it in 1951 by the Chinese. So now, you see, all six million Tibetans have been shaped by Chinese ruthlessness into a united body again, and this fact has made me realize that nations that suffer the most—here the Jewish people come to mind—become the toughest." He is silent a moment, then bursts into laughter. "Until recently the Chinese have called the Tibetans 'bandits.' Whether bandits or not, anyway, they are tough: they will never accept oppression."

The price of this toughness and political unity has been high. Many thousands of Tibetans—the actual number will probably never be known—have perished at Chinese hands or committed suicide in desperation. All but a handful of the country's 3,000 monasteries have been leveled, temples have been turned into warehouses, shrines have been pillaged and destroyed. Priceless images of gold, silver, and bronze have been stolen and sent to antique shops in Peking; clay images pulverized, made into bricks, and used in the construction of public lavatories; sacred scriptures shredded into pulp for newsprint, used as toilet paper and kindling. The hand-carved wooden blocks used for printing the Buddha's teachings, the biographies of the Dalai Lamas, the religious, historical, and political chronicles of Tibet have been hammered into furniture, nailed down as floorboards, carved into farm implements, burned as fuel. In private homes portraits of the Dalai Lama were torn down and replaced with those of Mao Tse-tung; *thonka* paintings displaced by posters bearing Maoist slogans; rosary beads, earrings, bracelets, charm boxes confiscated; braided hair derided as "the dirty black tail of serfdom" and chopped off; the possession of religious objects punishable by public humiliation, flogging, and imprisonment; gatherings of more than three people forbidden to eat together; Tibetan songs, dances, clothing, and customs banned and Tibetans forced to speak a Chinese–Tibetan patois; Lhasa Apsos shot or clubbed to death as undesirable relics of the past society.

Aware that the names of streets, houses, buildings, and monuments were derived from Tibet's religious and cultural heritage, the Chinese changed them and warned that any Tibetan discovered using the former names would be denounced as a reactionary and dealt with accordingly. The Norbulingka, site of the Dalai Lama's Summer Palace, became "People's Park"; Chakpori hill, site of the ancient medical college where thousands perished fighting the Chinese in the 1959 uprising, "Victory Peak"; the Tsugla Khang, central cathedral of the famed Jokhang Temple containing the priceless image of Jowo Rinpoche brought to Tibet 1,300 years ago by the Chinese bride of King Songtsen Gampo became "Guest House Number 5"; the Barkhor, Lhasa's main market street on which the Festival of Lights took place each New Year's, "Forward Path." The Potala was permitted to retain its name, but part of it was turned into a gruesome propaganda "museum" housing such displays as children being buried alive by monks in monastery cornerstones. People were forced to take new Chinese names containing a part of Mao's name: Mao, Tse, or Tung. The name Tenzin became "Mao's Red Thought"; Lobsang Dolma, "Red Mao-Lin"; Kechog Wangmo, "Great Leap Forward"; Chamba Kalsang, "Dependence on Mao's Idea of Class Struggle." Tibet itself has been divided into seven separate "autonomous" regions and its name changed to Xiazang.

Tibetans were required to carry a copy of the *Little Red Book* with them at all times and recite passages from "Mao Tse-tung Thought" on demand. Traditional seasonal fairs and religious festivals were banned; schoolchildren were encouraged to inform on their parents if they complained of Chinese rule and made to kill insects, dogs, birds, and other "parasites" so as to train them to show no compassion for living creatures; widespread starvation created by Peking's obtuse agricultural policies forced women to sell newborn infants for a basin of rice and ten Chinese dollars. At least one-quarter of the population was subjected to dreaded *thamzings*, so-called revolutionary struggle sessions in which Tibetans were forced by the Chinese into "reforming" the "reactionaries" among them by reviling, beating, kicking, and stoning them until they collapsed and were dragged away, dead or half dead, to prison; those showing reluctance to take part or sympathy to the victims were beaten and imprisoned. "Before the Chinese came into our country, a few Tibetans were slaves," the Dalai Lama says. "Now all are slaves."

Even this catalogue of horrors has not shaken the Dalai Lama's equanimity, attained through a lifetime of contemplation, meditation, observation, and study. There are many in this world, he knows, who out of ignorance or selfishness persist in taking actions that will ultimately harm them as much as, or even more than, their victims; and he speaks with quiet compassion of the need to understand and not condemn them. "We should think of our enemy as our greatest friend and teacher, for he tests our inner strength, our tolerance, our respect for others." Love for friends or family is primarily selfish, so that when our actions are not reciprocated as we might wish, we become sad and disappointed, hurt, and resentful. But love for an enemy is true love: "love without emotion or attachment, love with clear reason and feelings"; even though he may be trying to harm us, "we should be grateful to him and respond with kindness and patience."

Although he stresses the need for patience in the face of adversity, the Dalai Lama does not mean we must resign ourselves to defeat. "The very purpose of engaging in the practice of patience is to become stronger in mind, stronger in heart," he explains. "It is important to remain calm, for in an atmosphere of calmness you can use real human beings to learn wisdom." He pauses and looks off into the distance. "Wisdom is like ammunition, the calm mind like the weapon for firing," he says at last. "If you lose patience, if your brain founders by emotions, then you've lost the power to analyze. What doctor prescribes anger as a treatment for disease? What doctor says that by getting angry you can make yourself happy? It is better to forget than to hold anger. But if you are patient, from a basis of altruism, then you don't lose your strength of mind; you can even increase your strength of mind and then use your powers of analysis to figure out ways to overcome the negative force that is opposing you."

He has never expressed any doubt, nor does he admit to ever having had any doubt, that in time truth will triumph over brute force in his homeland. "As to the question of returning: since we are Tibetan, definitely we will return. But at the moment being in exile has some purpose. You see, my reason for coming out of Tibet was for our own country. I spent nine years with the Chinese before becoming a refugee in 1959; we could not serve our people from the inside, so instead we serve them from the outside. We are not anti-reform, anti-Communist, or even anti-Chinese; we are just fighting for our rights. So until the situation inside our country becomes truly, genuinely satisfactory, I will not return. I believe I can better serve our people, the six million people of Tibet, from the outside."

For somewhat less altruistic reasons Peking wants the man it once castigated as a reactionary and "wolf in monk's clothing" to do so from within. "The impetus behind the Tibetan national struggle was created by Chinese oppression of our people, not by the Dalai Lama," he says. "Now they want me to return to help them solve the problems they have brought about." In the last several years the Chinese have revived and intensified efforts begun in 1963 to bring about this return by proclaiming their culpability in having transformed a happy, peaceful, self-sufficient land into one of bleakness, misery, and starvation. Western publications, which for most of the past two decades have found it expedient to ignore the horror and devastation visited upon Tibet, are now carrying articles cataloguing these very horrors, and delegates from the Dalai Lama's government in exile have toured their homeland at the invitation of the Chinese government and confirmed them. At the same time Premier Deng Xiaoping has been ridding the country of the Chinese officials who presided over this disaster and enunciating a policy that bears a remarkable resemblance to a slogan Tibetans have been repeating stubbornly ever since the first Chinese troops set foot on Tibetan soil in 1950: "Tibet for Tibetans."

On the surface this seems like a step in the right direction. But more than three decades of Chinese lies, deception, and broken promises have embittered Tibetans to the point where they automatically dismiss anything Peking's leaders have to say. "Instead of creating happiness," says the Dalai Lama, "their efforts have brought suspicion, suffering, and animosity." In order to break down this barrier the Chinese must implement their promises, and to date they have failed to do so. While acknowledging that its savage attack on Buddhism was "our greatest mistake" and proclaiming that Tibetans are free once again to practice their religion, Peking has not discouraged the state-owned and -operated *Tibet Daily News* from carrying articles that editorialize on the uselessness of religion. While a handful of temples and monasteries have been reopened, they are available to the public for only a few hours each week, and these when the vast majority of Tibetans must be at work. While admitting their responsibility for "ten years of disaster" during the Cultural Revolution, they are at the same time trying to conceal the grim reality that they have in fact caused thirty-six years of disaster.

"Tibet is, without doubt, the worst example of a national minority area in China," wrote John Fraser, correspondent for the *Toronto Globe and Mail* upon his return from two years in the People's Republic. "[It] is a shocking indictment of a country that professes antipathy toward both colonialism and racism." Fraser's state-sponsored visit to Tibet with nineteen other journalists convinced him that "the oppression visited on the Tibetans, particularly during the Cultural Revolution and its aftermath, was at least the equal of—and probably far worse than—the melodramatic and mostly unbelievable crimes and persecution of the 'feudal Dalai Lama clique,' to quote Communist Party propaganda." Because the Tibetans steadfastly refuse to relinquish their national identity, states Fraser, "they represent a threat to the Chinese Government and therefore have to be controlled" and "anyone with an open mind and honest eyes learns quickly that it is a policy of containment first, ultimately leading to absorption. . . .

There is no doubt whatsoever that the desired final result, however long it takes, is total assimilation of all minority races into the Chinese mainstream."

Under such circumstances there can be no question of the Dalai Lama's returning to Tibet. "Deng Xiaoping has the courage to admit mistakes," he says. "In the past it was rare for the top Chinese leadership to speak with such realism about political matters. If China's leaders are now sincere about change, and hold to it for a generation, that will be very good. But I really doubt they will." There is good reason for his pessimism, for Peking has given similar assurances and later rescinded them as the result of ideological or personnel changes at the seat of government. Members of the three delegations sent to Tibet by the Dalai Lama in 1979 and 1980 were approached by Tibetans of all ages who, quivering with rage and with tears streaming down their faces, told them, "The Chinese said to us in the beginning that they would help the Tibetan people. Instead they have destroyed everything, taken whatever we had to China, and made us into Chinese serfs." Tugging at their pinky fingers to indicate that the Chinese were not to be trusted and stuffing crumpled notes into the pockets of the delegates which bore messages such as "My children can't live under the Chinese" and "We're not afraid to die," they pleaded with the delegates: "Tell His Holiness not to come back until Tibet is free." Can the Chinese premier be trusted to keep his word? Will Peking's policies be carried out by local officials in Tibet, who in the past have learned to move with extreme caution for fear that yet another shift of policy could cost them their positions, if not their lives? If the energetic eighty-two-year-old Deng dies, will his successor carry out his professed policies? If and when the Dalai Lama returns, there will no longer be a "Tibetan question," a fact of which both he and the Chinese are acutely aware; and while he does not expect to return as a king, neither does he wish to return as a pawn.

Assuming that there is some strong manifestation of good faith by Peking over a reasonable period of time—not a generation, perhaps, but long enough to demonstrate that the Chinese attitude toward Tibet has indeed changed—there is little doubt that then, and only then would the Dalai Lama consider returning. This is what he means by his oft-repeated statement that such an action on his part would be dependent on the happiness of the majority of Tibet's six million people. Yet some of those very people believe that "happiness" is synonymous with "independence." "To them," the Dalai Lama says, "I ask, 'What is the aim of independence? Happiness or unhappiness?' In any human society the most important goal is happiness. If we can achieve this through autonomy, all right; as part of a federation, all right; through independence, all right. During the past thirty-five years we have gained nothing from China; therefore it should be obvious why we wish to remain a separate country. But if the Chinese follow their words with actions, if we Tibetans derive more benefit by remaining a member of the Middle Kingdom community, I would be willing. Whether Tibet was independent or not doesn't matter so long as our people are happy. The fact that at the present moment our people are not happy is also more important than history. History can change. Look at your own country: first a group of British colonies, then a confederation, and finally a republic. Now if the Chinese attitude changes and they respect the Tibetan people's wishes and come to Tibet as liberators and helpers, we may think of some mutually beneficial terms. Before, they pursued an attitude that compelled us to make an effort to separate from them. If they now have something to offer us, the picture might be different—especially if we get some benefit from a union with them. After all, we are only six million people. We have no sea route. We are inaccessible because we live at such a high altitude. We are rich only in minerals, and you can't eat minerals."

To what kind of Tibet might the Dalai Lama return? Despite the fervent dreams of Tibetan nationalists, independence seems out of the question in the foreseeable future. A more likely prospect, if the Chinese are sincere about mending their ways, would be a form of union similar to that enjoyed by the Ukrainians and Belorussians within the U.S.S.R., and would include a seat in the United Nations. It is unlikely, however, that any such union would bear the name of People's Republic of China. "The word *China* means 'where Chinese people live,'" the Dalai Lama explains. "The people of Tibet, Mongolia, and East Turkestan are not Chinese; in fact there is not a single word in the Tibetan language which includes both China and Tibet. Throughout history the Chinese have emphasized the differences between China and the 'Middle Kingdom.' They said we Tibetans and the Chinese were equal as brothers, each part of the 'Middle Kingdom.' These days they say we Tibetans are also Chinese. This is nonsense."

But if Buddhism and Communism on the Roof of the World have failed to coexist peacefully in the past, how will these two seemingly antithetical systems be able to do so in the Tibet of the future? "Theoretically, original Marxism and Mahayana Buddhism, despite many differences, also had many points in common," the Dalai Lama believes. "The foremost is the emphasis on the common good of society. Buddhism is atheistic in the sense that a creator God is not accepted; rather, Buddhism presents a view of self-creation, that one's own actions create one's life situation. In this light, it has been said that Buddhism is not a religion, but a science of the mind. In Buddhism, it is explained that everything depends on one's karma. This means that one's life situation in the present depends upon one's actions and their motivations in the past and that one's future is thus capable of being molded through engaging in salutory actions with a pure motivation. Similarly, in Communist or Marxist theory everything is said to depend on one's own labor." Marxist economic theory, he points out, is concerned less with the accumulation of wealth and resources than with their proper use for the welfare of all, and thus bears a striking similarity to the Buddhist practice of placing the needs of others above those of the individual. In the past some followers of Marxism "destroyed one privileged social class only to create another in its place," just as some adherents of Buddhism turned monastic institutions from centers of learning into centers of commerce. But the Dalai Lama stresses that "a distinction must be made between systems and their practitioners" and counsels these practitioners to exercise tolerance and understanding. "Since the thrust of Marxist thought is not absolutely anti-religious, there is no point in religious persons' viewing Marxism as anti-religious, creating tension and distrust; the commonality of many aims should and must be stressed. Similarly, Marxists, out of ignorance and lack of personal experience, see religion as totally counterproductive, which is wrong. A real Marxist must discard narrow and dogmatic attitudes and be open to the value of spiritual teachings."

Any realistic solution to the Tibetan question—as well as to less pub-licized "questions" in Inner Mongolia, East Turkestan, and elsewhere—must take these things into account. "It is a reality of today's world that much of Buddhist civilization, stretching from the borders of Thailand to parts of Siberia, is under the sway of Communist ideology," the Dalai Lama points out. "This area is inhabited by more than a quarter of mankind, the vast majority of whom are Buddhists. History has shown that no single po-litical, economic, or social ideology has been sufficient. So it seems worth-while for the two great systems of this large expanse of the world to take points from each other. For the development of a peaceful, friendly human family of nations with a rich variety of faiths and political and economic systems, each of us has the responsibility to strive toward such harmony. There is no alternative."

He recognizes that in a future Tibet the size and role of the monkhood will of necessity be very different from what it was before the Chinese inva-sion. "In the past, most of our learned people were educated in the monas-teries," he says. "Although there were schools in the larger cities—in Lhasa alone there were more than twenty—in the rest of Tibet people had to enter a monastery in order to receive an education. This will not be necessary in the future, so there will probably be fewer people who will want to become monks or nuns. The number doesn't matter, of course: the important thing is quality. In the past our monk scholars did not work; instead they studied and prayed. But in the monasteries of the future I think monks and nuns should be involved also with social work and should play an active role in the social life of the country. In this sense we have much to learn from the West: the Christian fathers and nuns were strict religious practitioners, but at the same time they were of great service to the community."

Chinese officials have hinted that without the Dalai Lama's active partici-pation, their professed program to rehabilitate Tibet will be far more diffi-cult and consume many more years than it might should he decide to return. Yet that very return, should it take place, could precipitate a mass outpouring of long-repressed emotion that both the Chinese and the Dalai Lama might find difficult to control, as the following episode will attest. When the gray Toyota minibus containing members of the second delegation sent to Tibet by the Dalai Lama pulled up in front of Lhasa's state guest house in the summer of 1980, 2,000 Tibetans who had been waiting patiently for hours burst into a frenzy. Men thrust clenched fists into the air, women wept, children stuffed flowers into the hands of the five delegates; Chinese soldiers, unable to restrain the crowd, drew back in awe. "May the Dalai Lama's hopes and aspirations be fulfilled," began Phuntsog Wangyal, chairman of Great Britain's Tibetan community, after making his way through a sea of clutching hands and tearful embraces onto the steps of the guesthouse. Before he could continue, a young man jumped up and shouted, "Long live His Holiness the Dalai Lama!" The cry was taken up by the entire gathering, which echoed it in unison with such passion that the Chinese, frightened by the depth of the Tibetans' fervor, whisked the delegates from the scene and on the next day from the country as well; but for the presence of a contingent of foreign journalists in Lhasa that day, the incident would have been hushed up. "This was not an isolated incident," says Tenzin Tethong, leader of the delegation. "Wherever we went in Tibet, thousands came out illegally to greet us. The Chinese warned them not to, but they came anyway. They have nothing left to lose." This is precisely why the Chinese want so desperately for the Dalai Lama to return. "Now we know without doubt that we can wait as long as it takes," asserts Tethong, who is the Dalai Lama's representative at the Office of Tibet in New York. "Even the very young Tibetans, those who have only known foreign rule, are completely against the Chinese. They are helpless to fight them directly, but their resistance, their hatred, has only grown stronger over the years."

It is 7:30. The echoes of the monks' hand claps as they debate in the monastery courtyard fade into the dusk. Lights begin to flicker on in the marketplace; wisps of smoke rise like silvery chains into the darkening sky as people gather together for their evening tea. A gentle breeze blows down from the mountain, and the prayer flags flutter as they offer up invocations to the gods. For the Dalai Lama the time has come for an hour of prayer and meditation before bed. Like his predecessor, he is strict in his observance of religious practices, but unlike the autocratic Great Thirteenth—whose personality was ideally suited to the period of Tibetan history in which he lived and reigned—he understands the art of compromise. "In the present situation I think my nature is much more suitable. Right now, too much stubbornness is not good. And my determination and willpower are quite sufficient," he says, laughing. "Nobody knows, of course, what will be the future success of my actions. But so far, under an extremely difficult set of circumstances—the rise of Communism in China, twentieth-century power politics, twenty-seven years of exile—I think the main factor has been the Tibetan people's determination to survive as a nation; and in this context," he adds with a smile, "I believe the Dalai Lama has made some contribution."

After enjoying apparently robust health throughout his life, the Thirteenth Dalai Lama aged suddenly and died at fifty-seven. Many Tibetans believe that the reform-minded hierarch, upon finding his people stubbornly resistant to change, warned that unless they mended their ways, unsurpassed tragedy would befall Tibet, and, when they failed to heed his advice, chose to depart his earthly body in order to give time for his next embodiment to be discovered, grow to maturity, and lead the nation from the living hell that surely awaited it. "It is true he warned our people that terrible things would happen in Tibet," this new embodiment says, "but I do not think he willed his death; logically speaking it was a coincidence. Of course if you believe in the supernatural, which is rather illogical, then certainly it is possible: there are many accounts of spiritually advanced monks and lamas predicting the exact time they will become no more. Whether the Thirteenth Dalai Lama did so or not does not matter. The important thing is that my age, which seemed a great drawback when the Chinese invaded our country in 1950, has since proven to be ideal. I assumed my temporal responsibilities over thirty-five years ago, but I am still a young man." He bursts into laughter. "I've always felt I am from the younger generation. But now that I am fifty I think, 'What is young? What is old?'" His eyes close softly and he is silent for what is perhaps a minute but seems much longer. "So far," he says at last, "I have spent my best years, the cream of my life, as a refugee." His voice is soothing and gentle. "Serving our country, our people. Anyway, it is something sad, I think. Best period, remain outside." Sitting there in silence, he seems intensely human and vulnerable but at the same time like a painted or sculpted representation of the bodhisattva Chenresi, the herdsman whose flock includes all the living beings of the world, the deity who does not himself seek the shelter of the fold until the last of the flock has entered.

As the Dalai Lama awakens suddenly from his reverie, his eyes sparkle and his face takes on an expressive animation. "I do not want to be like a Tito," he laughs. "Better to retire at an early age. Mahatma Gandhi I admire: before India won her independence he was the leading figure, but afterward he chose to remain outside the government." He has often spoken with regret of how the force of circumstances has prevented him from spending more time in spiritual pursuits, how although he hopes each year to spend a week in retreat, he has managed to do so on only two or three occasions since arriving in Dharamsala more than two decades ago. "In the future my personal wish is to relinquish, if possible, my political responsibilities," he says, "and in some remote, pleasant place practice Yoga and meditation and study the teachings of Lord Buddha." Such an action would not be without precedent: the Fifth Dalai Lama followed a life of political activism with a solitary quest for inner peace, and the Eighth Dalai Lama rarely chose to exercise his political authority at all.

He pauses to adjust his posture and take a sip of tea from a large enamel mug bearing pictures of the snow mountains of Tibet, a few pine trees, and a solitary yak. "Now, if the institution of Dalai Lama is still something useful for Tibetans as well as for the Buddhist community in general, I think it would be better if we adopted a new system. A new Dalai Lama should be selected before the death of the old one." He takes another sip of tea, more, one suspects, to permit the full impact of his words to be realized than to quench his thirst. "In the past the system of choosing the Dalai Lamas as I myself was chosen did not always work out very well. The Seventh Dalai Lama acted for many years under the influence of his father, and the Ninth, Tenth, Eleventh, and Twelfth all died in their youth and left the governing of our country in the hands of regents. Now, the Fourth Dalai Lama—the Mongolian—came to Lhasa not as a monk but as a layman. His biography was written by the Fifth Dalai Lama, and in it the Fifth Dalai Lama hinted that if he had remained as a king rather than as a monk it might have been of some benefit. The strange behavior of the Fifth Dalai Lama's own reincarnation—the Sixth—was, I think, connected with this. If the Sixth Dalai Lama had been successful in his plan to give up the monkhood, remain as king, and pass on to one of his children the title of Dalai Lama, I think that the central Tibetan government would have been more stable and that the Manchus might never have come into our country. In recent years, of course, I believe the system of searching for a new reincarnation when the old one dies is more democratic, and I am proud of it."

But history can change. "You see, the name Dalai Lama belongs to me. I can give it to another person, and from then on that person will be the Dalai Lama." In such a case, what would become of Tenzin Gyatso, the Fourteenth Dalai Lama? "I will be a *bhiksu*," he says brightly, "a simple Buddhist monk!" The idea obviously delights him. "During the time of the Second Dalai Lama there was an indication that there were hundreds of reincarnations of the previous Dalai Lama," he says, warming to his subject. "Of these there was one outstanding one, who took the name Dalai Lama; the rest went out into the world to be benevolent. Now, in a wider sense," he continues, leaning forward intently, "the new Dalai Lama does not necessarily have to be my own reincarnation. He could be a mature and respected religious scholar, someone possessing an aura, a mysterious spiritual force we can feel but cannot see; a highly qualified person who has received the blessing just as I have. In fact it might be a good idea to replace a Dalai Lama every seven years, as we have always done with the position of Ganden Tri Rinpoche until the accession of my senior tutor, Ling Rinpoche." But how would the Tibetan people react? "At first I will probably meet some stubborn resistance. But after all, in the beginning there was no Dalai Lama; the very idea of Dalai Lama is involved in people's minds. Eventually they will get used to the idea."

While it is apparent that the Dalai Lama has given a great deal of consideration to making such a revolutionary break with the past, it would appear that his karma is against it. His decision whether to remain in exile or go back to the Land of Snows will doubtless be based, like all his actions in the past, on what he believes will be best for the Tibetan people, and these people need him now more than ever before. Whether or not one chooses to believe that he is a divine incarnation of the Bodhisattva of Mercy and Compassion, the fact remains that this gentle and resolute man has devoted his life to guiding his people and would not willingly abdicate that responsibility. Whether or not one chooses to believe in divine oracles, prophetic visions in sacred lakes, or mystical cloud formations, the fact remains that Kyitsang Rinpoche and his band of monks found what they were searching for in the little farmhouse in the snowcapped mountains of Amdo: the child who would embody the spirit of Chenresi, the patron saint of Tibet.

Epilogue

RATUK NGAWANG MANAGES the Kailash Hotel, a modest establishment in Dharamsala owned by an association of Chushi Gangdrug alumni. "There is not one of us who would not gladly give up his life to get back our homeland," says the Khampa freedom fighter, still looking remarkably fit at the age of fifty-three. He sips a cup of butter tea and gazes wistfully at the large framed portraits of the Dalai Lama and guerrilla chieftain Andruk Gompo Tashi, draped reverently with white *khata*s that hang on the wall opposite. "Until that time comes we must all stick together as His Holiness has told us."

Andruk Gompo Tashi succumbed at Darjeeling in 1964 to complications from the wounds suffered during the guerrilla campaigns in Lhoka as commander of the Chushi Gangdrug. His nephew Gyatso Wangdu, one of the four men parachuted into Kham in 1958, emerged in the following decade as the daring leader of Tibetan guerrilla forces in Mustang, a northwestern province of Nepal, before being killed in ambush by Nepalese soldiers in 1974.

Dorjee Tseten Tashi-Para retired from active government service in 1971 and now runs a restaurant in Dharamsala named Gakyi. "The name is a combination of the Tibetan words *gapo*, 'happy,' and *kyipo*, 'comfortable,' and means 'a place where people can be happy and comfortable,'" says the seventy-one-year-old former military commander who escorted the Dalai Lama into exile in 1959 before returning to carry on the fight. "I feel it describes not only my restaurant, but all of Dharamsala as well."

Ling Rinpoche spent the rest of his life in Dharamsala, where he continued to serve as senior tutor to the Dalai Lama until his death in 1984. "When I looked upon His Holiness for the first time, I was convinced he was the true incarnation of Chenresi," said the Ganden Tri Rinpoche, ninety-seventh in the line that began with the great reformer Tsong Khapa in the fourteenth century, shortly before he died. "Since then his development in both aspects of his role has been tremendous. As a spiritual leader he is one of the outstanding authorities on Tibetan Buddhism, and politically he has matured into a leader of great capability."

Trijang Rinpoche summoned his long-time secretary, Palden Tsering, to his bedside on a crisp November morning in 1981. "I shall not be making the trip to Mundgod after all," he announced in a deep, husky voice. Tears came to Palden Tsering's eyes, but he tried to hide them. "Shall I cancel the rail tickets, then?" he asked. The eighty-one-year-old junior tutor did not reply at once; instead he gazed at a *thonka* painting across the room and fingered his rosary. "Keep them," he replied at last. "I have an appointment there." The following day he died, and Tibetans believe that his next embodiment will be discovered at the refugee settlement at Mundgod in South India.

Lobsang Samden, the Dalai Lama's brother and playmate at the Potala, ran the Tibetan Medical Center until his death in September 1985 at the age of fifty-three. In 1979 he was a member of the first delegation sent to Tibet by the Dalai Lama. "What we saw there was unbelievable and shocking," he said upon his return. "I feel so sorry. Our history is destroyed. If Communism had helped the people after such destruction, all right. But it did not. They destroyed the old and gave us nothing in return."

Tsarong Shappé, once the most powerful lay official in Tibet, and always one of the most progressive Tibetans, chose to remain in Lhasa rather than follow so many of his countrymen into exile in the wake of the Tibetan National Uprising. At the age of seventy-four he thought himself too old to begin a new life in a foreign land. He was imprisoned by the Chinese and found dead in his cell the next morning.

Ngari Rinpoche finally got his wish and served in a special Tibetan unit of the Indian army, where he was known as much for his excellent marksmanship as for being the youngest brother of the Dalai Lama. He offered back his monastic vows several years ago and is now known as Tendzin Choegyal. Now thirty-nine, he lives in Dharamsala with his wife and two children and works for the Tibetan government.

Lobsang Tashi, the Chinese artillery officer who joined the Chushi Gangdrug in 1958, escaped from Tibet a few months after the National Uprising and has never been able to discover what became of the Lhasa gardener's daughter he was planning to marry. Now sixty-seven years old and married to a Chinese woman whose husband was killed by the P.L.A. in Lhoka, he lives in the Bylakuppe settlement in South India.

Tsepon Shakabpa lives in Kalimpong in the house he has owned since 1946 and has written a political history of Tibet. "His Holiness the Fourteenth Dalai Lama is the greatest of all the Dalai Lamas," says the seventy-eight-year-old former finance minister. "He is a man of extraordinary intelligence, wisdom, and strength of character: the only person capable of preserving the culture of our country in exile."

Gygyen Tharchin enjoyed cordial relations with the Thirteenth and, later, the Fourteenth Dalai Lama. After the Chinese invasion of Tibet, the pages of the *Tibet Mirror* were so outspoken in their outrage that an American newspaper described him as carrying on a "one-man war with Mao." The *Tibet Mirror* ceased publication in 1962, and Tharchin died in the late 1970s at the age of ninety.

Jetsun Pema Gyalpo heads the Tibetan Children's Village, following in the footsteps of her sister Tsering Dolma, who died of cancer in 1964. "When I reflect on what I saw and heard in Tibet," says the forty-four-year-old sister of the Dalai Lama, who visited there at his request in 1980, "and think about how much our people have suffered I realize how inadequate I am to retell their stories to the outside world."

Ngabo Ngawang Jigme continues to be the most controversial Tibetan of his time. The majority of Tibetans despise him as a "Second Lang Darma" and "Communist barbarian"; others believe him a patriot who has attempted to mitigate the treatment of the people of his homeland by the Chinese; all realize his potential importance in any future rapprochement between Dharamsala and Peking. Now seventy-six years old, he lives in Peking.

The Panchen Lama became acting chairman of the Preparatory Committee for the Formation of a Tibetan Autonomous Region upon the "abduction" of the Dalai Lama to India. In 1962 he handed to Mao Tse-tung his famous "70,000-character memorandum" demanding a halt to Chinese oppression of the Tibetan people. During the Monlam festival two years later, he prayed openly for Tibetan independence and for the long life and early return of the Dalai Lama, as a result of which he was subjected to a seventeen-day *thamzing* and jailed for having "organized a counterrevolutionary clique on behalf of the serf-owning class and engaged in wild activities against the people, the Motherland, and socialism." After thirteen years of solitary confinement and "reeducation" he was "rehabilitated" in 1978. Loved and venerated by the Tibetan people, who have realized that the Dalai Lama's enduring faith in him was fully justified, he is under virtual house arrest in Peking.

The Gyayum Chenmo never realized her dream to look again upon the statue of Jowo Rinpoche in Lhasa's Jokhang Temple, but passed away in Dharamsala in January 1981, two months short of her eighty-first birthday. The wooden casket containing her body was carried up into the mountains by a team of monks, where prayers were offered and it was placed upon a funeral pyre. Holding a stick whose end had been wrapped in a paraffin-soaked *khata* and set aflame, Lobsang Samden stepped forward and lit the blaze. As it burned, the villagers circled it slowly, intoning the mantra and placing *khata*s and incense upon it as offerings. When the last flame had flickered out, tea and *khabse*s were served by the monks and the mourners filed down the mountain to their homes. The people of Tibet had lost their Great Mother.

Some people say there is an ancient prophecy which states that the Tibetan people will lose both their country and the Dalai Lama, that they will regain it and the Dalai Lama, and that the Fourteenth Dalai Lama will be the last of the line.

"It is possible that I shall be the last," the Dalai Lama says with a smile, "although there is in fact no clear prophecy to that effect. But if I remain on earth another thirty or forty years, things are bound to change; as Buddhists we believe that all phenomena are impermament. Whether or not the Tibetan people choose a Dalai Lama is basically a question of the usefulness of the Dalai Lama as an institution. At the moment, the Dalai Lama is very important to Tibet, and it is my responsibility to fulfill my function to the utmost. This does not mean that the Dalai Lama is Tibet or Tibet the Dalai Lama. Not like that. The Dalai Lama is simply an individual.

"But as to the question of my own rebirth as a Mahayana Buddhist," he continues, with a twinkle in his eyes, "as long as there is suffering in the world, I shall be back.

"Whether or not I return as Dalai Lama," he adds, "is unimportant."

Appendixes

Tibet

City of Lhasa

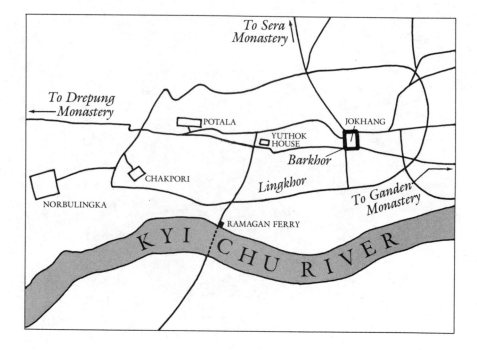

· APPENDIX C ·

The Dalai Lamas

    I. Gedün Truppa (*1391–1475*)

   II. Gedün Gyatso (*1475–1542*)

  III. Sonam Gyatso (*1543–1588*)

  IV. Yönten Gyatso (*1589–1617*)

   V. Ngawang Lobsang Gyatso (*1617–1682*)

  VI. Tsangyang Gyatso (*1683–1706*)

 VII. Kesang Gyatso (*1708–1757*)

VIII. Jampel Gyatso (*1758–1804*)

  IX. Luntok Gyatso (*1806–1815*)

   X. Tsultrim Gyatso (*1816–1837*)

  XI. Khendrup Gyatso (*1838–1856*)

 XII. Trinley Gyatso (*1856–1875*)

XIII. Thupten Gyatso (*1876–1933*)

XIV. Tenzin Gyatso (*1935–   *)

The Tibetan Calendar

1927 Fire-Hare Year	1957 Fire-Bird Year
1928 Earth-Dragon Year	1958 Earth-Dog Year
1929 Earth-Snake Year	1959 Earth-Pig Year
1930 Iron-Horse Year	1960 Iron-Mouse Year
1931 Iron-Sheep Year	1961 Iron-Bull Year
1932 Water-Ape Year	1962 Water-Tiger Year
1933 Water-Bird Year	1963 Water-Hare Year
1934 Wood-Dog Year	1964 Wood-Dragon Year
1935 Wood-Pig Year	1965 Wood-Snake Year
1936 Fire-Mouse Year	1966 Fire-Horse Year
1937 Fire-Bull Year	1967 Fire-Sheep Year
1938 Earth-Tiger Year	1968 Earth-Ape Year
1939 Earth-Hare Year	1969 Earth-Bird Year
1940 Iron-Dragon Year	1970 Iron-Dog Year
1941 Iron-Snake Year	1971 Iron-Pig Year
1942 Water-Horse Year	1972 Water-Mouse Year
1943 Water-Sheep Year	1973 Water-Bull Year
1944 Wood-Ape Year	1974 Wood-Tiger Year
1945 Wood-Bird Year	1975 Wood-Hare Year
1946 Fire-Dog Year	1976 Fire-Dragon Year
1947 Fire-Pig Year	1977 Fire-Snake Year
1948 Earth-Mouse Year	1978 Earth-Horse Year
1949 Earth-Bull Year	1979 Earth-Sheep Year
1950 Iron-Tiger Year	1980 Iron-Ape Year
1951 Iron-Hare Year	1981 Iron-Bird Year
1952 Water-Dragon Year	1982 Water-Dog Year
1953 Water-Snake Year	1983 Water-Pig Year
1954 Wood-Horse Year	1984 Wood-Mouse Year
1955 Wood-Sheep Year	1985 Wood-Bull Year
1956 Fire-Ape Year	1986 Fire-Tiger Year

The element which is the first part of the name of each year counts as "male" the first time and "female" the second. Thus 1960 is the "male" Iron-Mouse Year. Apart from these divisions into elements and animals there is also a cycle of sixty years. At the moment, according to the Tibetan calendar, we are living in the sixteenth cycle, which began in 1927 with the "female Fire-Hare year."

Glossary

chang   Tibetan barley beer.

Chenresi   Buddha of Compassion and patron saint of Tibet, the deity whom each Dalai Lama manifests in human form.

Chikyap Khenpo   The Dalai Lama's lord chamberlain; liaison between the aristocratic and monastic branches of government.

chörten   Cone-shaped masonry structure which often contains religious relics or the ashes of deceased lamas or monks who were great teachers.

Chushi Gangdrug   Tibetan guerrilla organization founded by Gompo Tashi Andrugtsang in 1958.

dob–dobs   Warrior monks.

dorje   Spiritual thunderbolt and scepter of the gods.

dzong   Administrative district of Tibet.

Dzongpons   District governors empowered by Lhasa to collect taxes and administer justice.

guru   Sanskrit word meaning "one who is heavy with knowledge" and moreover one who is benevolent with that knowledge.

lama	Tibetan word equivalent to the Sanskrit *guru*. Can be either a monk or a layman.
Kalon	Tibetan Council Minister, also known as Shappé ("Lotus-Foot").
Kalon Lama	The single ecclesiastic representative in the Kashag.
Kashag	The Dalai Lama's Council of Ministers, consisting of four officials, three aristocratic and one monastic.
khata	Ceremonial scarf.
Losar	Tibetan New Year's festival.
monk	One who has joined a religious order. In Tibetan, the equivalent word is *trapa;* in Sanskrit, *bhiksu.*
Monlam Chenmo	Great Prayer Festival of Tibet.
Norbulingka	Summer palace of the Dalai Lamas.
Potala	Winter palace of the Dalai Lamas, named after the spiritual abode of Chenresi.
ragyapa	Special community of beggars to whom was assigned the disposal of the dead.
Rinpoche	The highest titular honor in Tibet, conferred on persons believed to be reincarnations of famous religious teachers.
Shappé	Tibetan council minister; also known as Kalon.
Silon	Prime minister.
thonka	Ritualistic Tibetan Buddhist banner painting mounted on silk brocade.
Three Pillars	The three Gelugpa monasteries outside the city of Lhasa: Drepung, Sera, and Ganden.
Three Jewels	Buddha, Dharma (his teachings), and Sangha (the monkhood).

tsampa   Roasted barley flour; the staple food of all Tibet.

Tsepon   Tibetan finance minister.

Tsongdu   National Assembly of Tibet.

Tulku   Tibetan incarnation.

Bibliography

Andrugtsang, Gompo Tashi. *Four Rivers, Six Ranges: A True Account of Khampa Resistance to Chinese in Tibet* (Dharamsala, India, 1973).

Avedon, John F. *In Exile from the Land of Snows* (New York, 1984).

Barber, Noel. *From the Land of Lost Content: The Dalai Lama's Fight for Tibet* (London, 1969).

Bawden, C. R. *The Modern History of Mongolia* (New York, 1968).

Bell, Sir Charles. *Portrait of the Dalai Lama* (London, 1946).

————. *The People of Tibet* (London, 1928).

————. *The Religion of Tibet* (London, 1931).

————. *Tibet Past and Present* (London, 1924).

Bernard, Theos. *Penthouse of the Gods: A Pilgrimage into the Heart of Tibet and the Sacred City of Lhasa* (New York, 1939).

Bonavia, David, and Magnus Bartlett. *Tibet* (New York, 1981).

Bull, Geoffrey T. *When Iron Gates Yield* (London, 1964).

Butterfield, Fox. *China: Alive in the Bitter Sea* (New York, 1982).

Cammann, Schuyler. *Trade Through the Himalayas: the Early British Attempts to Open Lhasa* (Princeton, 1951).

Candler, Edmund. *The Unveiling of Lhasa* (New York, 1905).

Carrasco, Pedro. *Land and Polity in Tibet* (Seattle, 1959).

Chao, Shan. "Sunshine After Rain." *Peking Review,* 18 (May 5, 1959), 21–24.

"Chinese People Will Not Tolerate Foreign Intervention in Tibet." *Peking Review,* 17 (April 29, 1959), 8–9.

Chapman, Frederick Spencer. *Lhasa, the Holy City* (London, 1940).

Choedon, Dhondub. *Life in the Red Flag People's Commune* (Dharamsala, India, 1978).

Clark, Leonard. *The Marching Wind* (London, 1955).

Combe, G. A. *A Tibetan in Tibet* (New York, 1926).

Concerning the Question of Tibet (Peking, 1959).

Crosby, Oscar Terry. *Tibet and Turkestan* (New York, 1905).

Dalai Lama, the Fourteenth. *The Buddhism of Tibet and the Key to the Middle Way* (New York, 1975).

————. *The Opening of the Wisdom Eye* (Wheaton, Illinois, 1972).

————. *My Land and My People* (New York, 1962).

Dalvi, Brig. J. P. *Himalayan Blunder* (Bombay, 1969).

Das, Sarat Chandra. *Journey to Lhasa and Central Tibet* (London, 1902).

Deasy, H. H. P. *In Tibet and Chinese Turkestan* (New York, 1901).

Dolkar, Tseten, and John Windsor. *Girl from Tibet* (Chicago, 1971).

Dreyer, June Teufel. *China's Forty Millions* (Cambridge, 1976).

Ekvall, Robert B. *Fields on the Hoof: Nexus of Tibetan Nomadic Pastoralism* (New York, 1968).

———. *Religious Observances in Tibet* (Chicago, 1964).

Enders, Gordon B., and Edward Anthony. *Nowhere Else in the World* (New York, 1935).

Fleming, Peter. *Bayonets to Lhasa: The First Full Account of the British Invasion of Tibet in 1904* (London, 1961).

Ford, Robert. *Captured in Tibet* (London, 1957).

Franke, Herbert. "Tibetans in Yuan China." In *China Under Mongol Rule,* ed. John D. Langlois (Princeton, 1981), 296–328.

Fraser, John. *The Chinese: Portrait of a People* (New York, 1980).

Ginsburgs, George, and Michael Mathos. *Communist China and Tibet: The First Dozen Years* (The Hague, 1964).

Goldstein, Melvyn C. "An Anthropological Study of the Tibetan Political System." Unpublished Ph.D. dissertation, University of Washington, 1963.

Gould, Basil. *Report on the Discovery, Recognition and Installation of the Fourteenth Dalai Lama* (New Delhi, 1941).

———. *The Jewel in the Lotus* (London, 1957).

Goullart, Peter. *Land of the Lamas* (New York, 1959).

Harrer, Heinrich. *Seven Years in Tibet* (London, 1953).

———. "My Life in Forbidden Lhasa." *National Geographic,* 108 (July 1955), 1–48.

Hedin, Sven. *A Conquest of Tibet* (New York, 1934).

———. *Central Asia and Tibet: Towards the Holy City of Lassa,* 2 vols. (London, 1903).

Hermanns, Matthias. *Die Nomaden von Tibet* (Vienna, 1949).

Holdrich, Thomas H. *Tibet, the Mysterious* (London, 1904).

Hooker, Sir Joseph Dalton. *Himalayan Journals* (London, 1855).

"How General Tan's First Letter Was Brought to the Dalai Lama." *Peking Review,* 13 (April 3, 1959), 10–11.

"How the Tibetan Reactionaries Sabotaged the 17-Article Agreement." *Peking Review,* 19 (May 12, 1959), 16–19.

Howard, Harry Paxton. "Dalai Lama's Death Brings Crisis to Tibet." *The China Weekly Review,* 67 (January 27, 1934), 341–342.

Huc, E. *Travels in Tartary, Thibet, and China (1844–1848),* 2 vols. (London, 1879).

Hutheesing, G. P., ed. *Tibet Fights for Freedom: The Story of the March 1959 Uprising as Recorded in Documents, Despatches, Eye-Witness Accounts and World-Wide Reactions* (Bombay, 1961).

International Commission of Jurists. *The Question of Tibet and the Rule of Law* (Geneva, 1959).

———. *Tibet and the Chinese People's Republic: A Report to the International Commission of Jurists by Its Legal Inquiry Committee on Tibet* (Geneva, 1960).

Karan, Pradyumna P. *The Changing Face of Tibet* (Lexington, Kentucky, 1976).

Kawaguchi, Ekai. *Three Years in Tibet* (Benares, 1909).

Kolmas, Josef. *Tibet and Imperial China: A Survey of Sino-Tibetan Relations up to the End of the Manchu Dynasty in 1912* (Canberra, 1967).

Lamb, Alastair. *The China-India Border: The Origins of the Disputed Boundaries* (London, 1964).

———. *The McMahon Line: A Study in the Relations Between India, China, and Tibet, 1904 to 1914,* 2 vols. (London, 1966).

———. *Asian Frontiers: Studies in a Continuing Problem* (New York, 1968).

Bibliography

————. "Some Notes on Russian Intrigue in Tibet." *Journal of the Royal Central Asian Society,* XLVI (January, 1959), 46–65.

Landon, Perceval. *The Opening of Tibet* (New York, 1905).

Landor, A. Henry Savage. *In the Forbidden Land: An Account of a Journey into Tibet,* 2 vols. (New York, 1899).

Lang-Sims, Lois. *The Presence of Tibet* (London, 1963).

Lattimore, Owen. *Inner Asian Frontiers of China* (New York, 1940).

————. "China and the Barbarians." In *Empire in the East.* Ed. Joseph Barnes. New York, 1934, 3–36.

Le Palud, A. "What the Panchen Lama Told a French Newspaperman." *The China Weekly Review,* 67 (February 17, 1934), 456–457.

Levi, Werner. "Tibet Under Chinese Communist Rule." *Far Eastern Survey,* XXIII (January, 1954), 1–9.

Lhalungpa, Lobsang Phuntsok. "Buddhism in Tibet." In *The Path of the Buddha: Buddhism Interpreted by Buddhists.* Ed. Kenneth W. Morgan. New York, 1956, 237–306.

Li, Tieh-tseng. *Tibet Today and Yesterday* (New York, 1960).

————. *The Historical Status of Tibet* (New York, 1956).

Long, Jeff. "Going After Wangdu." *Rocky Mountain Magazine,* 33 (July/August 1981), 36–42.

Lu, Chang. "The Rebirth of the Tibetan People Cannot Be Halted." *Peking Review,* 18 (May 5, 1959), 8–11.

Macdonald, David. *The Land of the Lamas* (Philadelphia, 1929).

————. *Twenty Years in Tibet* (London, 1932).

MacGregor, John. *Tibet: A Chronicle of Exploration* (London, 1970).

McGovern, William Montgomery. *The Early Empires of Central Asia* (Chapel Hill, 1939).

————. *To Lhasa in Disguise: A Secret Expedition Through Mysterious Tibet* (New York, 1924).

Maisonneuve, Adrien. *Etudes Tibetaines* (Paris, 1971).

Maraini, Fosco. *Secret Tibet* (New York, 1952).

Markham, Clements R. *Narratives of the Mission of George Bogle to Tibet, and of the Journey of Thomas Manning to Lhasa* (London, 1879).

Mehra, Parshotam. *The Younghusband Expedition: An Interpretation* (Bombay, 1968).

Mehra, P. L. "Kazi U-Gyen: 'A Paid Tibetan Spy'?" *Journal of the Royal Central Asian Society,* LI (July–October 1964), 301–305.

————. "Tibet and Russian Intrigue." *Journal of the Royal Central Asian Society,* XLV (January 1958), 28–42.

Meng, C. Y. W. "Tibet After the Death of the Dalai Lama." *The China Weekly Review,* 67 (December 30, 1933), 204–208.

Migot, Andre. *Tibetan Marches* (New York, 1955).

Mitter, J. P. *Betrayal of Tibet* (New Delhi, 1964).

Moraes, Frank. *The Revolt in Tibet* (New York, 1960).

Moses, Larry William. *The Political Role of Mongol Buddhism* (Bloomington, Indiana, 1977).

Mullin, Chris. "Tibetan Conspiracy." *Far Eastern Economic Review,* 36 (September 5, 1975), 30–34.

Norbu, Dawa. *Red Star Over Tibet* (London, 1974).

————. "Strategic Development in Tibet: Implications for Its Neighbors." *Asian Survey,* XIX (March 1979), 245–259.

————. "The 1959 Tibetan Rebellion: An Interpretation." *The China Quarterly,* 77 (March 1979), 74–93.

Norbu, Jamyang. *Horseman in the Snow* (Dharamsala, India, 1979).
Norbu, Thupten Jigme, and Heinrich Harrer. *Tibet Is My Country* (New York, 1961).
Norbu, Thupten Jigme, and Colin M. Turnbull. *Tibet* (New York, 1968).
"On the So-Called 'Statement of the Dalai Lama.'" *Peking Review,* 16 (April 21, 1959), 1–2.
Paljor, Kunsang. *Tibet: The Undying Flame* (Dharamsala, India, 1977).
Patterson, George. "China and Tibet: Background to the Revolt." *The China Quarterly,* 1 (January–March 1960), 87–102.
———. *Tibetan Journey* (London, 1954).
———. *Tibet in Revolt* (London, 1960).
———. *Tragic Destiny* (London, 1959).
Peissel, Michel. *Cavaliers of Kham* (London, 1972).
Pemba, Tsewang. *Young Days in Tibet* (London, 1957).
Petech, Luciano. *Aristocracy and Government in Tibet 1728–1959* (Rome, 1973).
———. *China and Tibet in the Early XVIIIth Century* (Leiden, 1972).
———. *I Missionari Italiani nel Tibet e nel Nepal,* 2 vols. (Rome, 1952).
"Photocopies of the Originals: The Dalai Lama's Three Letters to General Tan Kuan-san." *Peking Review,* 15 (April 14, 1959), 8–9.
Prince Peter of Greece. *The Aristocracy of Central Tibet* (Kalimpong, 1954).
"Put Down the Rebellion in Tibet Thoroughly!" *People's Daily,* March 31, 1959.
Rahul, Ram. *Politics of Central Asia* (New York, 1974).
———. *The Government and Politics of Tibet* (New Delhi, 1969).
Rato, Khyongla Ngawang Losang. *My Life and Lives: The Story of a Tibetan Incarnation* (New York, 1977).
"The Rebirth of Tibet." *Peking Review,* 16 (April 21, 1959), 6–7.
"Rejoicing in Lhasa." *Peking Review,* 17 (April 29, 1959), 11.
Richardson, H. E. *A Short History of Tibet* (New York, 1962).
Riencourt, Amaury de. *Roof of the World: Tibet, Key to Asia* (New York, 1950).
Riggs, Fred W. "Tibet in Extremis." *Far Eastern Survey,* 19 (December 6, 1950), 224–230.
Rockville, William Woodville. *The Dalai Lamas of Lhasa and Their Relations with the Manchu Emperors of China* (Leiden, 1910).
———. *The Land of the Lamas* (New York, 1901).
Rosenthal, A. M. "Chou and the Lama: An Asian Drama." *The New York Times Magazine* (January 13, 1957).
Sen, Chanakya. *Tibet Disappears: A Documentary History of Tibet's International Status, the Great Rebellion and Its Aftermath* (London, 1960).
Shakabpa, Tsepon W. D. *Tibet: A Political History* (New Haven, 1967).
Shen, Tsung-lien, and Shen-chi Liu. *Tibet and the Tibetans* (Stanford, 1953).
Snellgrove, David, and Hugh Richardson. *A Cultural History of Tibet* (New York, 1968).
Stein, R. A. *Tibetan Civilization* (Stanford, 1972).
Tada, Tokan. *The Thirteenth Dalai Lama* (Tokyo, 1965).
Taring, Rinchen Dolma. *Daughter of Tibet* (London, 1970).
Teichman, Sir Eric. *Travels of a Consular Officer in Eastern Tibet* (Cambridge, 1922).
Thomas, Lowell Jr. *Out of This World: Across the Himalayas to Forbidden Tibet* (London, 1970).
———. *The Dalai Lama* (New York, 1961).
———. *The Silent War in Tibet* (New York, 1959).
———. *Tibet: 1950–1967* (Hong Kong, 1968).
———. *Tibet in the United Nations* (New Delhi, 1961).
———. *Tibet: No Longer Medieval* (Peking, 1981).
———. *Tibet: The Sacred Realm* (Philadelphia, 1983).

———. *Tibet Today* (Peking, 1974).

———. *Tibet Under Chinese Communist Rule* (Dharamsala, India, 1976).

———. *Tibetans in Exile: 1959–1969: A Report on Ten Years of Rehabilitation in India* (Dharamsala, India, 1969).

Tolstoy, Ilia. "Across Tibet from India to China." *National Geographic,* 90 (August 1946), 169–222.

Tucci, Giuseppe. *The Religions of Tibet* (London, 1980).

———. *To Lhasa and Beyond* (Rome, 1956).

Tung, Rosemary Jones. *A Portrait of Lost Tibet* (New York, 1980).

Van Geem, Isabell. *Crier Avant de Mourir: La Tragédie de Tibet* (Paris, 1977).

Varg, Paul A. *Open Door Diplomat: The Life of W. W. Rockhill* (Urbana, 1952).

———. "Tibet: An Unfortunate Vassal." *Current History,* 20 (February 1951), 90–94.

Waddell, L. Austine. *Lhasa and Its Mysteries: With a Record of the Expedition of 1903–04* (London, 1906).

———. *The Buddhism of Tibet, or Lamaism* (Cambridge, 1934).

Wangdu, Sonam. *The Discovery of the XIVth Dalai Lama* (Bangkok, 1975).

Winnington, Alan. *Tibet: Record of a Journey* (New York, 1957).

Younghusband, Francis. *India and Tibet* (London, 1910).

Index

Index

Index